www.wadsworth.com

wadsworth.com is the World Wide Web site for Wadsworth and is your direct source to dozens of online resources.

At *wadsworth.com* you can find out about supplements, demonstration software, and student resources. You can also send email to many of our authors and preview new publications and exciting new technologies.

wadsworth.com
Changing the way the world learns®

Readings in Social Research Methods

Second Edition

Diane Kholos Wysocki

University of Nebraska at Kearney

THOMSON
™
WADSWORTH

Australia • Canada • Mexico • Singapore • Spain
United Kingdom • United States

THOMSON

™

WADSWORTH

Executive Editor: *Sabra Horne*
Aquisitions Editor: *Robert Jucha*
Assistant Editor: *Stephanie Monzon*
Editorial Assistant: *Melissa Walter*
Technology Project Manager: *Dee Dee Zobian*
Marketing Manager: *Matthew Wright*
Project Manager, Editorial Production: *Katy German, Ray Crawford*
Print/Media Buyer: *Doreen Suruki*

Permissions Editor: *Sarah Harkrader*
Production Service: *Forbes Mill Press*
Text Designer: *Robin Gold*
Copy Editor: *Robin Gold*
Cover Designer: *Lisa Devenish*
Compositor: *Forbes Mill Press*
Cover Printer: *Webcom, Ltd.*
Printer: *Webcom, Ltd.*

Printed in Canada
1 2 3 4 5 6 7 06 05 04 03 02

For more information about our products, contact us at:
Thomson Learning Academic Resource Center
1-800-423-0563

For permission to use material from this text, contact us by:
Phone: 1-800-730-2214   **Fax:** 1-800-730-2215
Web: http://www.thomsonrights.com

Library of Congress Control Number:
2002115049

ISBN 0-534-61929-0

Wadsworth/Thomson Learning
10 Davis Drive
Belmont, CA 94002-3098
USA

Asia
Thomson Learning
5 Shenton Way #01-01
UIC Building
Singapore 068808

Australia
Nelson Thomson Learning
102 Dodds Street
South Melbourne, Victoria 3205
Australia

Canada
Nelson Thomson Learning
1120 Birchmount Road
Toronto, Ontario M1K 5G4
Canada

Europe/Middle East/Africa
Thomson Learning
High Holborn House
50/51 Bedford Row
London WC1R 4LR
United Kingdom

Latin America
Thomson Learning
Seneca, 53
Colonia Polanco
11560 Mexico D.F.
Mexico

Spain
Paraninfo Thomson Learning
Calle/Magallanes, 25
28015 Madrid, Spain

Contents

PART II ■ THE STRUCTURING OF INQUIRY 79

PART IV ■ ANALYZING DATA   257

Preface

I have been teaching research methods and working with students on their own research projects since I began teaching. I love working with undergraduates, just like you, to help them as they make sense of the world in which they live by conducting research. It's great fun to watch students think of a research question about something they see in their day-to-day lives and be able to turn that idea into research projects. However, I know that sometimes research can be difficult and that some students are even a little hesitant to take a research methods course. I worry about that. I want students to understand that research can be a lot of fun, and I want to help them enjoy it.

There are some great textbooks available about research methods. However, it has been my experience that students like to hear not only about the concepts they need to learn, but also how those concepts have been used in original studies. It has also been my experience that the more interesting the research topic and the more closely it connects with student's lives, the easier the material is to understand.

I cannot cover everything there is to know about research methods in this reader. I believe that would be an impossible undertaking and would just replicate what students learn from a textbook. Instead, I have compiled a series of brief readings that can be used to support the terms and concepts students will learn in their research methods class. You will find that these chapters parallel Earl Babbie's *The Practice of Social Research,* Tenth Edition, which makes this reader a perfect companion for Babbie's widely used text. However, this reader may also be used with any other research text currently on the market because the concepts this reader illuminates are those central to any course in research methods. *Readings in Social Research Method, Second Edition,* is intended for undergraduate students who are taking their first research methods course. The goal is to provide an introduction to the important issues and topics, while supporting those ideas with interesting original research articles.

I have many people to thank who have helped me with this book. To begin, I must thank Dr. Earl Babbie for his support with both editions of this book. It is truly an honor to have my reader paired with his textbooks. I also would like to thank the two best librarians around, Trudy de Goede and Mary Barton from the University of Nebraska, Kearney, library who were always ready and willing to get me whatever I needed, even at the last moment, and the Sociology secretary, Val Vierk, for her willingness to fax, copy, and send me everything I needed or forgot. Next, I must thank my outside reviewers who made numerous suggestions and comments about the first edition. Having been a reviewer myself, I know that a constructive review requires time away from other activities that are very important. To Ted Wagenaar, Miami University; David Folz, University of Tennessee; Joyce Tang, Queens College of the City University of New York; Robert Kapsis, Queens College of the City University of New York; Alisa Potter Mee, Concordia College; Jeffrey Burr, University of Massachusetts; Qi Jiang, Youngstown State University; and Sampson Lee Blair, Arizona

State University, I appreciate the time you took to make comments on the drafts of this book. I also would like to thank my copyeditor, Robin Gold, who has been great to work with during both editions, whom I have never met in person, but who has been a great "virtual pal" who has kept me on track and motivated throughout this process. I would also like to thank Bill Rasmussen who made sure I had everything I needed during the summer of 2002 while I was in Seattle to write this book. Not only did he provide me with love and support, but he also was willing to cook, clean and do laundry so I could write. And finally, there wouldn't be a need for a reader without students who have developed an interest in research and gone on to conduct their own projects with me over the years. Having students who love research as much as I do is what teaching is all about. So, with that said, thanks to Nicole Bleich, Jessica Reinert, Alicia Hausmann, Jennifer Thalken, and Christy Hinrichs, just to name a few, who remind me frequently why I love my job so much.

Readings in Social Research Methods

Second Edition

General Introduction

Anytime you read the newspaper or listen to a news report you hear about some type of research study. I read *The Denver Post* online and in the past few weeks alone I have read about the following research studies: caffeine, the chemical stimulant in coffee and tea, has been found to lower the risk of skin cancer in laboratory mice (Recer, 2002); top scientists have advised federal officials that there is "no evidence yet" that products from cloned animals are unsafe for human consumption (Garvey, 2002); an agent that could help detect an anthrax attack and serve as an antidote to the deadly disease has been developed by biologists at Rockefeller University (Wade, 2002); and in studying why cystic fibrosis is so much more deadly in girls than in boys, researchers found that on average, females are diagnosed with the disease four months later than boys (Auge, 2002).

Readings in Social Methods Research, second edition, is designed to help students, like you, learn about scientific research methods and how to decipher the studies that you hear about. Although you will be learning about research methods to reach your goal of completing this course, you will find that the things you learn, the way you will be taught to think, your ability to gather information and your capacity to draw your own conclusions, will go far beyond this class. I find that students are often quite fearful of taking a research methods course, and they come up with some preconceived ideas about how difficult the course will be. Sometimes they even *dig their heels in,* making it difficult for me to teach and difficult for them to learn. Furthermore, I have found that some textbooks are overwhelming for students and lack strong examples, primary sources, and exciting readings that will capture the attention of college students. My desire is to make research methods as fun for students to learn as it is for me to teach, so *Readings in Social Methods Research,* second edition, was designed as a reader with basic information and brief, stimulating, readings that will capture your attention, along with a variety of questions to help you incorporate what you have learned with what you have read.

Readings in Social Methods Research, second edition, is a reader suitable for students in basic research methodology classes who are just learning about research. The process of *reading* research is very important because most of us read much more research than we actually conduct. However, the ability to know how to read a research paper and understand it must be learned, be practiced, and is the basis for this reader.

Readings in Social Methods Research, second edition, can be used in any basic course or discipline and has been written to provide the student with plenty of information about the most popular social science research methods currently used. Instructors can use this reader as a supplement to any methods text on the market, but I designed it specifically to be used in conjunction with any of Earl Babbie's research methods books. You will notice that the table of contents is structured to match Babbie's books with only a few deviations. This reader may also be used with any other textbook on the market or as a stand-alone text that is supplemented with class lectures and outside reading.

Readings in Social Methods Research, second edition, provides a brief chapter intro-duction of methodological techniques and topics with the key concepts **boldfaced.** After each introduction there are a few questions that incorporate the subject matter with Info-Trac® College Edition, so students can gain practice finding sources on their own. After each chapter introduction, at least two articles that represent social science research—although sociology, criminal justice, gender studies, and social work are heavily repre-sented—show the student how the method is used in research. One of the things I have found in teaching is that the more interesting or controversial the research, the more inter-ested and excited my students are about learning. In my classes, I try to pick research to use as examples that will fulfill this goal. I did the same for this reader. The articles have been picked because I believe they are particularly interesting and engaging to students.

At the beginning of each article I have written a small abstract to help students under-stand what to look for while they are reading the article and to help them integrate what they have learned with the work researchers have conducted. Questions at the end of each article allow students to demonstrate their understanding of the methodological technique and how it has been used in the literature.

ORGANIZATION OF THE READER

Readings in Social Methods Research, second edition, is divided into 4 parts and has 12 chapters. This book is organized to follow the format of Earl Babbie's *The Practice of So-cial Research,* tenth edition, and can be used along with his textbook or by itself. What I have tried to do is gather articles that are relevant and that I thought would hold your inter-est. After each chapter introduction, there are InfoTrac College Edition assignments to help you use the concepts to work with each article. There are two to three articles in each chapter supporting the concepts discussed and three review questions at the end of each article. The glossary at the end of the book contains important terms that appear in bold type throughout the text.

Chapter 1, "Why Do You Need to Understand Research Methods," begins Part 1 and covers the basics about research. This chapter tells you that our ideas about the world around us might not be as accurate as our "commonsense" ideas would have us believe. You will learn that we all have two realities in our lives: one that is based on what we see and know to be real and the other that we believe to be real because someone else has told us they are real. In this chapter you will learn how important this idea is to research.

Chapter 2, "Combining Theory with Research Questions," focuses on the how the data we collect is empty and meaningless unless it is combined with theory. You will learn about four different paradigms that can be used in your research and learn the difference be-tween deductive and inductive theory.

I placed Chapter 3, "Ethics," early in this reader. Sometimes in other textbooks, you will see it as a chapter toward the end of the book or as an appendix. This leads me to be-lieve that ethics could be an afterthought. I believe that having a good grasp of the ethical problems in research is important to remember while you read this book. Thus, you will be able to think about important ethical issues as you design a project or read about some-one else's. You need to understand why participation should be voluntary, why you should not deceive or harm your subjects, and the role of the institutional review board. It is also important when you are reading the research of other people to be able to tell if they conducted their research ethically.

Part 2 begins with Chapter 4, "Research Design." In this chapter, you will learn that purpose of research is to explore, describe, and explain the phenomenon you want to study. You will also learn that units of analysis can be very confusing at times and the most common units of analysis are the individual, the group, the organization, the social category, the social artifact, the social institution, and the society. Finally, you will learn why time plays such an important role in research because it helps describe changes or differences in behaviors within a framework of different ages or stages across the life span.

Chapter 5, "Conceptualization and Operationalization," is somewhat difficult for some students, but will tell you how to take variables and put them into identifying concepts that you can ultimately measure during your project. For instance, if you are investigating religiosity, you can conceptualize that concept by giving it a definition. Let's say you define religiosity as someone who goes to his or her place of worship at least one time a week. You can then operationalize that concept and measure it, by asking the question: "How many times a week do you go to your place of worship?"

Once you know what you are studying, Chapter 6, "Indexes and Scales," can help you construct a way to measure your variables. You will also learn the difference between using an index and a scale and how to determine which would be best for your particular research question.

An important topic within research methods is in Chapter 7, "Sampling," where you will learn how you pick the group you want to conduct research on. Often it is impossible to pick the entire population because it is much too large. Therefore, you must somehow find a sample that represents the population. You will learn various sampling techniques and how to pick the best one for your project.

In Part 3, you will learn various modes of observations. Chapter 8 begins with "Experimental and Survey Research." Experiments are the easiest way to explain concepts that you need to know such as that the independent variable causes the dependent variable. This works well in controlled environments such as a lab, but when experiments are done on people, you have to think about other variables that can affect the dependent variable. Survey research is probably the most common method used in the social sciences and involves administering a questionnaire either in person, through the mail, or over the Internet.

Chapter 9 is about "Field Research and Unobtrusive Measures." Field research involves going where some type of action is happening and observing it. This action can be on a street corner, a public library, or a grade school playground. Narrative research involves listening to people's "voices" and letting them tell their own stories. As researchers, we sometimes are so busy asking questions that we forget to just listen and can miss what our subject is trying to tell us. Regardless, interviewing is important in research and you will learn various techniques for asking questions. In content analysis, you can analyze anything such as books, newspaper articles, pictures in magazines, or bumper stickers. For example, you might be interested in how women are portrayed in computer advertisements. What are their roles? Are they actually shown working with the computer or are they helping the male who is working with the computer?

In Chapter 10, "Existing Data and Evaluation Research," you will learn how existing data can support any type of research you are conducting. For instance, suppose you are interested in gender differences in 6th grade math classes. You can go to the Department of Education database where they have been surveying large numbers of students about their feelings and beliefs about their own math abilities. This type of existing data can support and guide your project. Evaluation research is used to find out how well programs are working to cause the desired change in either individual behaviors or programs.

Finally, Part 4 starts with "An Introduction to Statistics" in Chapter 11. You will learn basic information on how to use univariate, bivariate, and multivariate statistics. This chapter is not meant to be a complete course in statistics but, rather, a short overview to use in reading articles and understanding results.

Chapter 12 is new in this edition and is called "Reading and Writing a Research Paper." Because both reading and writing are so important and students are often confused about both, I have included this chapter. It will increase your knowledge about each part of an article, how to properly use citations and how to make sure you stay out of trouble with unintentional plagiarism.

And now with the overview complete, you are all set to learn about research methods. I hope you enjoy the journey.

REFERENCES

Auge, K. 2002, August 19. Tests for incurable cystic fibrosis illustrate debate. [Online] http://www.denverpost.com/Stories/0,1413,36%257E53%257E805408,00.html?search=filter

Garvey, M. 2002, August 21. Scientists: Cloned animals hold peril. [Online] http://www.denverpost.com/Stories/0,1413,36%257E23827%257E810291,00.html?search=filter

Recer, P. 2002. Caffeine may reduce skin cancer. [Online] http://www.denverpost.com/Stories/0,1413,36%257E23827%257E821341,00.html?search=filter

Wade, N. 2002, August 22. Scientists discover possible antidote to anthrax; could also detect attack. [Online] http://www.denverpost.com/Stories/0,1413,36%257E23827%257E812516,00.html?search=filter

PART I ■ AN INTRODUCTION TO INQUIRY

■

Chapter 1: Why Do You Need to Understand Research Methods?

Why are you taking this class in Social Research Methods? Is it because you are interested in the subject? Is it because you are required to take the course? Is it because you want to understand the articles that you have read for your school courses or for your job? You might be taking this class for the reasons already stated or for any number of your own new reasons. However, I believe that an important part of learning about research is to understand how the research is conducted and conclusions are found. The only way for you to understand the conclusions, however, is to learn how researchers both plan and conduct their research projects.

Just think about it . . . what type of questions do you have about the world in which you live? In March 2000, in Mount Morris Township, Michigan, a 6-year-old boy pulled a gun from his pants and shot a little girl to death in their first-grade classroom. This shooting took place in front of both teachers and classmates and resulted in the death of 6-year-old Kayla Rolland. As budding researchers, you might wonder what the motives and the effects of this disaster are on society. How can a 6-year-old carry a gun into a school, unnoticed by anyone in authority? Under what conditions are these children living and could those conditions, in any way, affect the resulting death of this little girl? Why would a child so young believe that shooting someone is the way to handle his problems? Did he learn this at home? Did he learn this from television? Can school shootings such as these be prevented? How do you go about finding out some of these answers? We are all curious about one thing or another, and the key to our curiosity is to find out if our ideas are correct, to learn which ones are not, and to make recommendations for change.

Here is another important reason to learn about research methods. We often see TV sales pitches that say "75 percent of doctors interviewed prescribed drug X for relief of arthritic pain." Would you believe this? Would this make you want to purchase drug X? What questions might you ask about this claim? Understanding research methods will help you figure out what questions you should ask about these findings. For instance, how many doctors were interviewed? What happens if the 75 percent of the doctors surveyed were actually based on only four interviews? Would you want to depend on a drug based on the fact that three doctors stated they liked it? What kinds of questions were the doctors asked about prescribing drug X? If the doctors were asked "Have you ever prescribed drug X?," were they just as likely to have prescribed drugs A, B, C, or D? Who interviewed the doctor?

If the manufacturers of drug X did the interviewing, were the doctors compensated for their participation in the study? Could compensation have swayed their responses? As you can see, you might think you have received the correct answers to the questions, but the answers might just be to encourage you to buy the product and have nothing to do with reality or truth.

DIFFERENT REALITIES

Research[1] is a series of steps, techniques, exercises, and events that can be applied to every sphere of life to help you understand the world in which you live. If you want to actually conduct research on doctors to determine how likely they are to prescribe drug X to their patients, you need to come up with some sort of plan to help guide your research. Your plan of action can also be called **research methods** because the methods you use are an essential set of skills, insights, and tools needed to answer any kind of questions. If you still think about the drug X study, you might ask some questions about the types of methods that were used to conclude that 75 percent of the doctors prescribed drug X. Who did the researchers actually talk to? How did they find the doctors to interview? If, before conducting the study, the researchers had a plan about how they were going to do their research, you could actually go back and look at their methods if you had a question or a doubt. The methods the researchers used could help you decide if the findings were reliable and could be trusted.

Why do you think methods sections are so important to research? One problem in research is that it is very easy for any of us to be uncertain about what is real and what isn't. How do you view the world around you? What kinds of practices, thoughts, values, and insights do you have about the world based on where you came from? Would they be different for someone who grew up in a different situation or a different culture? Where do you get your ideas about different cultures, people, and countries? Let me give you an example. A few years ago, I spent four weeks in Asia with my youngest son Jonathan, who was 19 years old at the time and had been backpacking around the world by himself. By the time I met up with him in Singapore, he had already been in numerous countries over a seven-month span. Anyway, as you can imagine, I was worried sick about him. Some countries that he planned on going to particularly concerned me because my reality about those countries was based on movies I had seen in the past. A very long time ago, I saw the movie *Midnight Express* (1978), in which a young American tourist was arrested by Turkish authorities after trying to smuggle hashish out of the country. This young man was sentenced to 30 years in prison where his realities were pretty harsh and his parents were unable to get him out and back into the United States. The things done to him in the prison were so terrible I had to leave the theater and couldn't watch the rest of the movie, but the memory stayed with me as my reality of a foreign country. In another film, *Return to Paradise* (1998), one American was arrested in Malaysia for a prankish misdemeanor. While he and his friends all shared in the prank, he took the rap for all of them and was sentenced to be hanged as a drug trafficker and was held for years in a terrible Malaysian prison. In the most current movie, *The Beach* (2000), Richard (Leonardo DiCaprio) traveled to Thailand where he ended up in

---

[1] Words in **boldface** are defined in the glossary at the end of the book.

grave danger on an island with some friends (I actually visited this island and it is very beautiful). Even though I am a sociologist and understand there are different types of realities, movies like these made me more concerned about my son going to Asia. This would be my **agreement reality** because the things I considered real were real only because I had learned about them through the media and people around me. This agreement reality took precedence over anything else. It wasn't until I actually went to Asia with my son and traveled all around, met the people, ate their food, and learned about the culture that I developed my **experimental reality,** where the things I knew were a function of my own direct experiences, rather than those experiences of others. I found that the things I had been concerned about originally were not as real as I had thought. The people were wonderful, they were helpful, I learned about new lifestyles that were different from my own, and my concerns were unfounded. When I left my son in Thailand and came back to Nebraska, I wasn't worried like I had been before I experienced the realities of these countries myself and found out the people were not out to capture young Americans and throw them into prisons never to be seen again. This doesn't however, mean that you can break the law in these countries and get away with it!!! The real reality is if you do something illegal in another country, you are subject to their laws and their punishments!!!

How then would two different realities affect the outcomes of research? Easy. It can blind you to things that might be right in front of your faces because you have preconceived ideas about the situations you are studying. You might also be looking at it from only one point of view and be completely blinded to other points of view. What do you think? Do you believe that your reality could affect the outcome of the research you are conducting? The methods used in research gave us an idea about the perspective the researcher comes from and the way the data was gathered so we could understand the methods and interpret the findings accurately.

HUMAN INQUIRY

Although your own reality plays a big part in the type of research, you are interested in and the conclusions you come up with, one thing you need to know is that you don't need to start over when you begin a research project. Furthermore, your topic doesn't have to be something no one else has ever thought about before. You already know some things for sure about the world around you. For instance, we all know that the world is round and if you drop something, it will fall. These ideas are based on **tradition**. So, if you accept what everyone around "knows" to be true, then you don't have to start from scratch. You could look at other research reports to see what other researchers have found previously because their findings could give you a basis for your own research. Although tradition is good, and saves some time and energy, it can also be bad. There is a good chance the findings might be inaccurate, which might stop you from looking far enough to find another "truth." Similarly, judgment errors can be made because all of us tend to believe people in **authority** and that authority is legitimate when, in fact, it might not be. Let's say you went to the doctor's office for a check up and you were told that something might be wrong with you and that you needed major surgery. Would you question the doctor who seems to be an authority on the subject? Or would you believe you have to have the surgery regardless of how you feel about it because the doctor is an authority figure and you believe the doctors' suggestions are legitimate?

STEPPING BACK

So, if you are reading about research, how can you see beyond your own personal realities and tradition and the authority of those who have conducted research previously? According to theorist C. Wright Mills, who in 1956 wrote *The Sociological Imagination,* we all have both **personal troubles** and **public issues** and must know the difference between the two. Personal troubles occur within all of us and within our immediate relationships with others. Public issues, on the other hand, have to do with the environments in which we live. If you get a job after graduating from college and the job doesn't pay enough money to support your children and help you purchase a home, you have a personal trouble. If you consider the fact that you might have been tracked in school to take home economics and shop classes rather than math and science and that it didn't happen just to you alone, but to many young people, which made it so you didn't have the skills for a better paying job, then it is a public issue (Claus, 1999).

How can you know the difference between personal troubles and public issues in your own research? Mills gives some basic steps to follow. You must first *distance yourselves* because often you are so immersed in your everyday life that it is difficult to see things that are right in front of your face. You need to "think yourselves out of the immediacy." Second, you must *engage in a systematic examination* of empirical methods and observations. This means you must conduct research to help you find answers to your questions. However, to do this you must also work within your own experiences. Third, you must eliminate **ethnocentrism.** Ethnocentrism is prejudicial attitudes between groups of people where there is the feeling and belief that one group's attitudes, customs, and behaviors are superior to those of the other groups. Do you believe you are better than people who live in a different social class from you? Let's say you grew up in a rural area and your assignment was to go observe gang members in the inner city. Would the fact that you had never been to an inner city and had never seen a gang member except in movies influence the conclusions you might draw about their behaviors? Fourth, you must *analyze the data* that you have collected. An analysis of your data may tell you that your commonsense ideas about a topic are actually incorrect. Finally, *action* should be taken. If you know something, you must do something about it. Improvements in society depend on this. Whether you take action by writing about your results in an academic journal or standing on a picket line, research works to help transform society.

REFERENCES

Claus, J. 1999. You can't avoid the politics: Lessons for teacher education from a case study of teacher-initiated tracking reform. *Journal of Teacher Education,* 50(1): 5.

Mills, C. Wright. 1956. *The sociological imagination.* New York: Oxford University Press.

INFOTRAC COLLEGE EDITION SUGGESTED READINGS AND DISCUSSION QUESTIONS

1. Look up the article by P. Cormack, 1999, Making the sociological promise: A case study of Rosemary Brown's autobiography. *Canadian Review of Sociology and Anthropology,* 36(3): 355. How does this article use C. Wright Mills' sociological promise?

2. Look up the article by S. Freud, 1999, The social construction of normality. (Knowledge Building) *Families in Society: The Journal of Contemporary Human Services,* 80(4): 333. Compare the way this author uses the social construction of normality to the way Berger uses the social construction of reality.

FROM THE SOCIOLOGICAL IMAGINATION

C. Wright Mills

C. Wright Mills believes that "the fruits of [our] imagination is the first lesson of the social sciences." Furthermore, he argues that while the social sciences are filled with what researchers have done in the past, the questions and conclusions that are found can be constructed differently depending on who conducts the research. Your own reality may influence the ways in which you look at life and could blind you to other possibilities. By using your sociological imagination, you can understand the larger context and how it affects individual lives. As you read the following article, you might think about how your life is affected by the bigger picture that Mills writes about.

Nowadays men often feel that their private lives are a series of traps. They sense that within their everyday worlds, they cannot overcome their troubles, and in this feeling, they are often quite correct: What ordinary men are directly aware of and what they try to do are bounded by the private orbits in which they live; their visions and their powers are limited to the close-up scenes of job, family, neighborhood; in other milieu, they move vicariously and remain spectators. And the more aware they become, however vaguely, of ambitions and of threats which transcend their mediate locales, the more trapped they seem to feel.

Underlying this sense of being trapped are seemingly impersonal changes in the very structure of continent-wide societies. The facts of contemporary history are also facts about the success and the failure of individual men and women. When a society is industrialized, a peasant becomes a worker; a feudal lord is liquidated or becomes a businessman. When classes rise or fall, a man is employed or unemployed; when the rate of investment goes up or down, a man takes new heart or goes broke. When wars happen, an insurance salesman becomes a rocket launcher; a store clerk, a radar man; a wife lives alone; a child grows up without a father. Neither the life of an individual nor the history of a society can be understood without understanding both.

Yet men do not usually define the troubles they endure in terms of historical change and institutional contradiction. The well-being they enjoy, they do not usually impute to the big ups and downs of the societies in which they live. Seldom aware of the intricate connection between the patterns of their own lives and the course of world history, ordinary men do not usually know what this connection means for the kinds of men they are

---

becoming and for the kinds of history-making in which they might take part. They do not possess the quality of mind essential to grasp the interplay of man and society, of biography and history, of self and world. They cannot cope with their personal troubles in such ways as to control the structural transformations that usually lie behind them.

Surely it is no wonder. In what period have so many men been so totally exposed at so fast a pace to such earthquakes of change? That Americans have not known such catastrophic changes as have the men and women of other societies is due to historical facts that are now quickly becoming "merely history." The history that now affects every man is world history. Within this scene and this period, in the course of a single generation, one sixth of mankind is transformed from all that is feudal and backward into all that is modern, advanced, and fearful. Political colonies are freed; new and less visible forms of imperialism installed. Revolutions occur; men feel the intimate grip of new kinds of authority. Totalitarian societies rise, and are smashed to bits—or succeed fabulously. After two centuries of ascendancy, capitalism is shown up as only one way to make society into an industrial apparatus. After two centuries of hope, even formal democracy is restricted to a quite small portion of mankind. Everywhere in the underdeveloped world, ancient ways of life are broken up and vague expectations become urgent demands. Everywhere in the overdeveloped world, the means of authority and of violence become total in scope and bureaucratic in form. Humanity itself now lies before us, the supernation at either pole concentrating its most coordinated and massive efforts upon the preparation of World War Three.

The very shaping of history now outpaces the ability of men to orient themselves in accordance with cherished values. And which values? Even when they do not panic, men often sense that older ways of feeling and thinking have collapsed and that newer beginnings are ambiguous to the point of moral stasis. Is it any wonder that ordinary men feel they cannot cope with the larger worlds with which they are so suddenly confronted? That they cannot understand the meaning of their epoch for their own lives? That—in defense of selfhood—they become morally insensible, trying to remain altogether private men? Is it any wonder that they come to be possessed by a sense of the trap?

It is not only information that they need—in this Age of Fact, information often dominates their attention and overwhelms their capacities to assimilate it. It is not only the skills of reason that they need—although their struggles to acquire these often exhaust their limited moral energy.

What they need, and what they feel they need, is a quality of mind that will help them to use information and to develop reason in order to achieve lucid summations of what is going on in the world and of what may be happening within themselves. It is this quality, I am going to contend, that journalists and scholars, artists and publics, scientists and editors are coming to expect of what may be called the sociological imagination.

The sociological imagination enables its possessor to understand the larger historical scene in terms of its meaning for the inner life and the external career of a variety of individuals. It enables him to take into account how individuals, in the welter of their daily experience, often become falsely conscious of their positions. Within that welter, the framework of modern society is sought, and within that framework the psychologies of a variety of men and women are formulated. By such means the personal uneasiness of individuals is focused upon explicit troubles and the indifference of publics is transformed into involvement with public issues.

The first fruit of this imagination—and the first lesson of the social science that embodies it—is the idea that the individual can understand his own experience and gauge his own fate only by locating himself within his period, that he can know his own chances in life only by becoming aware of those of all individuals in his circumstances. In many ways it is a terrible lesson; in many ways a magnificent one. We do not know the limits of man's capacities for supreme effort or willing degradation, for agony or glee, for pleasurable brutality or the sweetness of reason. But in our time we have come to know that the limits of human nature are frighteningly broad. We have come to know that every individual lives, from one generation to the next, in some society; that he lives out a biography, and that he lives it out within some historical sequence. By the fact of his living he contributes, however minutely, to the shaping of this society and to the course of its history, even as he is made by society and by its historical push and shove.

The sociological imagination enables us to grasp history and biography and the relations between the two within society. That is its task and its promise. And it is the signal what is best in contemporary studies of man and society. No social study that does not come back to the problems of biography, of history and of their intersections within a society has completed its intellectual journey. Whatever the specific problems of the classic social analysts, however limited or however broad the features of social reality they have examined, those who have been imaginatively aware of the promise of their work have consistently asked three sorts of questions:

1. What is the structure of this particular society as a whole? What are its essential components, and how are they related to one another? How does it differ from other varieties of social order? Within it, what is the meaning of any particular feature for its continuance and for its change?

2. Where does this society stand in human history? What are the mechanics by which it is changing? What is its place within and its meaning for the development of humanity as a whole? How does any particular feature we are examining affect, and how is it affected by, the historical period in which it moves? And this period—what are its essential features? How does it differ from other periods? What are its characteristic ways of history-making?

3. What varieties of men and women now prevail in this society and in this period? And what varieties are coming to prevail? In what ways are they selected and formed, liberated and repressed, made sensitive and blunted? What kinds of "human nature" are revealed in the conduct and character we observe in this society in this period? And what is the meaning for "human nature" of each and every feature of the society we are examining?

Whether the point of interest is a great power state or a minor literary mood, a family, a prison, a creed—these are the kinds of questions the best social analysts have asked. They are the intellectual pivots of classic studies of man in society—and they are the questions inevitably raised by any mind possessing the sociological imagination. For that imagination is the capacity to shift from one perspective to another—from the political to the psychological; from examination of a single family to comparative assessment of the national budgets of the world; from the theological school to the military establishment; from considerations of an industry to studies of contemporary poetry. It is the capacity to range from the most impersonal and remote transformations to the most intimate features of the human self—and to see the relations between the two. Back of its use there is always the urge to know the social and historical meaning of the individual in the society and in the period in which he has his quality and his being.

That, in brief, is why it is by means of the sociological imagination that men now hope to grasp what is going on in the world, and to understand what is happening in themselves as minute points of the intersections of biography and history within society. In large part, contemporary man's self-conscious view of himself as at least an outsider, if not a permanent stranger, rests upon an absorbed realization of social relativity and of the transformative power of history. The sociological imagination is the most fruitful form of this self-consciousness. By its use men whose mentalities have swept only a series of limited orbits often come to feel as if suddenly awakened in a house with which they had only supposed themselves to be familiar. Correctly or incorrectly, they often come to feel that they can now provide themselves with adequate summations, cohesive assessments, comprehensive orientations. Older decisions that once appeared sound now seem to them products of a mind unaccountably dense. Their capacity for astonishment is made lively again. They acquire a new way of thinking, they experience a transvaluation of values: in a word, by their reflection and by their sensibility, they realize the cultural meaning of the social sciences.

Perhaps the most fruitful distinction with which the sociological imagination works is between "the personal troubles of milieu" and "the public issues of social structure." This distinction is an essential tool of the sociological imagination and a feature of all classic work in social science.

What we experience in various and specific milieu, I have noted, is often caused by structural changes. Accordingly, to understand the changes of many personal milieu we are required to look beyond them. And the number and variety of such structural changes increase as the institutions within which we live become more embracing and more intricately connected with one another. To be aware of the idea of social structure and to use it with sensibility is to be capable of tracing such linkages among a great variety of milieu. To be able to do that is to possess the sociological imagination.

REVIEW QUESTIONS

1. What does C. Wright Mills mean when he says, "In this Age of Fact, information often dominates their attention and overwhelms their capacities to assimilate it"?

2. How can the fact that Mills believes each individual can understand his own experience and gauge his own fate by locating himself within his period affect the outcome of research?

3. Mills states "no social study that does not come back to the problems of biography, of history and of their intersections within a society has completed its intellectual journey." Using a topic that might be of interest to you to research, how does Mill's statement apply?

THE REALITY OF EVERYDAY LIFE

Peter Berger and Thomas Luckmann

Peter L. Berger and Thomas Luckmann explain that sociology involves the desire to understand the everyday social reality around us. We must understand the differences between our commonsense ideas about life and what is the "truth." Although reality is interpreted by each individual and adds meaning to his or her world, that reality of everyday life is often taken for granted and can influence our research questions and conclusions. While reading this article, think about how your commonsense reality might be different from actual reality and how the things that have happened in your life add to your commonsense ideas about the world.

Since our purpose in this treatise is a sociological analysis of the reality of everyday life, more precisely, of knowledge that guides conduct in everyday life, and we are only tangentially interested in how this reality may appear in various theoretical perspectives to intellectuals, we must begin by a clarification of that reality as it is available to the commonsense of the ordinary members of society. How that commonsense reality may be influenced by the theoretical constructions of intellectuals and other merchants of ideas is a further question. Ours is thus an enterprise that, although theoretical in character, is geared to the understanding of a reality that forms the subject matter of the empirical science of sociology, that is, the world of everyday life.

It should be evident, then, that our purpose is not to engage in philosophy. All the same, if the reality of everyday life is to be understood, account must be taken of its intrinsic character before we can proceed with sociological analysis proper. Everyday life presents itself as a reality interpreted by men and subjectively meaningful to them as a coherent world. As sociologists we take this reality as the object of our analyses. Within the frame of reference of sociology as an empirical science it is possible to take this reality as given, to take as data particular phenomena arising within it, without further inquiring about the foundations of this reality, which is a philosophical task. However, given the particular purpose of the present treatise, we cannot completely bypass the philosophical problem.

The world of everyday life is not only taken for granted as reality by the ordinary members of society in the subjectively meaningful conduct of their lives. It is a world that originates in their thoughts and actions, and is maintained as real by these. Before turning to our main task we must, therefore, attempt to clarify the foundations of knowledge in everyday life, to wit, the *objectivations* of subjective processes (and meanings) by which the *intersubjective* commonsense world is constructed.

For the purpose at hand, this is a preliminary task, and we can do no more than sketch the main features of what we believe to be an adequate solution to the philosophical problem—adequate, let us hasten to add, only in the sense that it can serve as a starting point for sociological analysis. The considerations immediately following are, therefore, of the nature of philosophical prolegomena and, in themselves, presociological. The method we consider best suited to clarify the foundations of knowledge in everyday life is that of phenomenological analysis, a purely descriptive method and, as such, "empirical" but not "scientific"—as we understand the nature of the empirical sciences.

The phenomenological analysis of everyday life, or rather of the subjective experience of everyday life, refrains from any causal or genetic hypotheses, as well as from assertions about the ontological status of the phenomena analyzed. It is important to remember this. Commonsense contains innumerable pre- and quasi-scientific interpretations about everyday reality, which it takes for granted. If we are to describe the reality of commonsense we must refer to these interpretations, just as we must take account of its taken-for-granted character—but we do so within phenomenological brackets.

Consciousness is always intentional; it always intends or is directed toward objects. We can never apprehend some putative substratum of consciousness as such, only consciousness of something or other. This is so regardless of whether the object of consciousness is experienced as belonging to an external physical world or apprehended as an element of an inward subjective reality. Whether I (the first person singular, here as in the following illustrations, standing for ordinary self-consciousness in everyday life) am viewing the panorama of New York City or whether I become conscious of an inner anxiety, the processes of consciousness involved are intentional in both instances. The point need not be belabored that the consciousness of the Empire State Building differs from the awareness of anxiety. A detailed phenomenological analysis would uncover the various layers of experience, and the different structures of meaning involved in, say, being bitten by a dog, remembering having been bitten by a dog, having a phobia about all dogs, and so forth. What interests us here is the common intentional character of all consciousness.

Different objects present themselves to consciousness as constituents of different spheres of reality. I recognize the fellowmen I must deal with in the course of everyday life as pertaining to a reality quite different from the disembodied figures that appear in my dreams. The two sets of objects introduce quite different tensions into my consciousness and I am attentive to them in quite different ways. My consciousness, then, is capable of moving through different spheres of reality. Put differently, I am conscious of the world as consisting of multiple realities. As I move from one reality to another, I experience the transition as a kind of shock. This shock is to be understood as caused by the shift in attentiveness that the transition entails. Waking up from a dream illustrates this shift most simply.

Among the multiple realities there is one that presents itself as the reality par excellence. This is the reality of everyday life. Its privileged position entitles it to the designation of paramount reality. The tension of consciousness is highest in everyday life, that is, the latter imposes itself upon consciousness in the most massive, urgent and intense manner. It is impossible to ignore, difficult even to weaken in its imperative presence. Consequently, it forces me to be attentive to it in the fullest way. I experience everyday life in the state of being wide-awake. This wide-awake state of existing in and apprehending the reality of everyday life is taken by me to be normal and self-evident, that is, it constitutes my natural attitude.

I apprehend the reality of everyday life as an ordered reality. Its phenomena are prearranged in patterns that seem to be independent of my apprehension of them and that impose themselves upon the latter. The reality of everyday life appears already objectified, that is, constituted by an order of objects that have been designated as objects before my appearance on the scene. The language used in everyday life continuously provides me with the necessary objectifications and posits the order within which these make sense and within which everyday life has meaning for me. I live in a place that is geographically designated; I employ tools, from can openers to sports cars, which are designated in the technical vocabulary of my society; I live within a web of human relationships, from my chess club to the United States of America, which are also ordered by means of vocabulary. In this manner language marks the co-ordinates of my life in society and fills that life with meaningful objects.

The reality of everyday life is organized around the "here" of my body and the "now" of my present. This "here and now" is the focus of my attention to the reality of everyday life. What is "here and now" presented to me in everyday life is the *realissimum* of my consciousness. The reality of everyday life is not, however, exhausted by these immediate presences, but embraces phenomena that are not present "here and now." This means that I experience everyday life in terms of differing degrees of closeness and remoteness, both spatially and temporally. Closest to me is the zone of everyday life that is directly accessible to my bodily manipulation. This zone contains the world within my reach, the world in which I act so as to modify its reality, or the world in which I work. In this world of working my consciousness is dominated by the pragmatic motive, that is, my attention to this world is mainly determined by what I am doing, have done or plan to do in it. In this way it is my world par excellence. I know, of course, that the reality of everyday life contains zones that are not accessible to me in this manner. But either I have no pragmatic interest in these zones or my interest in them is indirect insofar as they may be, potentially, manipulative zones for me. Typically, my interest in the far zones is less intense and certainly less urgent. I am intensely interested in the cluster of objects involved in my daily occupation—say, the world of the garage, if I am a mechanic. I am interested, though less directly, in what goes on in the testing laboratories of the automobile industry in Detroit—1 am unlikely ever to be in one of these laboratories, but the work done there will eventually affect my everyday life. I may also be interested in what goes on at Cape Kennedy or in outer space, but this interest is a matter of private, "leisure-time" choice rather than an urgent necessity of my everyday life.

The reality of everyday life further presents itself to me as an intersubjective world, a world that I share with others. This intersubjectivity sharply differentiates everyday life from other realities of which I am conscious. I am alone in the world of my dreams, but I know that the world of everyday life is as real to others as it is to myself. Indeed, I cannot exist in everyday life without continually interacting and communicating with others. I know that my natural attitude to this world corresponds to the natural attitude of others, that they also comprehend the objectifications by which this world is ordered, that they also organize this world around the "here and now" of their being in it and have projects for working in it. I also know, of course, that the others have a perspective on this common world that is not identical with mine. My "here" is their "there." My "now" does not fully overlap with theirs. My projects differ from and may even conflict with theirs. All the same, I know that I live with them in a common world. Most importantly, I know that there is an ongoing correspondence between my meanings and their meanings in this world, that we share a common sense about its reality. The natural attitude is the attitude of commonsense consciousness precisely because it refers to a world that is common to many men. Commonsense knowledge is the knowledge I share with others in the normal, self-evident routines of everyday life.

The reality of everyday life is taken for granted as reality. It does not require additional verification over and beyond its simple presence. It is simply there, as self-evident and compelling facticity. I know that it is real. While I am capable of engaging in doubt about its reality, I am obliged to suspend such doubt as I routinely exist in everyday life. This suspension of doubt is so firm that to abandon it, as I might want to do, say, in theoretical or religious contemplation, I have to make an extreme transition. The world of everyday life proclaims itself and, when I want to challenge the proclamation, I must engage in a deliberate, by no means easy effort. The transition from the natural attitude to the theoretical attitude of the philosopher or scientist illustrates this point. But not all aspects of this reality are equally unproblematic. Everyday life is divided into sectors that are apprehended routinely, and others that present me with problems of one kind or another. Suppose that I am an automobile mechanic who is highly knowledgeable about all American made cars. Everything that pertains to the latter is a routine, unproblematic facet of my everyday life. But one day someone appears in the garage and asks me to repair his Volkswagen. I am now compelled to enter the problematic world of foreign-made cars. I may do so reluctantly or with professional curiosity, but in either case I am now faced with problems that I have not yet routinized. At the same time, of course, I do not leave the reality of everyday life. Indeed, the latter becomes enriched as I begin to incorporate into it the knowledge and skills required for the repair of foreign-made cars. The reality of everyday life encompasses both kinds of sectors, as long as what appears as a problem does not pertain to a different reality altogether (say, the reality of theoretical physics, or of nightmares). As long as the routines of everyday life continue without interruption they are apprehended as unproblematic.

But even the unproblematic sector of everyday reality is so only until further notice, that is, until its continuity is interrupted by the appearance of a problem. When this happens, the reality of everyday life seeks to integrate the problematic sector into what is already unproblematic. Commonsense knowledge contains a variety of instructions as to how this is to be done. For instance, the others with whom I work are unproblematic to me as long as they perform their familiar, taken-for-granted routines—say, typing away at desks next to mine in my office. They become problematic if they interrupt these routines—say, huddling together in a corner and talking in whispers. As I inquire about the meaning of this unusual activity, there is a variety of possibilities that my commonsense knowledge is capable of reintegrating into the unproblematic routines of everyday life: they may be consulting on how to fix a broken typewriter, or one of them may have some urgent instructions from the boss, and so on. On the other hand, I may find that they are discussing a union directive to go on strike, something as yet outside my experience but still well within the range of problems with which my commonsense knowledge can deal. It will deal with it, though, as a problem, rather than simply reintegrating it into the unproblematic sector of everyday life. If, however, I come to the conclusion that my colleagues have gone collectively mad, the problem that presents itself is of yet another kind. I am now faced with a problem that transcends the boundaries of the reality of everyday life and points to an altogether different reality. Indeed, my conclusion that my colleagues have gone mad implies ipso facto that they have gone off into a world that is no longer the common world of everyday life.

Compared to the reality of everyday life, other realities appear as finite provinces of meaning, enclaves within the paramount reality marked by circumscribed meanings and modes of experience. The paramount reality envelops them on all sides, as it were, and consciousness always returns to the paramount reality as from an excursion. This is evident from the illustrations already given, as in the reality of dreams or that of theoretical thought. Similar "commutations" take place between the world of everyday life and the world of play, both the playing of children and, even more sharply, of adults. The theater provides an excellent illustration of such playing on the part of adults. The transition between realities is marked by the rising and falling of the curtain. As the curtain rises, the spectator is "transported to another world," with its own meanings and an order that may or may not have much to do with the order of everyday life. As the curtain falls, the spectator "returns to reality," that is, to the paramount reality of everyday life by comparison with which the reality presented on the stage now appears tenuous and ephemeral, however vivid the presentation may have been a few moments previously. Aesthetic and religious experience is rich in producing transitions of this kind, in as much as art and religion are endemic producers of finite provinces of meaning.

All finite provinces of meaning are characterized by a turning away of attention from the reality of everyday life. While there are, of course, shifts in attention within everyday life, the shift to a finite province of meaning is of a much more radical kind. A radical change takes place in the tension of consciousness. In the context of religious experience this has been aptly called "leaping." It is important to stress, however, that the reality of everyday life retains its paramount status even as such "leaps" take place. If nothing else, language makes sure of this. The common language available to me for the objectification of my experiences is grounded in everyday life and keeps pointing back to it even as I employ it to interpret experiences in finite provinces of meaning. Typically, therefore, I "distort" the reality of the latter as soon as I begin to use the common language in interpreting them, that is, I "translate" the non-everyday experiences back into the paramount reality of everyday life. This may be readily seen in terms of dreams, but is also typical of those trying to report about theoretical, aesthetic or religious worlds of meaning. The theoretical physicist tells us that his concept of space cannot be conveyed linguistically, just as the artist does with regard to the meaning of his creations and the mystic with regard to his encounters with the divine. Yet all these—dreamer, physicist, artist and mystic—also live in the reality of everyday life. Indeed, one of their important problems is to interpret the coexistence of this reality with the reality enclaves into which they have ventured.

The world of everyday life is structured both spatially and temporally. The spatial structure is quite peripheral to our present considerations. Suffice it to point out that it, too, has a social dimension by virtue of the fact that my manipulatory zone intersects with that of others. More important for our present purpose is the temporal structure of everyday life.

Temporality is an intrinsic property of consciousness. The stream of consciousness is always ordered temporally. It is possible to differentiate between different levels of this temporality, as it is intrasubjectively available. Every individual is conscious of an inner flow of time, which in turn is rounded on the physiological rhythm of the organism though it is not identical with these. It would greatly exceed the scope of these prolegomena to enter into a detailed analysis of these levels of intrasubjective temporality. As we have indicated, however, intersubjectivity in everyday life also has a temporal dimension. The world of everyday life has its own standard time, which is intersubjectively available. This standard time may be understood as the intersection between cosmic time and its socially established calendar, based on the temporal sequences of nature, and inner time, in its aforementioned differentiations.

There can never be full simultaneity between these various levels of temporality, as the experience of waiting indicates most clearly. Both my organism and my society impose upon me, and upon my inner time, certain sequences of events that involve waiting. I may want to take part in a sports event, but I must wait for my bruised knee to heal. Or again, I must wait until certain papers are processed so that my qualification for the event may be officially established. It may readily be seen that the temporal structure of everyday life is exceedingly complex, because the different levels of empirically present temporality must be ongoingly correlated.

The temporal structure of everyday life confronts me as a facticity with which I must reckon, that is, with which I must try to synchronize my own projects. I encounter time in everyday reality as continuous and finite. All my existence in this world is continuously ordered by its time, is indeed enveloped by it. My own life is an episode in the externally factitious stream of time. It was there before I was born and it will be there after I die. The knowledge of my inevitable death makes this time finite *for me*. I have only a certain amount time available for the realization of my projects, and the knowledge of this affects my attitude to these projects. Also, since I do not want to die, this knowledge injects an underlying anxiety into my projects. Thus I cannot endlessly repeat my participation in sports events. I know that I am getting older. It may even be that this is the last occasion on which I have the chance to participate. My waiting will be anxious to the degree in which the finitude of time impinges upon the project.

The same temporal structure, as has already been indicated, is coercive. I cannot reverse at will the sequences imposed by it—"first things first" is an essential element of my knowledge of everyday life. Thus I cannot take a certain examination before I have passed through certain educational programs, I cannot practice my profession before I have taken this examination, and so on. Also, the same temporal structure provides the historicity that determines my situation in the world of everyday life. I was born on a certain date, entered school on another, started working as a professional on another, and so on. These dates, however, are all "located" within a much more comprehensive history, and this "location" decisively shapes my situation. Thus I was born in the year of the great bank crash in which my father lost his wealth, I entered school just before the revolution, I began to work just after the great war broke out, and so forth. The temporal structure of everyday life not only imposes prearranged sequences upon the "agenda" of any single day but also imposes itself upon my biography as a whole. Within the co-ordinates set by this temporal structure I apprehend both daily "agenda" and overall biography. Clock and calendar ensure that, indeed, I am a "man of my time." Only within this temporal structure does everyday life retain for me its accent of reality. Thus in cases where I may be "disoriented" for one reason or another (say, I have been in an automobile accident in which I was knocked unconscious), I feel an almost instinctive urge to "reorient" myself within the temporal structure of everyday life. I look at my watch and try to recall what day it is. By these acts alone I re-enter the reality of everyday life.

REVIEW QUESTIONS

1. What is the social construction of reality?

2. How can your social construction of reality influence your research?

3. What does it take to step back from your own reality in research? Can you do this completely? Must you?

Chapter 2: Combining Theory with Research Questions

Why do you think research is conducted? The main reason is that researchers hope their findings will contribute to the discipline, while enhancing the various ways we all have of knowing about life and the world. I have found that theory is one of the least understood and most difficult terms for students who are learning about social science research. Regardless, it seems to me that the most important aspect for you to understand is to be able to describe various theories and to know how to use those theories in your research. A **theory** is basically nothing more than a system of ideas that help explain various patterns in the world. Let's say it is finals time and you believe that you learn more if you study for a few hours the night before the test rather than for an hour or two every night during the semester. That is a theory. As a result, theories guide you and give you clues about the direction in which to conduct research (Babbie, 2001).

Let me give you an example of how combining theories with research actually works. While I was in graduate school, I conducted a research project on transvestites (Wysocki, 1993). A transvestite is a person who wears the clothing of the opposite sex. I was investigating only males, who considered themselves to be heterosexual, but who liked to wear women's clothing. At first I thought I would just describe what they were telling me about their lives: when they started cross-dressing, why they cross-dressed, and how they cross-dressed. That would have been just **descriptive research,** which had already been done in other articles. I believed (and my thesis committee did as well) that a descriptive study would not have added much to the literature on transvestism. So, I went looking for the literature and found many different perspectives or theories that I could have drawn from to conduct this project. For instance, I could have used the medical model, which states there was some genetic problem within the man's body to make him want to cross-dress that can be *cured* by medicine (Rubenstein and Engel, 1996). Or I could have used the deviance literature that states that any behavior outside of the norm is considered deviant (Thio and Calhoun, 2001). Therefore, a man who wears the clothing of the opposite sex is deviant because what he does is not considered normal by society's standards. However, I consider myself a feminist sociologist, so I wanted to investigate transvestism from the social construction of sex, gender, and sexuality perspective, which states that we have all been taught how to portray ourselves based on what we have seen in the culture in which we live (Berger and Luckmann, 1966). So, the focus of my project changed when I used this theory as my guide. Instead of using a descriptive, medical, or deviant focus, I explored the aspects of femininity my respondents wanted to take on and the aspects of masculinity they wanted to get rid of (Wysocki, 1993).

LEVELS OF ANALYSIS AND THEORIES

There are many different ways to make sense of our social world and each way has resulted in different explanations. In 1970, T. S. Kuhn stated that scientists worked within paradigms. **Paradigms** are models or frameworks that help us observe and understand what we are studying. Paradigms are ways of viewing the world that dictate the type of scientific work that should be conducted and the kinds of theories that are acceptable. However, nothing stays the same, and over time, old paradigms are replaced by new ones (Kuhn, 1970).

As I stated earlier, theories involve constructing abstract interpretations that can be used to explain a wide variety of situations in the social world from various levels. Let me give you an example. Sagy, Stern, and Krakover (1996) examined the various factors that influenced the development of a sense of community in Israel. They looked at two different populations: 242 immigrants from the former USSR and 60 Israeli veterans who lived in five different temporary neighborhoods. First, the researchers used a **macrolevel analysis** that looked at large-scale social systems, such as the government or economic system and examined population size, population density, number of dwelling units in the site, urbanity of the area, ethnic heterogeneity, and peripheriality of the region. Second, they used a **microlevel analysis,** which looked at the everyday behavior in situations of face-to-face interactions, such as how people decide who to marry or how children communicate on a playground. In this study the researchers used three kinds of variables to accomplish their goals: (a) personal attitudes: evaluation of the dwelling unit and satisfaction with public services; (b) social networks; and (c) sociodemographic characteristics. As a result of using two different levels of analysis, they found some differences. For the veteran sample, only one macrolevel variable, the number of dwelling units in the site, and in the immigrant sample, three microlevel factors, evaluation of the dwelling unit, external network, and age, played a part in the underlying sense of community vary for different groups of people. Even though the Sagy et al. (1996) study didn't mention it, in between the macro and micro levels would be the **mesolevel analysis,** which focuses on social groups and organizations, such as the classroom or an office. In the Sagy et al. (1996) study, the mesolevel analysis might look at the two different groups to see how they interacted with each other.

Here is another example. Let's say you have an interest in researching education. If you investigated education from the macrolevel, you could ask the question "How does College A differ from College B?" From the microlevel, you could ask "How do women interact differently than men do in the classroom?," and from a mesolevel, you could ask, "How do computer science classes differ from sociology classes?"

Although you can use many different theories in your research, I am going to briefly mention only the major ones that you are most likely to come across in your readings. **Conflict theory** can be traced back to the writings of Karl Marx (1818–1883), who stated that power, ideology, and conflict are closely connected and that individuals are always in competition for resources or advantages. Those who hold the most power maintain their dominance over those without the power. If you want to study domestic violence, you might use the conflict theory to suggest that one person in the relationship has more power than the other does and, therefore, has more control over the situation that could lead to violence.

The **functionalist theory** was originally pioneered by Auguste Comte (1798–1857), who believed society was similar to an organism because it is made up of various parts that contribute to keep society functioning as a whole. If everything in society has a function, then society maintains equilibrium because everyone, and every social institution, has a job or a specific role to play. Think about your own family and how each member probably has his or her own job to do. One person might be responsible for taking out the trash, another for cooking dinner, and another for paying the bills. Everyone in the family has a function, and therefore the home retains its equilibrium if everyone does his or her part.

Symbolic interactionism was a theory that was influenced by the work of George Herbert Mead (1863–1931), who believed that language allows us to become self-conscious beings and that the key element in this process is the symbol. Social life actually depends on our ability to imagine ourselves in other social roles and our ability to communicate with others. One way to communicate is by using symbols and gestures. Having a common understanding of the symbols and gestures help us to make decisions about what is going on and how to respond in each situation. Have you recently told someone that you love him or her? Do you need to say this with words or are there symbols that mean the same thing? If you send a dozen long-stemmed roses to this person at work, would the roses be a symbol of your feelings? What about religious symbols worn on necklaces? What does the symbol tell you about the person? If you meet someone who is wearing a Star of David on his or her necklace, you might assume that the person you are talking to is Jewish without the person even telling you so. Could that symbol influence your behavior? How? Could it change or influence research?

I believe that **feminist theory** is an important theory to know about as well. The development of feminist theories has greatly influenced the way in which some researchers analyze women's positions in society (Ollenburger & Moore, 1998). Beginning with the women's movement of the 1960s and 1970s, feminist theory explores the variables of sex, gender, race, and sexuality and focuses on inequality in all areas of life. In other words, feminist theory involves questions about *identity* and *differences* (Reinharz, 1992). Research on gender differences will let you know why men and women tend to work in different areas of a production plant and don't often work side by side (Bielby & Baron, 1986), why women on average make less money than men who have the same amount of education (Bureau of Labor Statistics, 1998, 2001), and why the division of labor within the household is not equal (Berk, 1985). In my own work on various blood diseases (Wysocki, 2001), I focus on how women have been underdiagnosed and misdiagnosed when they show symptoms of a specific illness. The questions I ask are about the power differential between doctors and patients, and I explore whether or not women's complaints are minimized because they are women. Keep in mind that you don't have to be female or consider yourself a feminist to use a feminist perspective.

RESEARCH METHODS 101

While we are going to spend more time on these concepts in later chapters, I think it will be helpful for you as you read some of the articles in this reader to understand some of the key terms used in research. We have already talked about theories that guide us as we discover the "ins" and "outs" of the subject we are studying. We accomplish this task through the use of **concepts,** which are the mental images we have that summarize a set of similar observations, feelings, or ideas that is used to explain exactly what is meant by the term we are using in our project. Let's use the term "social class" and assume I ask you the question "what social class are you in?" What does this mean to you? Does it mean the

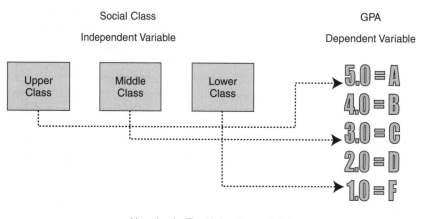

Hypothesis: The higher the social class a
person is in, the higher GPA they will have

Figure 2.1. The Relationship Between Social Class and GPA

same thing to you as it does to me? According to Wordnet (1997), social class is "people who have the same social or economic status." But how do we really know for sure what our social class would be? Do your parents say "We are lower class" or do you assume that because your parents are not paying for your college and you have to work to pay for your tuition that you are in a lower class?

To be able to measure social class, we need to have a **variable.** A variable is a characteristic that can change from one subject to another and must have at least two categories. So, the variable "social class" could have three categories that are "upper class," "middle class," and "lower class." Suppose we believe that the higher the social class of a person, the higher GPA they will have as shown in Figure 2.1.

This means that we have an expectation of what we will find when the research is completed. This expectation is stated in the form of a **hypothesis,** which is a statement about how two or more variables are expected to relate to each other. Notice that our hypothesis has two variables. One is the **independent variable** and the other is the **dependent variable.** The independent variable affects the change in the dependent variable and the dependent variable is changed. Which is which in our hypothesis? You are correct!!! Social class is the independent variable and GPA is the dependent variable. As you read the following articles, see if you can find the hypothesis, the independent variable, and the dependent variable. We will go into more detail about this in future chapters.

REFERENCES

Babbie, 2001. *The practice of social research* (9th edition). Belmont, CA: Wadsworth/Thomson Learning.

Berger, P., & Luckmann, T. 1966. *The social construction of reality: A treatise in the sociology of knowledge.* Garden City, NY: Doubleday.

Berk, S. F. 1985. *The gender factory: The apportionment of work in American households.* New York: Plenum.

Bielby, W., & Baron, J. N. 1986. Men and women at work: Sex segregation and statistical discrimination. *American Journal of Sociology,* 91: 759–799.

Bureau of Labor Statistics. 1998. Labor force statistics from the current population survey, Annual Average Tables from the January 1998 Issue of Employment and Earnings. [ONLINE] http://www.bls.gov/opub/mlr/1997/04/art2exc.htm#4a

Bureau of Labor Statistics. 2001. Median weekly earnings of full-time wage and salary workers by union affiliation, occupation, and industry. [ONLINE] http://stats.bls.gov/cps/cpsaat39.pdf

Kuhn, T. 1970. *The structure of scientific revolutions.* Chicago: University of Chicago Press.

Ollenburger, J. C., & Moore, H. A. 1998. *A sociology of women* (2nd edition). Upper Saddle River, NJ: Prentice Hall.

Reinharz, S. 1992. *Feminist methods in social research.* New York: Oxford University Press.

Rubenstein, E. B., & Engel, N. L. 1996. Successful treatment of transvestic fetishism with sertraline and lithium. *Journal of Clinical Psychiatry,* 57(2): 92.

Sagy, S., Stern, E., & Krakover, S. 1996. Macro- and microlevel factors related to sense of community: The case of temporary neighborhoods in Israel. *American Journal of Community Psychology,* 24(5): 657–677.

Thio, A., & Calhoun, T. 2001. *Readings in deviant behavior* (2nd edition). Boston: Allyn & Bacon.

WordNet® 1.6, © 1997 Princeton University "Definition of Social Class" [ONLINE] http://www.dictionary.com/search?q=social%20class

Wysocki, D. K. 1993. Construction of masculinity: A look into the lives of heterosexual male transvestites. *Feminism and Psychology,* 3(2): 374–380.

Wysocki, D. K. 2001. Gynecological and obstetrical complications in women with inherited bleeding disorders. *Female Patient,* 26: 13–15.

INFOTRAC COLLEGE EDITION SUGGESTED READINGS AND DISCUSSION QUESTIONS

1. Use keyword searches for the terms "research" and "theory" on InfoTrac College Edition. Find an article of interest to you. Can you describe the theory that the author used in the research project? How was it used? What other theories might have been used? Would using a different theory change the results of the project?

2. Look up the articles by T. Harris & P. Hill, 1998, "'Waiting to Exhale' or 'breath(ing) again': A search for identity, empowerment, and love in the 1990s," *Women and Language,* 21(2): 9. How has the theory in this article been used? What results do the authors find?

3. Look up articles in InfoTrac College Edition, such as "Dennis Rodman—'Barbie Doll gone horribly wrong': Marginalized masculinity, cross-dressing, and the limitations of commodity culture" or "'The nerd within': Mass media and the negotiation of identity among computer-using men." What kinds of research and theory are the authors using?

Delinquency of Chinese-Canadian Youth: A Test of Opportunity, Control, and Intergeneration Conflict Theories

Siu Kwong Wong

This reading uses three different theories to investigate youth of Chinese descent in North America. It is believed that these youth have a lower prevalence of delinquency than the average Canadian or American youth, probably because of the positive influence of their Chinese culture. This study used a sample of Chinese youth and adolescents in Winnipeg, Manitoba. Which three theoretical perspectives did the authors use? Notice how each of the perspectives changes the questions that are asked and the explanations that follow.

The number of immigrants who arrived in Canada from Southeast Asia, especially from Hong Kong, Taiwan, and China, has increased substantially in recent years. The population of Chinese in the major metropolises like Vancouver and Toronto has reached a significant proportion. However, there is relatively little research on immigrants and their children in Canada. What is known about these people has been influenced much by the media's reports of a handful of cases. Often, the media focuses on the extreme cases of immigrants' problems or achievements. At the one extreme, there are reports of criminal and exploitive activities in Chinatowns and neighboring ethnic communities such as gangland rivalry, drug trafficking, prostitution, smuggling of illegal immigrants, and exploitation of underground immigrant workers (Burton, Calabresi, & FlorCruz, 1993; Church, 1993; Liu, Gibney, Miller, & Morganthau, 1993). At the other extreme is the myth of Asian overachievers in Canadian and U.S. schools and universities. There is also a recent trend that Chinese Americans and Japanese Americans are depicted as "model minorities," since these groups seem to be doing much better socially and economically than other minority groups (Toupin & Son, 1991; Wong, 1985). Neither of these wholesale stereotypes, however popular, can accurately and justly represent the Chinese in North America.

Therefore, it is important to obtain a more accurate and balanced view of the prevalence of delinquency among Chinese youth and adolescents in North America, and to determine the extent to which the prevalence is explained by ethnicity or culture. The purpose of this study is to examine the relationship between delinquency and acculturation.

Prevalence of Delinquency

Studies on delinquency among Chinese youth in North America are relatively rare. Almost all of the existing studies were conducted in major metropolises in the United States such as New York, Los Angeles, or San Francisco. Moreover, many of those studies were based on small samples, official statistics, or evaluation of adolescents and youth by parents and teachers. Furthermore, there are concerns that delinquency and other problems among Chinese may be underreported.

Most of the recent studies on crime and delinquency among Chinese American youth focused on organized crime and gang activities (e.g., see Chin, 1990; Joe, 1994; Kelly, Chin, & Fagan, 1993). These studies focus mostly on gang members whose offenses tend to be specialized, such as drug dealing and trafficking, extortion, illegal gambling, gangland rivalry, and murder and massacre. Gang members are also quite different from the average Chinese youth in terms of their social and demographic characteristics. The typical member is an unemployed man in his late teens or early 20s with below average educational attainment (Joe, 1994). Thus, it is extremely difficult, if not impossible, to gauge the true prevalence of delinquency among Chinese youth based on a selected group of people.

With regard to the prevalence of delinquency in general, investigators tend to agree that North Americans of Asian origin have rather low rates of delinquency and behavior disorders (Abbott & Abbott, 1973; Chang, Morrissey, & Koplewicz, 1995; Cochrane, 1979; Kallarackal & Herbert, 1976; Kitano, 1973; Touliatos & Lindholm, 1980). However, there is also the possibility of underreporting that has caused the rates of delinquency to appear lower than they actually are. As a result, investigators are less certain as to the true prevalence of crime and delinquency among Asian American youth.

Explanations of Delinquency

Three explanations—opportunity theory, control theory, and intergeneration conflict theory—are identified as relevant to the study of the relationship between acculturation and delinquency.

Opportunity Theory. The thesis of opportunity theory is that ethnic minorities who have strong ties to their ethnic culture and community have access to illegitimate and legitimate opportunities provided by both conventional and unconventional organizations within the ethnic community. The availability of illegitimate opportunities, in turn, increases the likelihood of involvement in crime and delinquency.

In studies of gangs and organized crime, the typical gang member is depicted as someone who is low in English proficiency and has strong ties to the ethnic community, especially to the "tongs" or "triads." Gang members are often socially and economically disadvantaged, probably due to language barrier, lower class status, and discrimination by the larger society. Their opportunities, therefore, are confined to employment and providing services, either conventional or illicit, within the ethnic community. The opportunities and associations, especially those related to the tongs or triads, allow them to be involved in illegal activities such as drug dealing and trafficking and extortion (Joe, 1994; Kelly et al., 1993). In some cases, gang members may even offer protection to small businesses and individuals within the ethnic community from invading non-Chinese gangs (Kendis & Kendis, 1976). Based on opportunity theory, it is reasonable to hypothesize that adherence to Chinese culture increases access to illegitimate opportunities and the subsequent involvement in crime and delinquency.

Control Theory. Contrary to opportunity theory, control theory offers just the opposite view of the relationship between ethnic ties and delinquency. It states that adherence to one's ethnic culture reduces delinquency and acculturation to North American society increases delinquency. The underlying assumption of the theory is that Chinese culture is more keen on conformity, family solidarity, maintaining harmonious relationships, and respect for authority, particularly the unconditional respect for parents or filial piety (Fong, 1973). Chinese parents emphasize more physical control and restrictive rearing practices, whereas North American parents encourage individual freedom and choice (Kelley & Tseng, 1992).

Therefore, those who are committed to the traditional family and have strong ethnic values and strong ties to the ethnic community are shielded from deviant influences. Conversely speaking, those who deny their ethnic culture and detach from the ethnic community are likely to be marginalized and are susceptible to deviant influences.

Intergeneration Conflict Theory. The intergeneration conflict perspective addresses adjustment problems such as culture conflict, intergeneration conflict exacerbated by culture conflict, and adolescent identity crisis that minority and immigrant children face in a culture different from that of their parents (e.g., see Aronowitz, 1984). These problems may explain why some minority and immigrant children are more prone to psychiatric problems, behavior disorders, and delinquency.

The generation gap between parents and children may be widened by acculturation. Nguyen and Williams (1989) noted a substantial gap between Vietnamese American adolescents and their parents with regard to views on traditional values such as obedience to parents and respect for authority. Moreover, the longer the families were in the United States, the wider the value gap grew because parents kept their adherence to traditional values, whereas their children continued to acculturate to North American values. The gap in cultural values may exacerbate intergeneration conflict, which in turn weakens parental control and increases the likelihood of delinquency.

Another source of conflict may stem from the selective assimilation strategy many parents from Asia employ for their children (Portes & Zhou, 1993). On one hand, they expect their children to be proficient in English and to be successful in school and, later, in a promising career. On the other hand, they restrict their children from having too much contact with American friends and prevent them from being too "Americanized." Thus, even successful relationships with American peers can become a source of intergeneration conflict between parents and children (Charron & Ness, 1981). Also, children who fail to fulfill the dual expectations may become marginalized and susceptible to deviant influences (Hisama, 1980; Sue & Sue, 1973). Hence, a hypothesis is derived from the intergeneration conflict perspective that states that for those whose parents are less acculturated, acculturation increases the likelihood of involvement in delinquency (due to a widening intergeneration gap exacerbated by culture conflict); for those whose parents are more acculturated, acculturation has no effect on delinquency.

Method

Sample

The present analysis is based on a sample of 315 adolescents and youth of Chinese descent in Winnipeg, Manitoba. The sampling procedure began by drawing 2,000 single-syllable Chinese-sounding names from the city telephone directory. The households were contacted by telephone, and household members ages 10–20 with a Chinese background were identified. Of the 2,000 households contacted, a total of 477 eligible subjects were identified. Then, a subsequent mailed questionnaire was sent to the subjects up to four times until completion. Based on the number of respondents, refusals, and other non-responses, the response rate was about 70 percent.

Measurement

Acculturation. Acculturation refers to the adoption of the traits or patterns of another cultural group. Here, acculturation is viewed as an adaptation strategy or part of an adjustment process for individuals or the group as a whole to settle in a new social environment. Also, a rather broad definition of acculturation is used here that includes language, customs, habits and lifestyle, values, and family and peer relations.

In addition, moral values, commitment to the family, and association with Chinese friends also were examined as possible indicators of acculturation. Six questionnaire items were employed to measure moral values that included attitudes toward obedience to parents, respect for laws, tolerance of deviance, and the individual's freedom to smoke or drink. Presumably, those who have strong adherence to Chinese culture should score higher on items of obedience and conformity, and those who are acculturated to Canadian culture should score higher on items of tolerance and individualist values. Four items, including helping the family with housework, doing things for parents, and sensitivity to parents' opinion, were used to measure the respondents' commitment to the family. Association with Chinese friends was measured as the proportion of Chinese and Chinese-speaking friends.

Canadian-born respondents were compared with their foreign-born counterparts to show the extent to which the acculturation measures could discriminate between the two subsamples and yield a reasonable level of validity. The comparison revealed that Canadian-born respondents had significantly higher averages on the items of acculturation than foreign-born respondents. The differences were most notable in relation to customs, including ways of celebrating birthdays, relating to friends, and talking. In addition, native-born respondents had significantly fewer Chinese friends or friends who spoke Chinese than did foreign-born respondents. On the other hand, moral values and commitment to the family failed to differentiate foreign-born respondents from native-born respondents.

Parents' Acculturation. The effect of acculturation on delinquency by parents' level of acculturation was indicated by parents' English proficiency. Respondents were asked to state how well their parents could speak English. About 50 percent of the respondents reported that their father's level of English proficiency was "excellent" or "good," and 44 percent reported that their mother reached that level of proficiency. High level of parents' English proficiency was measured as both parents being in the "excellent" or "good" categories.

Delinquency. Respondents were asked to report the number of times they had committed delinquent acts, which ranged from skipping classes and cheating to assault and robbery, in the past 12 months. The sample as a whole had reportedly committed at least a total of

3,167 offenses, or an average of about 10 offenses per person. However, a majority of these offenses were quite minor, such as truancy (384 incidents), violation of copyright laws (809 incidents), and uttering threats of assault (273 incidents). Nonetheless, more serious offenses such as assaults (610 incidents) and thefts (376 incidents) were not uncommon among the respondents. About 85 percent of the respondents claimed that they had committed at least one of the 21 acts in the past year, and 40 percent of the respondents admitted committing at least 10 of the acts listed.

Findings

The opportunity hypothesis predicts that adherence to Chinese culture increases the likelihood of involvement in delinquency due to the increase in illegitimate opportunities. Conversely speaking, acculturation to Canadian society should reduce illegitimate opportunities and delinquency involvement. However, the results did not lend much support to this opportunity hypothesis. The observed effect of acculturation indicated that adherence to Chinese culture reduced rather than increased delinquency involvement. Therefore, the direction of the effect was just the opposite of what was predicted by opportunity theory.

The hypothesis derived from control theory proposes that adherence to Chinese culture reduces delinquency due to commitments to the traditional family and moral values. If that is true, then commitments to the family and moral values should mediate the effect of adherence to Chinese culture on delinquency. Once the effects of these mediating factors are removed, the effect of adherence to Chinese culture on delinquency should be significantly reduced. However, the effect of behavioral acculturation on delinquency did not decrease much even after controlling for the effects of moral values and family commitment. Therefore, it is reasonable to conclude that much of the effect of behavioral acculturation was not mediated by strong moral values or family commitment. This finding challenges control theory, which argues that Chinese are more conforming because of their cultural emphases on the traditional family and strong moral values.

To test the hypothesis derived from intergeneration conflict theory, the dependent variable of acculturation and subsample comparison was made based on the English proficiency of parents. The intergeneration conflict hypothesis predicts that the generation gap is widened by acculturation among those whose parents are less acculturated, and the widened gap, in turn, causes delinquency to increase. Consistent with this hypothesis, the observed effect of behavioral acculturation on delinquency was significant and positive for those whose parents had low English proficiency, whereas the effect was much weaker for the high-proficiency group. Perhaps the English proficiency of parents measures only one area of acculturation, and, given the limitation of the data, it may be more appropriate to concentrate on the language gap rather than the acculturation gap between parents and the child. Therefore, the effect of language acculturation on delinquency was estimated for the two subsamples. That is, those who used English more often were more likely to have committed delinquency, probably due to a widened language gap between them and their parents. On the other hand, for those whose parents were more proficient in English, language acculturation had no significant effect on delinquency, just as it was predicted by the theory. Again, the observed effect lends considerable support to the intergeneration conflict hypothesis.

Discussion

The results from the present study challenge some popular views on the relationship between culture and delinquency. It has been suggested in the literature that Chinese culture reinforces conformity due to the strong traditional family and cultural norms (Chang et al., 1995; Fong, 1973; Li & Rosenblood, 1994). As Chen and Yang (1986) summarized:

> Chinese culture, one of the world's oldest dating back to 4,000 years, traditionally emphasized loyalty to family, devotion to tradition, and greatly downplayed individual feelings (Hsu, 1981). American culture, one of the world's most recent with barely 400 years of history, emphasizes self-reliance, personal freedom, and glorifies the individual. (p. 19)

Contrary to this popular view, results from the present study do not show the suggested differences between Chinese and Canadian (North American) cultures. There were no observable differences between native-born and foreign-born respondents with regard to moral values and family commitment. Also, it has been demonstrated that moral values and family commitment did not mediate or explain the effect of acculturation. To that extent, the effect of culture on delinquency had little to do with differences in cultural norms or views on the traditional family.

If the above observation is true, then it is doubtful whether Chinese cultural norms and traditions per se can explain the low prevalence of delinquency among Chinese youth and adolescents in North America. Although a comparison between Chinese and North American cultural norms and traditions is beyond the scope of this study, the evidence from this study leads to the tentative conclusion that as a social control mechanism, Chinese cultural norms and traditions do not seem to be superior to those of Canadian or North American culture. However, more extensive evidence is needed before the preceding statement can be accepted as true. The lack of effect of association with Chinese peers on delinquency is also quite intriguing. Presumably, if Chinese adolescents and youth are more conforming than their non-Chinese counterparts, then association with the former should have greater restraining effects on delinquent behavior than association with the latter. Moreover, according to intergeneration conflict theory, association with non-Chinese peers should be a source of conflict between parents and the child because parents who employ the selective assimilation strategy for their children should disapprove of having too much contact with non-Chinese children. For either one of the above reasons, association with Chinese friends should reduce delinquency, whereas association with non-Chinese friends should increase delinquency. However, the evidence supported neither argument.

The evidence points to the possibility that peers, Chinese or non-Chinese alike, are not very effective enforcement agents of societal morality and norms. Also, non-Chinese peers do not have more deviant influence than Chinese peers. If that is true, then parents have little to worry about even when their children choose to have more non-Chinese than Chinese friends. Furthermore, it is possible that Chinese parents nowadays hold a more positive view toward non-Chinese than earlier Chinese immigrants did. Although racial discrimination is still a reality in North America, Chinese today do not share the same experience of open and outright discrimination directed at earlier immigrants (Li, 1988). Due to frequent interactions with residents in the inner city or the neighboring areas of

Chinatown, where they competed for the same jobs and resources, earlier immigrants had developed certain negative stereotypes about Caucasians and other non-Chinese, just as the non-Chinese held certain negative stereotypes about the Chinese (Kendis & Kendis, 1976). In contrast, the physical and social environment of the suburban areas, where many Chinese reside today, may contribute to a more positive view of Chinese parents toward their non-Chinese neighbors, and vice versa. Thus, Chinese parents may become more approving of their children's choice of non-Chinese friends. This explains why the child's association with non-Chinese friends does not necessarily lead to conflict between the generations.

The findings raise an even more fundamental question: To what extent are Chinese and Canadian or North American cultures different from each other? As far as this sample of respondents is concerned, the differences seem to be found in behavioral traits such as language, customs, habits, lifestyle, and friendship rather than cultural values and family relationship. Perhaps differences between Chinese and Canadian culture have been diminished due to increased interaction between cultural groups and exposure to different cultures. After all, immigrants from countries and places such as Taiwan, Hong Kong, and mainland China have been exposed to and practiced Western ideologies such as socialism and capitalism. Moreover, the availability of news and television broadcasts from Europe, Australasia, and North America has allowed the people in Taiwan, Hong Kong, and mainland China to be more or less internationalized even before they come to North America. The diminished cultural differences may explain why the results do not lend much support to control theory and offer only limited support to intergeneration conflict theory.

Nevertheless, culture is still a relevant explanation of delinquency for this particular sample of Chinese youth and the population they represent. At the very least, the findings have revealed some benefits of adherence to one's ethnic culture. It has been shown that adherence to Chinese culture, practicing Chinese customs in particular, reduced the involvement in minor offenses. Conversely, acculturation to Canadian society contributed to the increase in delinquency. Moreover, it has been shown that the language gap between parents and the child also contributed to the increase in delinquency.

In conclusion, results from this study challenge the "model minority" myth about people of Asian and Chinese origins in North America. Chinese culture is not a panacea for problems and it does not guarantee social and economic success. It is fair to say that children of minority ethnic origins, Chinese and non-Chinese alike, are at a higher risk of encountering personal problems than the average North American child. As we can see from the findings, even acculturation to the host society, a seemingly natural and harmless thing for a child to do in North America, can be a source of conflict between the generations. Thus, being Chinese does not reduce the problems and difficulties these children have to face and overcome. On the contrary, a long history of discriminatory government policy and the recent reduction of educational and occupational opportunities for Chinese and Asians make it more difficult for Chinese children to do well and succeed (Li, 1988; Wong, 1985). The fact that children of Chinese and Asian origins do not have a higher prevalence of delinquency than the average children in North America and that some of them are successful academically may be attributed to the tremendous efforts on the part of the individuals, the family and parents, and the ethnic community rather than the protective cushion of their ethnic culture.

References

Abbott, K. A., & Abbott, E. L. (1973). Juvenile delinquency in San Francisco's Chinese American community: 1961–1966. In S. Sue & N. Wagner (Eds.), *Asian-Americans: Psychological perspectives* (pp. 171–180). Palo Alto, CA: Science and Behavior Books, Inc.

Aronowitz, M. (1984). The social and emotional adjustment of immigrant children: A review of the literature. *International Migration Review, 18,* 237–257.

Burton, S., Calabresi, M., & FlorCruz, J. A. (1993, June 21). Where's the promised land? *Time,* pp. 35–36.

Chang, L., Morrissey, R. F., & Koplewicz, H. S. (1995). Prevalence of psychiatric symptoms and their relation to adjustment among Chinese-American youth. *Journal of the American Academy of Child and Adolescent Psychiatry, 34,* 91–99.

Charron, D. W., & Ness, R. C. (1981). Emotional distress among Vietnamese adolescents. *Journal of Refugee Resettlement, 1,* 7–15.

Chen, C. L., & Yang, D. C. Y. (1986). The self-image of Chinese-American adolescents: A cross-cultural comparison. *International Journal of Social Psychology, 32,* 19–26.

Chin, K.-L. (1990). *Chinese subculture and criminality.* Westport, CT: Greenwood.

Church, G. J. (1993, June 21). Send back your tired, your poor . . . *Time,* pp. 32–33.

Cochrane, R. (1979). Psychological and behavioral disturbance in West Indians, Indians and Pakistanis in Britain: A comparison of rates among children and adults. *British Journal of Psychiatry, 134,* 201–210.

Fong, S. L. M. (1973). Assimilation and changing social roles of Chinese Americans. *Journal of Social Issues, 29,* 115–127.

Hisama, T. (1980). Minority group children and behavior disorders: The case of Asian-American children. *Behavior Disorders, 5,* 186–196.

Hsu, F. L. K. (1981). *Americans and Chinese: Passage to differences* (3rd ed.). Honolulu: University Press of Hawaii.

Joe, K. A. (1994). The new criminal conspiracy? Asian gangs and organized crime in San Francisco. *Journal of Research in Crime and Delinquency, 31,* 390–415.

Kallarackal, A., & Herbert, M. (1976, February). The happiness of Indian immigrant children. *New Society,* pp. 422–424.

Kelley, M. L., & Tseng, H.-M. (1992). Cultural differences in child rearing: A comparison of immigrant Chinese and Caucasian American mothers. *Journal of Cross Cultural Psychology, 23,* 444–455.

Kelly, R. J., Chin, K.-L., & Fagan, J. A. (1993). The dragon breathes fire: Chinese organized crime in New York City. *Crime, Law and Social Change, 19,* 245–269.

Kendis, K. O., & Kendis, R. J. (1976). The street boy identity: An alternate strategy of Boston's Chinese. *American Urban Anthropology, 5,* 1–17.

Kitano, H. H. L. (1973). Japanese-American crime and delinquency. In S. Sue & N. N. Wagner (Eds.), *Asian-Americans: Psychological perspectives* (pp. 161–170). Palo Alto, CA: Science and Behavior Books, Inc.

Li, H. Z., & Rosenblood, L. (1994). Exploring factors influencing alcohol consumption: Patterns among Chinese and Caucasians. *Journal of Studies and Alcohol, 55,* 427–433.

Li, P. S. (1988). *The Chinese in Canada.* Toronto: Oxford University Press.

Liu, M., Gibney, F. Jr., Miller, S., & Morganthau, T. (1993, June 21). The new slave trade. *Newsweek,* pp. 34–41.

Nguyen, N. A., & Williams, H. L. (1989). Transition from East to West: Vietnamese adolescents and their parents. *The American Academy of Child and Adolescent Psychiatry, 28,* 505–515.

Portes, A., & Zhou, M. (1993). The new second generation: Segmented assimilation and its variants. *Annals, American Academy of Political and Social Sciences, 530,* 74–96.

Sue, S., & Sue, D. W. (1973). Chinese-American personality and mental health. In S. Sue & N. N. Wagner (Eds.), *Asian Americans: Psychological Perspectives* (pp. 111–123). Palo Alto, CA: Science and Behavior Books, Inc.

Touliatos, J., & Lindholm, B. W. (1980). Behavioral disturbance in children of native-born and immigrant parents. *Journal of Community Psychology, 8,* 28–33.

Toupin, E. S. WA., & Son, L. (1991). Preliminary findings on Asian Americans: "The model minority" in a small private East Coast college. *Journal of Cross-Cultural Psychology, 22,* 403–417.

Wong, E. F. (1985). Asian American middleman minority theory: The framework of an American myth. *Journal of Ethnic Studies, 13,* 51–88.

REVIEW QUESTIONS

1. What are some of the links between delinquency and conflict theory that were mentioned in this article?

2. Explain how the researchers used each of the three theories in their project.

3. What questions might the researchers have asked if they had used feminist theory in this project, rather than the three theories they used?

SCHOOL TRACKING AND STUDENT VIOLENCE

Lissa J. Yogan

There has been much attention in the media recently regarding violence in schools, espe-cially since the Columbine High School shootings in April 1999. As a result, it is important to find ways to curb this type of violence. Yogan used the theory of symbolic interactionism to explain the moral development children share with their teachers, how that moral devel-opment is affected by school practices, how these changes affect peer group interaction, how schools can positively influence and channel group formation, and ultimately reduce violence in schools. Can the explanations that Yogan used in her research decrease the violence in schools?

During the late 1990s, parents and educators alike became increasingly worried about the safety of schools. Their concern was warranted. The U.S. Department of Education reports that while the overall incidence of school crime had not greatly changed in recent years, there had been an increase in some types of school crime. School crime became more violent. Since 1992, there had been more than 211 school deaths associated with violence (Wolf, 1998). A few of these killings made the national news. When the suspects and victims were identified as small-town, white, middle-class children, the nation became alarmed. Over the past two years, there have been numerous cries to form national, state, and local task forces to confront the growing problem of school violence. Many of these task forces began to exam-ine school security systems, specifically the school's measures of crime prevention and con-trol. Were there enough metal detectors? Were the entrances locked? Were there enough security guards in place? While these security measures might prevent some incidents of vio-lence, they do nothing to help us understand why violent crime within schools has increased. In particular, they ignore the structure of the organization of schooling.

This article will focus on one aspect of school organizational structure: the effects that tracking (placing students in ability-based groups) has had on students' interactions with peers and adults. Looking at how and why students are tracked and how track place-ment affects their sense of self is one way of understanding the increase in school vio-lence, and it can suggest organizational changes as a way to combat it. I will begin by reviewing several theories and concepts that underlie the process of self-development. Un-derstanding how a person grows and develops and understanding how a school's structure may influence a person's self-development toward violent behavior can suggest organiza-tional changes that will ultimately result in decreased use of violence.

Symbolic Interactionist Theory and Student-Teacher Interaction

Social interaction, or, specifically, the interaction of students with peers and adults, is the subject matter of symbolic interactionism, one of the main branches of sociological theory.

Symbolic interactionism is based on the assumption that meaning and learning (education) are gained through interaction with others. How a person understands others, how others come to understand that person, and how the person comes to understand and identify himself or herself are part of the symbolic interaction process. It is through symbolic interaction that an individual develops a sense of self; who we are is partly a reflection of how others see us, as Charles Horton Cooley (1909) first pointed out. He called this idea the "looking glass self." In particular, we are shaped by our interactions with people who are significant to us. What is different for each of us is the group of people we consider to be significant; thus each of us undergoes a similar process to develop a unique self. Symbolic interactionism also delves into the role that perception and meaning play in these significant interactions.

We can use symbolic interactionism to understand the role of shared meaning in student-teacher interaction. Herbert Blumer (1969) states that symbolic interactionism rests on three simple premises. The first is that human beings act toward things on the basis of the meanings that the things have for them. The second premise is that the meaning of these things is derived from or arises out of the social interaction that one has with one's social counterparts. The third premise is that these meanings are handled and modified through an interpretive process used by the person in dealing with the things he or she encounters.

Using these three premises to look at teachers, it can be hypothesized that teachers will act toward students based on the meanings that students (as objects) have for them. This hypothesis was supported by the classic studies of Rosenthal and Jacobson (1968) and Rubovitz and Maehr (1971, 1975). In the Rosenthal and Jacobson study, the meaning that students had for teachers was controlled by the researchers. The researchers told the teachers that some of the students were likely to do well that year. In reality, the researchers randomly selected the students they labeled as likely to do well, yet the teachers acted toward the students based on the meanings that were given by the researchers (not by any actual measure of ability).

The second premise, that the meaning that students have for the teachers will be based on the social interaction that teachers have with their self-identified social counterparts, was also shown in the Rosenthal and Jacobson study. Teachers identified the researchers as their social counterparts and adopted their meanings rather than developing meanings independently.

The third premise, that the meanings given to students by the teacher's social counterparts will be modified through an interpretive process of the teacher, suggests that it is possible to change socially constructed meanings rather than simply adopt them. The changing of socially constructed meanings can be seen in the story of Jaime Escalante (Mathews, 1988). Escalante was the subject of the movie *Stand and Deliver* (1988). Escalante's social counterparts (other teachers) had decided that the Hispanic youths in their school would not be capable of learning, could not achieve at a college level, and would be doing well simply to graduate. He modified this interpretation and arrived at a new meaning. His new meaning of students was that these students could work college mathematical problems, could simultaneously manage school and home lives, and could succeed in high school. Escalante was able to modify the beliefs of his counterparts through the ideas he held about his abilities (self-evaluation) and through his beliefs about the barriers produced by racism and school ability groupings.

Understanding these three basic tenets of symbolic interaction is therefore helpful in formulating ideas about successful teacher-student interactions, but it does not completely address the process through which the three tenets are filtered. Two important questions that affect student-teacher interaction are (1) From where do groups of social counterparts (that is, teachers) derive their meanings of others? And (2) what are the interpretive processes that teachers use in modifying students' meanings?

George Herbert Mead (1934) provides one answer to the first question. He states that we each belong to a number of different socially functioning groups. Teachers and students may identify themselves as members of many different groups, including professional teachers' organizations, neighborhood communities, families, athletic organizations, and ethnic and religious groups. An individual identifies with a group or groups because he or she is able to understand the behaviors of members of these groups and integrate his or her own behavior with the behavior of the members. When individuals find it difficult to understand and integrate their behaviors with the behaviors of others, as sometimes happens in social interactions between students and teachers, it is likely that difficulty arises because the individuals are acting as members of two or more different social groups. In his description of social organization and the ideal of human society, Mead states, We often find the existence of castes in a community which make it impossible for persons to enter into the attitude of other people although they are actually affecting and are affected by these other people. The ideal of human society is one which does bring people so closely together in their interrelationships, so fully develops the necessary system of communication, that the individuals who exercise their own peculiar functions can take the attitude of those whom they affect. Remember that what is essential to a significant symbol is that the gesture which affects others should affect the individual himself in the same way. Human communication takes place through such significant symbols, and the problem is one of organizing a community which makes this possible.

This passage outlines two significant points that should be considered in teacher-student interactions. The first is that castes exist in communities and affect both members of the caste group and outsiders. Castes also exist in schools.[1] There are several ways castes at school are generated and affected, not least through race, class, and gender stereotypes in the wider society. However, one way these social forces come together to produce school castes that are found to be "virtually irreversible" is through tracking (Lawrence, 1998, 52; see also Schafer, Olexa, and Polk, 1972). Tracking is the placement of students into groups based on perceived intellectual ability or readiness to learn. However, because schools are not pure caste societies, it is assumed that the shared meaning described in Mead's ideal human society can be approximated within a carefully structured classroom environment.

The creation of this special classroom environment is the second key point of Mead's passage for the present analysis. For the creation of such an environment, it is necessary that the teacher (one who initiates interaction for the purpose of education) understand how his or her significant symbols of communication affect students differently. In addition, the teacher must understand when and why students are using different symbols to communicate. Thus knowledge of a student's primary social reference group and how that group differs from other students' reference groups and the teacher's social reference group is necessary for socially congruent instruction. If the instruction is not socially congruent, students are not likely to understand their teacher, and they are less likely to engage in the learning process.

The point is that current interactions are complicated by past interactions. Just as the literature on HIV and AIDS warns that when one has sexual intercourse with someone, one is, in effect, making sexual contact with all the previous partners of that person, the theory on social interaction tells us that we bring aspects of our past interactions into our present ones. It is precisely because of this link between the past and the present that interactions become both the problem of and the solution to school violence.

Students who enter the classroom with a history of exposure to violence may carry that violence and the ways of thinking that rationalize violence into all their interactions. They may interpret some actions through this way of thinking. A teacher, who typically is not living in a violence-filled community, may not understand how students interpret his or her actions, may not understand how students resolve and make sense of their own interactions, and may draw on stereotypes as a reference for meaning. Unless we change the organizational structure of schools to break down castes and create a more heterogeneous grouping of people, students who do not share the teacher's background are not likely to be influenced by that teacher or the institution that the teacher represents. A lack of bonding with an important societal institution such as school can lead to deviant behavior and to more serious forms of rule violation involving violence.

Violence that results in death is an extreme form of deviance. Deviance or delinquency among youths has been studied for many years. Hirschi's social control theory (1969) says that delinquency occurs when youths fail to bond with conventional social institutions. Within society, there are several conventional institutions; one of these is the institution of education represented by schools and schoolteachers. Strong bonds with school, described by Hirschi as the individual's relationship with school or teachers, and the amount of time spent on school-related activities compared to the amount of time spent on non-school-related activities contribute to an individual's willingness to conform to societal conventions. When individuals are bonded to conventional institutions, they are less likely to act in deviant ways. Thus one of the keys to reducing violence within schools is to increase the bonds that students feel to the school or to conventional others within the school. However, one of the aspects of school organization that reduces bonding for certain groups is tracking.

Tracking

Increasing the bonds that students form to school through teachers is made more difficult by the process of tracking. "Tracking" is a word that is used to describe the ability groups established by the schools. Theoretically, these ability groups are supposed to enable more effective education because students with similar ability levels and readiness to learn will be taught together to their optimum level of academic performance. Teachers can concentrate on just one type of student instead of having to prepare lesson plans that account for more than one type, such as advanced, average, and remedial students.

In reality, however, tracking has not made education more effective. Instead, it has created and perpetuated many of society's problems. The institutional practice of tracking that is now common in most public schools has numerous effects on both teachers and students. It has been found to affect how students view themselves (self-identity), how they evaluate themselves (self-image), and how others view them (public identity) (Kelly and Pink, 1982, 55; Lawrence, 1998, 52). It has been criticized for the following reasons:

> More minority and lower income students are in the basic or low-ability tracks; placement in the track tends to be permanent, with little movement up or down in spite of students' learning and progress; and tracking has a labeling and stigmatizing effect so that teachers expect less of lower tracked students and frequently their expectations are correct. (Lawrence, 1998, 52)

Many of these effects can be related to self-development and social bonding. Tracking affects teachers' expectations of students' performance (Oakes, 1985; Kelly and Pink, 1982; Rosenthal and Jacobson, 1968). The concept of self-fulfilling prophecy tells us that if students are labeled as educationally inferior or superior, that is how they will perform. Thus tracking sends messages to students about inferiority and superiority.

Tracking also separates students on variables other than intellectual ability (Alexander, Cook, and McDill, 1978), including race, class, father's occupation, misconduct, and past academic record rather than IQ (Kelly and Grove, 1981). This means that students are denied the opportunity to interact in the classroom with a heterogeneous group of students. The odds are good that those in their classes will mirror their socioeconomic and minority or majority status.

Tracking also has produced qualitative and quantitative instructional differences (Gamoran, 1986; Karweit, 1987). For those at the top, the belief is that their way is best, and their educational achievement provides all the evidence of success they need. For those at the bottom, school becomes yet another hurdle to achieving self-esteem and developing a positive sense of self. Studies have documented the harmful effects of tracking on the academic achievement of those students in the lower tracks (Oakes, 1985, 1990). Tracking has also created a structure in which students do not receive equal knowledge, skills, or credentials for success beyond high school. Those in the upper tracks usually receive an education that prepares them for college, while those in the bottom tracks receive an education that focuses on remedial skills, or what Willis (1993) described as "learning to labor."

In addition to the inequality in educational outcome associated with tracking, studies show that placement in tracks reflects a student's race and socioeconomic status. Low-income, African American, and Latino children are more frequently placed in low-level classes (regardless of achievement) than Euro-American children with higher family incomes (Oakes and Guiton, 1995; Welner and Oakes, 1996). Indeed, evidence suggests that, even controlling for IQ and previous ability, "blacks and low income students were still more likely to be found in the basic or low ability tracks" (Lawrence, 1998, 52; see also Schafer, Olexa, and Polk, 1972). Because tracking favors the students in the upper tracks over those in the lower tracks, it is easy to hypothesize that those in the lower tracks will be less likely to bond with the institution of school. It is still likely, however, that the students will bond with other students within their ability group, or track, especially those of similar racial, ethnic, gender, or class background. This is one of the problems of interaction: it is an ongoing process that can produce negative as well as positive outcomes, if organizational arrangements do not take account of its existence.

If students form bonds with other students who are similar to them, they are not as likely to diversify and expand their thinking as are students who bond with students who are dissimilar to them. Our knowledge grows as our range of experiences, both vicarious and real, grow. Each new experience or new way of thinking to which we are exposed may cause us to reevaluate that which we thought we knew (Perry, 1970). When we receive more supports than challenges, our thinking becomes stagnant. Thus students who are surrounded by students who share their social, ethnic, and class position in society (a support) are less likely to be challenged in their thinking. Stagnant thinking is not the goal of education.

One possible way to remedy this situation is for the students to form bonds with the teacher, who can then challenge their ways of thinking and help them grow. However, this option is complicated by reality. As discussed earlier, often the teacher is different from the student in age—sometimes by many years—as well as in other demographic characteristics. Not only are these differences magnified by tracking; they also may reflect differences in socioeconomic status and race. Even though the majority of students in many urban schools belong to a minority group, teachers continue to be predominantly white (U.S. Department of Education, 1993). Also, teachers belong to the middle class, but many students (particularly those in lower tracks) belong to the lower class. Thus it takes great effort and desire on the part of the student and the teacher to form a common bond. It is more likely that students will initially bond with other students. If we are to change thinking processes, students have to be given more opportunities to bond with other students who are both similar and dissimilar to them. The opinions of other students matter. How others see us affects our development of self. How others view us also affects our self-esteem.

Self-Esteem

Social interactions and the development of self are linked to self-esteem and the process of self-development described earlier. The concept of self-esteem is embedded in the theory of symbolic interaction. Self-esteem is also a conceptual component of the more inclusive process of self-conception. The process of self-conception is considered a key element in the relationship between individual behavior and the social organization of which the individual is a part. Linkages have been made between self-esteem and racial bias (Ashmore and Del Boca, 1976; Harding et al., 1969) and between self-esteem and teacher effectiveness (Edeburn and Landry, 1976). In both instances, the link between a person's self-evaluation and subsequent behavior can be seen.

At an individual level, needs for self-esteem and superior status are considered to be among the major causes and perpetuators of prejudice and racial discrimination (Allport, 1954; Ashmore and Del Boca, 1976; Harding et al., 1969; Tajfel and Turner, 1979). Self-esteem works through group identification to produce discriminatory behaviors in some individuals. All people desire positive evaluation by others and self. Tajfel and Turner (1979) have shown that people who have low self-esteem tend to seek positive evaluation by identifying a uniqueness (positive specialness) for their in-group over an identified out-group. In the United States, this often takes the form of (perceived) positive white in-group norms compared to (perceived) negative black out-group norms.

However, this identification can also take the reverse form. In the reverse form, minority students perceive or declare their culture and its norms as superior to those of their white, middle-class teacher. This need for positive distinctiveness leads to perceived intergroup competition and motivates prejudice and discriminatory behaviors. Within school, the need for positive distinctiveness may lead students and teachers in upper-level tracks to perceive the tracks as a form of competition and thus develop a prejudice against those in lower-level tracks. This phenomenon was demonstrated by Finley (1984), who noted that a competition existed between teachers for high-level or high-status students.

It has also been noted that a particular anti-achievement culture has developed among African American students, who are typically placed in lower tracks (Suskind, 1998; Fordham, 1988). The ideology within this culture says that to succeed academically is to become "white." Thus, within some groups that are typically relegated to the lower tracks, the need for positive distinctiveness leads to the formation of a culture that is the antithesis of the culture of the teacher, the educational process, and the school's perceived culture of academic success (Cohen, 1955).

Self-esteem has also been linked to achievement and performance. Research has shown a positive correlation between self-esteem and school achievement (Stevens, 1956; Fink, 1962; Williams and Cole, 1968; Simon and Simon, 1975). Additional studies have shown that teacher-student interaction is an important variable in the student's self-esteem and achievement. Edeburn and Landry (1976) state that teachers who themselves have a positive self-image affect their students more positively than do teachers who have a low or negative self-image. Davidson and Lang (1960) found that the more that children perceive their teachers' feelings toward themselves as positive, the better the academic achievement of the children. Thus positive teacher self-esteem is an important variable in reducing culturally induced prejudicial attitudes and is important in the successful educational interaction of teachers and students.

Unfortunately, tracking sends a message to those in the lower tracks that they are not as good as other students. Teachers all too often support this message as they talk down to students or dumb down the course requirements. Power (1993) found that track level does have a direct effect on self-esteem; as track level increases, so does self-esteem. Her analyses also indicate that a student's self-esteem is susceptible to the effects of track placement even years after the placement occurred. Students who were placed in the lower tracks in elementary school still showed decreased self-esteem in high school. This tells us that, although students age, they rarely are able to overcome the negative effects of tracking.

What has been described so far is theory and research evidence on self-formation, an explanation of why some students become deviant, and the relationship of tracking to the development of self and to the development of bonds with schools or with individuals in schools. I would now like to discuss how these processes can lead to both the expression of violence and the elimination of violence by linking theory and research with the reality of life in today's society.

Schools, Society, and Violence

During the 1990s, many people pointed to the change in the family as the cause of violence.[2] They suggested that the increase in one-parent households and two-income families had led to decreased attention to what our youths were doing. Of course, this change in family structure is linked to both political and economic changes in society. Through the implementation of no-fault divorce laws, the political system has made it easier for men and women to end marriages. The increased divorce rate has led to an increase in one-parent households. Our economic structure has increased opportunities for women to become employed outside the home, and downsizing and technological advances have made two incomes in a family more of a necessity than in the past. Thus the change in adult family members' ability to spend time with children reflects more than just a change in the institution of the family. It reflects much broader changes in society.

From their beginnings, schools have mirrored society. The school model still commonly used is one that is based on the structure of factories. Students enter at a set time (similar to punching a time clock); they move down the assembly line of reading, writing, and arithmetic; and they emerge at graduation as a finished product. Through tracking, schools reflect the economic and racial segregation of society. School districts are tied to place of residence, and school funds are commonly tied to property taxes. Both districts and their property taxes reflect the extreme residential segregation common in the United States. What is intriguing is why schools mirror society when they do not have to do so.

One of the American school's early tasks was to socialize immigrants. In other words, early in the history of public education, schools were seen as the institution most able to change individuals. Schools could socialize and make those deemed inferior (immigrants) into model citizens who would understand and support the norms and values (such as democracy and equality for all) of their new culture. Somewhere along the way, schools quit socializing into model citizens those deemed inferior and instead instituted processes that maintained the inferior student's entering status. Today, when students graduate, their master status is still likely to be their race or socioeconomic status. In the past, an immigrant's ethnicity or socioeconomic status became less important if he or she were educated. In large part, society's acceptance of an immigrant was due to the fact that the immigrant had been socialized through heterogeneous interaction. That interaction took place in schools where there were no tracks. There was simply a heterogeneous group of students who interacted with and learned about each other over the course of several years. Both immigrant and native born were changed by the experience. Values and norms merged, and, at the end, both immigrant and native born had roughly the same status in society.

Remember that symbolic interactionists tell us that who we are is determined by our social interactions with significant others. If I have a family and friends who are moral, law-abiding, happy people who tell me consistently good things about myself, I am probably a person who is moral, law abiding, and happy. But if I have family, friends, or a society that tells me I am worthless, that breaking some laws is acceptable, and that others' lives are not worth much, then I am likely to become a person that is angry, disobedient, and potentially dangerous. What happens if I am isolated? I get the message that society does not want to be with me, and I might interpret that in such a way as to become jealous of or angry with society. Insofar as tracking contributes to this separation and isolation, it also contributes to the general level of school violence, although evidence of a direct relationship between tracking and delinquency remains unclear (Lawrence, 1998). Schools are the one institution that have in the past proved themselves successful at transforming individuals' place in society. They did this through carefully structured interactions between students and teachers. Today, instead of mirroring society's faults, schools should use the opportunity and time given to them to model a more positive society.

They can and should help create a society in which students from all different educational, racial, and economic backgrounds interact. Tracking does not do this. Currently tracking reinforces social class and racial segregation patterns. Moreover, it does not just separate; it tells one group that it is better than another. One of the most common ways that peer groups and friendships are formed is through classroom formation and shared experiences. It is critical to the development of self and to cognitive growth that individuals are exposed to diverse ways of thinking. Good teachers can make this happen.

Clearly, there is also a strong need for leadership within schools and, specifically, within classrooms. In recent years, the teaching profession has not attracted the nation's best and brightest. This is a serious problem. Teachers may be one of the few adults whom children have in their lives on any consistent basis. The economic demand on parents, particularly mothers, has decreased the amount of time they have to spend with their children. Thus the responsibility of teachers to be role models and moral guides is increased. Teachers need to take time to talk about what is right and wrong. They need to help teach citizenship, civility, respect, and compassion for others. They need to offer thoughtful critiques of society and the media and thought-provoking questions about how to handle difficult situations without resorting to violence. As a society, we cannot afford for teachers to be moral relativists. Too many children do not have enough adults willing or present to offer solid moral teaching and guidance. If students are taught problem-solving skills by watching action films or by other teens who see multiple reasons why it is acceptable to use violence against someone else, they are more likely to resort to violence when they face a problem. Students today need more than heterogeneous groupings within their schools. They need strong teachers who know how to connect with them and how to simultaneously build their self-esteem and challenge their ways of thinking and problem solving.

Notes

1. Castes might also operate in subgroups at schools, such as jocks, preppies, skaters, thespians, gangstas, goths, and so on.
2. In a nonscientific survey of Internet users, a CNN (1999) poll reported that parents were seen as the leading cause of school violence by 29 percent of the 59,698 respondents, followed by access to guns and the media.

References

Alexander, Karl L., Martha Cook, & Edward L. McDill. 1978. Curriculum tracking and educational stratification: Some further evidence. *American Sociological Review,* 43: 47–66.

Allport, Gordon W. 1954. *The nature of prejudice.* Reading, MA: Addison-Wesley.

Ashmore, Richard D., & Frances K. Del Boca. 1976. Psychological approaches to understanding intergroup conflicts. In *Towards the elimination of racism,* ed. Phyllis A. Katz. New York: Pergamon.

Blumer, Herbert. 1969. *Symbolic interactionism: Perspective and method.* Berkeley: University of California Press.

CNN. 1999. CNN Interactive Quickvote. Available http://www.cnn.com/

Cohen, Albert. K. 1955. *Delinquent boys: The culture of the gang.* New York: Free Press.

Cooley, Charles Horton. 1909. *Social organization.* New York: Scribner.

Davidson, Helen H., & Gerhard Lang. 1960. Children's perceptions of their teachers' feelings toward them related to self-perception, school achievement, and behavior. *Journal of Experiential Education,* 29: 107–118.

Edeburn, Carl E., & Richard G. Landry. 1976. Teacher self-concept and student self-concept in grades three, four, and five. *Journal of Educational Research,* 69: 372–375.

Fink, Martin B. 1962. Self-concept as it relates to academic underachievement. *California Journal of Education Research,* 13: 57–62.

Finley, Merrilee K. 1984. Teachers and tracking in a comprehensive high school. *Sociology of Education,* 57: 233–243.

Fordham, Signithia. 1988. Racelessness as a factor in Black students' school success: Pragmatic strategy or pyrrhic victory? *Harvard Educational Review,* 58: 54–84.

Gamoran, Adam. 1986. Instructional and institutional effects of ability grouping. *Sociology of Education,* 59: 185–198.

Harding, John, Harold Prochansky, Bernard Kutner, & Isidor Chein. 1969. Prejudice and ethnic relations. In *Handbook of social psychology,* ed. Lindzay Gardner & Elliot Aronson, 2nd ed., Vol. 5. Reading, MA: Addison-Wesley.

Hirschi, Travis. 1969. *Causes of delinquency.* Berkeley: University of California Press.

Karweit, Nancy. 1987. Diversity, equity, and classroom processes. In *The social organization of schools,* ed. Maureen T. Hallinan. New York: Plenum.

Kelly, Delos H., & Winthrop D. Grove. 1981. Teachers' nominations and the production of academic "misfits." *Education,* 101: 246–263.

Kelly, Delos H., & William T. Pink. 1982. School crime and individual responsibility: The perpetuation of a myth? *Urban Review,* 14(1): 47–63.

Lareau, Annette. 1989. *Home advantage: Social class and parental intervention in elementary education.* Washington, DC: Falmer.

Lawrence, Richard. 1998. *School crime and juvenile justice.* New York: Oxford University Press.

Lee, Valerie E., & Julia B. Smith. 1995. Effects of high school restructuring and size on early gains in achievement and engagement for early secondary school students. *Sociology of Education,* 68: 241–270.

Mathews, Jay. 1988. *Escalante: The best teacher in America.* New York: Henry Holt.

Mead, George Herbert. 1934. *Mind, self, and society: From the standpoint of a social behaviorist.* Chicago: University of Chicago Press.

Oakes, Jeannie. 1985. *Keeping track: How schools structure inequality.* New Haven, CT: Yale University Press.

Oakes, Jeannie. 1990. *Multiplying inequalities: The effects of race, social class, and tracking on opportunities to learn math and science.* Santa Monica, CA: Rand.

Oakes, Jeannie, & Gretchen Guiton. 1995. Matchmaking: The dynamics of high school tracking decision. *American Educational Research Journal,* 32(1): 3–33.

Perry, William, Jr. 1970. *Intellectual and ethical development in the college years.* New York: Holt, Rinehart & Winston.

Power, Ann Marie R. 1993. *The effects of tracking on high school students' self-esteem.* Master's thesis, University of Notre Dame.

Ray, Karen. 1995. *Grant High School case report.* Los Angeles: University of California at Los Angeles, Center for Research for Democratic School Communities.

Rosenthal, Robert & Lenore Jacobson. 1968. *Pygmalion in the classroom: Teacher expectation and pupils' intellectual development.* New York: Holt, Rinehart & Winston.

Rubovitz, Pamela C., & Martin L. Maehr. 1971. Pygmalion analyzed: Toward an explanation of the Rosenthal-Jacobson findings. *Journal of Personality and Social Psychology,* 19: 197–203.

Rubovitz, Pamela C., & Martin L. Maehr. 1975. Teacher expectations: A special problem for Black children with White teachers? In *Culture, child, and school: Sociocultural influences on learning,* ed. Martin L. Maehr & William M. Stallings. Monterey, CA: Brooks/Cole.

Schafer, Walter, Carol Olexa, & Kenneth Polk. 1972. Programmed for social class: Tracking in high school. In *Schools and delinquency,* ed. Kenneth Polk & Walter Schafer. Englewood Cliffs, NJ: Prentice Hall.

Simon, William E., & Marilyn G. Simon. 1975. Self-esteem, intelligence, and standardized academic achievement. *Psychology in the Schools,* 12: 97–100.

Stand and Deliver. 1988. *An American Playhouse* Theatrical Film, Menendez/Musca & Olmos Production. Burbank, CA: Warner Brothers.

Stevens, Peter H. 1956. *An investigation of the relationship between certain aspects of self-concept and student's academic achievement.* Ph.D. diss., New York University, 1956. Abstract in Dissertation Abstracts 16: 2531–2532.

Suskind, Ron. 1998. *A hope in the unseen: An American odyssey from the inner city to the Ivy League.* New York: Broadway Books.

Tajfel, Henri, & John C. Turner. 1979. An integrative theory of intergroup conflict. In *The social psychology of intergroup relations,* eds. William G. Austin & Stephen Worchel. Monterey, CA: Brooks/Cole.

U.S. Department of Education. National Center for Education Statistics. 1993. *Digest of education statistics.* Washington, DC: Government Printing Office.

Van Galen, Jane. 1987. Maintaining control: The structuring of parent involvement. In *Schooling in social context: Qualitative studies,* ed. G. W. Noblit & W. T. Pink. Norwood, NJ: Ablex.

Wells, Amy Stuart, & Jeannie Oakes. 1998. Tracking, detracking, at the politics of educational reform: A sociological perspective. In *Sociology of education: Emerging perspectives,* ed. Carlos Alberto Torres & Theodore R. Mitchell. Albany: State University of New York Press.

Welner, Kevin G., & Jeannie Oakes. 1996. (Li)ability grouping: The new susceptibility of school tracking systems to legal challenges. *Harvard Educational Review,* 66(3): 451–470.

Williams, Robert L., & Spurgeon Cole. 1968. Self-concept and school adjustment. *Personnel and Guidance Journal,* 46: 478–481.

Willis, Paul E. 1993. Learning to labour: How working class kids get working class jobs. Aldershot, United Kingdom: Ashgate.

Wolf, Stephen M. 1998. Curbing school violence: Our youth, and our schools, need support before an incident occurs—Not after. *Attache* (*U.S. Airways*) Sept. 9.

REVIEW QUESTIONS

1. How did Yogan use the theory of symbolic interactionism in this paper? What would have been different if the author had used another theory?

2. What does the author mean when she states that "teachers will act toward students based on the meanings that students (as objects) have for them?"

3. Can you come up with your own questions and thoughts about a study you might consider on school violence? What theory would you use and why?

MURDER FOLLOWED BY SUICIDE IN AUSTRALIA, 1973–1992: A RESEARCH NOTE

Jo Barnes

This paper reports on the findings of a study of murder-suicide in Australia from a feminist perspective. The study is based on the analysis of 188 events in four states of Australia spread over a period of 20 years from 1973 to 1992 and focuses on two types of murder-suicide—those events in which a male offender kills his female partner and those events in which a parent kills his or her child or children. The motivations of men and women who commit murder and then kill themselves are qualitatively different. Suicide is often studied from criminal justice and a mental health perspective, as well as those studies that are purely descriptive. Notice how the focus of murder-suicide changes when it is studied from a feminist perspective.

Introduction

Murder-suicide has been a somewhat neglected topic of study in sociology and has mainly been the domain of mental health and epidemiology studies. As a consequence, the conclusions drawn have concentrated on the occurrence of murder-suicide as a rare event that

Barnes, J. "Murder Followed by Suicide in Australia, 1973–1992: A Research Note," *Journal of Sociology,* 36n(1), pp. 1–12. Copyright © 2000 ASA: Australian Sociological Association. Reprinted by permission of Sage Publications, Ltd.

is perpetrated by a mentally unstable person who has finally lost control. This has meant that the social circumstances that surround the event have been ignored or accepted as a given. This study focuses on intimate and familial murder-suicide and places these types of murder-suicide in a feminist framework in order to add an extra dimension to existing explanations.

A general overview of the literature reveals three distinct approaches to the study of murder followed by suicide. The first approach is the comparison of murder-suicide with the separate acts of murder and suicide (e.g. Wolfgang 1958; West 1965; Mackenzie 1961; Wallace 1986). The second approach is that which accounts for murder-suicide in terms of mental illness (e.g. Berman 1979; Goldney 1977; Rosenbaum 1990). And finally, there have been a number of empirical studies which seek to describe murder-suicide in terms of the profiles of offender and victim, the relationship of the offender to the victim, and the context in which the murder-suicide took place (e.g. Palmer and Humphrey 1980; Allen 1983; Easteal 1994).

The various studies have been useful in identifying the actors involved in murder-suicide and in describing the relationships and circumstances that surround many of the events. Murder-suicide is a gendered activity—in the majority of cases men are the instigators of murder-suicide and women and children are the victims. It is also familial—the victims are predominantly intimately involved with the offender or they are the children of the offender. Expressions of jealousy, frustration and hostility that culminate in violence, which is often an ongoing factor within the relationship, are also recognized as important components in the murder-suicide event. Yet previous researchers have taken their existence for granted and have failed to question why men should feel jealous or hostile towards their wives or lovers. Why is it that men, in particular, are so determined not to allow their partner to leave? Why do the male offenders feel jealous and hostile to such an extent that they would rather kill the one they love and die themselves than accept that their partner no longer wishes to be part of their lives? The social context within which notions of ownership and control have developed and the use of violence to enforce them is an important element which needs to be addressed in relation to the murder-suicide event.

There has generally been a lack of gender differentiation in the studies of murder-suicide. The lack of concentration on women as offenders is understandable because of the much smaller incidence of women offenders in the murder-suicide event. However, the omission of a discussion around gender from the descriptions of murder-suicide results in two outcomes. First, an assumption is made that the conditions of women's lives are essentially the same as those of men and therefore an analysis that reflects men's experience is basis enough to describe the role of men and women in the murder-suicide event. Second, although the conditions of women's lives may differ from those of men, these differences are not seen as pertinent to the murder-suicide event.

While some studies acknowledge that children are often the victims in murder-suicides, most researchers have concentrated on the intimate relationship between offender and victim. This has meant that general descriptions of murder-suicide have tended to include male and female offenders as one category with only passing reference to the fact that while male offenders tend to murder adult females and sometimes their own children, female offenders are much more likely to kill only their children. Although the question of why women who kill their intimate partners rarely kill themselves is beyond the scope of the present study, we need to ask why in the majority of female initiated murder-suicides the victims are children? Why is it that women take such positive steps to kill their own children—an act that is contrary to the strong emphasis on the mothering role that is inherent in a modern capitalist society such as Australia?

Method

Although the definition of murder-suicide appears to be a simple one in which one person kills one or more people and then kills himself or herself, it is still problematic. Murder-suicide is a not a monolithic act. The event itself has many dimensions and it is the varying conditions within murder-suicide that confound the attempt to understand all murder-suicides within a single explanation. Indeed what is defined as murder-suicide, often by those who investigate the crime, can also be seen variously as murder and suicide as separate events; murder that is followed by the suicide of the offender in an act of remorse; double suicide in which one persons kills another and himself or herself in collusion with that person; or murder-suicide as an entity in itself, in which both the murder and the suicide are planned and carried out. It is with this latter definition of murder-suicide that this research is concerned.

Data for this project were collected on each event classified by the State Coroner as a murder-suicide. A function of the Coroner is to investigate every aspect of any death that is reported to him or her in order to ascertain and confirm the deceased's identity, the circumstances surrounding the death, the clinical cause of death, and the identity of any person who may have contributed to that death. In order to do this, the Coroner is assisted by specialist investigators such as police experts, scientists, forensic pathologists and other specialists who may be needed. In each state the Coroner collects information on both the offender and victim which usually consists of personal details such as age, gender and other demographic details, a detailed account of the discovery of the bodies, accounts by witnesses and relatives that may offer some background information, as well as copies of suicide notes and autopsy reports.

Using the Coroner's records, demographic details such as age, gender, occupation and nationality were examined. In addition, background information such as accounts from witnesses and relatives, copies of suicide notes and autopsy reports were also studied. Problems related to the data must be acknowledged when using them for purposes other than that for which they were collected. The information is collected by police officers in order to ensure that no prosecuting actions need to be taken and it is these officials whose decisions impact on what information is collected. At the same time, researchers are totally reliant on the objectivity of those collecting the information initially. It is these officials who make decisions as to which information is important in terms of what they require. Additionally, many of the witness statements are written in language that is stilted and concise, reflecting police procedure, rather than the emotive language that can be assumed to have been exhibited so shortly after such a traumatic event. Nevertheless, in most cases statements by relatives and friends often give detailed information on relationships and circumstances which, at least in the police and Coroner's minds, contexualize the event so that he or she is able to conclude that a verdict of murder-suicide is appropriate.

TABLE 1. NUMBER OF KNOWN MURDER-SUICIDE EVENTS IN EACH STATE 1973–1992

Year	South Australia	Victoria	Western Australia	Tasmania	New South Wales	Total
1973	0	6	N/A	N/A	10	16
1974	2	6	N/A	N/A	5	13
1975	3	6	1(#)	N/A	5	15
1976	5	8	1(#)	N/A	13	27
1977	1	7	0(#)	N/A	6	14
1978	3	3	1(#)	1	7	15
1979	3	11	1(#)	1	8	24
1980	0	9	1(#)	1	11	22
1981	1	5	1(#)	1	11	19
1982	2	7	1(#)	1	8	19
1983	3	8	2(#)	N/A	5	18
1984	2	10	1(#)	N/A	12	25
1985	1	6	2(#)	N/A	14	23
1986	2	11	0(#)	2	7	22
1987	3	14	2	3	12	34
1988	2	11	1	N/A	5	19
1989	2	6	2	1	8	19
1990	0	6	3	1	7	17
1991	3	5	4	1	11	24
1992	3	3	5	2	7	20
Total	41	148	29	15	172	405

(#) Perth only—country areas not available

Source: Data collected by author from Coroners' records in each state except NSW where it was collected by the NSW Bureau of Crime Statistics and Research.

Findings

As can be seen from Table 1, a total of 405 known murder-suicides were recorded as such between the years 1973 and 1992 in five states. The number of incidents ranged from 13 in 1974 to 34 in 1987, with an average of 20 per year. It is apparent that NSW (average 8.6) and Victoria (average 7.4) have the greatest number of murder-suicides each year while South Australia averages two murder-suicides per year. Because of the lack of complete figures for Western Australia and Tasmania it would be unwise to calculate statistics for these states, however, if the available figures are extrapolated to those missing periods one could estimate that Western Australia averages approximately two murder-suicides per year and Tasmania one per year. While overall the number of murder-suicides remains fairly consistent each year, 1987 inexplicably stands out as having an abnormally high number of reported murder-suicide events in Victoria and NSW.

Of the 188 cases in the present sample there were 188 offenders (those who murdered and subsequently committed suicide) and 250 murdered victims. The most distinctive feature overall was that 90 percent (170) of the offenders were male while 70 percent (177) of the victims were female. Male offenders were older than female offenders—the mean age of male offenders being around 43 years (n=169), while the mean age of female offenders was about 32 years (n=17). The majority of male offenders (53 percent) were in the 30–49 age group, while the majority (82 percent) of female offenders were in the 20–39 age group. Male victims, too, were generally older than female victims. The mean age of male adult victims was 43 years (n=37), while the mean age of female adult victims was 39 years. Around 28 percent of the victims were aged 15 years or less.

Of the 250 victims in this sample, 50.4 percent were or had been in an intimate relationship with the offender (intimates are defined as present and past spouses, defactos and lovers). The second largest category (29 percent) was that of "own child." An interesting observation arising out of the data is that the victim of a male offender is more likely to be an intimate of the offender (54 percent), while the victim of a female offender is more likely to be her own child (75 percent). Those victims in an existing relationship with the offender accounted for 40 percent of all victims, while victims who had terminated their relationship with the offender totaled 10 percent of all victims. About 29 percent of all victims were the child of the offender and 7 percent of all victims were related to the offender either by blood or marriage. In four cases the victim was a son or daughter of a partner or ex-partner. In addition, there were six cases in which the victim was a perceived sexual rival of the offender. In 16 cases both the partner or ex-partner and at least one child were murdered by the offender, while in 14 cases the offender killed two or more of his own children. There were only six cases in which the victim was a stranger.

The data indicated that the mode of death differed according to the gender of the offender. Male offenders were more likely to use what are considered to be more violent ways of committing both murder and suicide. For male offenders, a firearm was the favored weapon for both murder (73 percent) and suicide (74 percent). This contrasts with female offenders who were less likely to use firearms for the murder (15 percent) or the suicide (17 percent). A more "passive" mode of murder and suicide was favored by female offenders—carbon monoxide poisoning or suffocation accounted for 39 percent of murders and 28 percent of suicides.

Murder-suicide is essentially a domestic event and this is reflected in the number of murder-suicides which take place in the home (69 percent). Both the murder and the suicide occurred in most cases away from public gaze or at least in close proximity to the offenders' and/or victims' homes. Many of the events (43 percent) took place in the home where both the victim and the offender were living at the time; 14 percent took place in the victim's home, often following the victim's departure from the family home and 10 percent took place at the offender's home. Often in these cases the victims had returned to collect their belongings from the family home or perhaps to discuss the break-up of the relationship. The nature of murder-suicide is reflected in the location of its occurrence.

As in studies on domestic violence, the privacy of the home makes it difficult to research the circumstances in which murder-suicide takes place. Previous violence is a feature of some murder-suicides (37 percent) and can be categorized into two types—that which was a characteristic of the relationship generally and that which preceded the murder-suicide. In some cases both types of violence were present while in others the violence could be seen as part of the process of the murder-suicide. Studies of domestic violence have persistently agreed that it is impossible to know precisely how much violence actually exists. Alternatively, while the actual murder-suicide cannot be ultimately hidden it is impossible to gauge how close domestic violence becomes to being murder and perhaps suicide. As Rod (1980) argues, it is often a matter of luck that intimate violence does not become murder.

The over-consumption of alcohol has often been used in our culture as an excuse for a loss of self-control but there is no scientific evidence that alcohol is the cause of violent behavior—the popular notion that alcohol transforms the male into a violent brute has not been substantiated. According to MaxAndrew and Edgerton (1969), alcohol intoxication affects the sensorimotor abilities but its effects on behavior are determined by socialization. There are very few cases in which it can be said that alcohol or drugs were the "cause" of murder-suicide. This is not to say that alcohol does not play some part in some murder-suicides but it seems that alcohol in most cases is a facilitator, that is, it enables the offender to act in a way which may not have occurred at that time had the offender not been drinking.

Mental and physical illness, despite earlier studies that argue to the contrary, did not appear to be prevalent in the majority of murder-suicides in the Australian sample. Reference to the offender's mental condition occurred in only 25 percent of the cases in this study. In only 13 percent of cases the offender had been treated by doctor prior to the murder-suicide. Diagnoses ranged from "nerves" and depression to paranoid schizophrenia. In a number of cases the "nerves" and depression had been reported as being the outcome of circumstances such as relationship breakup, unemployment or child custody battles.

Above all else, murder-suicide is gendered. In the current study male offenders numerically account for 90 percent of all murder-suicides while females make up 71 percent of victims in the event. The relationship between the offender and victim has been seen as an important issue in this study because in the majority of cases murder-suicide involves couples who are in an intimate relationship. Murder-suicide as a single act seems to be most prevalent in circumstances where the offender kills his spouse and/or children and shortly after, as part of that same motivation, kills himself.

Daly and Wilson's (1988) account of the masculine and intimate features of homicide can usefully be applied to murder-suicide. Developing a conceptual framework that describes the masculine element of homicide, Daly and Wilson argue that women are viewed by their partners in proprietary terms and as such are regarded as men's exclusive property. They argue that sexual jealousy and rivalry are the dominant motives in homicides in which men are the offenders and women the victims, and deaths are often prompted by separation or the threat of separation. Masculine proprietariness, often founded on violence, pervades the stories of intimate murder-suicide in this study—the female partner becomes a possession that must be taken along on the journey to death.

An ingredient of the masculine possessiveness of female victims by their male partners is jealousy. Often reported in the accounts of murder-suicide is a statement such as, "He was very jealous about her and he told me if he could not have her no one else would." At the same time, in many cases the victim has left the relationship or announced an intention to leave. Broken relationships in murder-suicide are predominant and in many cases the victim had left or was threatening to leave the offender. In 35 percent of cases the main factor in the murder-suicide event was the fact that the victim had left the relationship or was threatening to leave. Despite other factors being present (such as jealousy, the threat of violence, etc.), it is the departing threat or action that triggers the sequence of events. There are several reasons (and these are not necessarily mutually exclusive) why the victim has resolved to leave her partner—it may be that the relationship has broken down, it may be because of violence shown towards the victim, or it may be that the victim has begun a relationship with another man.

The following selected case studies illustrate the points made above.

Case 1. A 19-year-old male offender and his 18-year-old female victim had known each other for approximately 12 months and had been engaged to be married for three months. For a short time they lived together. However, following repeated arguments and fights which included physical abuse by the male partner, the female victim broke off the engagement and the offender left their apartment to return to his parents' home. Over the following month the offender made repeated attempts to contact his ex-fiancée who shunned his approaches and sought to avoid him. Finally the offender approached his victim outside her home and an argument took place during which the offender put a rifle to his victim's head and fired causing fatal head injuries. He then turned the gun on himself. In a letter written earlier in the day to his parents the offender wrote: "I was going to ask her one more time [to come back to him] and if she didn't it was the only way out because I wasn't having no other guy handling my [victim]."

Case 2. A 39-year-old female forced her 47-year-old husband to leave the home and an abusive marriage. Three weeks later the husband returned and shot his wife. He later rang the police and said "I just had to do it. We've been separated you know. I just couldn't stand it." He then shot himself.

Although it would appear that murder-suicides involving children as the victims of male and female parents have similar qualities, there are nevertheless some important differences. Men appear to plan the murder and the suicide as a single act so that they will retain possession of their children and, in some cases, purposefully act out of spite towards the partner they can no longer have. The notion of possession and/or control flow through into murder-suicides involving child victims. Like the intimate murder-suicide, men who kill their children in murder-suicide cases often do so as a reaction to the loss of those children. The children are often the objects of a custody battle that the men are losing or have lost. Again, the concepts of possession and jealousy are primary here and the idea of "If we cannot live together, we will die together" has significant strength.

Case 3. The offender's wife had left him approximately 12 months before the murder-suicide took place and the couple had recently attended the Family Court in which custody of their three children had been awarded to the wife. The couple exhibited bitter feelings towards each other concerning which the family court judge wrote:

> The hearing virtually turned into a forum for each party involved to participate in character assassination, and despite the real purpose of the case, the continuing

welfare of the children, they made bitter accusations against one another with almost no thought of the children in mind.

In what was apparently a pre-arranged plan when he failed to gain custody, the offender took his three children aged five, three and two years old for a drive (under the custody arrangements) and did not return. The offender and his children were found dead approximately a week later, the offender having administered sleeping tablets to the children and himself and then asphyxiating them all in the car in a state forest. He wrote to his mother: "If A, B and C and I cannot be together in life we are together in peace."

According to earlier research (Wolfgang 1958; Wallace 1986), women who kill their adult male partners rarely commit suicide and this is confirmed by this study in which there are only four cases in which a female offender killed her male partner. Rather, it is young children who are the victims of female initiated murder-suicides. In this study 69 victims (28 percent) were aged 15 years or less and female offenders were responsible for the deaths of 18 (26 percent) of these young people.

For women, it would seem that it is suicide that is the prime objective of a female initiated murder-suicide but in her quest to end her own life she does not relinquish her responsibility for the welfare of her children. Because children are the most likely victims of female offenders in murder-suicide cases, the general belief has been that women who kill their own children must by definition be somehow mentally unfit. I would argue that although the motivations of men and women who kill their children and then themselves are qualitatively different they both occur within a context of patriarchal norms. Chodorow's (1978) thesis of object relations—in which qualities for successful nurturing become embedded in personality based on gender identity, coupled with a basic theory of socialisation—allows the construction of a scenario in which women have suicide as their ultimate aim, and in order to protect their children they take them out of this life. Women who kill their own children are acting out their mothering role to its consummate level

Conclusion

This research has been an attempt to "step back" and determine why offenders should feel the need to cling to ideas of dominance, possession and protection of their partners and children. Although in the final analysis it is still necessary to consider why individuals should commit murder-suicide in preference to any alternative course of action, it is argued that the patriarchal nature of our society provides the fertile context for an individual to kill a loved one and then commit suicide. For a more complete understanding of this tragic phenomenon of murder-suicide, the empirical analysis needs to be placed in a combined psychological and sociological framework.

References

Allen, N. H. (1983) "Homicide Followed by Suicide; Los Angeles, 1970–1979." *Suicide and Life Threatening Behaviour* 13(3): 55–165.

Berman, A. L. (1979) "Dyadic Death: Murder-Suicide." *Suicide and Life Threatening Behaviour* 9(1): 15–23.

Chodorow, N. (1978) *The Reproduction of Mothering: Psychoanalysis and the Sociology of Gender.* Berkeley: University of California.

Daly, M., and M. Wilson (1988) *Homicide.* New York: Aldine de Gruyter.

Easteal, P. (1994) "Homicide-Suicides Between Adult Sexual Intimates: An Australian Study." *Suicide and Life Threatening Behaviour* 24(2): 140–151.

Goldney, R. D. (1977) "Family Murder Followed by Suicide." *Forensic Science* 9: 219–228.

Mackenzie, R. W. (1961) *Murder and the Social Process in New South Wales 1933–1957.* Unpublished Doctoral Thesis, Sydney: University of Sydney.

MaxAndrew, C., and R. B. Edgerton (1969) *Drunken Comportment: A Social Explanation.* Chicago: Aldine.

Palmer, S., and J. A. Humphrey (1980) "Offender-Victim Relationship in Criminal Homicide Followed by Offender's Suicide, North Carolina 1972–1977." *Suicide and Life Threatening Behaviour* 10(2): 106–118.

Rod, T. (1980) "Marital Murder" in J. Scutt (ed.) *Violence in the Family: A Collection of Conference Papers.* Canberra: Australian Institute of Criminology.

Rosenbaum, M. (1990) "The Role of Depression in Couples Involved in Murder-Suicide and Homicide." *American Journal of Psychiatry* 147(8): 1036–1039.

Wallace, A. (1986) *Homicide: The Social Reality.* Sydney: NSW Bureau of Crime Statistics and Research, Attorney General's Department.

West, D. J. (1965) *Murder Followed by Suicide.* London: Tavistock Publications.

Wolfgang, M. E. (1958) "An Analysis of Homicide-Suicide." *Journal of Clinical and Experimental Psychopathology* xix(3): 208–218.

REVIEW QUESTIONS

1. This research was based on feminist theory. However, the researchers stated that murder suicides could be investigated from other perspectives. What were those perspectives?

2. If you were to conduct a similar study using other perspectives besides feminist, what types of questions would you ask? Who would you ask the questions? What kind of results do you think you would get?

3. What were the methods described in this study? If you had to design a similar study, how would you do it?

Chapter 3: Ethics

I believe that a discussion about ethics is very important and must be covered before you begin learning about research design. It is imperative that you understand why research must be conducted ethically, what kind of research is unethical, and how to know the difference.

Ethics are the rules or standards that govern the conduct of a person or the members of a profession (Dictionary.com 2002). Ethics tell us what is morally good and bad and right and wrong. However, often the ethics, or lack of ethics, used in research projects seem to be connected to the researchers' own personal values, which can be problematic. If you think back to the first chapter, C. Wright Mills said you must step out of your own world and work within your limited experiences to really understand how other people live, how they might think, and how they feel. If you can't do this, there might be a problem if your own values and ethics are not aligned with conducting ethical research. Furthermore, both values and ethics are always open to negotiation and change. What is ethical for one person might not be ethical for another, and what is considered ethical in some societies might not be ethical in others.

Your discipline has its own **code of ethics** set up to help guide your research. You can find your code of ethics by looking up your national organization on the Internet.[1] Ethical considerations in research developed as a direct result of unethical experimentation on humans. During World War II, there were many unethical experiments conducted by the Nazis who used people in their experiments because "the guinea pigs, were, of course, the prisoners" (Aroneanu, 1996: 85). Often experiments were done on people without anesthetic and were intended to maim or kill the individual. For instance, in one experiment air was injected into the veins of people who were in concentration camps to see exactly how much compressed air could be injected into a person without causing an embolism (Aroneanu, 1996). In another experiment, paddles were placed on either the temple or the forehead and the neck, then an electric current was given to test which method of electric shock worked the best (Aroneanu, 1996). In the Nuremberg trials, which took place after WWII, an International Military Tribunal tried high Nazi officials for their actions toward humans during the war (Aly, Chroust, and Pross, 1994). Twenty-one officials who went to trial were sentenced to death (Foner and Garraty, 1991). The Nuremberg trials were in the mid 1940s, so the ethical issues that came up then should have made researchers aware of the need to keep subjects safe and free from harm. However, since that time there have been many more experiments, even in the United States, that have had devastating consequences, with little regard for human life.

One individual who believed strongly in experimentation on humans was Andrew C. Ivy, an eminent researcher and vice president of the University of Illinois Medical School.

---

[1] For instance, if you are a sociologist, you can find your code of ethics at http://www.asanet.org/members/ecoderev.html or if you are a social worker, you can find your code of ethics at http://www.socialworkers.org/pubs/code/code.asp.

He had been asked by the American Medical Association to be its representative at the Nuremberg Doctors' Trial and was the prosecution's key witness on American medical ethics. Ivy testified to the high ethical standards of American researchers during the war, including those working in penal institutions. However, Ivy also believed that prisoners were good subjects to use in experiments. In fact, Ivy did not believe that official coercion was necessary in a prison environment and that prisoners in the United States were available, easily "handled," and should be used. Prisoners ended up as subjects of experiments for studies of athlete's foot, infectious hepatitis, syphilis, malaria, influenza, and flash burns (Hornblum, 1997).

The list of experiments on people without their knowledge or consent has been unbelievably long. In one case, during the 1940s and 1950s, 40 people were injected with radioactive isotopes, including plutonium and uranium to investigate the occupational dangers that faced nuclear workers (Gordon, 1996). In another case in 1945, a black male cement worker was in a car accident in Tennessee. He was taken to the Manhattan Project Army Medical Center to have his bones set and stayed in the hospital for a few weeks. During his time there, he became the first of eighteen unsuspecting patients to become injected with plutonium in various highly distinguished medical institutions around this country to investigate plutonium's health effects on the body (Moreno, 2000; Welsome, 1999). Similarly, in the "Green Run" study, radioactive gas was deliberately and secretly discharged over Washington State from a government nuclear plant. Even though this study didn't kill anyone, the local vegetation and animals absorbed high levels of radiation. It is believed that the radiation increased the incidence of cancer (Gordon, 1996).

Probably one of the most famous studies in the United States that you might have heard about was called the "Tuskegee Syphilis Study." This study was begun in 1932 by the United States Public Health Service when 399 very poor, mostly illiterate African American sharecroppers in Alabama became part of an experiment without their knowledge or consent. All these men were in the later stage of syphilis when the study began, but they were told they had "bad blood." They did not give consent to be in this study because they didn't even know there was a study. Instead, the men were followed over the next 40 years, were kept from any kind of treatment, given diagnostic spinal taps, aspirins, and even free lunches so researchers could study untreated syphilis in black men (Reverby, 2000). This study was exposed in 1972 to the public, but it wasn't until 1997 that President Bill Clinton gave an apology to the final eight survivors.

A bit farther from the United States, a study was conducted in India from 1976 to 1988, in which the researcher attempted to study rates of progression of uterine cervical dysplasias to malignancy in 1158 Indian women. The lesions progressed to invasive cancer in 9 of the women, and 62 women developed carcinoma of the cervix before they were treated. It has been alleged that the researcher had neither informed the women that their lesions were known to progress to cancer nor offered them treatment at the outset (Mudur, 1997).

ETHICAL ISSUES IN RESEARCH

To make sure researchers adhere to the standards of a specific discipline, the first rule of research is that all participation involving humans should be **voluntary**. Subjects should be asked to participate in the study and *must* give their consent. Because respondents may have revealed personal information about themselves or been given something that could have long-lasting effects on them physically or mentally, it is important that they know they are part of a study. Is it ethical to go into an Internet chat room and collect conversations between individuals without telling them you are watching them? Although some researchers are, in fact, doing this, others believe that if you are watching or participating as a researcher you must tell your subjects you are watching what they do and what they say and ask them for their permission (Wysocki, 1999). This means that participants must give their **informed consent** only *after* the participants have been informed of the purpose of the study, who the researchers are, who they work for, and exactly what will be done during the study. Informed consent didn't become a reality until 1947 after those who were involved in the Manhattan Project wanted to declassify some of their secret reports (Moreno, 2000). As a result, a new policy stated that no "substance, known to be, or suspected of being, poisonous or harmful should be used in human subjects unless all of the following were met: (a) that a reasonable hope exists that the administration of such a substance will improve the condition of the patient, (b) that the patient give his complete and informed consent in writing, and (c) that the responsible next of kin give in writing a similarly complete and informed consent, revocable at any time during the course of the treatment" (Moreno, 2000: 141).

The second rule of research is that researchers have an obligation to *do no harm* to their respondents, either physically or psychologically. In 1971, Phillip Zimbardo began "The Prison Experiment," where college-aged men, who were willing subjects, were picked up at their homes, charged with a crime, spread-eagled against the police car, and handcuffed before being placed in a makeshift "jail" in the basement of Stanford University. The young men were randomly assigned to being guards or inmates to study the psychological effects of prison life. Then the trouble began and "in less than 36 hours into the experiment, Prisoner #8612 began suffering from acute emotional disturbance, disorganized thinking, uncontrollable crying, and rage" (Zimbardo, 1999). What has been so controversial since this study has been whether or not true harm was done to the respondents. A similar experiment, also known as the BBC, was recently done in Britain that seemed to have replicated the Zimbardo Prison Experiment. This experiment also had many critics and had to be terminated early because of concerns about the emotional and physical well being of the subjects (Galbraith, 2002).

The third rule is that researchers must *protect the identity* of their subjects. As researchers, you must make sure that while information is gathered and data is collected, you provide the research subjects either with **anonymity** or **confidentiality.** It is important for you to understand the distinction between these two terms. *Anonymity* is when no one, not even the researcher, knows the identity of the respondent. An example of this is when a survey is conducted on the Internet. The respondent completes the survey and returns it via email, however the email is sent to a third party where any identifying information is removed and the email is then forwarded to the researcher. This is all done electronically and no person comes in contact with the data until it reaches the researcher. *Confidentiality,* on the other hand, is when the researcher knows who the respondents are, but their identities are not revealed. This can be done in a number of ways. Remember the transvestite study I mentioned in the previous chapter? My respondents were not concerned that I knew their identities. The surveys were not anonymous. I had assured them confidentiality; when they submitted their surveys to me, I assigned them numbers and removed their names. I then kept a computer file of the numbers, along with their names and other identifying information. Once the study was complete, I deleted that information from my computer, placed it on a disk, and locked it away so no one else could have access to it.

The fourth rule is to not *deceive subjects.* Do you have the right to lie about who you are and engage in research without the knowledge of the respondent? Deceiving people is unethical. Stanley Milgram (1969) conducted a study on obedience, where the subject was told to obey a set of increasingly callous orders to shock another individual if the wrong answer was given to a question. The subjects were deceived because they were not told they were actually the subjects in the experiment and that the experiment was staged to set up the proper conditions for observing the behavior. Although the findings in this study have been valuable for society, the subjects were deceived and showed signs of psychological harm.

The final rule of ethical research involves *analysis and reporting.* As researchers, you have ethical obligations to your subjects and to your colleagues to report both positive and negative findings (Babbie, 2001). For instance, in 1995, Marty Rimm, a Carnegie Mellon undergraduate, published the results of his study about pornography on the Internet in the *Georgetown Law Journal* (Rimm, 1995). Rimm's findings, however, were found to be either misleading or meaningless after the study was published. Rimm had inflated the amount of pornographic images stored on the Internet and his methodology was in question (Elmer-Dewitt, 1995). Unfortunately, the "findings" of this study were cited in Congressional hearings as evidence that the Internet should be controlled to reduce "indecent" material. Rimm was also invited to present his findings before Congressional hearings in support of the "Communications Decency Act" as an "expert." The consequences for the research, the researcher, the journal, and the institution were severe.

As a result of these rules and the problems with research, **Institutional Review Boards** (IRB) have been established at any agency that receives federal research support. The IRB is made up of a panel of people, usually faculty, who review all research proposals to make sure that the rights and interests of the subjects are protected, that the research is ethical, and that no harm comes to the subjects.

REFERENCES

Aly, G., Chroust, P., & Pross, C. 1994. *Cleansing the Fatherland: Nazi medicine and racial hygiene.* Baltimore: Johns Hopkins University Press.

Aroneanu, E. (Translated by Thomas Whissen) 1996. *Inside the camps: Eyewitness accounts of life in Hitler's death camp.* Westport, Connecticut: Praeger.

Babbie, E. 2001. *The practice of social research,* 9th ed. Belmont, CA: Wadsworth/Thomson Learning.

Caplan, A. L. 1992. When evil intrudes. (Twenty years after: The legacy of the Tuskegee syphilis study). *Hastings Center Report,* 22(6): 29–33.

Dictionary.com. 2002. Ethics. [ONLINE] http://www.dictionary.com/search?q=ethics

Elmer-Dewitt, P. 1995. On a screen near you: Cyberporn. *Time Magazine,* July 3: 38–43.

Foner, E., & Garraty, J. A. 1991. Nuremberg trials (1945–1946 trials of Nazi officials). *The reader's companion to American History,* p. 802. Boston: Houghton-Mifflin.

Galbraith, K. 2002. 2 British professors stir criticism with prisonlike "experiment" for reality TV show. Chronicle of Higher Education Online [ONLINE] chronicle.com/daily/2002/01/2002012905.htm

Gordon, D. 1996. The verdict: No harm, no foul. *Bulletin of the Atomic Scientists,* 52(1): 33–41.

Hornblum, A. 1997. They were cheap and available: Prisoners as research subjects in twentieth century America. *British Medical Journal,* 315(7120): 1437–1442.

Milgram, S. 1969. *Obedience to authority.* New York: Harper & Row.

Moreno, J. D. 2000. *Undue Risk: Secret State Experiments on Humans.* New York: W. H. Freeman.

Mudur, G. 1997. Indian study of women with cervical lesions called unethical. *British Medical Journal,* 314(7087): 1065.

Reverby, S. 2000. *Tuskegee's Truths: Rethinking the Tuskegee Syphilis Study.* Chapel Hill, NC: University of North Carolina Press.

Rimm, M. 1995. Marketing pornography on the information highway: A survey of 917,410 images, descriptions, short stories, and animations downloaded 8.5 million times by consumers in over 2000 cities and territories. *Georgetown Law Journal,* 83: 1849–1934.

Welsome, E. 1999. *The plutonium files: America's secret medical experiments in the Cold War.* New York: Dial Press.

Wysocki, D. K. 1999. Virtual sociology: Using computers in research. *Iowa Journal of Communication,* 31(1): 59–67.

Zimbardo, P. 1999. The Stanford Prison Experiment. [ONLINE] http://www.prisonexp.org/slide-22.htm

INFOTRAC COLLEGE EDITION SUGGESTED READINGS AND DISCUSSION QUESTIONS

1. Use InfoTrac College Edition to find the article "Psychology's Tangled Web: Deceptive Methods May Backfire on Behavioral Researchers." What research used deception? Can you find any more examples of unethical research using InfoTrac College Edition?

2. Confidentiality and anonymity are important in conducting research. Two articles deal with these issues. Find "Social Services Can Act on Anonymous Information about Abuse" and "Factors Associated with HIV Testing Among Sexually Active Adolescents: A Massachusetts Survey." How do the researchers resolve these issues?

3. Use InfoTrac College Edition to find out about the Tuskegee Institute, now Tuskegee University, which is where the syphilis study took place. For instance, there is an article about Dr. Frederick D. Patterson who was the founder of the United Negro College Fund and also was president of Tuskegee Institute from 1935–1955. What else can you find out about the Institute's role in the project?

NUREMBERG AND THE ISSUE OF WARTIME EXPERIMENTS ON U.S. PRISONERS: THE GREEN COMMITTEE

Jon M. Harkness

This article deals with the final report of the Green Committee of 1948 that you read about earlier in the chapter. In this report, a U.S. physician, who headed this committee and testified at the Nuremberg Medical Trials, refuted Nazi claims that research done on prisoners in the United States was as questionable as the "research" conducted by the Nazis. The problem is that this final report was published in the Journal of the American Medical Association *(JAMA), a very reputable medical journal, which then convinced doctors in the United States that experiments done on prisoners were ethical. Notice how the researchers justify their decisions during the research project.*

Defense attorneys at the Nuremberg Medical Trial argued that no ethical difference existed between experiments in Nazi concentration camps and research in U.S. prisons. Investigations that had taken place in an Illinois prison became an early focus of this argument. Andrew C. Ivy, M.D., whom the American Medical Association had selected as a consultant to the Nuremberg prosecutors, responded to courtroom criticism of research in his home state by encouraging the Illinois governor to establish a committee to evaluate prison research. The governor named a committee and accepted Ivy's offer to chair the panel. Late in the trial, Ivy testified—drawing on the authority of this committee—that research on U.S. prisoners was ethically ideal. However, the governor's committee had never met. After the trial's conclusion, the committee report was published in JAMA, where it became a source of support for experimentation on prisoners.

The most famous document resulting from the Nuremberg Medical Trial is the Nuremberg Code, and the most celebrated element of this Code is the opening consent clause, which states that a research subject "should be so situated as to be able to exercise free power of choice, without the intervention of any element of force, fraud, deceit, duress, over-reaching, or other ulterior form of constraint or coercion."(1) When one views this pronouncement in the abstract, the continuation—indeed, the vast expansion—of medical experimentation in U.S. prisons during the quarter century immediately following the trial can seem a mystifying contradiction. In this article, I will attempt to unravel an element of this mystery—if not resolve the contradiction—by examining another documentary product of the trial.

The U.S. prosecutors took several weeks as the Nuremberg Medical Trial began in the late 1946 to present their case against the defendants. On January 27, 1947, near the end of this early phase in the proceedings, the prosecution team put Dr. Werner Leibbrandt on the stand. Leibbrandt was a German physician and medical historian who had been persecuted by the Nazis during the war for "racial reasons." (2) The prosecutors

Harkness, Jon. M. 1996. Nuremberg and the issue of wartime experiments on U.S. prisoners: The Green Committee. *JAMA,* 276(20), 1672–1676. Reprinted with permission from the American Medical Association.

intended that Leibbrandt would testify on "the effect of the Nazi dictatorship on the German medical profession and medical standards." (3)

During much of Leibbrandt's examination by the prosecution, he labored to make a claim that the Hippocratic Oath contained implicit guidelines for medical scientists engaged in nontherapeutic research with human subjects. (2) The cross-examination of Leibbrandt by Robert Servatius, defense counsel for Dr. Karl Brandt (who had been Hitler's personal physician), was the opening volley in an attempt by some of the defendants, and their attorneys, to equate U.S. wartime research on prisoners with Nazi experiments on concentration camp inmates. In short, the German physicians on trial wanted to argue that they were no more guilty of experimental improprieties than U.S. medical scientists who had relied on prisoners as research subjects during the war. (By exploring this episode, I am not endorsing the validity of the parallel that the Nazi medical defendants attempted to make during the trial.) Servatius began by asking—in hypothetical terms—for Leibbrandt's thoughts on the use of prisoners as research subjects:

> QUESTION: Witness, are you of the opinion that a prisoner who had over ten years sentence to serve will give his approval to an experiment if he receives no advantages there from? Do you consider such approval voluntary?
>
> ANSWER: No. According to medical ethics this is not the case. The patient or inmate [is] basically brought into a forcible situation by being arrested.
>
> QUESTION: Are you of the opinion that eight hundred prisoners under arrest at various places who give their approval for an experiment at the same time do so voluntarily?
>
> ANSWER: No.
>
> QUESTION: You do not distinguish as to whether the experiments involve permanent damage . . . or whether it is temporary?
>
> ANSWER: No . . .
>
> QUESTION: If such prisoners are infected with malaria because they have declared themselves willing, do you consider that . . . admissible?
>
> ANSWER: No, because I do not consider such a declaration of willingness right from a point of view of medical ethics. As prisoners[,] they were already in a forced situation. (2)

Servatius had Leibbrandt just where he wanted him at this point. The crafty trial attorney then presented Leibbrandt with a copy of an article on wartime malaria experiments conducted on prisoners at Stateville Prison in Illinois from the June 4, 1945, issue of *Life* magazine. Servatius spent several minutes laying out the details of the article: He read aloud the entire text, which recounted in laudatory terms the work of the scientists and the sacrifices made by the prisoner-subjects, and he described in detail each of the several photographs accompanying the article. (4)

At the conclusion of his review of the *Life* piece, Servatius had a simple—and obvious—question for Leibbrandt: "Now will you please express your opinion on the admissibility of these experiments?" Servatius had set a trap, and Leibbrandt did not demonstrate any particular effort to escape the snare; he maintained consistency with a blunt condemnation of the Stateville research:

"On principle[,] I cannot deviate from my view mentioned before on a medical, ethical basis. I am of the opinion that even such experiments are excesses and outgrowths of biological thinking." (2) Earlier in his testimony, Leibbrandt had described his view of "biological thinking": "Under biological thinking . . . a physician . . . does not take the [human] subject [of an experiment] into consideration at all . . . the patient has become a mere object so that the human relation no longer exists and a man becomes a mere object like a mail package." (1,2) Conceivably, the prosecution team could have dismissed Leibbrandt's criticism entirely by arguing that any ethical shortcomings that might be identified in the use of U.S. prisoners as research subjects paled in comparison to the atrocities committed by the Nazi medical scientists on trial. It might also seem that prosecutors could have ignored criticism of human experimentation in the United States as essentially irrelevant to a trial concerning medical research in Germany. But a closer examination of the prosecution's case suggests that such responses would have been seen as problematic by the U.S. attorneys.

The prosecution was burdened by a fundamental disadvantage in arguing its case: the absence of preexisting and widely recognized written rules for human experimentation. Without such clearly articulated standards, prosecutors attempted (with limited success) to claim that other codes of medical ethics, such as the Hippocratic Oath, provided unambiguous guidance to medical researchers working with human subjects. But, more importantly, the U.S. prosecution team suggested that written rules were not really necessary because researchers outside Nazi Germany had for many years universally and unerringly followed an unwritten set of rules "by common agreement and practice" when experimenting with human subjects. This line of argument appears to have made it difficult for the U.S. prosecution team to accept any ethical criticism of human experimentation in the United States. (5)

The specific challenge of Leibbrandt's unexpected testimony prompted a particular—and involved—response. Exactly who masterminded this plan is not clear, but the central figure was indisputably Andrew C. Ivy, M.D., a respected medical researcher and vice president of the University of Illinois in charge of the Chicago professional schools. The American Medical Association (AMA) had responded to a request from the Nuremberg prosecutors for expert advice on matters of medical science and medical ethics by naming Ivy as the official AMA consultant for the proceedings. (6–8) A contemporary piece in *Time* magazine discussing Ivy's role in the Nuremberg Medical Trial described him both as "one of the nation's top physiologists" and as "the conscience of U.S. science." (9)

Andrew Ivy was in the Nuremberg courtroom in late January of 1947 to hear Leibbrandt condemn prison research in Ivy's home state of Illinois. Shortly afterward, Ivy returned to Chicago and proceeded to contact Illinois Governor Dwight H. Green with an idea. Ivy suggested that he would be willing to chair a committee to examine the ethics of the malaria research that had taken place at Stateville Prison during the war. Based on events that would unfold during the next few months, it seems likely that Ivy instigated the formation of this committee largely in anticipation of an opportunity that he would have to rebut Leibbrandt's testimony in Nuremberg. Governor Green was probably not aware of this scheme, but he went along with Ivy's suggestion. Green was more likely motivated by a desire to have some advice on the question of whether to pardon any of the Illinois prisoners who had participated in the research. He was almost certainly not worried about the morality of the research itself, as the use of U.S. prisoners in medical research was generally held in high regard by the public at the time. (1,10)

On March 13, 1947, Governor Green wrote to several Illinois citizens to see if they would be willing to serve on a committee chaired by Ivy. (11) The opening of Green's letter makes clear that establishing the committee was Ivy's idea: "At the suggestion of Dr. Andrew C. Ivy, Vice-President of the Chicago Professional Colleges of the University of Illinois, I have decided to appoint an Advisory Committee . . ." (11) On April 27, Ivy wrote his first letter to the 6 men who had agreed to join him on a committee that would advise the governor on "the ethical considerations involved" in medical experimentation with Illinois state prisoners. (12) The group included 2 physicians (in addition to Ivy), Robert S. Berghoff, M.D., a prominent Chicago cardiologist, and Morris Fishbein, M.D., then editor of *JAMA;* a Chicago rabbi named George Fox; Ralph A. Gallagher, a Catholic priest and chair of the Department of Sociology at Loyola University; Oscar G. Mayer, president of the large meatpacking company bearing his name; and Kaywin Kennedy, a prosperous lawyer from Bloomington, Illinois. Ivy closed his letter to his fellow committee members with a promise to contact the group "within two to three weeks" to arrange "a convenient date and time" for their first meeting. (12)

In mid June, near the end of the Nuremberg Medical Trial, Ivy appeared before the tribunal as a rebuttal witness. With him, Ivy had the report of the so-called Green Committee—a committee that had not yet found "a convenient date and time" for it's first meeting. (13) In introducing Ivy to the court, the prosecution was careful to establish him as Leibbrandt's equal in general and his superior in judging the particulars of U.S. medical experimentation. Under friendly questioning, by the prosecution, Ivy spoke in glowing terms about the experimentation that had taken place in U.S. prisons during the war. He listed among his own qualifications to testify the fact that he was "chairman of the committee appointed by Governor Green in the State of Illinois to consider the ethical conditions under which prisoners and penitentiaries may be used ethically as subjects in the medical experiments." (12) Ivy implied that the Green Committee had carefully considered and approved the Stateville research; he never volunteered that the prestigious Green Committee had never met. (14)

Under the more pointed questioning of the defense attorneys, Ivy took on Leibbrandt more directly. At one point he stated plainly, "I do not agree with . . . Professor Leibbrandt . . . he assumes that prisoners cannot be motivated to take part in medical experiments by humanitarian incentives. This is contrary to our experience." (14) Servatius, the attorney who had led Leibbrandt to condemn the wartime prison research in Illinois, attempted to ask Ivy some probing questions about the nature of the Green Committee's deliberations. Ivy avoided outright misrepresentation by responding—somewhat awkwardly—in the first-person singular:

QUESTION: In your commission with the Green Committee, you probably debated how the volunteers should be contacted; is that not so?

ANSWER: Yes.

QUESTION: On this occasion was there not discussions of the question that you should assure yourself that no coercion was being exercised, or that the particular situation to which [sic] the person found himself who applied was being exploited?

ANSWER: Yes, I was concerned about that question.

QUESTION: There were discussions about that?

ANSWER: Not necessarily with others, but there was always consideration of that in my own mind. (1,14)

Servatius also raised questions about the origins of the Green Committee and the relation of the committee to the Nuremberg Medical Trial. In responding to these queries, Ivy flirted with perjury:

QUESTION: May I ask when this committee was formed?

ANSWER: The formation of this committee, according to the best of my recollection, occurred in December 1946 . . .

QUESTION: Did the formation of this committee have anything to do with the fact that this trial is going on . . . ?

ANSWER: There is no connection between the action of this committee and this trial. (1,14)

Under cross-examination by Servatius, Ivy also read the "conclusions" of the committee into the trial record:

Conclusion 1: The service of prisoners as subjects in medical experiments should be rewarded in addition to the ordinary good time allowed for good conduct, industry [sic], fidelity, and courage, but the excess time rewarded should not be so great as to exert undue influence in obtaining the consent of the prisoners. To give an excessive reward would be contrary to the ethics of medicine and would debase and jeopardize a method for doing good. Thus the amount of reduction of sentence in prison should be determined by the forbearance required, by the experiment, and the character of the prisoner. It is believed that a 100% increase in ordinary good time during the duration of the experiments would not be excessive in those experiments requiring the maximum forbearance.

Conclusion 2: A prisoner incapable of becoming a law abiding citizen should be told in advance, if he desires to serve as a subject in a medical experiment, not to expect any reduction in sentence. A prisoner who perpetrated an atrocious crime, even though capable of becoming a law abiding citizen, should be told in advance, if he desires to serve as a subject in a medical experiment, not to expect any drastic reduction in sentence. (1,14)

The first conclusion represented an early—perhaps the first—public enunciation by a prominent U.S. medical researcher of the potential ethical problems associated with granting a prisoner a large sentence reduction in exchange for participation in an experiment. Ivy, in essence, conceded the possibility of coercion by excessive reward in prison research; he denied, however, Werner Leibbrandt's assertion that experimentation on prisoners was, by definition, unethical. In the second conclusion, Ivy captured the U.S. public's most common concern about experimentation with prisoners up until the 1960s (which had nothing to do with exploitation or coercion): the worry that vicious felons might be rewarded too greatly merely for participating in an experiment.

The Green Committee After Nuremberg

The attempt of defense lawyers at Nuremberg to parallel the experimental crimes of their clients with the research conducted by U.S. scientists in prisons during the war almost certainly did not have a significant impact on the final outcome of the Nuremberg Medical Trial. There is no evidence that the 3 U.S. citizens who constituted the judicial panel found this defense tactic compelling. However, evidence clearly demonstrates that Ivy perceived the strategy as a serious threat. Less than 2 weeks after testifying in Nuremberg, Ivy returned to Chicago and wrote a letter dated June 24, 1947, to the other members of the Green Committee. In the letter, Ivy explained, without apology that he had prepared the committee report on his own because of the demands of his role at Nuremberg (13):

> I should indicate that it was necessary for me to prepare . . . the report . . . in my capacity as a rebuttal witness at the Nuremberg medical trials, since the German defense attorneys raised the issue of the conditions under which prisoners might be used as subjects in medical experiments and could be considered as volunteers. The German defense attorneys were attempting to develop the idea that when we in the U.S.A. used prisoners in the Federal and State prisons . . . we were doing the same thing which the Nazi physicians did during the War. That defense was, of course, refuted by my testimony, a part of which consisted in pointing out the conditions under which the use of prisoners is ethical and that these conditions have been exercised in all the work done in the U.S.A.

Ivy enclosed a copy of the report with his letter and suggested that "perhaps a formal meeting of the Committee may be considered unnecessary" after each member of the committee had read what he had already prepared. (13)

The members of the Green Committee were not, in fact, completely satisfied with Ivy's report. Some committee members corresponded with Ivy through the summer and fall of 1947, and the group actually met twice—in November and December 1947—before submitting the report to the governor. (15) The final report altered each of the 2 conclusions that Ivy had presented in Nuremberg in minor ways, but there is no evidence that anyone on the committee challenged the fundamental premise that the group was created to endorse: that prison research American-style was ethically acceptable. In fact, the final report of the committee judged the wartime research on Illinois prisoners as more than ethically acceptable. These experiments were cited by the group as "an example of human experiments which were ideal because of their conformity" with the highest standards of human experimentation, which included a proviso that "all subjects have been volunteers in the absence of coercion in any form." (16)

The final report also did much more than grant the experiments a stamp of approval within the confines of the Illinois state administration. *JAMA* editor Fishbein, who was a member of the Green Committee, decided to publish the report as a Special Article in the February 14, 1948, issue of THE JOURNAL. (16) The Green Committee, which had begun as a response to an unexpected condemnation of prison research in Illinois during the Nuremberg Medical Trial, ended its work with an authoritative declaration that this same research had been "ideal." For years to come, advocates of prison experimentation in this country could point to the Green Committee report as a strong source of support for the practice—almost certainly, none knew its true origin.

Conclusion

The Green Committee report arose from the Nuremberg Medical Trial because Ivy refused to concede even a remote moral similarity between the experimental atrocities committed in Nazi concentration camps and the medical tests that had been carried out in U.S. prisons during the war. Indeed, Ivy held to this position so steadfastly in the trial that it seems he was willing to risk perjury—or, at least, avoid the truth—to hold his ground. Ivy's stance can be seen as a symptom of a broader refusal among U.S. medical scientists to draw lessons about their own actions from the Nuremberg Medical Trial. (17) But Andrew Ivy's posture was more than just representative; Ivy also helped to create this widespread attitude. His thoughts and deeds during the trial, especially as eventually reflected in the Green Committee report that appeared in *JAMA,* contributed to a widespread failure among U.S. medical scientists to grapple with the difficult ethical questions about their own work that the Nuremberg Medical Trial might have raised. In effect, as Ivy assured the judges in Nuremberg that there was nothing ethically suspect about experimentation with prisoners in the United States, he sent the same message to his U.S. colleagues.

References

1. Trials of War Criminals Before the Nuremberg Military Tribunal. Vol. 2: Military Tribunal, Case 1, *United States v Karl Brandt,* et al, October 1946–April 1949. Washington, D.C.: U.S. Government Printing Office; 1950. For more complete references to the material in this article, see Harkness, J. M., *Research Behind Bars: A History of Nontherapeutic Research on American Priso*ners. Madison: University of Wisconsin—Madison; 1996:137–152. Thesis.

2. Leibbrandt testimony. In *Complete Transcripts of the Nuremberg Medical Trial, National Archives* Microfilm, M587 (microfilm reel 3), January 27, 1947, pp. 1961–2028.

3. Taylor, T. Final Report to the Secretary of the Army on the Nuremberg War Crimes Trials. Washington, D.C.: U.S. Government Printing Office; 1949: 89.

4. Prison Malaria: Convicts Expose Themselves to Disease So Doctors Can Study It. *Life.* June 4, 1945: 43–44, 46.

5. Ivy, A. C. Report on War Crimes of a Medical Nature Committed in Germany and Elsewhere on German Nationals and the Nationals of Occupied Countries by the Nazi Regime During World War II. 1946. (A copy of this unpublished report can be found at the National Library of Medicine and in the Archive of the American Medical Association.)

6. Dragstedt, C. A. Andrew Conway Ivy. *Q Bull Northwestern Univ Med School.* Summer 1944:139–140.

7. Grossman, M. I. Andrew Conway Ivy (1893–1978). *Physiologist.* April 1978: 11–12.

8. Bill, D. B. A. C. Ivy-reminiscences. *Physiologist.* October 1979: 21–22.

9. Citizen doctor. *Time.* January 13, 1947: 47.

10. Annas, G. J., and Grodin, M. A. *The Nazi Doctors and the Nuremberg Code: Human Rights in Human Experimentation.* New York: Oxford University Press; 1992: 204.

11. Letter from Governor Dwight H. Green to Morris Fishbein, March 13, 1947. Archives of the University of Chicago Library, Morris Fishbein Papers, Box 98: 2.

12. Letter from Andrew C. Ivy to Rev Ralph A. Gallagher, S J; Rev. Ralph Wakefield; Dr. G. George Fox; Dr. Morris Fishbein; Mr. Kaywin Kennedy; Dr. Robert S. Berghoff; and Mr. Oscar G. Mayer, April 21, 1947. Archives of the University of Chicago Library, Morris Fishbein Papers, Box 98: 2.

13. Letter from Andrew C. Ivy to Dr. Robert S. Berghoff, Dr. Morris Fishbein, Rabbi George Fox, Father Ralph Gallagher, Mr. Kaywin Kennedy, and Mr. Oscar Mayer, June 24, 1947. Archives of the University of Chicago Library, Morris Fishbein Papers, Box 98: 2.

14. Ivy testimony. In *Complete Transcripts of the Nuremberg Medical Trial,* National Archives Microfilm, M887 (microfilm reels 9 and 10), June 12–16, 1947, pp. 9029–9324.

15. Archives of the University of Chicago Library, Morris Fishbein Papers, Box 98: 2.

16. Ethics Governing the Service of Prisoners as Subjects in Medical Experiments: Report of a Committee Appointed by Governor Dwight H. Green of Illinois. *JAMA.* 1948; 136: 457–458.

17. Advisory Committee on Human Radiation Experiments. *Final Report of the Advisory Committee on Human Radiation Experiments.* Washington, D.C.: U.S. Government Printing Office; 1995: 137–154.

REVIEW QUESTIONS

1. Why did the AMA use Ivy to represent the United States on medical experimentation during the Nuremberg Medical Trials?

2. What does Ivy say about using prisoners for medical experimentation? How does he justify this?

3. Do you think it is important to read about something that took place so long ago? Why do we have to go over things that have happened in history?

PROBLEMS OF ETHICS IN RESEARCH

Stanley Milgram

Stanley Milgram carried out his study on obedience at Yale University from 1960 to 1963. In reaction to the "systematic slaughter on command" of so many people during World War II, Milgram wanted to determine why individuals would actually obey authority even when they knew what they were being asked to do was wrong. This experiment involved a "teacher," who was the real focus of the experiment, instructed to shock the "learner" when a wrong answer was given. The point of the experiment was to see how far a person would go when ordered to inflict pain on the "learner." As you read the article, you might keep in mind whether or not this project truly did hurt the participants.

The purpose of the inquiry described here was to study obedience and disobedience to authority under conditions that permitted careful scrutiny of the phenomenon. A person was told by an experimenter to obey a set of increasingly callous orders, and our interest was to see when he would stop obeying. An element of theatrical staging was needed to set the proper conditions for observing the behavior, and technical illusions were freely employed (such as the fact that the victim only appeared to be shocked). Beyond this, most of what occurred in the laboratory was what had been discovered, rather than what had been planned.

For some critics, however, the chief horror of the experiment was not that the subjects obeyed but that the experiment was carried out at all. Among professional psychologists a certain polarization occurred. The experiment was both highly praised and harshly criticized. In 1964, Dr. Diana Baumrind attacked the experiments in the *American Psychologist,* in which I later published this reply:

> In a recent issue of *American Psychologist, a* critic raised a number of questions concerning the obedience report. She expressed concern for the welfare of subjects who served in the experiment, and wondered whether adequate measures were taken to protect the participants.
>
> At the outset, the critic confuses the unanticipated outcome of an experiment with its basic procedure. She writes, for example, as if the production of stress in our subjects was an intended and deliberate effect of the experimental manipulation. There are many laboratory procedures specifically designed to create stress (Lazarus, 1964), but the obedience paradigm was not one of them. The extreme tension induced in some subjects was unexpected. Before conducting the experiment, the procedures were discussed with many colleagues, and none anticipated the reactions that subsequently took place. Foreknowledge of results can never be the invariable accompaniment of an experimental probe. Understanding grows because we examine situations in which the end is unknown. An

investigator unwilling to accept this degree of risk must give up the idea of scientific inquiry.

Moreover, there was every reason to expect, prior to actual experimentation, that subjects would refuse to follow the experimenter's instructions beyond the point where the victim protested; many colleagues and psychiatrists were questioned on this point, and they virtually all felt this would be the case. Indeed, to initiate an experiment in which the critical measure hangs on disobedience, one must start with a belief in certain spontaneous resources in men that enable them to overcome pressure from authority.

It is true that after a reasonable number of subjects had been exposed to the procedures, it became evident that some would go to the end of the shock board, and some would experience stress. That point, it seems to me, is the first legitimate juncture at which one could even start to wonder whether or not to abandon the study. But momentary excitement is not the same as harm. As the experiment progressed there was no indication of injurious effects in the subjects; and as the subjects themselves strongly endorsed the experiment, the judgment I made was to continue the investigation.

Is not the criticism based as much on the unanticipated findings as on the method? The findings were that some subjects performed in what appeared to be a shockingly immoral way. If, instead, every one of the subjects had broken off at "slight shock," or at the first sign of the learner's discomfort, the results would have been pleasant, and reassuring, and who would protest?

A very important aspect of the procedure occurred at the end of the experimental session. A careful postexperimental treatment was administered to all subjects. The exact content of the dehoax varied from condition to condition and with increasing experience on our part. At the very least, all subjects were told that the victim had not received dangerous electric shocks. Each subject had a friendly reconciliation with the unharmed victim, and an extended discussion with the experimenter. The experiment was explained to the defiant subjects in a way that supported their decision to disobey the experimenter. Obedient subjects were assured of the fact that their behavior was entirely normal and that their feelings of conflict or tension were shared by other participants. Subjects were told that they would receive a comprehensive report at the conclusion of the experimental series. In some instances, additional detailed and lengthy discussions of the experiments were also carried out with individual subjects.

When the experimental series was complete, subjects received a written report which presented details of the experimental procedure and results. Again, their own part in the experiments was treated in a dignified way and their behavior in the experiment respected. All subjects received a follow-up questionnaire regarding their participation in the research, which again allowed expression of thoughts and feelings about their behavior.

The replies to the questionnaire confirmed my impression that participants felt positively toward the experiment. In its quantitative aspect (see Table 8), 84% of the subjects stated they were glad to have been in the experiment; 15% indicated neutral feelings; and 1.3% indicated negative feelings. To be sure, such findings are to be interpreted cautiously, but they cannot be disregarded.

TABLE 8. EXCERPT FROM QUESTIONNAIRE USED IN A FOLLOW-UP STUDY OF THE
OBEDIENCE RESEARCH

Now that *I* have read the report, and all things considered	Defiant %	Obedient %	All %
1 I am very glad to have been in the experiment	40.0	47.8	43.5
2 I am glad to have been in the experiment	43.8	35.7	40.2
3 I am neither sorry nor glad to have been in the experiment	15.3	14.8	15.1
4 I am sorry to have been in the experiment	0.8	0.7	0.5
5 I am very sorry to have been in the experiment	0.0	1.0	0.5

Note: Ninety-two percent of the subjects returned the questionnaire. The characteristics of the non-respondents were checked against the respondents. They differed from the respondents only with regard to age; younger people were overrepresented in the non-responding group.

Further, four-fifths of the subjects felt that more experiments of this sort should be carried out, and 74% indicated that they had learned something of personal importance as a result of being in the study.

The debriefing and assessment procedures were carried out as a matter of course, and were not stimulated by any observation of special risk in the experimental procedure. In my judgment, at no point were subjects exposed to danger and at no point did they run the risk of injurious effects resulting from participation. If it had been otherwise, the experiment would have been terminated at once.

The critic states that, after he has performed in the experiment, the subject cannot justify his behavior and must bear the full brunt of his actions. By and large it does not work this way. The same mechanisms that allow the subject to perform the act, to obey rather than to defy the experimenter, transcend the moment of performance and continue to justify his behavior for him. The same viewpoint the subject takes while performing the actions is the viewpoint from which he later sees his behavior, that is, the perspective of "carrying out the task assigned by the person in authority."

Because the idea of shocking the victim is repugnant, there is a tendency among those who hear of the design to say "people will not do it." When the results are made known, this attitude is expressed as "if they do it they will not be able to live with themselves afterward." These two forms of denying the experimental findings are equally inappropriate misreading of the facts of human social behavior. Many subjects do, indeed, obey to the end, and there is no indication of injurious effects.

The absence of injury is a minimal condition of experimentation; there can be, however, an important positive side to participation. The critic suggests that subjects derived no benefit from being in the obedience study, but this is false. By their statements and actions, subjects indicated that they had learned a good deal, and many felt gratified to have taken part in scientific research they considered to be of significance. A year after his participation one subject wrote: "This experiment has strengthened my belief that man should avoid harm to his fellow man even at the risk of violating authority."

Another stated: "To me, the experiment pointed up . . . the extent to which each individual should have or discover firm ground on which to base his decisions, no matter how trivial they appear to be. I think people should think more deeply about themselves and their relation to their world and to other people. If this experiment serves to jar people out of complacency, it will have served its end."

These statements are illustrative of a broad array of appreciative and insightful comments by those who participated.

The 5-page report sent to each subject on the completion of the experimental series was specifically designed to enhance the value of his experience. It laid out the broad conception of the experimental program as well as the logic of its design. It described the results of a dozen of the experiments, discussed the causes of tension, and attempted to indicate the possible significance of the experiment. Subjects responded enthusiastically; many indicated a desire to be in further experimental research. This report was sent to all subjects several years ago. The care with which it was prepared does not support the critic's assertion that the experimenter was indifferent to the value subjects derived from their participation.

The critic fears that participants will be alienated from psychological experiments because of the intensity of experience associated with laboratory procedures. My own observation is that subjects more commonly respond with distaste to the "empty" laboratory hour, in which cardboard procedures are employed, and the only possible feeling upon emerging from the laboratory is that one has wasted time in a patently trivial and useless exercise.

The subjects in the obedience experiment, on the whole, felt quite differently about their participation. They viewed the experience as an opportunity to learn something of importance about themselves, and more generally, about the conditions of human action.

A year after the experimental program was completed, I initiated an additional follow-up study. In this connection an impartial medical examiner, experienced in outpatient treatment, interviewed 40 experimental subjects. The examining psychiatrist focused on those subjects he felt would be most likely to have suffered consequences from participation. His aim was to identify possible injurious effects resulting from the experiment. He concluded that, "although extreme stress had been experienced by several subjects, none was found by this interviewer to show signs of having been harmed by his experience. . . . Each subject seemed to handle his task (in the experiment) in a manner consistent with well-established patterns of behavior. No evidence was found of any traumatic reactions." Such evidence ought to be weighed before judging the experiment.

At root, the critic believes that it is not proper to test obedience in this situation, because she construes it as one in which there is no reasonable alternative to obedience. In adopting this view, she has lost sight of this fact: A substantial proportion of subjects do disobey. By their example, disobedience is shown to be a genuine possibility, one that is in no sense ruled out by the general structure of the experimental situation.

The critic is uncomfortable with the high level of obedience obtained in the first experiment. In the condition she focused on, 65% of the subjects obeyed to the end. However, her sentiment does not take into account that within the general framework of the psychological experiment obedience varied enormously from one condition to the next. In some variations, 90% of the subjects disobeyed. It seems to be not only the fact of an experiment, but the particular structure of elements within the experimental situation that accounts for rates of obedience and disobedience. And these elements were varied systematically in the program of research.

A concern with human dignity is based on a respect for a man's potential to act morally. The critic feels that the experimenter *made* the subject shock the victim. This conception is alien to my view. The experimenter tells the subject to do something. But between the command and the outcome there is a paramount force, the acting person who may obey or disobey. I started with the belief that every person who came to the laboratory was free to accept or to reject the dictates of authority. This view sustains a conception of human dignity insofar as it sees in each man a capacity for choosing his own behavior. And as it turned out, many subjects did, indeed, choose to reject the experimenter's commands, providing a powerful affirmation of human ideals.

The experiment is also criticized on the grounds that "it could easily effect an alteration in the subject's . . . ability to trust adult authorities in the future." . . . However, the experimenter is not just any authority: He is an authority who tells the subject to act harshly and inhumanely against another man. I would consider it of the highest value if participation in the experiment could, indeed, inculcate a skepticism of this kind of authority. Here, perhaps, a difference in philosophy emerges most clearly. The critic views the subject as a passive creature, completely controlled by the experimenter. I started from a different viewpoint. A person who comes to the laboratory is an active, choosing adult, capable of accepting or rejecting the prescriptions for action addressed to him. The critic sees the effect of the experiment as undermining the subject's trust of authority. I see it as a potentially valuable experience insofar as it makes people aware of the problem of indiscriminate submission to authority.

Yet another criticism occurred in Dannie Abse's play, *The Dogs of Pavlov,* which appeared in London in 1971 and which uses the obedience experiment as its central dramatic theme. At the play's climax, Kurt, a major character in the play, repudiates the experimenter for treating him as a guinea pig. In his introduction to the play, Abse especially condemns the illusions employed in the experiment, terming the setup "bullshit," "fraudulent," "cheat." At the same time, he apparently admires the dramatic quality of the experiment. And he allowed my rejoinder to appear in the foreword to his book. I wrote to him:

> I do feel you are excessively harsh in your language when condemning my use of illusion in the experiment. As a dramatist, you surely understand that illusion may serve a revelatory function, and indeed, the very possibility of theater is founded on the benign use of contrivance.

One could, viewing a theatrical performance, claim that the playwright has cheated, tricked, and defrauded the audience, for he presents as old men individuals who are, when the greasepaint is removed, quite young; men presented as physicians who in reality are merely actors knowing nothing about medicine, etc., etc. But this assertion of "bullshit," "cheat," "fraud" would be silly, would it not, for it does not take into account how those exposed to the theater's illusions feel about them. The fact is that the audience accepts the necessity of illusion for the sake of entertainment, intellectual enrichment, and all of the other benefits of the theatrical experience. And it is their acceptance of these procedures that gives you warrant for the contrivances you rely upon.

So I will not say that you cheated, tricked, and defrauded your audience. But, I would hold the same claim for the experiment. Misinformation is employed in the experiment; illusion is used when necessary in order to set the stage for the revelation of certain difficult-to-get-at truths; and these procedures are justified for one reason only: they are, in the end, accepted and endorsed by those who are exposed to them . . . When the experiment was explained to subjects they responded to it positively, and most felt it was an hour well spent. If it had been otherwise, if subjects ended the hour with bitter recriminatory feelings, the experiment could not have proceeded.

This judgment is based, first, on the numerous conversations I have had with subjects immediately after their participation in the experiment. Such conversations can reveal a good deal, but what they showed most was how readily the experience is assimilated to the normal frame of things. Moreover, subjects were friendly rather than hostile, curious rather than denunciatory, and in no sense demeaned by the experience. This was my general impression, and it was later supported by formal procedures undertaken to assess the subjects' reaction to the experiment.

The central moral justification for allowing a procedure of the sort used in my experiment is that it is judged acceptable by those who have taken part in it. Moreover, it was the salience of this fact throughout that constituted the chief moral warrant for the continuation of the experiments.

This fact is crucial to any appraisal of the experiment from an ethical standpoint.

Imagine an experiment in which a person's little finger was routinely snipped off in the course of a laboratory hour. Not only is such an experiment reprehensible, but within hours the study would be brought to a halt as outraged participants pressed their complaints on the university administration, and legal measures were invoked to restrain the experimenter. When a person has been abused, he knows it, and will quite properly react against the source of such mistreatment.

Criticism of the experiment that does not take account of the tolerant reaction of the participants is hollow. This applies particularly to criticism centering on the use of technical illusions (or "deception," as the critics prefer to say) that fails to relate this detail to the central fact that subjects find the device acceptable. Again, the participant, rather than the external critic, must be the ultimate source of judgment.

While some persons construe the experimenter to be acting in terms of deceit, manipulation, and chicanery, it is, as you should certainly appreciate, also possible to see him as a dramatist who creates scenes of revelatory power, and who brings participants into them. So perhaps we are not so far apart in the kind of work we do. I do grant there is an important difference in that those exposed to your theatrical illusions expect to confront them, while my subjects are not forewarned. However, whether it is unethical to pursue truths through the use of my form of dramaturgical device cannot be answered in the abstract. It depends entirely on the response of those who have been exposed to such procedures.

One further point: the obedient subject does not blame himself for shocking the victim, because the act does not originate in the self. It originates in authority, and the worst the obedient subject says of himself is that he must learn to resist authority more effectively in the future.

That the experiment has stimulated this thought in some subjects is, to my mind, a satisfying consequence of the inquiry. An illustrative case is provided by the experience of a young man who took part in a Princeton replication of the obedience experiment, conducted in 1964. He was fully obedient. On October 27, 1970, he wrote to me:

"Participation in the 'shock experiment' . . . has had a great impact on my life. When I was a subject in 1964, though I believed that I was hurting someone, I was totally unaware of why I was doing so. Few people ever realize when they are acting according to their own beliefs and when they are meekly submitting to authority. . . . To permit myself to be drafted with the understanding that I am submitting to authority's demand to do something very wrong would make me frightened of myself. . . . I am fully prepared to go to jail if I am not granted Conscientious Objector status. Indeed, it is the only course I could take to be faithful to what I believe. My only hope is that members of my board act equally according to their conscience."

He inquired whether any other participants had reacted similarly, and whether, in my opinion, participation in the study could have this effect.

I replied:

"The experiment does, of course, deal with the dilemma individuals face when they are confronted with conflicting demands of authority and conscience, and I am glad that your participation in the study has brought you to a deeper personal consideration of these issues. Several participants have informed me that their own sensitivity to the problem of submission to authority was increased as a result of their experience in the study. If the experiment has heightened your awareness of the problem of indiscriminate submission to authority, it will have performed an important function. If you believe strongly that it is wrong to kill others in the service of your country, then you ought certainly to press vigorously for CO status, and I am deeply hopeful that your sincerity in this matter will be recognized."

A few months later he wrote again. He indicated, first, that the draft board was not very impressed with the effect of his participation in the experiment, but he was granted CO status nonetheless. He writes:

"The experience of the interview doesn't lessen my strong belief of the great impact of the experiment on my life. You have discovered one of the most important causes of all the trouble in this world. . . . I am grateful to have been able to provide you with a part of the information necessary for that discovery. I am delighted to have acted, by refusing to serve in the Armed Forces, in a manner which people must act if these problems are to be solved. With sincere thanks for your contribution to my life . . .

In a world in which action is often clouded with ambiguity, I nonetheless feel constrained to give greater heed to this man, who actually participated in the study, than to a distant critic. For disembodied moralizing is not the issue, but only the human response of those who have participated in the experiment. And that response not only endorses the procedures employed, but overwhelmingly calls for deeper inquiry to illuminate the issues of obedience and disobedience.

References

Lazarus, R. 1964. A laboratory approach to the dynamics of psychological stress. *American Psychologist,* 19: 400–411.

REVIEW QUESTIONS

1. This study is controversial and has been for years. Do you believe that the benefits outweighed the risks in this study? Why or why not?

2. Do you agree with Milgram that this study was not harmful to the subjects? Explain your answer.

3. Why wouldn't this study be considered ethical today?

THE ETHICS OF CONDUCTING SOCIAL-SCIENCE RESEARCH ON THE INTERNET

James C. Hamilton

The Internet and the World Wide Web have advanced our ability to gain information at an amazing rate. Each year, more and more individuals have either their own personal computers or access to computers in their schools, libraries, or places of work. With technological advances comes the possibility for researchers to connect with people who might otherwise be difficult to reach either because of the proximity to the researcher or the desire of the individual to remain anonymous. Even though more and more researchers are using the Internet to gather data, change doesn't happen without the possibility of the problems that are addressed in this article by Hamilton. If the things individuals write on the Internet are available to the public, then should a researcher really have to deal with ethics on the Internet?

Over the past four or five years, the amount of social-science research conducted on the Internet has increased exponentially. More than 100 World Wide Web sites now invite visitors to participate in a wide variety of scientific research, or in activities that resemble scientific research, including personality tests, intelligence tests, and opinion surveys.

Other sites bear a superficial resemblance to those used for legitimate research, but are designed solely for entertainment purposes. For instance, visitors to the Free Internet Love Test site (http://www.lovetest.com) can provide information—including astrological signs—about themselves and their partners, and receive feedback about their compatibility.

The growth of research on the Internet has outpaced the efforts of researchers—and advocates for the ethical treatment of research participants—to understand the implications of this new methodology and to develop guidelines for its responsible use. The Internet clearly is a very powerful research tool, and its benefits—such as the ability to reach large numbers of people, at very low cost—are alluring. But like all powerful tools, it can be destructive if it is not used properly, or if it falls into the wrong hands.

An Internet search that I conducted suggests that on-line researchers are not consistently employing the safeguards that are used to protect participants in traditional research. For example, in studies not conducted on line, participants must read and sign a statement that describes the research and explains their rights. Although on-line researchers could easily convey the same type of information on a Web page, many on-line research sites dispense with that important safeguard.

Complicated studies often require that researchers give participants additional information, beyond the informed-consent statement. In practice, many studies are so complex that it is impossible to give participants a full explanation of the research before they participate, without running the risk of skewing the results. As an example, participants who are told that a study concerns how the race of a defendant influences jurors' decisions are

Hamilton, James C. 1999. The ethics of conducting social-science research on the Internet. *Chronicle of Higher Education,* Dec. 3, 1999 46 (15) p. B6(2). Used with permission.

likely to alter their responses to appear unprejudiced. Therefore, many researchers give participants a post-experimental debriefing—that is, they provide a full explanation of the research only after the participants have completed the experiment. On-line researchers could design their Web sites to send participants to a debriefing page after they are finished, but many do not.

What's more, even if researchers include a debriefing page, they cannot make participants read it. That problem highlights some of the ethical issues raised by the fact that researchers have so little control over the nature of participants' experiences in on-line research. In face-to-face studies, researchers can see if participants have an adverse reaction to the study and can take steps to assist them—perhaps by terminating their participation and debriefing them with extra care. In on-line studies, it is not possible for researchers to safeguard the emotional well-being of participants in the same way. Many researchers have opted to address that limitation by providing disclaimers, which state that people should not participate if they feel that they cannot handle the emotional impact of the procedure or of any feedback they might receive.

Although that might seem to be a sensible way to deal with the problem, current ethical guidelines prohibit the use of such disclaimers. Federal agencies that support research—as well as scientists' professional organizations—assert that researchers must protect the rights of their participants, and that they cannot simply ask people to sign away those rights.

Another ethical risk posed by on-line research has to do with the confidentiality of data collected over the Internet. In general, most Internet users enjoy complete anonymity. Unless someone provides personal information voluntarily, there is almost no practical way to determine the identity of a visitor to a given Web site. Although it is possible to identify the Internet address from which a particular message was sent, that address rarely belongs to a single identifiable individual. Even at academic institutions in which professors' computers are connected directly to the Internet, a machine might well use a different address each time the professor turns it on.

The anonymity that is common on line makes it possible for individuals to submit data on multiple occasions—either accidentally or intentionally—with virtually no chance of being detected. Because such multiple responses on a wide scale can invalidate a study, researchers may ask participants for identifying information, such as e-mail addresses. Or a researcher might use something called a cookie to identify the computer from which each participant submitted his or her response. However, both of those methods compromise the researcher's ability to guarantee the confidentiality of the data.

Even worse, computer hackers can easily intercept participants' responses to online studies. If they also intercept identifying information, the results for the participants could be disastrous—particularly if the study deals with sensitive issues, such as criminal or sexual behavior.

Usually institutional review boards—which work to insure that all research involving human subjects complies with applicable legal and ethical standards—save researchers from any breaches of confidentiality and other ethical lapses. However, some on-line research is being conducted without the required approval of an IRB. Recently, a doctoral student at a major U.S. university confided to me that neither he nor his dissertation chairman had thought to secure IRB approval for his on-line dissertation research. Even when IRBs are consulted about on-line research, they may be ill-equipped to evaluate the studies.

Based on my correspondence with members of IRBs around the country, I estimate that roughly half of the members have received proposals for on-line research, while only a few of the members have reported that their IRB had developed guidelines for evaluating ethical risks and safeguards in such research.

Careful evaluation of proposals for online research requires considerable expertise in the area of Internet hardware and software. To properly evaluate those proposals, IRB members need to know who will run the Web site: the researcher, from his or her own computer; the staff of a university's computer center; or a third party. If the researcher does not have complete control of the computer serving the site, the IRB must know the identities of everyone who will have access to the data, and how confidentiality will be maintained.

Beyond those general issues, IRB members need to deal with specific technical questions. These include whether data are collected only when the participant hits the "submit" button, or before the participant decides that he or she is finished; whether the participant is automatically referred to a debriefing page if he or she quits in the middle of the study; and whether participants can delete their data after they learn the purpose of the study. It takes considerable technical savvy to know enough to ask such questions, let alone to evaluate the answers.

As technology becomes increasingly sophisticated, more experimenters will be able to have on-line research sites, but the danger is that fewer will have adequate knowledge of how their sites work, in order to insure the well-being of the participants. As a result, IRBs will also have to begin evaluating the technical credentials of on-line researchers, to insure that they—or their technological consultants—have sufficient expertise to implement the appropriate technical safeguards.

Perhaps the greatest threat to on-line research is the danger to its credibility posed by data-collection sites established primarily for commercial or entertainment purposes.

Those Web sites far outnumber academic-research sites, and in many cases, it is not easy to sort out which is which.

Although many commercial data-collection sites are forthcoming about who is sponsoring the research and how the data will be used, several such sites attempt to make money by deceiving participants. For example, several commercial sites appear to offer free personality or intelligence testing—but after completing the tests, participants are informed that they need to pay for a full report of their performance. Other commercial sites promise more-elaborate feedback to visitors who provide identifying information for the sponsor's database. Sites that employ such deceptive tactics may make the public suspicious of all data-collection sites, including those that serve legitimate scientific purposes.

Data-collection sites that are designed primarily for entertainment (such as the Pooh-Piglet Psychometric Personality Profiler, at http://www.ggw.org/donor-ware/pooh/, where you can discover whether you are more like Pooh, Piglet, Tigger, or Eeyore) might have an equally damaging effect on the public's attitude toward on-line scientific research. Most of the entertainment sites are operated by private individuals for their own amusement, and are designed to provide feedback to visitors, not data for the site's owner. It is likely that visitors might fill out the forms several times, with different data, to see what kinds of feedback they get—about whether they're introverted or extroverted, say, or what kind of person they should marry.

Such sites may not lead Web surfers to believe that it is important to respond accurately or honestly to on-line tests, questionnaires. Or surveys—or even to respond only once. Were participants in on-line scientific experiments to take the same approach, the data they provided would be of no use. Rather than trying to enforce higher standards on such sites, academic researchers should put their efforts into doing a better job of identifying the scholarly nature of their sites. Few researchers make use of design elements that would help reassure potential participants about the legitimacy of their research. Those elements include the prominent display of the name and logo of the researcher's university, information allowing participants to contact the researcher, and links to other sites with information about the researcher's credentials, such as the Web page of his or her department and the site of the IRB that approved the study.

We need guidelines to help researchers and members of IRBs alike insure that online research is both scientifically and ethically sound. Professional and governmental organizations that advocate support for science, such as the American Association for the Advancement of Science and the National Science Foundation, as well as groups that promote research in the social sciences, such as the American Psychological Society, should work together to establish such guidelines.

At a minimum, the guidelines should require all on-line researchers to provide information that would permit participants to contact the researcher, a means for obtaining participants' fully informed consent, full disclosure of any risks to their confidentiality, a post-experimental debriefing page, and a way for the participants to learn about the results of the study. The guidelines also should include up-to-date information on the technologies used to conduct on-line research and a set of criteria for evaluating the technical aspects of proposed on-line studies.

Ideally, the guidelines would standardize on-line research in a way that would help Internet users to distinguish academic-research sites from other kinds. It would also be useful for IRBs to maintain a list—on line, of course—of on-line studies that they have approved.

Once the guidelines have been put into practice, we will need to educate the public about them, and about making well-informed decisions on participating in online research. The organizations that created the guidelines could set up a Web site for the public that would explain the risks and benefits of on-line research, and make potential participants aware of ways to distinguish legitimate, scientific-research sites from commercial or entertainment sites. Researchers could provide a link from their sites to that public-education site.

On-line research holds much promise for many academic disciplines. However, we will not serve the interests of science if we do not make sure that such research is conducted ethically. We must not forget our responsibilities to our participants, even when we meet them only in cyberspace.

REVIEW QUESTIONS

1. Find a survey on the Internet. Can you tell if the survey is from an academic institution? Has it been approved by an IRB? How can you tell?

2. Can research on the Internet be anonymous? Does it need to be? Explain your reasoning in detail.

3. Do you think observing behaviors in an Internet chat room should have IRB approval before the observations begin? Why or why not?

PART II ■ THE STRUCTURING OF INQUIRY

■

Chapter 4: Research Design

Before you actually begin learning about specific research designs, it is important to have an understanding about some of the terms that you will hear throughout your research methods class. There are numerous reasons to conduct research. In fact, there are almost as many reasons as there are researchers. Furthermore, research studies may have multiple purposes; however, the most common reasons for conducting research are to explore, describe, and explain the phenomenon that is being studied (Babbie, 2001).

THE REASONS FOR RESEARCH

Exploratory research may be the first stage of a research project to give the researcher new knowledge about a phenomenon so that he or she can design a more in-depth secondary study. For instance, one exploratory study was conducted to investigate the experiences of 40 HIV-positive mothers. The study was specifically set up to explore the social service agencies designed to help the women, to learn how the women coped with the infection, particularly as it related to parenting, and to determine their concerns, preferences, and plans for the future care of their children. The researchers explored the lives of the women who talked about their problems at the individual and family level, the organizations and providers level, and the policy and community level. Then the researchers were able to make recommendations for providers and design new studies to see which recommendations were most helpful (Marcenko & Samost, 1999). Other exploratory studies have been done that explore the various types of violence inflicted on women who live in public housing because these are typically areas where gendered power relations are played out, and the influence of drugs has increased the degradation and abuse of women (DeKesseredy, Alvi, Schwartz, and Perry, 1999), that explore how police-community relationships improve the citizens attitudes toward the police (Palomiotto and Unninthan, 2002), and that used vignettes to explore how gender affects the ethical decision made by two groups of students (Byers and Powers, 1997).

Descriptive research allows the researcher to develop ideas about a topic and then describe the phenomenon in question. Descriptive research usually begins with a well-defined topic that leads to the research being conducted to describe the topic accurately. For instance, Nnorom, Esu-Williams, and Tilley-Gyado (1996) studied HIV, tuberculosis, and syphilis in Nigeria to determine the distribution by age group and to establish any association between these diseases. The researchers also wanted to estimate the male-to-female ratio of HIV and syphilis infections in Nigeria and to estimate the urban-to-rural ratio of HIV and syphilis infections in Nigeria. The researchers accomplished this task by using the results generated from the 1993/94 national HIV/Syphilis sentinel survey that was carried out in 17 of the 30 states in Nigeria. The results from this descriptive study allowed researchers to make recommendations about where to focus HIV/STD interventions and where more diagnostic, prophylactic, and therapeutic interventions should be encouraged. In another study, Ensign (2000) looked at homeless adolescent women who were at high risk for negative health outcomes. Ensign used semi-structured interviews and focus groups to hear the personal experiences concerning health, self-care, and fertility control. The results from this study enabled the researcher to describe problems specific to these young homeless women in order to make changes in the way health care providers are trained in how to ask about sensitive subjects. Without a description of the problem, it is impossible to find a solution.

The third purpose of research is to provide an explanation **(explanatory research)** of some phenomenon. After you have explored a topic and have a fairly good description of it, you might begin to wonder about it. You might want to know why it happens the way it does. Does it really always happen the way you think? If something else were around, would the results be different? For example, think about the researchers I just described who studied the distribution of TB, syphilis, and HIV in Nigeria. Now they might want to explain why some areas have higher incidences of these diseases than other areas do. Could it be the lack of health care in some areas? Could it be the lack of education? Would putting more education in some of the areas with the highest infection rates ultimately lower the rates of infection?

UNITS OF ANALYSIS

Another aspect of research that can be somewhat confusing is that of **units of analysis.** Units of analysis refer to the type of unit researchers use when measuring variables to describe and explain the differences among them. The most common units of analysis are the individual, the group, the organization, the social category, the social artifact, the social institution, and the society.

The most typical unit of analysis is the *individual,* such as students who are asked in a survey to rate teachers in a university. In another example, Johnson (2000) investigated a randomly selected group of individuals who lived in Indiana to find out what types of people supported the *Promise Keepers,* a religious group of men who gather to discuss their place in their homes. The results of this study suggested that for those who had lower education levels, the self-esteem they gained from being a member was important, and for those with higher education levels, the political nature of Promise Keepers was most important.

Using *groups* as the unit of analysis, Winfree, Bernat, and Esbensen (2001) conducted a systematic comparison of gang-related attitudes and behavior of youths who lived in two different cities. The researchers explored the attitudes and orientations of both gang and non-gang eighth-grade students. Even though the statistical comparisons supported the position that the children in one city expressed higher levels of pro-gang attitudes, there did not appear to be significant differences in self-reported gang membership. However, Hispanic youths in both cities were more pro-gang in their attitudes and orientations, and they reported higher levels of gang membership.

Organizations as the unit of analysis can also provide some interesting comparisons in many different areas. One of those areas is health care because the health maintenance organizations (HMO) program has grown rapidly in recent years. However, some have concerns about the quality, access, and satisfaction of care patients actually receive from these big organizations. Because there are believed to be widespread variations in the patients between HMOs or fee-for-services (FFS), Riley, Potosky, Klabunde, Warren, and Ballard-Barbash (1999) compared the care the women received from both organizations. The researchers found that although there was no difference in the diagnosis of the disease between the two providers, there was a difference in the treatment plans.

I believe using social artifacts as the unit of analysis is always fun, especially for students. Social artifacts can include bumper stickers, newspapers, books, and the news media. For instance, Scharrer (2001), studied more than 300 male characters in police and detective television dramas from 1970 to 1990 to examine their levels of hypermasculinity and antisocial behavior. The results of this study indicated a strong association for all male characters between physical aggression/antisocial behaviors and hypermasculinity. In another example using textbooks as the social artifacts, Zittleman and Sadker (2002) investigated the treatment of gender in 23 teacher education textbooks published between 1998 and 2001. What they found was that the progress made was minimal and that introductory/foundation texts provided slightly more than 7 percent of their content to gender issues, whereas the methods texts average little more than 1 percent. Although the researchers found that a commitment to gender fairness was verbalized in several of the textbooks, specific resources and strategies to achieve that goal were often absent, whereas inadequate, stereotypic, and inaccurate treatment of gender was commonplace. The results of using textbooks as a unit of analysis in the study suggest that although student teachers may learn that equity in the classroom is important, they do not get the information in the textbooks they use to make it a reality.

Using the correct unit of analysis is very important in your research. There are typically two types of problems associated with using the wrong unit of analysis: the **ecological fallacy** and **reductionism.** The ecological fallacy is when an inference is made about individuals when the data actually came from groups. Reductionism, on the other hand, is when a complex phenomenon is seen and explained in terms of a single, narrow concept, thus *reducing* to a simple explanation what is actually quite complex. Here is an example. Let's say you want to compare the blood pressure of two groups of patients, so you take the blood pressure on each arm of each patient. The unit of analysis is the patient, but if you actually use each of the blood pressures taken on, say 50 patients, you would have 100 blood pressures. What would this do to the analysis? It can lead to problems in the interpretations. It might, in fact, be better and more accurate, to analyze the mean of the two blood pressures for each patient (Bland and Altman, 1995). But knowing your unit of analysis is most important to your results.

THE TIME DIMENSION

Time plays an important role in research because it helps describe changes or differences in behaviors within a framework of different ages or stages across the life span. You might want to know if marriage is the same now as it was 50 years ago. Maybe you found a study about how individuals picked their mates during the 1920s. Can you use that study to see if there is a change in the way individuals currently pick their mates?

The **longitudinal method** allows you to assess the change in behavior of one group of subjects at more than one point in time. Let's say you wanted to test a group of 10-year-olds, who live with parents who smoke, in 1980 to see if they smoked. Then you wanted to test them again in 1982, 1984, 1986, and so on until they were 21-years-old. This would be considered longitudinal because you are examining the changes in smoking habits in these children over an extended period. The advantage of this type of study is that it allows for changes over a long time; however, the main disadvantage to this type of study is that it is expensive because you must keep track of the subjects for the duration of the study. Furthermore, the dropout rate for this type of study may be high because people move, they don't leave forwarding addresses, or they change their minds about participating in the study.

The **cross-sectional method,** however, examines several groups of people at one point in time. So, if you wanted to conduct the same study about smoking habits that we just mentioned, you might conduct the study in 1990 on 10-year-olds, 12-year-olds, 14-years-olds, and all the way up to 21-year-olds. If all your subjects grew up in households where people smoke, you might be able to tell when the children made a decision to smoke or not smoke themselves. The major advantages of this type of study are that it is inexpensive, it involves a short time span, and there is a lower dropout rate. The disadvantages, however, are that it reveals nothing about the continuity of the phenomenon on a person-by-person case, the subjects may be the same chronological age, but may be of different maturational ages, and it gives no ideas which direction of change that a group might take.

REFERENCES

Babbie, E. 2001. *The practice of social research,* 9th edition. Belmont, CA: Wadsworth/Thomson Learning.

Bland, M., & Altman, D. G. 1995. Comparing methods of measurement: Why plotting difference against standard method is misleading. *Lancet,* 346 (8982): 1085–1087.

Byers, B., & Powers, W. G. 1997. Criminal justice and ethical ideology: An exploration of a loyalty-truthfulness dilemma. *Journal of Criminal Justice,* 25 (6): 527–541.

DeKesseredy, W. S., Alvi, S., Schwartz, M. D., & Perry, B. 1999. Violence against and the harassment of women in Canadian public housing: An exploratory study. *Canadian Review of Sociology and Anthropology,* 36 (4): 499.

Ensign, J. 2000. Reproductive health of homeless adolescent women in Seattle, Washington, USA. *Women and Health,* 31 (2/3): 133.

Johnson, S. D. 2000. Who supports the Promise Keepers? *Sociology of Religion,* 61 (1): 93–104.

Marcenko, M. O., & Samost, L. 1999. Living with HIV/AIDS: The voices of HIV positive mothers. *Social Work,* 44(1): 36.

Masheter, C. 1998. Friendships between former spouses: Lessons in doing case-study research. *Journal of Divorce & Remarriage,* 28 (3–4): 73–97.

Nnorom, J. A., Esu-Williams, E., & Tilley-Gyado, A. 1996. HIV, tuberculosis and syphilis in Nigeria: A descriptive study. *AIDS Weekly Plus,* Sept 23: 28.

Palmiotto, M. J., & Unninthan, N. P. 2002. The impact of citizen police academies on participants: An exploratory study. *Journal of Criminal Justice,* 30 (2): 101–107.

Riley, G. F., Potosky, A. L., Klabunde, C. N., Warren, J. L., & Ballard-Barbash, R. 1999. Stage at diagnosis and treatment patterns among older women with breast cancer: An HMO and fee-for-service comparison. *JAMA, The Journal of the American Medical Association,* 281 (8): 720–733.

Scharrer, E. 2001. Tough guys: The portrayal of hypermasculinity and aggression televised police dramas. *Journal of Broadcasting & Electronic Media,* 45 (4): 615–635.

Winfree, T. L., Bernat, F. P., & Esbensen, F. 2001. Hispanic and Anglo gang membership in two southwestern cities. *Social Science Journal,* 38 (1): 105–117.

Zittleman, K., & Sadker, D. 2002. Gender bias in teacher education texts: New (and old) lessons. *Journal of Teacher Education,* 53 (2): 168–181.

INFOTRAC COLLEGE EDITION SUGGESTED READINGS AND DISCUSSION QUESTIONS

1. Use InfoTrac College Edition to locate any articles that interest you. If you are interested in domestic violence, you could refer to the article called "Drinking and Marital Aggression in Newlyweds: An Event-Based Analysis of Drinking and the Occurrence of Husband Marital Aggression," or if you are interested in nutrition, you could refer to the article "2-Year Tracking of Children's Fruit and Vegetable Intake." After locating an article, see if you can figure out the independent and dependent variables. What about the units of analysis?

2. Locate a longitudinal study such as "A Longitudinal Study of Hong Kong Adolescents' and Parents' Perceptions of Family Functioning and Well-Being" on InfoTrac College Edition. What was the hypothesis? What would be the consequences of having the study take place over a long period? How would you design the study without it being longitudinal? Now look for a cross-sectional study called "Cross-Validation of the Temptation Coping Questionnaire: Adolescent Coping with Temptations to Use Alcohol and Illicit Drugs." Can you talk about the differences between the two types of research designs?

Public Assistance Receipt Among Immigrants and Natives: How the Unit of Analysis Affects Research Findings

Jennifer Van Hook, Jennifer E. Glick, and Frank D. Bean

For this article, Van Hook, Glick, and Bean studied the differences in rates of public assistance between immigrant and native households. Using the 1990 and 1991 panels of the Survey of Income and Program Participation, the researchers found the differences were only significant at the level of larger units of analysis. Therefore, the way the researcher defined the unit of analysis could have played a major role in the results of the study and the lives of people. In this article, notice how the researchers describe the units of analysis that they used.

Why choose one unit of analysis or presentation over another? In analyzing data or presenting results on welfare usage, a researcher might select individuals or a unit that involves the collection of individuals in some more aggregate form, such as families or households. Most studies that compare immigrants' and natives' welfare use rely on such aggregate-level units. In these studies, if one or more individuals within the unit receive public assistance income, the entire unit is classified as a welfare-receiving unit. There are several reasons for selecting such aggregates as the unit of analysis and presentation. First, household and resident family members often share resources and amenities (Greenhalgh, 1982; Lloyd, 1995) and are often grouped together for determining eligibility for welfare. Second, for administrative purposes, public officials may require statistics that use aggregate-level units such as families because these units better approximate eligibility units. Third, researchers and advocates of the poor may find statistics that use aggregate units particularly meaningful for assessing the determinants of public assistance receipt. This is because welfare use arguably derives from the characteristics of the units of eligibility (i.e., the circumstances of the family and the ability of potential earners in the family to support their dependents), not necessarily from the characteristics of each of the individuals, particularly the children.

Four kinds of aggregate-level units that have been or can be used for presenting statistics on welfare receipt are the household, family household, family, and minimal household unit. The household has been the most frequently used unit for analyzing and presenting data on immigrants' welfare receipt. Research on household recipiency clearly shows that receipt among immigrant households has increased over the last two decades (Bean, Van Hook, & Glick, 1997; Borjas, 1994; Borjas & Trejo, 1991; Trejo, 1992). By 1980, immigrants' recipiency had surpassed natives,' a trend that has continued during the 1980–1990 decade. A disadvantage of comparisons involving all households is that some contain unrelated individuals who may not share resources or participate in decisions relating to long-

Van Hook, J., Glick, J. E., & Bean, F. D. 1999. Public assistance receipt among immigrants and natives: How the unit of analysis affects research findings. *Demography,* 36(1): 111–120. Used with permission from the Population Association of America.

term resource consumption or production (Greenhalgh, 1982; Kuznets, 1978). One solution is to present results for family households, or households containing individuals related through blood, marriage, or adoption (Kuznets, 1978). The presentation of results for family households typically excludes single-person households and households containing unrelated individuals (Blau, 1984; Jensen, 1988; Tienda & Jensen, 1986). Compared with studies based on households, studies based on family households report similar patterns but smaller immigrant-native differences (Jensen, 1988; Tienda & Jensen, 1986).

The presentation of results at the household or even the family household level, however, may misrepresent the level of recipiency, both because multiple sources of recipiency can exist within the same household or family household and because unrelated individuals are excluded. For example, most analyses simply examine whether any member of a household receives welfare without considering the number of welfare grants going to the household. A single-recipient household may contain one recipient or several, depending upon the complexity of the household. Further, samples restricted to family households could omit some types of welfare receipt. Because samples restricted to family households do not include single individuals (who may be eligible for SSI but not AFDC), they may be more likely to detect recipiency of AFDC than of SSI.

The family (or subfamily) has been considered an appropriate unit of analysis and presentation because families, rather than individuals or households, are used to determine eligibility for AFDC (Simon, 1984). Families are defined as co-residential units containing the family head, spouse (if present), and dependent children. Multiple-family units may reside within the same household. Welfare eligibility is based on the resources of one family regardless of the potential recipients' access to the resources of co-residential or nonresidential extended family members. Therefore, it may be more accurate to consider the characteristics of spouses, partners, and dependent children than to consider those of the entire household or family household when examining welfare use. As with samples of family households, however, samples of families do not include single or unrelated individuals and therefore exclude many SSI recipients.

An alternative is to use the minimal household unit. The minimal household unit, often relied on in research on extended family households, refers to the smallest identifiable unit within a household that has the potential to reside independently of others (Biddlecom, 1994; Ermisch & Overton, 1985; Glick, Bean, & Van Hook, 1997). Families as well as single individuals are counted as separate units. Presenting results for minimal household units offers the advantage of using families (i.e., they approximate the unit used to determine eligibility) while including data for single, unrelated individuals.

As the preceding discussion implies, the goal among many researchers studying immigrants' welfare receipt has been to focus on units that approximate co-residential groups that share resources or that are considered as a single unit when applying for welfare (e.g., Bean et al., 1997). This goal, however, may not be appropriate for addressing some kinds of research questions. For instance, researchers attempting to compare the per capita costs of welfare recipiency between immigrants and natives might be best served by presenting results for samples of individuals. Because welfare grants to families and couples increase with the number of dependents (U.S. House of Representatives, 1994), researchers presenting results for households or families in order to compare the "welfare burden" of two groups may reach erroneous conclusions to the degree that household or family size and recipient density differ appreciably between the two groups. Further, in analyses of the fiscal implications of immigration, the National Research Council recommends relying on individuals (Smith & Edmonston, 1997) because aggregate-level units are temporally unstable. Researchers using longitudinal analyses of welfare use may have difficulty tracking families or households over time when they break apart and re-form (Citro & Michael, 1995; Lloyd, 1995).

More important for present purposes, not all persons grouped together in aggregate level units are identical with respect to welfare receipt and other important social indicators such as nativity status. In many cases, a welfare-receiving household is counted as one household no matter how many recipients it contains, and immigrant households are counted as receiving welfare even if no immigrant household members received welfare (i.e., if U.S.-born household members received welfare). Such heterogeneity within households is no small issue. Although most immigrants live in households headed by immigrants and most natives live in households headed by natives (over 95% in both cases), 25% of adults and 80% of children living in households headed by immigrants are U.S.-born citizens (estimated from the 1990 U.S. Public Use Micro-data Sample). The extent to which unit nativity composition is problematic largely depends on how researchers treat U.S.-born children living in immigrant households. If researchers adopt the household (or other aggregate units) as the unit of analysis and define its nativity based on the nativity of the householder (e.g., Borjas, 1994) or the nativity of the householder or the householder's spouse (e.g., Bean et al., 1997), they assume, intentionally or not, that native-born children are immigrants. Because nativity-related eligibility criteria for AFDC and other public assistance for children are based on children's place of birth, not the nativity of parents, and because immigrant parents are not eligible for AFDC benefits in their first five years of residence in the United States, some immigrant households can be classified as households receiving welfare only because of the presence of a native-born child.

Data and Measures

To examine the extent to which comparisons of immigrant and native recipiency are affected by the unit of presentation, we use data from the 1990 and 1991 panels of the Survey of Income and Program Participation (SIPP). One major reason for using the SIPP, as opposed to the CPS or U.S. census data, to study the consequences of presenting results for individual-, family-, and/or household-level units is that it is the only large data source that contains detail regarding which children and other dependents are covered by public assistance payments. We combine the 1990 and 1991 panels to obtain enough cases to allow the calculation of reliable estimates for immigrants by type of assistance received.

The unit of analysis is the individual because welfare recipiency is determined from SIPP data for each person. For the presentation of results, we construct samples of individuals, family members (individuals residing with relatives), minimal household units, families, households, and family households. We group individuals into units according to their living arrangements and familial relationships as of January 1990 or 1991 (depending on the year of the SIPP panel). Minimal household units are co-residential family units and single individuals. Thus, the primary family unit (containing the householder; spouse; and any single, dependent children under age 25), additional family units in the household (married couples with or without dependent children, single parents with a child or children), and single adults aged 25 or older are all counted as separate units. Each single adult, including unmarried parents living in the homes of their adult children, is classified as a separate unit. Families are defined as minimal household units that contain two or more related individuals. The household sample contains all households as defined by the U.S. Census Bureau. Family households are the subset of households that contain two or more individuals related to the household head. Finally, family members are individuals who reside with relatives. The family, family household, and family member samples differ from the others in that the units in the family samples are composed of family members, not the full set of persons interviewed in the SIPP as are the units in the individual, minimal household unit, and household samples. Hereafter, we refer to the samples of family members, families, and family households as the family samples.

Immigrants are broadly defined as foreign-born persons living in the United States, and natives are defined as U.S.-born persons. Individuals born abroad of American parents and those born in U.S. outlying areas (e.g., Puerto Rico) are counted as native born. Unfortunately, the SIPP does not collect country-of-birth information for children under age 15. For most of these children, we use mother's, and in some cases, father's, place of birth as a proxy: If the child's natural mother is foreign born and immigrated after the child was born, then the child is classified as foreign born; otherwise, the child is classified as U.S. born. We are unable to match 12% of the children with their natural mothers. For this group, we use the natural father's or a guardian's nativity as a proxy. Using these procedures, we classify 98% of children as either foreign born or U.S. born. The remaining 2% of children are classified as having the same nativity as the head of their family unit. The weighted percentage of children classified as foreign born following these procedures is 3.3%, a figure that is larger than the percentage calculated from 1990 U.S. census data (2.7%; the two estimates are significantly different at $p < .05$). Units in which the head or the spouse of the head is foreign born are classified as immigrant, and the remaining units are defined as native. Units in which the head or spouse was born in an outlying area or is a foreign-born post-secondary student are excluded from the sample, and persons living in such units are excluded from the individual-level samples. Hence, even though persons born in U.S. outlying areas are initially classified as native born, most are eventually excluded from the samples of individuals. The number of cases in each of the samples are presented separately by nativity in Table 1.

The SIPP collects monthly data on who in each household receives various types of cash public assistance benefits and which dependents, if any, are covered by the welfare payments. We define recipients as those who report receiving, or are reported as having received, at least one type of public assistance income during the month of January 1990 or 1991 (depending on year of the SIPP panel). The types of public assistance that we count as welfare are the three primary cash assistance programs: AFDC, SSI, and General Assistance. Recipient units are defined as those in which at least one member is a recipient. We differentiate between recipients of the two major types of cash assistance, AFDC and SSI, because the two programs serve different populations and involve different types of policy responses. We define AFDC and SSI recipients and recipient units in the same way as described previously for recipiency of any type of public assistance. For example, AFDC recipients are those who are reported as having received or as having been covered by AFDC in January and AFDC recipient units are those containing at least one AFDC recipient.

TABLE 1. UNWEIGHED NUMBERS OF CASES IN EACH SAMPLE, BY NATIVITY

Sample	Immigrants	Natives
Households	3,268	26,643
Minimal Household Units	4,017	31,624
Individuals	6,463	71,138
Family Households	2,680	18,608
Families	2,670	18,067
Family Members	5,509	59,841

Source: [U.S. Bureau of the Census, 1993] Survey of Income and Program Participation, 1990 and 1991 panels.

Results

Rates of public assistance receipt among immigrants and natives are presented in Table 2 for households, minimal household units, individuals, family households, and families. In the case of the individual-level statistics presented in Table 2, we treat children as immigrant or native based on their estimated place of birth, not the birthplace of their parents or household head. As shown in the top panel of the table, use of any type of public assistance among immigrants exceeds that among natives when larger units of aggregation are used. In both the household-based comparisons (i.e., households, minimal household units, and individuals) and the family-based comparisons (i.e., family households, families, and family members), the level of welfare receipt for immigrants is significantly higher than that for natives only in the cases of the most aggregated units (household or family households). Welfare receipt is not significantly higher among immigrants than among natives in the cases of the smaller units. Thus, research comparing welfare receipt of immigrants and natives can reach divergent conclusions based solely on the use of different units of analysis or presentation.

Does this finding hold up when we examine different types of welfare receipt? When all sources of welfare are separated into cash assistance received from AFDC, from SSI, or from other sources (not examined here), the patterns observed for "any type of public assistance" are generally replicated, especially in the case of SSI: The use of larger-sized units makes immigrants' receipt appear higher relative to natives' than does the use of smaller-sized units. When nativity differences are examined, the differences involving AFDC are not statistically significant for any of the units, although in each of the three aggregate units involving families, AFDC receipt of natives exceeds that of immigrants. In the case of SSI, however, immigrants' receipt exceeds natives' receipt, irrespective of the unit examined. Thus, as we have argued elsewhere (Bean et al., 1997), the findings of research based on immigrant-native comparisons of welfare receipt also depend on the type of welfare receipt examined. We cannot determine why immigrant-native comparisons are affected by using different units of presentation from simple examinations of units. For the sake of brevity, we focus only on how assessments of immigrant levels of receipt vary

TABLE 2. PUBLIC ASSISTANCE RECIPIENCY AMONG IMMIGRANTS AND NATIVES, BY UNIT OF PRESENTATION AND PUBLIC ASSISTANCE PROGRAM, JANUARY 1990/1992

	Percentage Who Received Public Assistance Benefits			
	Immigrants	Natives	Immigrants –Natives	Standard Error of the Difference
Any Type of Public Assistance				
Households	8.30	6.62	1.68*	.536
Minimal Household Units	6.85	6.19	.66	.439
Individuals	6.52	5.75	.77	.527
Family Households	8.56	7.02	1.54*	.610
Families	6.86	6.41	.45	.553
Family Members	6.60	5.85	.75	.575
AFDC				
Households	3.38	3.06	.32	.353
Minimal household units	2.79	2.70	.09	.287
Individuals	3.42	3.75	-.33	.391
Family Households	4.15	4.31	-.16	.440
Families	4.29	4.67	-.38	.447
Family Members	4.03	4.44	-.41	.459
SSI				
Households	4.78	3.48	1.30*	.413
Minimal household units	3.88	3.23	0.65*	.334
Individuals	2.79	1.66	1.13*	.348
Family Households	4.42	2.83	1.59*	.443
Families	2.61	1.74	0.86*	.343
Family Members	2.30	1.12	1.18*	.342

Source: [U.S. Bureau of the Census, 1993] Survey of Income and Program Participation, 1990 and 1991 panels.

* Difference is statistically significant ($p < .05$).

depending on whether household-level versus individual-level units are used. To estimate the magnitude of the contribution of nativity differences in household size, in the average number of recipients per receiving unit, and in household nativity composition to household-level differences in welfare receipt, we decompose the differences following the procedure outlined by Das Gupta (1993). Although the overall nativity differences in AFDC receipt are not statistically significant, some of the separate components might be. Hence, we repeat the decomposition analyses for each of the three welfare measures:

overall welfare, AFDC, and SSI receipt. Because age is important in different ways for AFDC and SSI receipt, we examine children and adults separately.

The difference in overall welfare recipiency between immigrants and natives measured at the household level is 1.68 percentage points, a gap that is statistically significant. Much of the difference in welfare is due to (a) differences in rates measured at the individual level, (b) differences in household size, (c) differences in recipient clustering, (d) differences in household nativity composition, and (e) differences in recipient nativity composition. Because households contain both adults and children, each of the components (except the individual-rate component) is further broken down into a part due to adults and a part due to children. The numbers in the far right-hand column of the table can be interpreted as the amount and direction of the immigrant-minus-native difference if immigrants and natives were identical on each of the other variables examined. The other factors also contribute to the immigrant-native difference, some operating to increase it and others to reduce it. For example, the higher recipient clustering within immigrant households reduces the household differential by nearly three fourths of a percentage point (0.70), indicating that the household-level differences would be even larger if welfare receipt were not more concentrated within immigrant households. Similarly, if the lower homogeneity of households (i.e., lower proportions of immigrants in immigrant households than of natives in native households) were the only factor at work, the direction of the difference between immigrants and natives would be reversed.

Summary and Discussion

The results show that immigrant-native comparisons of welfare recipiency depend on the unit chosen for the analysis and presentation of data. When welfare receipt is evaluated at the level of larger units, such as households or families, immigrants exceed natives in the extent to which they receive welfare. In the cases of smaller units, however, there are no differences between immigrants and natives in overall welfare receipt. However, immigrants exceed natives in SSI but not AFDC receipt, irrespective of the unit of analysis or presentation used. The findings also indicate that if immigrants and natives had identical living arrangements, immigrants' receipt would not significantly exceed natives' receipt in the case of AFDC, but it would exceed natives' receipt more in the case of SSI. The nativity difference in AFDC receipt would even reverse direction (although the difference would not be statistically significant) if immigrants and natives had identical living arrangements. Aggregate-level comparisons of welfare receipt by nativity thus tend to overstate use of AFDC but to understate use of SSI among immigrants in comparison with natives. However, nativity differences are also affected by group differences in children's nativity. When native-born children in households headed by immigrants are treated as foreign born, AFDC receipt of immigrant households is statistically significantly lower than that of native households.

Broadly speaking, the work presented here illustrates a set of problems that can occur in many research situations. Group comparisons of rates can be sensitive to the choice of unit of analysis or presentation, and discrepancies in results between studies using different units of analysis or presentation can arise from group differences in living arrangements.

Moreover, multivariate analyses do not adjust for the confounding influences of group differences in characteristic clustering or aggregate unit size. For instance, one may use a sample of households to estimate models that control for household size and composition and that adjust the independent variable to take into account multiple recipients per receiving household. Estimates of the group differentials produced by such models, however, fail to replicate the standardized differentials estimated by the method used in this paper (e.g., see Das Gupta, 1993). The reason is that, unlike the standardized differentials, multivariate models do not hold the individual-level rate constant. Rather than treat only the aggregate unit size as a measure of the dispersion of a population of persons and characteristics across households, multivariate models treat covariates, such as household size, as determinants of the probability that one or more individuals in a household display a given characteristic. The predicted prevalence rates differ from those observed because different aggregate unit sizes have different levels of association with the rates, not because a fixed number of persons and recipients are redistributed across households. Hence, rather than rely only on multivariate modeling to fix the problems associated with using a particular unit of analysis, researchers should be selective about their choices of the units of analysis and presentation.

References

Bean, F. D., J. V. W. Van Hook, & J. E. Glick. 1997. Country-of-origin, type of public assistance and patterns of welfare recipiency among U.S. immigrants and natives. *Social Science Quarterly,* 78: 432–451.

Biddlecom, A. E. 1994. *Immigration and co-residence in the United States since 1960.* Paper presented at the annual meeting of the Population Association of America, Miami.

Blau, F. 1984. The use of transfer payments by immigrants. *Industrial and Labor Relations Review,* 37(2): 222–239.

Borjas, G. J. 1994. The economics of immigration. *Journal of Economic Literature,* 32: 1667–1717.

Borjas, G. J., & S. J. Trejo. 1991. Immigrant participation in the welfare system. *Industrial and Labor Relations Review,* 44(2): 195–211.

Citro, C. F., & R. T. Michael, eds. 1995. *Measuring poverty: A new approach.* Washington, DC: National Academy Press.

Das Gupta, P. 1993. *Standardization and decomposition of rates: A user's manual.* U.S. Bureau of the Census, Current Population Reports, Series P23–186. Washington, DC: U.S. Government Printing Office.

Ermisch, J. F., & E. Overton. 1985. Minimal household units: A new approach to the analysis of household formation. *Population Studies,* 39: 33–54.

Fix, M., & J. S. Passel. 1994. Perspective on immigration: A series of three op-ed articles. *Los Angeles Times,* August 1–3.

Glick, J. E., F. D. Bean, & J. V. W. Van Hook. 1997. Immigration and changing patterns of extended household/family structure in the United States: 1970–1990. *Journal of Marriage and the Family,* 59: 177–191.

Goldscheider, F. K., & L. J. Waite. 1991. *New families, no families? The transformation of the American home.* Berkeley/Los Angeles: University of California Press.

Greenhalgh, S. 1982. Income units: The ethnographic alternative to standardization. *Population and Development Review,* 8(Supplement): 70–91.

Jensen, L. 1988. Patterns of immigration and public assistance utilization, 1970–1980. *International Migration Review,* 22(1): 51–83.

King, M., & S. H. Preston. 1990. Who lives with whom? Individual versus household measures. *Journal of Family History,* 15(2): 117–132.

Kuznets, S. 1978. Size and age structure of family households: Exploratory comparisons. *Population and Development Review,* 4(2): 187–223.

Levitan, S. A. 1985. *Programs in aid of the poor* (5th ed.). Baltimore: Johns Hopkins University Press.

Lloyd, C. B. 1995. Household structure and poverty: What are the connections? Population Council, Social Science Research, Research Division Working Papers, No. 74.

Ruggles, P. 1990. *Drawing the line: Alternative poverty measures and their implications for public policy.* Washington DC: Urban Institute Press.

Simon, J. 1984. Immigrants, taxes, and welfare in the United States. *Population and Development Review,* 10(1): 55–69.

Smith, J. P., & B. Edmonston, eds. 1997. *The New Americans: Economic, demographic, and fiscal effects of immigration.* Washington, DC: National Academy Press.

Tienda, M., & L. Jensen. 1986. Immigration and public assistance participation: Dispelling the myth of dependency. *Social Science Research,* 15: 372–400.

Trejo, S. J. 1992. Immigrant welfare recipiency: Recent trends and future implications. *Contemporary Policy Issues,* 10(2): 44–53.

U.S. Bureau of the Census. 1993. *Survey of income and program participation (SIPP) 1990 waves 1–8 longitudinal microdata file technical documentation.* Washington, DC: U.S. Bureau of the Census.

U.S. Commission on Immigration Reform. 1994. *U.S. immigration policy: Restoring credibility, report to Congress.* Washington, DC: U.S. Commission on Immigration Reform.

U.S. Commission on Immigration Reform. 1997. *Becoming an American: Immigration and immigrant policy, report to Congress.* Washington, DC: U.S. Commission on Immigration Reform.

U.S. House of Representatives, Committee on Ways and Means. 1994. *1994 Green Book: Background material and data on programs within the jurisdiction of the Committee on Ways and Means.* Washington, DC: U.S. Government Printing Office.

REVIEW QUESTIONS

1. What units of analysis were used for this study?

2. What were the differences in the results based on the units of analysis used?

3. Could the researchers have used another unit of analysis? What would it have been? Do you think it would have shown different results?

CONSEQUENCES OF PARTICIPATING IN A LONGITUDINAL STUDY OF MARRIAGE

Joseph Veroff, Shirley Hatchett, and Elizabeth Douvan

In this study, Veroff, Hatchett, and Douvan suggest there might be some consequences to conducting longitudinal studies. Using the data from a 4-year study of black and white newlyweds, couples were randomly selected to be in either a large study group or a smaller control group. The subjects in the larger study groups received more frequent and intense interviewing during the study. Notice how more interaction over a longer period could affect that outcome of the study.

There are some issues that researchers who use survey methodology would like to repress. Perhaps the most disturbing of these is the possibility that the methods they use may actually cause a short- or long-term change in the very phenomenon they are trying to measure—in other words, that certain survey research designs, particularly longitudinal ones, may comprise an unintentional intervention that changes attitudes or behavior or both. Here we present research from an experimental manipulation in a 4-year longitudinal study of marital adjustment and stability among black and white urban newlyweds that suggests that such effects may occur.

We incorporated this experimental design in response to a concern raised by human subjects review boards at both the University of Michigan and the National Institute of Mental Health. Both groups wondered whether long-term, in-depth inquiry into the bases of affection, conflict, difficulties and problems in a marriage, perceptions of each other, attitudes toward gender roles, general levels of well-being in the marriage, and the like could raise concerns in a married couple about each other that would not have been considered had we not asked about them.

In research directly relevant to the question, Wilson et al. (1984) found that having undergraduates explain their dating relationships (i.e., telling them to "list all the reasons you can think of why your relationship . . . is going the way it is") had a disruptive effect on attitude-behavior consistency—that is, the relationship between feelings toward their partners and whether the couple is dating several months later, as compared to a control group. Wilson, Kraft, and Dunn (1989) have reanalyzed the data and have found that the disruptive effect occurs only for couples who had been dating a short amount of time. Various explanations are offered. The ones given greatest credence focus on the assumption that people in longer relationships probably have more consistent schemas about the relationship and hence are less likely to generate new material about the relationship in the interview that would disrupt the connection between present attitude and future behavior. This should be less true for the shorter relationships. The implication of these results for our study is that interviewing newlyweds who had known each other a long time might be

Veroff, J., Hatchett, S., & Douvan, E. 1992. Consequences of participating in a longitudinal study of marriage. *Public Opinion Quarterly,* 56: 325–327. Reprinted by permission of University of Chicago Press.

less disruptive of their ongoing relationship than interviewing newlyweds who have been in shorter relationships. One might have similar expectations with regard to whether or not the couples lived together before marriage. We might assume that cohabitation would give the couples broader experiences to develop schemas that are more resistant than those of couples who did not live together.

Wilson et al. (1989) are doing parallel research on other attitude objects besides dating partners—particularly political figures. In that context, they find that there is a bi-directional attitude change when subjects are asked to generate explanations for their attitudes. Some become more positive over time; some more negative. Following Wilson's lead, we would expect an increased variance on measures of marital well-being over time for couples we intensively interviewed at more points than for a control group interviewed less intensively and for a shorter period of time.

Thus, there is some evidence to suggest that the kind of effect that concerned the human subjects board might result from our 4-year prospective study of newlyweds in first marriages. Little is known about attitudinal or behavioral change resulting from data collection. However, we generated two general hypotheses about what types of effects we might find when we examine marital adjustment and well-being among randomly sampled couples in our main study and control groups. First, following Wilson et al.'s (1989) lead, we explored whether there was greater variance in marital quality measures in the second year among the study group compared to the control group. Second, we felt that the general effect of more frequent and intensive interviews would be positive by the fourth year, with the main study group having better marital adjustment and stability than the control group. We felt that both of these effects would be smaller for couples who had considered themselves a couple for a longer period of time as Wilson, Kraft, and Dunn's (1989) research suggested.

Method

Two samples—a main study group and a control group—were each randomly selected from a sampling frame of eligible couples applying for marriage licenses in Wayne County, MI, during a 3-month period (April–June 1986). To be eligible, the marriage had to be the first for both, and the wife had to be 35 or younger. In the first and third years of the study, both spouses in the main study group were first interviewed using standard structured questionnaires containing both open and fixed response questions. These face-to-face interviews averaged 80 minutes. Later, on another day, they were interviewed together using two innovative techniques. They were first asked to construct a joint narrative, to "tell the story" of their relationship, and then they participated in a revealed differences task (explained further below). These interviews were audiotaped and averaged 30 minutes. In years 2 and 4, spouses were interviewed separately by telephone for an average of 15 minutes, again using structured questionnaires.[1] Race of interviewer and respondent were matched for the face-to-face interviews.

In comparison, the control group was interviewed minimally over the 4-year period. In order to get baseline data for the control group, wives received a short structured interview averaging 7 minutes in the first year. In years 2 and 4, the control couples were contacted by phone using the same method as for the main study group. However, in year 2, the controls were asked only a subset of the questions (all closed-ended) with the inter-

TABLE 1. RESPONSE RATES AND BASES OF ATTRITION FOR STUDY AND CONTROL
RESPONDENTS (BY YEAR)

	Number of Respondents in Eligible Sample [a]	Responded %	Refused %	Not Located or Interviewed
Year 1:				
Study	1,148	65	22	13
Control	172[b]	69	9	22
Year 2:				
Study	746	92	3	4
Control	114	92	0	7
Year 3:				
Study	681	85	8	7
Control[c]	—	—	—	—
Year 4:				
Study	559	90	5	5
Control	102	86	7	7

[a] In year 1, this was the original listed sample minus all those respondents who turned out not to be married or not living in Wayne County; in years 2–4 this represented the number of people who were interviewed in the prior year and were still married.

[b] Only the wives in the couples listed were interviewed; the response rate, noninterviews, and refusals are based on the wives only.

[c] The control sample not interviewed in year 3. Control sample responded at a significantly lower rate than the white control sample. Within race, the response rates for study and control samples are comparable.

views averaging 5 minutes, compared to the 15 minutes for the main study. Between waves, study group couples were sent an anniversary card with an enclosed postcard to be returned if they had moved or changed phone numbers. No contact was made with the control group between waves.

In the first year of the study, 373 main study couples—199 black and 174 white— were interviewed in their homes 3–7 months after they were married. The overall response rate for the study was 66 percent,[2] which is high given that the cooperation of both spouses was needed for inclusion in the study. Fifty-nine wives in the control group, 36 percent of them black, were interviewed during the same period in the first year. Table 1 presents, for the study group and the control group separately, the eligible sample of respondents[3] for that year; response rate (the number interviewed/the number of eligible respondents); percent refusals; and percent not interviewed, which could be for a variety of reasons (sickness, impossible to locate, moved too far away for interviewing). There were no significant differences in response rates in black and white study samples, but the black control sample responded at a significantly lower rate than the white control sample. Within race, the response rates for study and control samples are comparable.

The topics in the structured questionnaires in years 1 and 3 for the main study included the following: the quality and density of couples' networks; the way they interact with each other, with considerable focus on how they handle conflicts; their feelings about their relationship, including irritations, sexual tensions, and ways they care for each other; how they assign household chores and their attitudes toward these arrangements; their perceptions of themselves and each other, and their ideals for themselves and each other; their general well-being and specific marital well-being; and much more. The questionnaires in years 2 and 4 contained mostly closed format questions, which represented replications of items included in main marital well-being measures, significant life events, and selected other topics.

As noted earlier, the couple interview included two novel procedures. In the narrative, the couple told an open-ended story of their relationship using only a storyboard with topical markers cuing coverage of their first meeting, their courtship, the wedding, life after the wedding, and hopes for the future. This was a difficult task for some couples, who gave less involved or merely descriptive stories. However, most couples became involved in the storytelling task, which for them presented a chance to pull together many strands of their relationship. Some spouses were surprised to hear each other's version of their experience as a couple. In the second procedure, husbands and wives separately rated the importance of a number of marital ideals (e.g., "If you're fighting, cool off before you say too much") and then had to resolve their differences. This procedure often elicited large differences in attitudes toward marriage. We were interested in the way the couples resolved their differences, but the couples were clearly interested in how they differed on important marital issues and ideals.

Results

We evaluated our general hypotheses using two approaches. First, we examined the variance on overall attitudinal indicators of marital well-being for the study and control group to see if, like Wilson et al. (1989), we found bi-directional changes between the first and second year. Next, we looked at the effects of being in the main study or the control group on marital stability and on several indicators of marital adjustment or well-being.

The first approach yielded some evidence supporting Wilson et al.'s (1989) findings that explaining art attitude can enhance that attitude in some people but disrupt it in others and hence induce an increased variance in that attitude. Whereas there were no study group-control group differences in the variances on a measure of marital satisfaction in the first year, by the second year the variance on that measure was significantly higher in three of the four gender x race groups. And again by year 4 there were no significant study group-control group differences in variance. These results thus gave us some indirect evidence that our main study methodology may have had disruptive effects on the marital well-being of some respondents. Although it was plausible to think that the amount of time a couple lived together as a couple would be a moderating factor in affecting this pattern (the variance effect should be minimal for long-term couples and clearest for couples who had not lived together before marriage), an analysis testing this hypothesis using a question asked of the couples about their cohabitation history yielded no significant findings.

Our second approach yielded non-significant results with regard to marital stability over the 4 years but did yield some provocative results using attitudinal assessments of marital experience in the fourth year. When we compared the separation and divorce rates of couples at the end of the study, we found that the main study couples appeared to have fared worse than the control couples. We found that 9 percent of the original control sample and 15 percent of the original study sample were known to be divorced or separated at the end of the study. This difference proved to be non-significant in a logit analysis of the divorced/separated versus married status of couples at year 4, which included two other variables known to be significantly related to both the couple's study status and fourth-year marital status: race (black couples were more likely to become divorced and were proportionally more represented in the study sample); and wives' initial feelings about the ease of talking with their husbands (lower in the divorced couples and higher in the control sample). Even if we included those respondents who are nonascertained on marital status as part of the divorced/separated group,[4] the predictive power of study status is not significant, although the trend becomes stronger. Testing a model that includes race as a factor interacting with study status also yields no significant results, nor does a model that includes how long a couple lived together before marriage as an interacting factor. Thus, the initial study status difference in marital stability washes out with proper controls.

A different picture emerges when we compare the attitudes that study versus control status couples express about their marital quality the fourth year. Many of couples not interviewed at the end of the study were those who were non-respondents or who were not followed because they separated or divorced over the first 3 years. Admittedly, this would leave us with couples who are on the whole better off. However, there still could be differences in the marital quality of study and control group couples that could speak to our overall hypothesized effect.

How to measure marital quality in the fourth year? We had many options, since the control sample was given more attitudinal questions in the fourth year than they were given in previous panels. Crohan and Veroff (1989) distinguished four factors for the overall perceptions and feelings about marriage measured in our study. These reflect (1) the couple's general happiness; (2) the sense of competence each spouse feels in the spouse role; (3) perceptions of equity in the relationship; and (4) the sense of control each spouse feels to make things right in the relationship. The following presents one prototypic item for each dimension of marital well-being:

Marital happiness (five items). "Taking things altogether, how would you describe your marriage?" Would you say your marriage is very happy, a little happier than average or not too happy?"

Marital competence (two items). "Since you have been married, how often have you felt you were not as good a (wife/husband) as you would like to be—often, sometimes, rarely or never?"

Marital equity (two items). "All in all, considering how much each of you put into your marriage, who would you say gets more out of being married—you, your (wife/husband) or both of you equally?"

Marital control (two items). "Every (wife/husband) experiences times when things between (herself/himself) and (her husband/his wife) are not going as well as (she/he) would like. When such times come up for you, how often do you feel that you can do or say something to make things better—most of the time, sometimes or hardly ever?"

To evaluate our hypothesis of better marital quality as the result of being involved in the study group versus the control group, we used these four measures of overall marital quality and two measures tapping specific aspects of the relationship—the sexual aspect and an index of marital tension.

These two indices were two of five factors emerging from a factor analysis of all specific marital qualities not assessed in the Crohan and Veroff (1989) indices. These were the only two significantly correlated with the central measure of marital happiness and, hence, relevant to assessing well-being. Prototypic items for each of these scales are listed below.

Negative aspects of sexual life (three items). "How often in the past month did you feel upset about the way the two of you were getting along in the sexual part of your relationship—often, sometimes, rarely, or never?"

Marital tension (four items). "During the past month, how often did you feel irritated or resentful about things your (wife/husband) did or didn't do—often, sometimes, rarely or never?"

When certain aspects of marital quality or well-being were assessed, the study group marriages appear to have fared better than those of the control group. For marital equity, we found a significant main effect for study status and a significant interaction effect of gender, race, and study status. Study group couples perceived more equity in their marriages at the end of the study than did control couples. The significant interaction comes from the fact that the main effect was particularly true for black wives. Also, wives and husbands in the study group felt more competent in their spousal roles than those in the control. The other results suggest that marital tensions are higher in control couples and that black study group wives are less likely than black control wives to perceive their sex life as negative. All in all, these results suggest that better-adjusted marriages may have developed among study couples as a result of the more frequent and more involved interviewing.

Summary and Discussion

Apart from trying to assess whether our marriage study design had negative or positive effects on the marriages we were monitoring, we were also attempting to address a more general question of whether longitudinal survey studies of social phenomenon can inadvertently effect short- or long-term changes in the natural course of things.

Our evidence suggests that being part of an intensive, longitudinal study focused on feelings one has about his or her marriage, and perceptions of the feelings of one's spouse, may result in both attitudinal and behavioral changes among newlywed couples. Similar to Wilson et al. (1989), we found some significant results that suggest negative effects on the natural life course of the marriages of our respondents. Although we realize the negative effect (the greater variance in marital satisfaction expressed by the study group compared to the control group) is merely suggestive, we think it is important to consider. We also found clear evidence of positive effects of being in the study. The marriages of study group couples after 4 years seem more adjusted. Perhaps the study group interviewing experience caused couples to focus on a number of issues earlier in their marriage than they would have done naturally. We had no control over spouses talking after the interviewers left. And it may be that the marriages of couples that remained intact to the end of the study were better off as a consequence of their having reflected on these issues. While Wilson's research suggested that those who had been in relationships for shorter time periods were more susceptible to either positive or negative changes, we found no such evidence.

Using how long the couple lived together before marriage as an indicator of length of intimate association, we found no significant results or even marginal trends for relationship length as a moderator on the effects of study status on increased variance in satisfaction, stability, or fourth year marital quality.

Whether results of this study would generalize to less extensive and intensive surveys of marriage or other interpersonal relationships is an open question. Nevertheless, the results should alert survey researchers, who have become increasingly interested in asking respondents complex questions about significant people, that the topics they probe may linger as issues in their respondents' lives.

This study may also alert researchers to parallel effects that may occur when surveys inquire in depth about any topic that has not been well considered prior to the survey. Wilson and his colleagues have evidence that asking people about their reasons for supporting certain political figures can disrupt their original attitudes. Although their work has been primarily with undergraduate students, similar results could be found in the general population. Their research strongly suggests that political voting preferences, not just voting behavior, may be affected by a survey interviewer asking respondents why they have a particular view. More than a quarter of our marriage study was composed of similar open-ended questions.

Although the results presented here are tentative, researchers should consider the possibility that their studies, especially if they use in-depth interviews about personal matters, may unintentionally trigger new perspectives in respondents and subsequently change their lives. We are too tempted to see respondents as passive beings dutifully conforming to their role in the survey interview. They may be more reactive than we think.

Notes

1. Because the telephone interviewing staff was almost all white, an experiment was conducted in the second year to detect race of interviewer effects among blacks interviewed over the phone. The black sample was randomly split into two groups, one done by white telephone interviewers and the other by black field interviewers using their home telephones. No race of interviewer effects were found.

2. This couple response rate is larger than one would expect if an 80 percent response rate was obtained for each spouse separately. The joint probability of getting the couple given this individual rate would be .64 or 64 percent.

3. In the first year, this figure excluded those who, in the original listing obtained from the county clerk office, did not get married or whose address at time of interviewing was not in Wayne County; in subsequent years it excluded those from whom there was no interview in the prior year or having been interviewed in the prior year said they were separated or divorced or that their spouse had died.

4. There would be reason to believe that there were numerous unhappy, if not divorced and separated, couples among those who were not interviewed because we could not contact them or they refused to be interviewed. Evidence for this assertion comes from an analysis of whether an index of expressed marital happiness in a preceding year differentiates those who were and were not interviewed in the subsequent year. For years 2–4, consistent results, most of them significant at the .05 level: compared to those who were interviewed, those not interviewed reported being less happy in the preceding year when they were interviewed.

References

Anderson, Barbara A., Brian D. Silver, & Paul R. Abramson. 1988. The effects of the race of the interviewer on measures of electoral participation by Blacks in SRC national election studies. *Public Opinion Quarterly,* 52: 53–83.

Clausen, Aage. 1968. Response validity: Vote report. *Public Opinion Quarterly,* 41: 56–61.

Crohan, Susan E., & Joseph Veroff. 1989. Dimensions of marital well-being among White and Black newlyweds. *Journal of Marriage and the Family,* 51: 373–384.

Kraut, Robert E., & John B. McConahey. 1973. How being interviewed affects voting: An experiment. *Public Opinion Quarterly,* 37: 381–398.

Traugott, Michael W., & John P. Katosh. 1979. Response validity in surveys of voting behavior. *Public Opinion Quarterly,* 43: 359–377.

Wilson, Timothy D., Dana S. Dunn, Jane A. Bybee, Diane B. Hyrnan, & John A. Roloado. 1984. Effects of analyzing reasons on attitude-behavior consistency. *Journal of Personality and Social Psychology,* 47: 5–16

Wilson, Timothy D., Dana S. Dunn, Delores Kraft, & Douglas J. Lisle. 1989. Introspection, attitude change and attitude-behavior consistency: The disruptive effects of explaining why we feel the way we do." In *Advances in Experimental Social Psychology,* ed. L. Berkowitz, 22: 287–343. Orlando, FL: Academic Press.

Wilson, Timothy D., Dolores Kraft, & Dana S. Dunn. 1989. The disruptive effects of explaining attitudes: The moderating effect of knowledge about the attitude object." *Journal of Experimental Social Psychology,* 25: 379–400.

Yalch, Richard F. 1976. Pre-election interview effects on voter turnout. *Public Opinion Quarterly,* 40: 331–336.

REVIEW QUESTIONS

1. What did the researchers find that was problematic with this longitudinal study?

2. What was the difference between the control group and the research group? How did that difference affect the outcome of the project?

3. Would it have been better to do a cross-sectional design? Why or why not?

Chapter 5: Conceptualization and Operationalization

Regardless of how you collect your data, it will be in the form of *raw data.* This means that the data has not been processed in any way at all. It is really pretty impossible to do much with raw data. Suppose you have a class and you have some basic information about class members such as this:

Student #	Name	Feelings About the Class	GPA	Final Grade
1	Sam	Hated It	2.5	54
2	Lucy	Bored by It	3.8	87
3	Wilbur	Love the Class	4.0	100
4	Fran	Hated It	4.0	98
5	Craig	Bored by It	2.9	76

The table has raw data. You really don't know what any of it means, and you must find out. In **quantitative research,** the raw data that has been gathered must be converted into some type of numerical equivalents before you can do some type of analysis and statistical testing. These numerical equivalents are necessary to describe the data and to explain whether or not the data supports your hypothesis, which we will be discussing a little later. For instance, in the previous table, you can convert the GPAs of all the students to find the class GPA average. In **qualitative research,** on the other hand, the data is collected from notes, observations, and interviews, and it usually is not summarized by numbers or analyzed with statistics. In this chapter, we will be focusing on how you begin to define a concept so you can gather the raw data you will need for your project.

Suppose you heard a news report that said, "Students who believe in God and go to a place of worship have higher GPAs." Would you be curious about it and want to know if it is true? What kind of questions could you ask? You would first need to come up with a **hypothesis,** which is a tentative statement about the empirical relation that involves a relationship between two or more **variables.** The variable is a characteristic or property that can vary by taking on different values. The **independent variable** is the variable hypothesized to cause, or lead to, a variation in the dependent variable. The **dependent variable,** on the other hand, is the variable whose variation is hypothesized to depend on or be influenced by the independent variable.

Forming a research question involves defining the **concept** or the mental image that summarizes a set of similar observations, feelings, or ideas. How will you know exactly how to design your research project unless you understand exactly what you are going to measure? Research questions tend to revolve around concepts and variables, which are often not easy to distinguish between, so they must be carefully defined so others will understand precisely what you mean and what you are measuring.

Let's say that your hypothesis is as follows: "The more religious a person is, the better his or her success in college will be." In this case, your dependent variable would be success, which you believe would be influenced by your independent variable, which is religiosity. Many students find it easier to visualize this with an arrow.

(Independent Variable)   (Dependent Variable)

Religiosity   Success

The term religiosity is very abstract. What do you think it really means? You first need to conceptualize religiosity. **Conceptualization** means that you will identify and define the concept so you can study it. So, you can conceptualize religiosity as someone who goes to a house of prayer at least one time a week, says prayers every night before going to bed, follows the ten commandments exactly, and believes in a higher power. With those ideas in mind, you now have a working agreement about what the term religiosity means. Now that you have conceptualized religiosity, you are able to indicate the presence or absence of the concept by specifying one or more indicators. An **indicator** is what you choose to be the reflection of the variable you are studying. Thus, praying every night would be an indicator of how religious a person is. But maybe you and your classmates don't have the same ideas about religiosity. Therefore, you might want to group this concept into "feelings of religiosity" and "actions of religiosity. " These groups would be called **dimensions.** As a result, it is possible to divide the concept of religiosity according to different sets of dimensions.

Now that you have your variable figured out, you have to decide how you are going to **operationalize** it for your particular study. To operationalize your variable, you must say exactly how you will be measuring the variable. To find out how religious a person really is, you might ask the following questions:

1.   How many times have you been to a place of worship in the last month?

2.   Do you believe in a praying every night before you go to bed?

So, you have gone from abstractly thinking about a term that you want to research to figuring out exactly what you want to know about the term, and how you will measure it to find out if your hypothesis is correct.

Another aspect that is very important to the research process is to find out how valid your measurements are. To measure the **validity** of a question, you must be sure that what you are using to operationalize your variable is actually measuring the variable you have stated you were studying. You want to make sure the measurement you use is measuring the entire variable, not just part of the variable. Let's say you want to study success in your research methods class. If you use only the question "what grade did you get in research methods?," does that really tell you how successful a student is? What other questions would you need to ask to measure this? I believe there are a number of ways to measure a student's success and that grades are only part of it. What other indicators can be used to measure a person's success in a class? To have **reliability,** on the other hand, means that if a particular technique is applied over and over again to the same object, the results will be the same each time. There are a few ways to check the reliability of a measurement. One way is to test and then retest the object being measured. Another way is with **interobserver** or **interrater reliability** where the reliability of a measurement is compared with the results obtained by at least two different observers.

CONSTRUCTING QUESTIONS

You might think it is easy to ask people questions. In fact, you probably ask questions all the time. However, when you are writing questions for a research project you must consider certain things. For instance, you wouldn't want to ask the question "Are you religious?" Why wouldn't you? What types of answers would you receive? Would everyone's responses really answer the question you want to ask?

There are many kinds of questions. Some questions are **open-ended,** where the respondents are asked to provide their own answers to the question. Other questions are **close-ended,** where the respondents are asked to select an answer from a list of possible answers. Some questions are very good, and others are not useful. It is important that you know the difference. Questions should also be relevant to your hypothesis and variables. If the question has nothing to do with either, then it shouldn't be in your **questionnaire.** Questions should be clear and asked in a straightforward manner, such as "What grade did you receive on your last methods test?"

What about this question: "Do you know how to design a questionnaire, and what grade did you receive on your methods test?" This question is **double-barreled** because it has an *and* in it. Therefore, the question actually becomes two questions, making it difficult for the respondents to know what they are answering. How would you answer this question?: "Do you never not want chocolate for dinner?" This question would be considered a **double negative** and would also be difficult for your respondents to answer. Finally, you need to consider the **social desirability** of your question. If you ask the question, "Do you beat your animals?," do you think anyone would actually answer the question positively?

INFOTRAC COLLEGE EDITION SUGGESTED READINGS AND DISCUSSION QUESTIONS

1. Using the variable "social class," find articles such as "Stratification, class and health: Class relations and health inequalities in high modernity" or "The social networks and resources of African American eighth graders: Evidence from the National Education Longitudinal study of 1988". Can you tell how these articles operationalize the variable? Can you locate other articles in the InfoTrac College Edition database that use social class?

2. Everyone falls in love with someone. Look up the word "love" on InfoTrac College Edition. Your search should result in giving you a few options. Look up various articles on love such as "Three-dimensional love." "T'ang Chun-i's philosophy of love," and "Urban African American adolescent parents: Their perceptions of sex, love, intimacy, pregnancy, and parenting." How is love operationalized in each of these articles? Is there a difference?

CONCEPTUALIZATION OF TERRORISM

Jack P. Gibbs

As you have learned, conceptualizing a variable is not always easy to do. There are many different ways to conceptualize the same term. Therefore, it is important to state how you are using the concept in the project you are conducting. In this article, Gibbs discusses the issues and problems that surround the conceptualization of terrorism. Most definitions are based on purely personal opinions, but Gibbs goes beyond a definition of terrorism by emphasizing the definition's bearing on five major conceptual questions, each of which introduces a major issue or problem.

Definitions of terrorism are controversial for reasons other than conceptual issues and problems. Because labeling actions as "terrorism" promotes condemnation of the actors, a definition may reflect ideological or political bias (for lengthy elaboration, see Rubenstein, 1987). Given such considerations, all of which discourage attempts to define terrorism, it is not surprising that Laqueur (1977, p. 5) argued that

> A comprehensive definition of terrorism does not exist nor will it be found in the foreseeable future. To argue that terrorism cannot be studied without such a definition is manifestly absurd.

Even granting what Laqueur implies—that terrorism is somehow out there awaiting definition—it is no less "manifestly absurd" to pretend to study terrorism without at least some kind of definition of it. Leaving the definition implicit is the road to obscurantism.

Even if sociologists should overcome their ostensible reluctance to study terrorism (for a rare exception, see Lee, 1983), they are unlikely to contribute to its conceptualization. The situation has been described succinctly by Tallman (1984, p. 1121): "Efforts to explicate key concepts in sociology have been met with stifling indifference by members of our discipline."

There are at least two reasons why sociologists commonly appear indifferent to conceptualizations. First, Weber and Parsons gave the work a bad name in the eyes of those sociologists who insist (rightly) on a distinction between substantive theory and conceptual analysis. Second, conclusive resolutions of conceptual issues are improbable because the *ultimate* justification of any definition is an impressive theory that incorporates the definition. Nonetheless, it is crippling to assume that productive research and impressive theories are possible without confronting conceptual issues and problems. The argument is not just that theorizing without definitions is sterile, nor merely recognition that theory construction and conceptualization should go hand in hand. Additionally, one can assess definitions without descending to purely personal opinion, even when not guided by a theory.

Systematic tests of a theory require definitions of at least *some* of the theory's constituent terms; but test findings, even those based on the same units of comparison, will

Gibbs, J. P., "Conceptualization of Terrorism," *American Sociological Review,* 54 (3), 1989, pp. 329–340. Used with permission.

diverge if each definition's empirical applicability is negligible, meaning if independent observers disagree when applying the definition to identify events or things. To illustrate, contemplate a question about any definition of terrorism: How much do independent observers agree in judging whether or not President Kennedy's assassination was terrorism in light of the definition? As subsequent illustrations show, simple definitions may promote agreement in answers to the Kennedy question and yet be objectionable for theoretical reasons; but the immediate point is that an empirically applicable definition does not require a theory. By contrast, given evidence that a definition promises negligible empirical applicability, no theory can justify that definition.

Still another "atheoretical" criterion is the definition's consistency with convention. That criterion cannot be decisive, because it would preclude novel definitions; but it is important when the field's professionals must rely on "outsiders" for data and, hence, presume appreciable congruence between their definitions and those of the outsiders. That consideration is particularly relevant here, because in analyzing terrorism social scientists often rely on reports of government officials, journalists, and historians.

Conceptual issues and problems haunt virtually all major terms in the social and behavioral sciences, and any definition is ambiguous if it does not answer questions bearing on those issues and problems. There are at least five such questions about terrorism. First, is terrorism *necessarily* illegal (a crime)? Second, is terrorism *necessarily* undertaken to realize some particular type of goal and, if so, what is it? Third, how does terrorism *necessarily* differ from conventional military operations in a war, a civil war, or so-called guerrilla warfare? Fourth, is it *necessarily* the case that only opponents of the government engage in terrorism? Fifth, is terrorism *necessarily* a distinctive strategy in the use of violence and, if so, what is that strategy?

The questions are answered in light of a subsequent definition of terrorism, but more than a definition is needed. The pursuit of a theory about terrorism will be furthered by describing and thinking about terrorism and all other sociological phenomena in terms of one particular notion, thereby promoting the recognition of logical and empirical associations. The most appropriate notion is identified subsequently as "control," but a defense of that identification requires a definition of terrorism (*not* of "terror").

A Definition of Terrorism

Terrorism is illegal violence or threatened violence directed against human or nonhuman objects, provided that it:

1. was undertaken or ordered with a view to altering or maintaining at least one putative norm in at least one particular territorial unit or population;

2. had secretive, furtive, and/or clandestine features that were expected by the participants to conceal their personal identity and/or their future location;

3. was not undertaken or ordered to further the permanent defense of some area;

4. was not conventional warfare and because of their concealed personal identity, concealment of their future location, their threats, and/or their spatial mobility, the participants perceived themselves as less vulnerable to conventional military action; *and*

5. was perceived by the participants as contributing to the normative goal previously described (*supra*) by inculcating fear of violence in persons (perhaps an indefinite category of them) other than the immediate target of the actual or threatened violence and/or by publicizing some cause.

Clarification, Issues, and Problems

In keeping with a social science tradition, most definitions of terrorism are set forth in a fairly brief sentence (see, e.g., surveys by Oots, 1986, pp. 5–8, and Schmid & Jongman, 1988, pp. 32–38). Such definitions do not tax the reader's intellect or patience, but it is inconsistent to grant that human behavior is complex and then demand simple definitions of behavioral types.

The Illegality of Terrorism. Rubenstein's definition (1987, p. 31) is noteworthy if only because it makes no reference to crime or illegality: "I use the term 'terrorism' . . . to denote *acts of small-group violence for which arguable claims of mass representation can be made.*" However, even granting that terrorism is an illegal action, there are two contending conceptions of crime, one emphasizing the *reactions* of officials as the criterion and the other emphasizing normative considerations (e.g., statutory law). Because of space limitations, it is not feasible to go much beyond recognizing the two contending conceptions. It must suffice to point out that an action may be illegal or criminal (in light of statutes and/or reactions by state officials) because of (1) where it was planned; (2) where it commenced; and/or (3) where it continued, especially in connection with crossing a political boundary. Such distinctions are relevant even when contemplating the incidence of terrorism.

One likely reaction: But why is terrorism *necessarily* a crime? The question suggests that *classes* of events or things exist independently of definitions. Thus, it may appear that "stones" and "humans" denote ontologically *given* classes, but in the context of gravitational theory, stones and humans are *not* different. However, to insist that all definitions are *nominal* is not to imply that conventional usage should be ignored; and, again, the point takes on special significance when defining terrorism. The initial (unnumbered) part of the present definition is consistent with most other definitions and also with this claim: most journalists, officials, and historians who label an action as "terrorism" evidently regard the action as illegal or criminal. However, it is not denied that two populations may differ sharply as to whether or not a particular action was a crime. As a *necessary* condition for an action to be terrorism, only the statutes and/or reactions of officials in the political unit where the action was planned or took place (in whole or in part) need identify the action as criminal or illegal.

Violence and Terrorism. Something like the phrase "violence or threatened violence" appears in most definitions of terrorism (see Schmid & Jongman, 1988, p. 5). As in those definitions, the phrase's key terms are here left as primitives; and whether they must be defined to realize sufficient empirical applicability can be determined only by actual attempts to apply the definition.

Despite consensus about violence as a *necessary* feature of terrorism, there is a related issue. Writers often suggest that only humans can be targets of violence, but many journalists, officials, and historians have identified instances of destruction or damage of nonhuman objects (e.g., buildings, domesticated animals, crops) as terrorism. Moreover, terrorists pursue their ultimate goal through inculcation of fear and humans do fear damage or destruction of particular nonhuman objects.

The Ultimate Goal of Terrorists. The present definition indicates that terrorists *necessarily* have a goal. Even though it is difficult to think of a human action that is not goal oriented, the consideration is controversial for two reasons. One reason is the allegation that terrorists are irrational or mentally ill (see, e.g., Livingston, 1978, pp. 224–239; and Livingstone's commentary, 1982, p. 31 on Parry), which raises doubts as to whether terrorists have identifiable goals. The second reasons why part 1 of the definition is controversial: many sociologists, especially Durkheimians, do not emphasize the purposive quality of human behavior, perhaps because they view the emphasis as reductionism. In any case, a defensible definition of virtually any term in sociology's vocabulary requires recognition of the relevance of internal behavior (e.g., perception, beliefs, purpose). Thus, without part 1 of the present definition, the distinction between terrorism and the *typical* robbery becomes obscure. The typical robber does not threaten violence to maintain or alter a putative norm; he or she is concerned only with behavioral control in a particular situation.

A defensible definition of a norm is not presumed (see Gibbs, 1981, pp. 9–18, for a litany of difficulties). Rather, it is necessary only that at least one of the participants (those who undertake the violent action or order it) view the action as contributing to the maintenance or alteration of some law, policy, arrangement, practice, institution, or shared belief.

Part 1 of the definition is unconventional only in that goals of terrorists are *not* necessarily political. Many definitions create the impression that all terrorism is political (for a contrary view, see Wilkinson, 1986, p. 51*)*, but the very term "political terrorism" suggests at least two types. The concern of social scientists with terrorism typologies is premature (see, e.g., the commentary by Oots [1986, pp. 11, 301 on Mickolus's notions of international, transnational, domestic, and interstate terrorism). No terrorism typology amounts to a *generic* definition (see the survey in Schmid & Jongman, 1988, pp. 39–59), and without the latter the former is bound to be unsatisfactory.

Military Operations and Terrorism. To repeat a previous question: How does terrorism *necessarily* differ, if at all, from conventional military operations in a war, civil war, or so-called guerrilla warfare? The question cannot be answered readily because there are no clearly accepted definitions of conventional military operation, war, civil war, and guerrilla warfare. "Guerrilla" is especially troublesome because journalists are prone to use the word without defining it but such as to suggest that it is synonymous with terrorism (a usage emphatically rejected by Laqueur, 1987, and Wilkinson, 1986).

Conventional military operations differ from terrorism along the lines indicated by parts 2, 3, and 4 of the definition. However, the definition does not preclude the possibility of a transition from terrorism to civil war. One tragic instance was the Easter Rising in Ireland (1916), when rather than perpetuate the terrorism tradition, a small group of Irish seized and attempted a permanent defense of government buildings in Dublin, vainly hoping that the populace would join them in open warfare. Today, it is terrorism rather than civil war that haunts Northern Ireland, and the term "guerrilla warfare" has no descriptive utility in that context.

Terrorism as a Special Strategy. One feature of terrorism makes it a distinctive (though not unique) strategy is violence. That feature is described in part 5 of the definition.

Part 5 is controversial primarily because it would exclude action such as this threat: "Senator, if you vote for that bill, it will be your death warrant." Why would such a threat not be terrorism? A more theoretically significant answer is given subsequently. Here it must suffice to point out that scores of writers have emphasized "third-party" or "general" intimidation as an essential feature of terrorism; and journalists, officials, or historians only rarely identify "dyadic intimidation" (X acts violently toward Y but *not* to control Y's behavior) as terrorism.

"State Terrorism" as a Special Issue. Zinam's definition (1978, pp. 244–45) illustrates one of many reasons why definitions of terrorism are so disputable: "[Terrorism is] the use or threat of violence by individuals or organized groups to evoke fear and submission to obtain some economic, political, sociopsychological, ideological, or other objective." Because the definition would extend to the imposition of legal punishments by government officials to prevent crimes through *general* deterrence, in virtually all jurisdictions (see Morris, 1966, p. 631) some aspects of criminal justice would qualify as terrorism; and Zinam's definition provides no basis for denying that it would be "state terrorism. " Even granting that a state agent or employee acts for the state only when acting at the direction or with the consent of a superordinate, there is still no ostensible difference between the use or threat of violence in law enforcement and Zinam's terrorism.

Had Zinam defined terrorism as being *necessarily* illegal or criminal, then many instances of violence by a state agent or employee at the direction or with the consent of a superordinate would not be terrorism. However, think of the numerous killings in Nazi Germany (Ernst Roehm, the Storm Troop head being a well-known victim) during the Night of the Long Knives (June 30, 1934). Hitler ordered the slaughter, and *at rite time* the killings were illegal in light of German statues; but Hitler publicly acknowledged responsibility, and the only concealment was that perceived as necessary to surprise the victims. Surely there is a significant difference between such open, blatant use of coercion by a state official (dictator or not) and the situation where regime opponents are assassinated but officials disavow responsibility and the murders are so secretive that official complicity is difficult to prove. The "rule of terror" of Shaka, the famous Zulu chief, is also relevant. Shaka frequently ordered the execution of tribal members on a seemingly whimsical basis, but the orders were glaringly public (see Walter, 1969). Shaka's regime illustrates another point: in some social units there may be no obvious "law" other than the will of a despot, in which case there is no basis to describe the despot's violence as illegal. The general point: because various aspects of government may be *public* violence, to label all of those aspects "terrorism" is to deny that terrorism has any secretive, furtive, or clandestine features.

Given the conceptual issues and problems that haunt the notion of state terrorism, it is hardly surprising that some writers attribute great significance to the notion, while others (e.g., Laqueur, 1987, pp. 145–146) seem to reject it. The notion is not rejected here, and the following definition does not make it an extremely rare phenomenon. State terrorism occurs when and only when a government official (or agent or employee) engages in terrorism, as previously defined, at the direction or with the consent of a superordinate, but one who does *not* publicly acknowledge such direction or consent.

The foregoing notwithstanding, for theoretical reasons it may prove desirable to limit the proposed definition of terrorism (*supra*) to *nonstate* terrorism and to seek a quite different definition of *state* terrorism. Even so, it will not do to presume that all violence by state agents is terrorism. The immediate reason is that the presumption blurs the distinction between terrorism and various kinds or aspects of law enforcement. Moreover, it is grossly unrealistic to assume that all instances of genocide or persecution along racial, ethnic, religious, or class lines by state agents (including the military) are terrorism regardless of the means, goals, or circumstances. Nor is it defensible to speak of particular regimes (e.g., Stalin's, Hitler's, Pol Pot's) as though all of the related violence must have been state terrorism. For that matter, granted that the regimes were monstrous bloodbaths, it does not follow that the state agents in question made no effort whatever to conceal any of their activities and/or their identity. Readers who reject the argument should confer with American journalists who attempted to cover Stalin's Soviet Union, Hitler's Germany, or Pol Pot's Cambodia. Similarly, it is pointless to deny that secretive, clandestine, or furtive actions have been characteristic of "death squads" (many allegedly "state") in numerous Latin American countries over recent decades. It is commonly very difficult to prove that such groups murder with the knowledge and/or consent of state officials; but the difficulty is one justification for identifying the murders as terrorism, even though the state-nonstate distinction may be debatable in particular instances.

Difficulties in Empirical Application

One likely objection to the present definition of terrorism is its complexity; but, again, demands for simplicity are inconsistent with human behavior's complexity. Nonetheless, application of the definition does call for kinds of information that may not be readily available. Reconsider a previous question: Was President Kennedy's assassination terrorism? The present definition does not permit an unequivocal answer, largely because there are doubts about the goals of the assassination and whether or not it was intimidation. If terrorism were defined as simply "the illegal use or threat of violence," an affirmative answer to the Kennedy question could be given; but the definition would also admit (*inter alia*) all robberies and many child abuses. Similarly, the phrase "for political purposes" would justify an affirmative answer to the Kennedy question; but the implication would be a tacit denial of *apolitical* terrorism, and divergent interpretations of "political" are legion. Finally, although a definition that specifically includes "murder of a state official" would maximize confidence in an affirmative answer to the Kennedy question, there must be doubts about the feasibility of such an "enumerative" definition of terrorism. And what would one make of the murder of a sheriff by his or her spouse?

The general point is that a *simple* definition of terrorism tends to delimit a class of events so broad as to defy valid generalizations about it (reconsider mixing presidential assassinations, robberies, and child abuses) or so vague that its empirical applicability is negligible. In the latter connection, the Kennedy illustration indicates the need to grant this methodological principle: the congruence dimension (but not the feasibility dimension) of a definition's empirical applicability is enhanced when independent observers agree that the definition cannot be applied in a particular instance because requisite information is not available. If that principle is not granted, sociologists will try to make do with simple definitions and whatever data are readily available.

Presumptive and Possible Terrorism. Comparative research on terrorism commonly is based on the use of the term "terrorism" by journalists or officials. Hence, insofar as the use of data on *presumptive* terrorism can be justified, a definition's utility is enhanced by its correspondence with the use of the term "terrorism" by journalists and officials. Although only potentially demonstrable, my claim is that the present definition corresponds more with such use of the term than does any simpler definition, such as: terrorism is illegal violence.

Even when terrorism research is based on *descriptions* of violent events, as in newspaper stories, there may be cases that can be designated as *possible* terrorism even though the information is not complete; and a definition's empirical applicability can be assessed in terms of agreement among independent observers in such designations. In that connection, the present definition points to the kind of information needed for truly defensible research on terrorism, which is not the case when investigators try to make do with a much simpler definition, or no definition at all.

References

Durkheim, Émile. 1949. *The division of labor in society.* New York: Free Press.

Gibbs, Jack P. 1981. *Norms, deviance, and social control.* New York: Elsevier.

Harris, Marvin. 1979. *Cultural materialism.* New York: Random House.

Laqueur, Walter. 1977. *Terrorism.* London: Weidenfeld and Nicolson.

Laqueur, Walter, 1987. *The age of terrorism.* London: Weidenfeld and Nicolson.

Lee, Alfred M. 1983. *Terrorism in Northern Ireland.* Bayside, NY: General Hall.

Livingston, Marius H., ed. 1978. *International terrorism in the contemporary world.* Westport, CT: Greenwood.

Livingstone, Neil C. 1982. *The war against terrorism.* Lexington, MA: Heath.

Morris. Norval. 1966. Impediments of penal reform. *University of Chicago Law Review,* 33: 627–656.

Noakes, Jeremy. 1986. The origins, structure and function of Nazi terror. Pp. 67–87 in *Terrorism, ideology, and revolution,* edited by Noel O'Sullivan. Brighton, England: Harvester.

Oots, Kent L. 1986. *A political organization approach to transnational terrorism.* Westport, CT: Greenwood.

Parsons, Talcott. 1951. *The social system.* New York: Free Press.

Rubenstein, Richard E. 1987. *Alchemists of revolution.* London: I. B. Tauris.

Schmid, Alex P., and Albert J. Jongman. 1988. *Political terrorism.* Rev. ed. Amsterdam: North-Holland.

Skocpol, Theda. 1979. *States and social revolution.* London: Cambridge University Press.

Tallman, Irving. 1984. Book review. *Social Forces* 62: 1121–1122.

Walter, Eugene V. 1969. *Terror and resistance.* New York: Oxford University Press.

Weber, Max. 1978. *Economy and society.* 2 vols., continuous pagination. Berkeley: University of California Press.

Wilkinson, Paul. 1986. *Terrorism and the liberal state.* 2nd ed. New York: New York University Press.

Zinam, Oleg. 1978. Terrorism and violence in light of a theory of discontent and frustration. Pp. 240–268 in *International terrorism in the contemporary world,* edited by Marius H. Livingston. Westport, CT: Greenwood.

REVIEW QUESTIONS

1. What are some of the problems and issues that occur with personal definitions of terrorism?

2. How did Gibbs end up conceptualizing terrorism?

3. What type of research can be done based on the new definitions of terrorism?

A SYSTEMATIC QUALITATIVE EVALUATION OF LEVELS OF DIFFERENTIATION IN FAMILIES WITH CHILDREN AT RISK

Yeudit Avnir and Ron Shor

For this article, the researchers wanted to increase their understanding of the dynamics within the parent-child relationship in families whose children were at risk because their parents' child-rearing practices were dysfunctional. Once again, it is important to define the concept, and these researchers address the issue of using the concept of differentiation and describe how they operationalized this variable. Before reading this article, think about how you would describe differentiation and then how you would measure it. Is it the same or different than how the author operationalizes this concept.

Different theoretical frameworks have been implemented in the development of research and assessment strategies of situations of children at risk. A review of these frameworks reveals two major deficits. The first is that there is lack of sufficient attention to the nature of the dynamics within the focal system (i.e., the parent-child system) in cases of child maltreatment. The second related deficit is that these models most often do not provide specific and concrete guidelines about how to analyze daily events in parent-child relationships. Such events can serve as a basis for assessing problems in parent-child relationships and for assessing change in parenting approach as a result of therapeutic work. The ecological model, for example, when applied to the area of child maltreatment illuminates the importance of including multidimensional factors in assessing situations of risk of

Avnir, Y. & Shor, R. 1998. A systematic qualitative evaluation of levels of differentiation in families with children at risk. *Families in Society: The Journal of Contemporary Human Services* 79(5): 504–514. Used with permission.

abuse and neglect of children (e.g., Browne, 1988; Thomlison, 1997), but it does not focus on or provide specific guidelines for assessing the dynamics of parent-child relationships. Other theories, such as attachment and psychodynamic theories, do relate to the focal system of parent-child relationships, but they focus mainly on specific aspects that may lead to child maltreatment such as deficits in empathy or in the connectedness between a parent and a child (e.g., Fashenbach, 1989; Steele, 1980; Tuohy, 1987). Such specific perspectives do not provide a sufficient base as to what to observe and how to analyze the problems in the complex and diverse daily dynamics of the parent-child relationship in situations of children at risk.

In this paper, application of the concept of differentiation to the context of families with children at risk will be presented as a central concept for analyzing the difficulties of parents in relating to their children. In addition, a systemic qualitative framework for assessing parents' levels of differentiation and for assessing changes in their approach towards their children will be presented. This framework was implemented in research that evaluated the level of differentiation of parents who participated in a short-term therapeutic group program for families with children at risk, under the auspices of the Social Welfare Department of Jerusalem. The main objective of the program was to improve the parents' relationships with their children, thus reducing the risk for child maltreatment.

Differentiation is a concept that was included in Bowen's family systems theory (Bowen, 1978) and describes individuals in terms of interactive relationship patterns (Aylmer, 1986). According to Bowen, a family that has a balanced relationship between separateness and connectedness is a family with a high level of differentiation (Kerr & Bowen, 1988). The concepts of separateness and connectedness have been used also by other theoreticians and researchers of family relationships (e.g., Minuchin, 1974; Olson, Sprenkle & Russel, 1979), although each of their perspectives is somewhat different, both in terminology and conception. Differentiation is reflected primarily in the family system's interactional patterns for maintaining interpersonal distance, and thus, in the system's tolerance for both individuality and intimacy, and it exists on a continuum from high to low levels of differentiation (Kerr & Bowen, 1988). Within families that have a low level of differentiation, the boundaries are regulated in extreme ways: enmeshment patterns in which an insufficient separateness or faulty boundaries prevent autonomy and individuality, or disengagement patterns in which rigid boundaries between family members allow autonomy at the expense of intimacy, support, and responsiveness (Minuchin, 1974). Hoffman (1975) describes these poorly differentiated patterns as either "too richly cross-joined" or "too poorly cross-joined." Poorly differentiated patterns are reflected in family members' preoccupation with self and absence of empathy, regard, and respect for the uniqueness and individuality of others. Behaviors often reflect assumptions that other members are either not capable of functioning in accordance with their developmental levels, or are capable of functioning well beyond their developmental levels (Anderson & Sabatelli, 1990).

A central quality of a relationship that has a high degree of differentiation is a relationship in which there is a dialogue. Dialogue relates to the ability of two people to relate to each other in an open manner and to exchange ideas around subjects that are important to them while respecting the unique self of each of them (Friedman, 1992). Bowen uses the term "person to person" to describe such relationships (Bowen, 1978). Boszormenyi-Nagy & Krasner (1987) note that "genuine dialogue" is thought to be the necessary context for mature individuation to occur. A genuine dialogue, with its emphasis on fairness, trust, and ongoing relatedness offers both the potential for self-delineation (the definition of self in relation to significant others) and self-validation (affirming one's self worth through caring for others). Both disengagement and enmeshment characterize lack of differentiation by the fact that there is no constructive dialogue enabling the uniqueness of the family member to be actualized.

The concept of differentiation, when applied to parenting, describes an age-appropriate balance of separateness and connectedness for children. Differentiated relationships between parents and children can be defined as those in which the parent is able to differentiate between the emotional world of the parent and that of the child, to allow the child to develop autonomy, to be sensitive to the child's needs, and to develop a dialogue including communication of confirmation and respect. Parent-child interactions in well-differentiated families allow children to experience and express their individuality while remaining intimately connected to the parent (Sabatelli & Mazor, 1985). The parent is able to build a relationship with a child in which processes such as the extent of dependence, decision making regarding family matters and areas of interests will indicate a balance in the family relationships between cohesiveness and uniqueness. In poorly differentiated enmeshed systems, parental intrusiveness and a blurring of personal boundaries work against individual autonomy and individuality that may in time interfere with the child's development. Parental control and authority are often stressed in response to the child's effort to act autonomously. In the disengaged pattern the lack of involvement and care may lead to neglect of children (Anderson & Sabatelli, 1992; Minuchin, 1974).

Practice experience indicates that among parents who participated in the therapeutic groups for parents with children at risk in Jerusalem, a dialogue with their children has often been missing, and a low level of differentiation was observed. In such families, the child is often perceived by his/her parents in a mechanical way. Parents approach their children as though they can activate them according to their wishes and plans without taking into consideration the child's self and his/her right to actualize his/her uniqueness. The child's "failure" to fulfill the parents' wishes could lead to maltreatment.

Studies also indicate a relationship between low level of differentiation and the risk of child maltreatment. Abusive mothers have been shown in studies to have difficulty interacting with their children in developmentally appropriate ways (Crittenden & Bonvillian, 1984; Bousha & Twentyman, 1984). These mothers were described as having difficulties to interact reciprocally with their children and to pace their interactions to their children's needs. They appeared to be responding to their own internal needs, rather than being able to accurately perceive and respond to the child's cues. Dore and Fagan (1993) found that neglecting mothers also have difficulty interacting with their children in a developmentally appropriate way. The neglecting mothers in their sample were less developmentally appropriate than non-maltreating mothers in play interactions with their children. For example, they tended to either overwhelm their children with quick responses or were too slow in responding to them, and they frequently used many more controls and directions than were developmentally appropriate. Support for the relationships between low level of differentiation and child maltreatment could be drawn also from studies in which depressed affect and internalizing behaviors of adolescents have been linked to parents' controlling behavior and failure to grant sufficient autonomy to their children (Allen, Hauser, Eickholt, Bell, & O'Connor, 1994; Fauber, Forehand, Thomas, & Weirson, 1990; Gjerde and Block, 1991).

A Framework for Research and Assessment of Levels of Differentiation

A common research methodology used to assess the dynamics of parent-child relationships relies on the responses of family members to questionnaires. However, problems in accurate reporting have been noted with maltreating parents (Reid, Kavanagh, & Baldwin, 1987). Self-report methods often reflect more the wish of the parents for relationships than the actual way that they approach the relationships. In a western society that emphasizes ideals of tolerance, openness, and pluralism between parents and children, there is a chance that parents will provide desirable responses that may stand in sharp contradiction to what actually occurs within a family. To overcome this limitation, a qualitative method was developed and applied in research used to evaluate changes in the parenting approach of participants in a short-term therapeutic group program (the group consisted of three couples and four single mothers). This method relied on content analysis of the descriptions by the parents themselves of their relationships with their children. The descriptions were documented during the therapeutic process and in nonstructured interviews before and after the group therapy. The utilization of this method was based on the assumption that as much as the person describes his/her relationship with another in an open manner, it is possible to receive a closer look at the unique quality of the relationship.

Operationalization of Differentiation

The first stage in the development of the systemic qualitative evaluation of parents' differentiation (SQEPD, Avnir, 1997) was the operationalization of the dimensions contained in differentiation in parent-child relationships, in a way enabling analysis of daily events between parents and children. This served as the basis for the content analysis of the parents' descriptions.

The operationalization of the dimensions of differentiation attempted to capture specific patterns of the relationship between parents and children. A parent helps a child develop into an adult each day and each hour, while doing activities that have significance and importance in shaping the internal and external world of the child. The main dimensions of differentiation developed for the analysis of the daily dynamics in a parent-child relationship were based on Bowen's theory as well as on other theoreticians and researchers of family relationships (e.g., Karpel, 1976; L'abate, 1976; Olson, Sprenkle & Russel, 1979). They are as follows:

1. *Continual need for familiarity with the uniqueness of the child.* This relates to the continual need to learn about and be familiar with the child's world. In an undifferentiated approach with an enmeshment pattern, because of the over-involvement between family members, the parent may perceive his/her familiarity with the child's world as a given and, may, for example, interpret the child's wishes according to his/her own wishes, fears, and beliefs. In the disengaged pattern in an undifferentiated approach, the parent may be disconnected from the child's world and may, for example, ignore the cues and expressions of the child.

2. *Adjusting pace.* This relates to the need to consider the pace of the child and to adjust the parent's pace to that of the child. An example of an undifferentiated enmeshed

pattern could be conducting the family's activities according to the parent's pace, and an example of an undifferentiated disengaged pattern could be that there is a lack of connection between the parents' and the child's activities.

3. *Privacy.* This relates to the parents' respect for the child's need for privacy in the emotional, cognitive, and behavioral areas. In an undifferentiated enmeshed pattern, the parent can intrude into each aspect of the child's life, while in the undifferentiated disengaged pattern, there is almost no opportunity to share feelings, thoughts, and activities between parents and children.

4. *Accepting differences.* This relates to the parent's recognition of the child's right to be different from what the parent wishes and expects, and that the parent perceives the child as different from the other siblings in the family. An example of an undifferentiated enmeshed approach could be for the parent to demand that the child will fit a set standard and to demand sameness among all of his/her children without considering the uniqueness of each child. In the undifferentiated disengaged approach, there could be a distance that does not allow the parent to recognize the child's differences from other children.

5. *Autonomy of choice.* This relates to the parents' enabling the child to make choices according to his age level. In the enmeshed form of lack of differentiation, the parent could make decisions regarding the child's life without considering the child's choices and needs. In the disengaged form of lack of differentiation, the parent could be totally uninvolved in the child's decisions.

6. *Enabling relationships with others.* This relates to the parent enabling the child to develop relationships with other members of the family and with people outside the family. In an undifferentiated enmeshed form of relationship, the parent may demand exclusiveness in his/her relationship with the child or he/she may include the child in coalitions that are aimed to serve the parent's fights with others. The undifferentiated disengaged form could be manifested by lack of involvement or support by the parent for the child as he/she explores the possibilities for the development of relationships with others.

7. *Personal power.* This relates to the extent and kind of power that the parent perceives that he/she and the child have. A supportive approach of a parent in a child's development of his/her unique characteristics requires a belief by the parent that the child has internal sources of personal power allowing him/her to function independently in the world. An impasse to such a supportive approach could be not only lack of belief by the parent in the child's personal power, but also lack of belief by the parent in his/her own personal power to function independently without the children. The undifferentiated enmeshed dynamic could be manifested when a parent perceives that he/she has total power and the child is totally powerless. In such situations there is no opportunity for expression of the child's individuality. The opposite situation which could be present in this dynamic could be when the parent feels powerless and dependent on his/her children. In the undifferentiated disengaged dynamic, because of the distance from the child, there could be situations in which the parent feels total power without recognizing the resources of the power of the child.

8. *A mediating factor.* This relates to the fact that dialogue could be a mediating factor in each of the above dimensions. It could demonstrate the parent's willingness to get to know the child and give expression to his/her individuality. When differentiation exists through dialogue, there is a balance between the needs of the parent (parents' self) and those of the child (child's self). Both the undifferentiated enmeshed dynamic and the undifferentiated disengaged dynamic could be characterized as lacking a functional dialogue between a parent and a child. In the undifferentiated enmeshed dynamic, the self of the parent and self of the child could be experienced as one system and, therefore, the parent may not feel the need for a dialogue. The flow of information in this case could be unidirectional in the form of lecturing about the parent's thoughts or giving instructions without any opportunity for the child to express his/her thoughts. In the undifferentiated disengagement dynamic, the self of the parent and the self of the child could be experienced as two foreign selves. There could be situations in which there are almost no conversations between a parent and a child.

Evaluation of Levels of Differentiation

The systemic qualitative evaluation of parents' differentiation (SQEPD) for content analysis of parents' descriptions of their relationship with their children was developed. This framework enabled determination of the level of differentiation in the analyzed descriptions and the relating of this level to the relevant dimensions of differentiation. The parents' descriptions were taped and transcribed both in the interviews conducted before and after the therapeutic program and also during the therapeutic sessions (content analysis was done only for the interviews). Since the contents of the descriptions of each family were analyzed separately, the analysis of each family was defined as a case study. The unit of analysis was stories in which the parents described their relationships with their children (the word "story" relates to descriptions of thoughts or events that focus on one subject of the parent-child relationship; 299 stories were analyzed). The level of differentiation was analyzed in each story according to the following components: (a) the subject of the story, (b) participants in the story, (c) general characteristic of the story, (d) the parent's perception of the activity of the other, (e) the meaning of the activity of the other for the teller, (f) the emotional experience of the parent, (g) the focus of the difficulty/achievement according to the parent, (h) the parent's feeling of power, (i) the parent's way of coping with the presented situation.

For each of the dimensions a detailed guide for categorizing and evaluating the content of the parents' descriptions was developed. To illustrate the application of this systemic framework, content analysis on one story from each of the interviews conducted with one mother is presented. The aim of the analysis of these examples is to demonstrate how the systemic framework can be used when examining case studies to determine the levels of differentiation in a parent's relationship with his/her child and to assess change in the parent's approach.

The stories in the following examples relate to the descriptions by Sara, a mother of two daughters, who participated in the group with her husband Uri. The couple's two daughters are Daniela, who is four-and-a-half years old, and Liora, who is three years old. The couple was referred to the social welfare department as a result of a report from a hospital of an incident of physical violence by the mother toward Daniela. In the first story from the first interview conducted prior to the treatment, the interviewer began by asking the mother about her view of her relationship with her daughter Daniela.

The mother: "Daniela, because of her smartness, her sharpness, her smartness [sic] and her understanding, is probably independent. She is independent as a result of this and strong. Therefore it is very difficult for me with her in many things. I have difficulties around decisions. It is difficult for me even to cooperate with her to do something, even regarding a small example: a game. She decides and she wants and she is first. And even if I did not explain the game to her, she does not let me get close to her, not even to show her the game. And of course in every thing she always thinks that I am wrong. Every thing is a burden for me. Everything is difficult for me because of her smartness, and when I talk with her and explain things to her, she even tries to respond and tell me what she is thinking about. And it is very difficult for me to tell her what to do during the day, she does not like it and does not want it because of her smartness and her desire to be independent."

Analysis of the mother's level of differentiation in this story according to the SQEPD follows:

- The subject of the story: How the mother views her relationship with Daniela.
- Participants in the story: The mother and Daniela.
- General characteristic of the story: Negative experiences.
- Activity of the other from the parent's perception: Daniela is smart, sharp, independent, and strong.
- The meaning of the activity of the other for the teller: Negative, it is difficult for the parent.
- Emotional experience of the parent: Anger.
- The focus of the difficulty/achievement: Difficulty with the child.
- The parent's feeling of power: Powerlessness.
- Ways of coping: An attempt to coerce the mother's desires; there is no dialogue.
- Conclusion: Undifferentiated enmeshment with a focus on the powerlessness of the parent (the personal power dimension).

The mother's response indicated that the girl's desire for autonomy and independent activities was experienced by the mother as negative and made her angry. The word "smartness" was repeated several times. Each time, smartness and independence were experienced as negative characteristics that created difficulties. The girl, for example, did not allow her mother to explain the game, and this was perceived as a competition about who knows what and who does not know. There was no indication of pride about the girl's capabilities, only feelings of frustration and anger. The mother was not able to develop a dialogue with the girl. It made her angry that the girl expressed her thoughts when the mother wanted to explain things. She felt that in this way the girl devalued her. On the other hand, she at the same time devalued the legitimacy of the desire of the girl for independence. In this story, there is no direct report of violence but of a dynamic that could lead to frustrated reactions by the mother and, in fact during the interview, there were other descriptions in which Sara talked about outbursts, swearing and beating of the girl.

The second interview, which was conducted after the group therapy, reflected a more differentiated approach by the mother towards Daniela. There was better recognition of the personal power of the girl and better adjustment to the girl's pace. In addition, the mother focused to a greater degree on her other daughter with an attempt to understand her. The following description demonstrates the change:

The mother: "Before, I acted as if I am the mother, and I can decide, and this [is] it. The rules were very strong and difficult. Today, when I see and understand, and receive explanations from you and from other persons about what a child is, and that she is, in fact, a person with her own feelings, decisions, mind and ability for expression, and can even correct me. Today, I see that she is this person, I accept and understand it in the best way, so I am changing. I am listening to the child. For example, at 9:30 she called me from her room since she was probably afraid to come out since she knows that I don't permit her. It made me feel very good. I saw what kind of a girl she is. She said that she cannot fall asleep. I thought, I did not know what to say, and then I gave her something to read. You know what you could do, draw or write or do what ever you want in your room. Since this is the way that I had been given explanations, I see it as the right way. You can not force a person to fall asleep. So, like myself when I can not fail asleep, I know no matter what, I will not fall asleep. Therefore I gave her freedom." [Sara described that she allowed the girl to be in the living room a little bit since the girl could not fall asleep after reading books.] "Then she was totally satisfied. It was excellent for her, and she went to sleep. Then I was satisfied, and she was satisfied. So if I can do this, if I can activate my mind and thoughts at the same time, then the results are good. So today I understand that she has feelings and wants. And she went to sleep with happiness, she said 'good night father, good night mother.' So I felt very good; all of us benefited from this."

Analysis of the mother's level of differentiation in this story according to the systemic framework follows:

- The subject of the story: Difficulties of the girl to fall asleep.
- Participants in the story: The mother and Daniela.
- General characteristic of the story: Positive experiences.
- Activity of the other from the parent's perception: The daughter has desires.
- The meaning of the activity of the other for the teller: Positive for the girl and for the mother.
- Emotional experience of the parent: Positive.
- The focus of the difficulty/achievement: Achievement of the parent in relating to the child.
- The parent's feeling of power: Satisfying.
- Ways of coping: Learning from messages, enabling activity according to the pace of the girl, there is no anger.
- Conclusion: Differentiation with the focus on the continual need for familiarity dimension.

The mother's response in the beginning of the story was one of recognition of the individuality of the child and the need to be attuned to her; throughout the story she described actual implementation of this perception. This story demonstrated recognition by Sara that it is not possible to coerce her daughter to sleep. Through a process of exploration and learning from the girl's cues, she succeeded in finding an adaptive solution.

This process also indicated a situation in which the power was not perceived as being totally within the daughter or within the mother. As Sara said, "all of us benefited from it. "

A Framework for Assessing Change and for Comparison

To receive a more complete picture of the level of differentiation expressed in the interviews and to provide a base for comparison among the interviews, a framework for summarizing the analyses of the stories in each interview was developed. The identification of the overall pattern in each interview could provide a base not only for comparison of the level of differentiation at two points of time in one family (assessing change), but also for comparing the level of differentiation among different families.

A framework was developed to show the conclusions that were received from the analyses of all the stories in each interview. There are four categories for the levels of differentiation along the different dimensions which are differentiation, dilemmas, undifferentiated enmeshed patterns, and undifferentiated disengaged patterns. The last two categories included two components—the child's self and the parent's self—that relate to the balance between the focus on the child's self or the parent's self. (In differentiation, a balance exists between these two factors, and there is no significant emphasis on either the child's self or parent's self.)

The category of dilemmas was added during the content analysis after questions were raised about whether sections of the case studies could be characterized by one unified pattern (differentiation or lack of differentiation) and about whether the move from lack of differentiation to differentiation was total. Initial analysis of the stories indicated that responses were usually not pure. There were stories that expressed differentiation, enmeshment or disengagement. However, it became clear that an intermediate category was needed that would relate to dilemmas around the attempts to reach differentiation. Dilemmas and attempts to reach differentiation (such as a parent's awareness of a specific need of his/her child but not knowing how to respond) were marked on the borders between differentiation and undifferentiation.

The analysis of the first interview (in which Sara felt that her own self was devalued) was defined in the level of differentiation category as lack of differentiation enmeshment with a focus on the parent's self and in the dimension of differentiation category as personal power. The analysis of the second interview (in which Sara coped with the difficulty of Daniela's falling asleep) was defined in the level of differentiation category as differentiation and in the dimension of differentiation category as continual need for familiarity.

A summary of the data was used to compare the general patterns of the levels of differentiation in each interview. Since the number of analyzed stories in each interview was not equal and since there was a need to create a basis for comparing the two interviews, the percentage of the number of the analyzed stories in each level of differentiation was calculated. In the presented case study of Sara, for example, a summary of the levels of differentiation of the two interviews shows that 26% (n = 6) of the stories in the second interview, as opposed to 5% (n = 1) of the stories in the first interview, were classified as differentiation. The first interview clearly reflects a dominant pattern of lack of differentiation. In the second interview, it was possible to see an increase in the indications of differentiation that implies a change toward a more functional parenting approach.

Conclusions

Two main factors were found to be essential in developing and applying the concept of differentiation of self into a relevant assessment and research instrument in families with children at risk. The first is the way in which this relatively abstract concept was operationalized, and the second is the nature of the qualitative method that was developed for content analyses of the case studies.

The multidimensional operationalization of the concept of differentiation provided a concrete and specific framework for examining the ongoing daily events and problems in parent-child relationships on one hand and captured the complex issues in parent-child dynamics on the other. In addition, it provided a base to examine common patterns among families with children at risk (such as difficulties in developing a dialogue), as well as the unique problems of each family. The focus of the dimensions of differentiation on daily aspects of parents' relationship with their children removes the emphasis of the therapeutic work from issues to which the parents may have difficulties changing (e.g., the history of the parents) to the parents' daily struggles in their relationship with their children. Coping with these struggles could be perceived as feasible and desirable for the parents.

The SQEPD was found to be an effective way to study sensitive issues among at-risk families within the context of social welfare services. In studying problems such as parents' malfunctioning relationship with their children, parents may have a tendency not to reveal patterns that are generally considered to be inappropriate in responding to direct and structured questions (e.g., self-report questionnaires). However, by analyzing the content of the parents' free descriptions before and after the therapeutic process, and by conducting the interviews as an integral part of the participation in the therapeutic program, the risk for responses reflecting social desirability was reduced. In addition, the potential for insight into parents' views and family processes was increased. A limitation of this method is that it could be affected by the practitioner-researcher's subjective interpretation of the analyzed situations. However, the SQEPD assisted in reducing the subjectivity of the analyses.

By use of the SQEPD, it was possible to evaluate the level of differentiation in a manner that did not interfere with the treatment. The focus was the subjective world of the parents and the issues that concerned them. This evaluation could serve as a helpful tool for social workers in the family and child welfare field in assessing the problems in a parent-child relationship. It could also provide a tool to assess therapeutic progress and a database for setting new therapeutic objectives (for example, analyses of the case studies indicated a need to work with the parents on ways to develop a dialogue with their children and to become familiar with their children's unique characteristics). This method of analysis could provide an accessible nonintrusive instrument for practitioners and researchers in evaluating practices with families and children at risk.

References

Allen, J. P., Hauser, S. T., Eickholt, C., Bell, K. L., & O'Connor, T. G. (1994). Autonomy and relatedness in family interactions as predictors of expressions of negative adolescent affect. *Journal of Research on Adolescence,* 4(4), 535–552.

Anderson, S. A, & Sabatelli, R. (1990). Differentiating differentiation and individuation: Conceptual and operation challenges. *American Journal Family Therapy,* 18(1), 32–50.

Anderson, S. A., & Sabatelli, R. M. (1992). The differentiation in the family system scale (DIFS). *American Journal of Family Therapy,* 20(1), 77–89.

Avnir, Y. (1997). *Perception of the child as a differentiated person: A criterion for the evaluation of change in a group-work program for improvement of parents-children relations in children-at-risk families.* Unpublished master's thesis, The Hebrew University of Jerusalem, Israel.

Aylmer, R. C. (1986). Bowen family systems marital therapy. In N. S. Jacobson, & A. S. Gurman (Eds.), *Clinical handbook of marital therapy* (pp. 107–148).

Bousha, D. M., & Twentyman, C. T. (1984). Mother-child interactional style in abuse, neglect, and control groups: Naturalistic observations in the home. *Journal of Abnormal Psychology,* 93(1), 106–114.

Bowen, M. (1978). *Family therapy in clinical practice.* New York: Aronson.

Boszormenyi-Nagy, I., & Krasner, B. (1987). *Between give and take: An introduction to contextual therapy.* New York: Brunner Mazel.

Browne, D. H. (1988). High risk infants and child maltreatment: Conceptual and research model for determining factors predictive of child maltreatment. *Early Child Development and Care,* 31, 43–53.

Crittenden, P. M., & Bonvillian, J. D. (1984). The relationship between maternal risk status and maternal sensitivity. *American Journal of Orthopsychiatry,* 54(2), 250–262.

Dore, M. M., & Fagan, J. (1993). Mother-child play interactions in neglecting and nonneglecting mothers. *Early Child Development and Care,* 87, 59–68.

Fashenbach, N. D. (1989). Empathy and physical abuse. In D. C. Cicchetti (Ed.), *Child Maltreatment.* Cambridge: Cambridge University Press.

Fauber, R., Forehand, R., Thomas, A. M., & Wierson, M. (1990). A mediational model of the impact of marital conflict on adolescent adjustment in intact and divorced families: The role of disrupted parenting. *Child Development,* 61, 1112–1123.

Friedman, M. (1992). *Dialogue and the human image.* London: Sage.

Gjerde, P. E., & Block, J. (1991). Preadolescent antecedents of depressive symptomatology at age 18: A prospective study. *Journal of Youth and Adolescence,* 20, 217–223.

Hoffman, L. (1975). Enmeshment and too richly cross-joined system. *Family Process,* 14, 457–468.

Karpel, M. (1976). Individuation: From fusion to dialogue. *Family Process,* 15, 65–82.

Kerr, M. E., & Bowen, M. (1988). *Family evaluation: An approach based on Bowen theory.* New York: Norton.

L'abate. (1976). *Understanding and helping the individual in the family.* New York: Grune & Stratton.

Minuchin, S. (1974). *Families and family therapy.* Cambridge, MA: Harvard University Press.

Olson, D. H., Sprenkle, D. H., & Russel, C. S. (1979). Circumplex model of marital and family systems: Cohesion and adaptability dimensions, family types, and clinical applications. *Family Process,* 18(1), 3–27.

Reid, J. B., Kavanagh, K., & Baldwin, D. V. (1987). Abusive parents' perceptions of child problem behaviors: An example of parental bias. *Journal of Abnormal Child Psychology,* 15, 457–466.

Sabatelli, R. M., & Mazor, A. (1985). Differentiation, individuation, and identity formation: The integration of family system and individual developmental perspective. *Adolescence,* 20(79), 619–633.

Steele, B. (1980). Psychodynamic factors in child abuse. In C. H. Kempe & E. Melfer (Eds.), *The battered child* (pp. 49–86). Chicago: University of Chicago Press.

Thomlison, B. (1997). Risk and protective factors in child maltreatment. In M. W. Fraser (Ed.), *Risk and resilience in childhood: An ecological perspective.* Washington, DC: NASW Press.

Tuohy (1987). Psychoanalytic perspective on child abuse. *Child and Adolescent Social Work,* 4(1), 25–40.

REVIEW QUESTIONS

1. How did these researchers operationalize the concept *differentiation?*

2. What dimensions of differentiation did they use?

3. Can you think of another way they could have operationalized the concept of differentiation?

SCALE FOR ASSESSING EMOTIONAL DISTURBANCE: LONG-TERM TEST-RETEST RELIABILITY AND CONVERGENT VALIDITY WITH KINDERGARTEN AND FIRST-GRADE STUDENTS

Michael H. Epstein, Philip D. Nordness, Douglas Cullinan, and Melody Hertzog

This study addresses the psychometric characteristics of the Scale for Assessing Emotional Disturbance (SAED), which is a standardized, norm-referenced instrument that is based on the federal definition of emotional disturbance (ED). The main purpose of the SAED is to assist practitioners in identifying children with emotional disturbance by operationally defining ED as stated in the Individuals with Disabilities Education Act Amendments of 1997. The first study investigates the long-term test-retest reliability of the SAED over a seven-month period. The second study examines the convergent validity of the SAED by comparing it with several subscales of the Systematic Screening for Behavior Disorders, a multigate screening system to identify children at risk of behavior problems. Keep in mind as you read this article that both the validity and reliability of a study is very important, and in this study, the results indicate that the SAED is a reliable and valid instrument for identifying young children who may qualify for the federal definition of ED.

Children with emotional disturbance (ED) constitute one of the fastest growing populations served in school systems across the United States. As the number of students identified with ED increases, so does the need for psychometrically sound instruments to assist in identifying children with ED. Currently, there are a number of scales available for assessing children with ED, but none of them were developed to operationally define the federal criteria of ED. The Individuals with Disabilities Education Act (IDEA) of 1990 and its Amendments of 1997 define emotional disturbance as follows:

(i) a condition exhibiting one or more of the following characteristics over a long period of time and to a marked degree, which adversely affects educational performance:

   (A) An inability to learn which cannot be explained by intellectual, sensory, or health factors.

   (B) An inability to build or maintain satisfactory relationships with peers and teachers.

   (C) Inappropriate types of behaviors or feelings under normal circumstances.

   (D) A general pervasive mood of unhappiness or depression.

   (E) A tendency to develop physical symptoms or fears associated with personal or school problems.

(ii) The term includes children who are schizophrenic. The term does not include children who are socially maladjusted, unless it is determined that they are emotionally disturbed. (U.S. Department of Education, 1998, p. II-46)

The federal definition has fostered much discussion and criticism over the years (Coleman & Webber, 2002; Kauffman, 1997). The primary issues involve the differing purposes of the definition; the exclusion of children who are socially maladjusted; the meaning of the terms long period of time, marked degree, and adversely affects; and perhaps most significantly, how to measure the various conditions in a reliable and valid manner.

Although a number of instruments and strategies have been used to assist school staff to make identification and placement decisions, few if any of them have specifically addressed in a psychometrically sound manner the central feature of the federal definition. Nonetheless, local education agencies need an empirically based, norm-referenced, and functional assessment instrument to guide them in operationalizing the federal definition. The Scale for Assessing Emotional Disturbance (SAED; Epstein & Cullinan, 1998) was developed specifically to meet these needs by operationally defining ED as stated in IDEA. The SAED is a standardized, norm-referenced scale that assists in the identification of children who qualify for the federal special education category of ED (Epstein & Cullinan, 1998). The SAED contains five subscales, each corresponding to one of the five characteristics that may identify a student as having ED by the federal definition. The five subscales are termed Inability to Learn, Relationship Problems, Inappropriate Behavior, Unhappiness/Depression, and Physical Symptoms/Fears. The SAED also measures two other features of the federal definition, using a subscale that operationalizes Social Maladjustment and a single item that assesses the extent to which the student's behavior Adversely Affects educational performance. The SAED also contains a seven-item subscale measuring Overall Competence (student strengths and resources).

The construction of the SAED was performed in a systematic, logical manner and in accordance with the psychometric standards established by the American Psychological Association (1985). The SAED was developed systematically using the following procedures. The authors began by identifying the constructs to be measured. These included the five federal characteristics of ED, Overall Competence, and Social Maladjustment. Then a literature search was conducted of professional writings and research on the emotional and behavioral disorders of children (Achenbach, 1995; American Psychiatric Association, 1994; Breen & Fiedler, 1996; Cicchetti & Cohen, 1995a, 1995b; Kauffman, 1997; Merrell, 1994; Quay, 1986; Witt, Elliot, Kramer, & Gresham, 1994). Next, the authors examined existing rating scales, checklists, and other strategies that measure behavioral problems of children to analyze their content for format and wording (Achenbach, 1991a, 1991b; Brown & Hammill, 1990; Quay & Peterson, 1996; Reynolds & Kamphaus, 1992). Finally, the authors examined the federal definition of ED and related publications (IDEA, 1997). These activities resulted in the development of a prototype scale of 85 items that addressed children's emotional and behavioral problems.

Reliability and Validity

A psychometrically sound instrument should be able to demonstrate validity and reliability over time and across settings in a consistent manner. The more consistent and stable an instrument's validity and reliability remain over time and across settings, the more believable the results from the instrument are. Initial research on the SAED demonstrated good content validity (Epstein & Cullinan, 1998) and short-term reliability (Epstein, Cullinan, Harniss, & Ryser, 1999) of the instrument. However, given the importance of the decisions that professionals must make when a student is being considered for special education because of emotional disturbance, assessment instruments such as the SAED need extensive research on their psychometric characteristics. Of particular interest may be the convergent validity and long-term reliability of the instrument.

Convergent validity refers to the relationship between measures of the same construct using different assessment techniques (Crocker & Algina, 1986; Salvia & Ysseldyke, 1998; Harniss, Epstein, Ryser, & Pearson, 1999). *Long-term reliability* refers to an instrument's stability over a period of at least 6 months. With respect to the SAED, only about 6% of the students with ED in the norming sample were ages 5, 6, and 7 years. Thus, the psychometric characteristics of the SAED with young children, particularly kindergarten and first-grade students, need to be assessed.

The purpose of the present studies was to assess the long-term test-retest reliability of the SAED and the convergent validity of the SAED with children in kindergarten and first grade. In Study 1, we investigated the long-term test-retest reliability of the SAED to determine the stability of the measure over time. In Study 2, we examined the convergent validity of the SAED by comparing it with several subscales of the Systematic Screening for Behavior Disorders (SSBD; Walker & Severson, 1990), a multigate screening system to identify children at risk of behavior problems.

Study 1

Method

Participants and Setting. Participants in the study consisted of 270 kindergarten and first-grade students drawn from three elementary schools in a small midwestern city. Participants were 135 boys and 135 girls enrolled in general education classrooms. The number of students per grade level was 130 kindergarten students and 140 first graders ranging from 4 to 8 years of age with a mean age of 5.7 years.

Measure. The SAED is a standardized, norm-referenced rating scale that assesses the emotional and behavioral problems of children and adolescents by operationalizing the federal definition of ED. Individuals completing the SAED respond to 7 Overall Competence items, 45 Emotional-Behavioral items, and 1 Adversely Affects item using Likert-type scales. The SAED items are designed to be rated by adults who are knowledgeable about the student. The rater reads each statement and marks the rating that best describes the student's status at the time and over the last 2 months. The instrument is designed to be completed in 10 minutes or less by a teacher or by other individuals who have worked with the student. Once the rater has completed the scale, the raw scores are calculated for each subscale. Using simple tables in the SAED manual, the rater converts each subscale raw score to a percentile rank and a standard score with a mean of 10 and a standard deviation of 3. The subscales reported in the present study included the five federal definition characteristics of ED—Inability to Learn, Relationship Problems, Inappropriate Behavior,

Unhappiness/Depression, Physical Symptoms/Fears—plus the Overall Competence subscale. The Social Maladjustment subscale was not used in this study because this subscale is appropriate for students age 11 years and older.

Procedure. The ratings were conducted in the fall and spring of the 1999–2000 academic school year. All of the raters were general education teachers. Before the first rating in October, teachers were trained in completing the SAED. The training involved a 1-hour workshop where teachers were instructed on the definition of ED, how to read the instructions for the SAED, and how to rate each of the items. Teachers were then asked to complete the SAED for each student in their classroom and given 1 week to complete the task. The scales were then collected and scored. In May, teachers were given a second SAED scale to complete on the same students they had rated in October. The time between ratings was approximately 7 months.

Analysis, Results and Discussion

The dependent measure for the study was the standard score for each SAED subscale. Means and standard deviations for each administration of the SAED subscales of Inability to Learn, Relationship Problems, Inappropriate Behavior, Unhappiness/Depression, Physical Symptoms/Fears, and Overall Competence are presented in Table 1. Long-term test-retest reliability is an indication of a measure's stability over time. The results of this study indicate that the SAED is a highly stable measure over a long period of time (7 months). The finding that the SAED produces significant results after an interval of 7 months increases the confidence with which test users may generalize the findings of an initial administration to later administrations.

Study 2

Method

Participants. The participants were 123 kindergarten and first-grade students drawn from three elementary schools in a small midwestern city. Participants were 64 boys and 59 girls selected from general education classrooms. The number of students per grade level was 59 kindergarten and 64 first-grade students, ranging from 5 to 8 years of age, with a mean age of 5.58 years.

Measures. The convergent validity of the SAED was assessed by comparing its standard scores with the scores from three of the scales of the Systematic Screening for Behavior Disorders (SSBD; Walker & Severson, 1990). The SSBD is a systematic screening and identification assessment instrument for use in identifying elementary school-age students at risk of school dropout or behavior disorders of an externalizing or internalizing nature. The SSBD consists of three "gates" that provide progressively more intensive levels of screening, whereby only those students meeting or exceeding the predetermined cutoff criteria move on to the next step. At Gate 1, teachers rank-order all the students on their class roster to identify the three students who best evince externalizing characteristics and the three students who best evince internalizing characteristics of behavior disturbance. At Gate 2, teachers complete three scales (Critical Events, Maladaptive Behavior, and Adaptive Behavior)

TABLE 1. LONG-TERM TEST-RETEST RELIABILITY OF THE SCALE
FOR ASSESSING EMOTIONAL DISTURBANCE

	First Testing		Second Testing		
Subscale	**M**	**SD**	**M**	**SD**	**r**
Inability of Learn	9.71	2.09	9.93	2.08	.750
Relationship Problems	9.03	1.88	9.20	1.92	.728
Inappropriate Behavior	10.34	2.03	10.52	2.15	.838
Unhappiness/Depression	8.82	1.56	8.89	1.50	.511
Physical Symptoms/Fears	8.73	1.45	8.87	1.61	.625
Overall Competence	9.54	2.80	10.16	2.99	.818

Note: All correlations were statistically significant at the $p < .001$ level.

on the three highest externalizing and internalizing students identified in Gate 1. The Critical Events checklist includes 33 externalizing (e.g., steals, sets fires) and internalizing (e.g., exhibits painful shyness, exhibits sad affect) items that measure low-frequency, high-intensity behavior problems. The checklist indicates whether the critical event has occurred or not occurred within the last 6 months (Walker & Severson, 1990). The Adaptive Behavior scale includes 12 items that assess teacher-related and peer-related behavioral adjustment (e.g., follows established classroom rules). The Maladaptive Behavior scale includes 11 items that assess teacher-related and peer-related problem behavior (e.g., pouts or sulks). The Adaptive Behavior and Maladaptive Behavior scales measure the frequency of the student's behavior within the last month. Students who exceed the normative criteria on the three scales move on to Gate 3, where direct observations are made of the child's behavior in the classroom and on the playground (Walker & Severson, 1990).

The SSBD was selected to assess the convergent validity of the SAED because of its sound psychometrics. Other researchers have found that the SSBD discriminates between externalizing and internalizing behavior problems and identifies preschool and elementary school students who have or are at risk of severe behavior problems (Feil, Walker, & Severson, 1995; Walker et al., 1994).

Procedure. The ratings were collected in the fall of 1999. Twenty-one general education teachers were trained in administering the SSBD and the SAED. The training involved a 1-hour workshop where the teachers were instructed on the definitions of ED and internalizing and externalizing behavior disorders and on how to read and interpret the instructions for the SAED and SSBD and how to rate each of the items on the scales. The teachers completed the SSBD Gates 1 and 2 as part of the screening process to identify students at risk of ED at the end of October 1999. This process resulted in the teachers' completing the three scales of the SSBD on six students in their class. One week later, they were asked to rate the same six students in their class on the SAED. The SSBD and the SAED were completed on 123 students.

Results and Discussion

Correlations between SAED and SSBD were found to be low, middle, or high across the subscales, ranging from a low of .105 between the SAED subscale of Unhappiness/Depression and the SSBD subscale of Maladaptive Behavior and a high of .810 between the SAED subscale of Inappropriate Behavior and the SSBD subscale of Maladaptive Behavior. Most (16 of 18) of the correlations were statistically significant either at the .01 or .001 level (two-tailed). However, the Overall Competence and Unhappiness/Depression SAED subscales did not show a significant correlation with the Maladaptive Behavior subscale of the SSBD.

For a correlation coefficient to be cited as evidence of validity, it should equal or exceed .35 (Hammill, Brown, & Bryant, 1989). Several of the SAED subscales (i.e., Relationship Problems, Inappropriate Behavior, and Inability to Learn) easily meet this criterion. As would be expected, correlations were strongest between subscales that assessed similar constructs. For example, correlations were highest between SAED Inappropriate Behavior and SSBD Maladaptive Behavior (.810), SAED Relationship Problems and SSBD Critical Events (.700), and SAED Inability to Learn and SSBD Adaptive Behavior (–.540). It is interesting that the other SAED subscales (Overall Competence, Unhappiness/Depression, and Physical Symptoms/Fears) demonstrated low to moderate correlations with the SSBD subscales, although many of these were significant. Given the challenge of assessing internalizing types of emotions and behaviors with a rating scale, the low to moderate correlations were not surprising.

General Discussion

The findings from these investigations into its long-term test-retest reliability and convergent validity strengthen the believability of the Scale for Assessing Emotional Disturbance (Epstein & Cullinan, 1998) as a psychometrically sound instrument for assessing young children with or at risk of ED. The SAED demonstrated significant stability over a 7-month time period. This suggests that teachers and other decision makers can accurately identify areas of emotional or behavioral concern for general education students with the SAED and that those areas of concern that were identified by the SAED are stable over time. The convergent validity of the SAED and the SSBD was less significant.

Several limitations of these studies should be noted. First, these two studies were conducted in a midsized midwestern town. It is possible that the findings may not generalize to other students in other geographical regions or to a national sample. Second, teachers were asked to complete the rating forms on several students at a time, which differs from the situation when a teacher is asked to assess a single student who is being considered for special education services. Third, it is important to recognize that some of the correlations were low and must be interpreted with caution and within the context of other data sources.

Developing effective methods of identifying young children who are at risk of ED is an essential first step for intervening early as emotional or behavioral problems begin to manifest. Early identification can reduce and amend the future adjustment and performance problems of at-risk children. The findings from our studies suggest that the SAED is a reliable instrument that may be useful to educators and school personnel in a number of ways.

To begin with, the SAED can be used as an instrument to help identify young children who may qualify for services under the federal definition of ED. This would be particularly useful for school districts, because the SAED measures ED following federal guidelines. As with any instrument, the SAED should not be the sole determining factor of whether a child qualifies for special education under the ED definition. Using the SAED scores along with other relevant information, such as parent interviews, teacher reports, observations, and other assessment instruments, is an important part of the process of identifying students with ED.

References

Achenbach, T. M. (1991a). *Manual for the Child Behavior Checklist/4–18 and 1991 profile.* Burlington: University of Vermont, Department of Psychiatry.

Achenbach, T. M. (1991b). *Manual for the Teacher's Report Form and 1991 profile.* Burlington: University of Vermont, Department of Psychiatry.

Achenbach, T. M. (1995). Developmental issues in assessment, taxonomy, and diagnosis of child and adolescent psychopathology. In D. Cicchetti & D. J. Cohen (Eds.), *Developmental psychopathology: Volume 1. Theory and methods* (pp. 57–80). New York: Wiley.

American Psychiatric Association. (1994). *Diagnostic and statistical manual of mental disorders* (4th ed.). Washington, DC: Author.

American Psychological Association. (1985). *Standards for educational and psychological testing.* Washington, DC: Author.

Breen, M. J., & Fiedler, C. R. (Eds.). (1996). *Behavioral approach to assessment of youth with emotional/behavioral disorders.* Austin, TX: PRO-ED.

Brown, L., & Hammill, D. R. (1990). *Behavior rating profile.* Austin, TX: PRO-ED.

Cicchetti, D., & Cohen, D. J. (Eds.). (1995a). *Developmental psychopathology: Volume 1. Theory and methods.* New York: Wiley.

Cicchetti, D., & Cohen, D. J. (Eds.). (1995b). *Developmental psychopathology: Volume 2. Risk, disorder, and adaptation.* New York: Wiley.

Coleman, M. C., & Webber, J. (2002). *Emotional and behavioral disorders: Theory and practice* (4th ed.). Boston: Allyn & Bacon.

Crocker, L., & Algina, J. (1986). *Introduction to classical and modern test theory.* New York: Holt, Rinehart & Winston.

Cronbach, L. J. (1951). Coefficient alpha and the internal structure of tests. *Psychometrika, 16,* 297–334.

DelCarmen-Wiggins, R., & Carter, A. S. (2001). Assessment of infant and toddler mental health: Advances and challenges. *Journal of the American Academy of Child and Adolescent Psychiatry, 40*(1), 8–10.

Epstein, M. H., & Cullinan, D. (1998). *Scale for assessing emotional disturbance.* Austin, TX: PRO-ED.

Epstein, M. H., Cullinan, D., Harniss, M. K., & Ryser, G. (1999). The Scale for Assessing Emotional Disturbance: Test-retest and interrater reliability. *Behavioral Disorders, 24,* 222–230.

Feil, E. G., Walker, H. M., & Severson, H. H. (1995). The early screening project for young children with behavior problems. *Journal of Emotional and Behavioral Disorders, 3,* 194–202.

Feil, E. G., Walker, H., Severson, H., & Ball, A. (2000). Proactive screening for emotional/behavioral concerns in Head Start preschools: Promising practices and challenges in applied research. *Behavioral Disorders, 26,* 13–25.

Forness, S. R., & Kavale, K. (2000). Emotional or behavioral disorders: Background and current status of the E/BD terminology definition. *Behavioral Disorders, 25,* 264–269.

Hammill, D. D., Brown, L., & Bryant, B. R. (1989). *A consumer's guide to tests in print.* Austin, TX: PRO-ED.

Hamiss, M. K., Epstein, M. H., Ryser, G., & Pearson, N. (1999). The behavioral and emotional rating scale: Convergent validity. *Journal of Psychoeducational Assessment, 17,* 4–14.

Individuals with Disabilities Education Act Amendments of 1997, 20 U.S.C. 1400 et seq. (1997).

Kauffman, J. (1997). *Characteristics of emotional and behavioral disorders of children and youth* (6th ed.). Columbus, OH: Merrill.

Knitzer, J. (2000). Early childhood mental health services: A policy and systems development perspective. In J. P. Shonkoff & S. J. Meisels (Eds.), *Handbook of early childhood intervention* (2nd ed., pp. 416–438). Cambridge: Cambridge University Press.

Merrell, K. W. (1994). *Assessment of behavioral, social, and emotional problems.* White Plains, NY: Longman.

Merrell, K. W. (1996). Social-emotional assessment in early childhood: The preschool and kindergarten behavior scales. *Journal of Early Intervention, 20*(2), 132–145.

Quay, H. C. (1986). Classification. In H. C. Quay & J. S. Werry (Eds.), *Psychopathological disorders of childhood* (3rd ed., pp. 1–34). New York: Wiley.

Quay, H. C., & Peterson, D. (1996). *Revised Behavior Problem Checklist, PAR edition. Professional manual.* Odessa, FL: Psychological Assessment Resources.

Reynolds, C. R., & Kamphaus, R. W. (1992). *Behavior assessment system for children.* Circle Pines, MN: American Guidance Service.

Salvia, J., & Ysseldyke, J. (1998). *Assessment* (7th ed.). Boston: Houghton Mifflin.

U.S. Bureau of the Census. (1990). *Statistical abstract of the United States.* Washington, DC: Author.

U.S. Department of Education. (1998). *Twentieth annual report to Congress on the implementation of the Individuals with Disabilities Education Act.* Washington, DC: Author.

U.S. Department of Education. (1999). *Digest of education statistics* (NCES Publication No. 2000–031). Washington, DC: National Center for Educational Statistics, Office of Educational Research and Improvement.

Walker, H. M., & Severson, H. H. (1990). *Systematic screening for behavior disorders* (2nd ed.). Longmont, CO: Sopris West.

Walker, H. M., Severson, H. H., Nicholson, F., Kehle, T., Jenson, W. R., & Clark, E. (1994). Replication of the Systematic Screening for Behavior Disorders procedure for the identification of children. *Journal of Emotional and Behavioral Disorders, 2,* 66–77.

Witt, J. C., Elliot, S. N., Kramer, J. J., & Gresham, F. M. (1994). *Assessment of children: Fundamental methods and practices.* Madison, WI: Brown & Benchmark.

REVIEW QUESTIONS

1. Explain convergent validity and how it is used in this study.

2. Why did the researchers need to check for both reliability and validity of the instrument?

3. How was the data gathered for the studies?

Chapter 6: Indexes and Scales

In the last chapter, you learned some of the foundations for **quantitative research.** Quantitative research uses a numerical representation and manipulation of the variables to describe and explain the topic being studied. In this chapter, you will learn how to create reliable **measurement techniques,** so you can transform your concepts into variables. You already know that virtually any social phenomenon can be studied. However, the key to designing a research project is to make sure that you can accurately measure your variables, either directly or indirectly.

A Few More Things to Think About

Before we begin, a few terms and concepts need to be explained. Not all variables are **mutually exclusive,** where they fit neatly into attributes of the variable. For instance, suppose you wanted to know the marital status of your respondents. The **variable** "marital status" would have the attributes of married, divorced, single, widowed and in some cases even cohabitating. Now, if you wanted to ask a question about the variable "religion," you might not want to list all the possibilities. Instead, you may have an **exhaustive** attributes list where you list only the most common religions such as Jewish, Catholic, and Methodist. You can also add "other" to the list and allow your respondents to fill in their own religions.

What happens, however, if the variable you are measuring isn't as easy to measure as the two previous examples? Let me give you an example. Many of my students are very concerned with their grades. In fact, some don't want to take a research methods course, and even avoid taking it until their senior years, because they don't want it to hurt their grade point average (GPA). Well, I always ask them how they define "success" in a class. How do you define it? Is it based only on your GPA? For some, it might be. However, I would **operationalize** the abstract concept of "success" in other ways, as well. In fact, I would operationalize "success" as a student who understands the definitions taught in class and knows how to put those concepts to use in his or her own research project. So, what kinds of response would I get if I asked my students, "Are you successful in this research methods class?" Unless I have operationalized success for them, their definitions might be different from each other's and my definition. So, based on my definition of success, I might ask them a few questions such as, "What was your last test grade in the class?," "Define an independent variable and a dependent variable," "Design an experiment and state the hypothesis and the variables that you would use." If students can do all of these things, then they fit into my definition of the concept of "success." But there is more to think about than just asking a few questions.

SCALES AND INDEXES

Scales and **indexes** are often interchanged and therefore can be confusing. Both give re-searchers information about the variables they are studying and make it possible to as-sess the quality of the measurement. Scales and indexes tend to increase **reliability** and **validity,** as we learned in the previous chapter, while they condense and simplify the data that is collected. An *index* is a combination of items into a single numerical score. This score is obtained when various parts of the construct are each measured and then com-bined into one measure. For example, *U.S. News and World Report* evaluates Ph.D. pro-grams in five major disciplines almost every year. They rank the programs using objective measures such as the entering students' test scores, faculty/student ratio, and reputation ratings from both inside and outside of academia. Various people also judge the overall academic quality of the programs on a scale of 1 (marginal) to 5 (distinguished). Once all the indicators are measured, researchers re-scale the final score to rank each of the pro-grams (Garrett, Morse, & Flanigan, 1999). If you visit the *U.S. News and World Report* Web site http://www.usnews.com/usnews/edu/grad/rankings/rankindex.htm you will see that in 1998 the top ten Ph.D. programs in Sociology were as follows:

University of Wisconsin—Madison	4.8
University of California—Berkeley	4.7
University of Chicago	4.7
University of Michigan—Ann Arbor	4.5
University of North Carolina—Chapel Hill	4.5
University of California—Los Angeles	4.3
Harvard University (MA)	4.2
Stanford University (CA)	4.2
Princeton University (NJ)	4.1
Northwestern University (IL)	4.0

Scales refer to a special type of measurement, where the numbers are assigned to positions that indicate varying degrees of the variable being considered. In other words, scales can measure the intensity or pattern of a response along a continuum and are often used when the researcher wants to measure the respondents' feelings about something. For instance, in a study to assess the associations between quality of life and attitudes to-ward sexual activities in adolescence, *The Comprehensive Quality of Life Scale* was used. This scale measured students' objective and subjective quality of life in seven areas: mate-rial well-being (possessions), health, productivity, intimacy, safety, place in the community, and emotional well-being. Subjective quality of life was assessed on two dimensions: satis-faction (responses were made on a 7-point scale ranging from delighted to terrible) and im-portance (responses were made on a 5-point Likert scale ranging from could not be more important to not at all important).

The **Likert Scale** is one of the most common scales, and one you have probably even seen. This scale was developed in the 1930s by Rensis Likert and asks the respondent to indicate whether they agree or disagree with a statement. For example, you may have completed a student evaluation where you rate your professor at the end of a semester. The evaluations at my school look like this:

Overall, how would you rate the teaching in this course?

A = Superior

B = Above Average

C = Average

D = Below Average

E = Unsatisfactory

The **Bogardus Social Distance Scale** measures the social distance separating groups from one another. Emory Bogardus developed the scale in the 1920s to measure the willingness of members from one ethnic group to associate with members of another ethnic group. Other groups can include religious, political, or deviant groups. This scale assumes that a person who refuses contact or is uncomfortable around a person from the group in question will answer negatively as the items move closer. For instance, you might ask the question, "Do you like getting to know people from other cultures?" The individual you asked might say "no." However, using the Bogardus social distance scale, you could use the following series of questions:

Please state yes or no to the following statements about how comfortable you would be having a person from (another country):

_____ As a student enrolled in your college

_____ As a student in your class

_____ As a student sitting next to you in class

_____ As a student living in the same dorm as you do

_____ As your roommate

If you find your respondents begin answering no as the questions become closer in proximity, then you might see that the respondents are uncomfortable with people from other countries as they get closer to them.

The **semantic differential** is very similar to the Likert scale because it asks the respondents to choose between two opposite positions. For instance, LaRocca and Kromrey (1999) investigated the perceptions of sexual harassment of 296 students as well as perceptions of both perpetrator and victim character traits. The students were asked to read a scenario and describe behavior and character traits for perpetrator and victim using a seven-point semantic differential scale. An example of some of their opposites were as follows:

	Very Much	Somewhat	Neither	Somewhat	Very Much	
Weak	❏	❏	❏	❏	❏	Strong
Naïve	❏	❏	❏	❏	❏	Sophisticated
Powerful	❏	❏	❏	❏	❏	Powerless
Insincere	❏	❏	❏	❏	❏	Sincere
Hostile	❏	❏	❏	❏	❏	Friendly

Having students rate these opposites showed that female students perceived the scenario as more sexually harassing than male students, even though both men and women judged female perpetrators less harshly than male perpetrators. Furthermore, LaRocca and Kromrey found that both men and women were influenced by perpetrator attractiveness and they perceived an attractive opposite gender perpetrator as less harassing than a same gender attractive perpetrator.

COMPUTERS TO ANALYZE DATA

Currently, one of the most common ways to analyze data is by using the computer. Many different computer programs are available for both qualitative and quantitative analysis. Some of the programs might already be on your computer if you have Microsoft Office, with Word, Excel, and PowerPoint. These programs can do some simple calculations and allow you to work with text and graphics, while storing large quantities of verbal and quantitative data. However, beyond the capabilities of these programs, you might need to get involved in some of the more specifically designed programs for data analysis such as MicroCase, SAS, STATA, or SPSS, which is the most popular. To get a better idea about using statistical programs in social science research you might refer to some of the following books:

1. *Adventures in social research: Data analysis using SPSS for Windows 95/98* by Earl Babbie, Fred Halley, and Jeanne Zaino. 2000. Thousand Oaks, CA: Pine Forge Press.

2. *SPSS for Windows step by step: A simple guide and reference, 11.0 update* by Darren George and Paul Mallery. 2003. Boston: Allyn & Bacon.

3. *Data analysis using SPSS for Windows: A beginner's guide* by Jeremy J. Foster. 1998. London: Thousand Oaks, CA: Sage.

4. *Using SPSS for Windows and Macintosh: Analyzing and understanding data* by Samual Green, and Neil Salkind. 2003.Upper Saddle River, NJ: Prentice Hall.

REFERENCES

Garrett, G., Morse, R. J., & Flanigan, S. M. 1999. How we rank graduate schools. *U.S. News and World Report,* [ONLINE] http://www.usnews.com/usnews/edu/beyond/gradrank/gbrank.htm

LaRocca, M. A., & Kromrey, J. D. 1999. The perception of sexual harassment in higher education: Impact of gender and attractiveness. *Sex Roles: A Journal of Research,* 40 (11): 921.

INFOTRAC COLLEGE EDITION SUGGESTED READINGS AND DISCUSSION QUESTIONS

1. Type the words "Survey Design" into InfoTrac College Edition. You should come up with several articles. Read some of them and see if you can locate how they talk about their survey instruments. How was their survey distributed? Did they do follow-up mailings? What were the results?

2. Make a spreadsheet with the following headings: (1) Subjects, (2) Age range of subjects, (3) Distribution method used, (4) Subject of study, (5) Response rate. After locating the following articles and filling in the information under the appropriate heading for each article, can you make any statement about what subjects and which methods result in the highest response rate?

   Prenatal consultation: Role and Perspective of the Pediatric Surgeon

   Sexuality of the Spina Bifida Male: Anonymous Questionnaires of Function and Knowledge

   No Exit? The Effect of Health Status on Dissatisfaction and Disenrollment from Health Plans

   Alcohol Use and Psychosocial Well-Being among Older Adults

   Soft Drink Consumption among U.S. Children and Adolescents: Nutritional Consequences

3. Find five more articles on your own by typing "Response rate" into InfoTrac College Edition, and add them to your spreadsheet.

ENVIRONMENTAL WASTE: RECYCLING ATTITUDES AND CORRELATES

Knud S. Larsen

In this article, a Likert-type scale was developed and used to measure attitudes toward recycling among 452 male and female undergraduates. The instrument had high correlations and satisfactory reliability. There was a predictable relationship between attitudes toward recycling and attitudes toward environmental issues, rights issues, and political participation. As you are reading this article, think about why the author used a Likert scale and ask yourself if any other scale would have been better or useful.

Solutions to the increasingly serious problem of environmental waste in the United States are at least partially dependent on attitudes about recycling. In their comprehensive review of the literature, Van Liere and Dunlap (1980) concluded that positive attitudes and behaviors regarding recycling are most prevalent among people who are young, politically liberal, and from large households. These findings have also been supported by the studies of Samdahl and Robertson (1989) and by that of Howenstein (1993), although Howenstein concluded that there is considerable recycling potential in almost all demographic groups, provided there is sufficient motivation.

Knud S. Larsen, "Environmental waste: Recycling attitudes and correlates," *Journal of Social Psychology,* 135(1), 1995, pp. 83–89. Reprinted with permission of the Helen Dwight Reid Educational Foundation. Published by Heldref Publications, 1319 Eighteenth St., NW, Washington DC 20036-1802. Copyright © 1995.

That environmental awareness and a sense that the environment is personally relevant lead to an increased incidence of recycling has been documented in a number of studies. Baldassare and Katz (1992) noted that perceived environmental threat is highest among younger respondents, women, liberals, and Democrats, but that those most likely to recycle perceive environmental waste as a serious threat to their personal health and well-being. The relationship between recycling and environmental awareness and personal relevance has also been demonstrated by Lansana (1992). Oskamp, Harrington, Edwards, and Sherwood (1991) found that demographic variables did not predict participation in recycling programs but that knowledge about environmental conservation did. Owning a house and intrinsic motives to recycle were also related to recycling behavior (Oskamp et al., 1991; Lansana, 1992).

Simmons and Widmar (1990) found that recyclers were more likely than nonrecyclers to believe in environmental conservation and to feel personally responsible for the condition of the environment but that such positive attitudes may not result in recycling if knowledge about recycling is lacking. Likewise, Vining and Ebreo (1992, 1994) found that recyclers' behavior was motivated more by concern about the environment than by financial incentives or other rewards. Thus, environmental awareness and a sense of personal responsibility for the environment are critical to a successful recycling program.

Positive attitudes about recycling may also be related to other environmentally relevant attitudes, such as negative attitudes toward transporting nuclear waste on the nation's highways (Larsen, 1994a) or positive attitudes toward protecting the depleted salmon runs in the Pacific Northwest (Larsen, 1994b). People who have positive attitudes toward recycling tend to be politically liberal. Thus positive attitudes toward recycling may be correlated with the protection of prisoners' rights and positive attitudes toward birth control.

Because the aforementioned studies (which yielded relationships between environmental awareness, attitudes, and recycling behavior) were based on survey questions, it was not possible to evaluate reliability and validity. In addition, whereas previous research indicates only tendencies and individual differences, researchers need to explore deviations from central tendencies and to assess group differences more adequately. With these goals in mind, I developed a Likert-type scale to measure attitudes toward recycling environmental waste.

Method

A total of 452 undergraduates (195 men, 257 women) at Oregon State University participated in the five phases of the study. The participants' mean age was 21.22 years. The scales I used in the five phases of the present study were of the Likert type and were administered with the usual instructions.

Phase 1: Item Analyses. The item pool consisted of 81 statements, 40 keyed in a positive direction and 41 in a negative direction. The statements were edited independently by a five-person research team, using Edwards's (1957) a priori criteria for unidimensional statements. The item pool was administered to 49 male and 51 female undergraduates (mean age = 20.80). Item analysis yielded 20 items (10 positive, 10 negative).

Attitudes Toward Recycling (ATR) Scale and Part-Whole Correlations

Part-Whole Items	Statement correlation + /–
1. I only generate a small amount of waste, so I don't believe I am responsible for clean up.	.81–
2. I would recycle magazines.	.76 +
3. We should not clean up all waste disposal sites.	.75–
4. Enough is being done to clean up the environment.	.75–
5. The world's oceans are not in need of cleaning up by people.	.74–
6. Recycling is too much of a hassle to bother with.	.73–
7. People should share the responsibility of cleaning up the environment.	.72 +
8. I would recycle plastics.	.72 +
9. I would take an active role in recycling.	.71 +
10. I see no reason to recycle.	.70–
11. I would take advantage of recycling programs available to me.	.70 +
12. I think all packaging, no matter what the cost, should be recyclable.	.70 +
13. I would recycle even if pick up services for recycling were not available.	.69 +
14. Some people exaggerate the true amount of pollution in the world.	.69–
15. Non-recycled waste created in the past is not an issue worth addressing.	.68–
16. I would use water saving devices in my home.	.68 +
17. If I were asked to volunteer for a clean up group, I would.	.67 +
18. I would use phosphate free laundry detergent.	.67 +
19. I would not vote in favor of a measure to ban Styrofoam packaging.	.67–
20. I see no purpose in sorting garbage.	.67–

Phase 2: Reliability and Construct Validity—Attitudes Toward the Transportation of Nuclear Waste and Pro-Environmental Paradigms. A survey consisting of (a) the 20-item Attitudes Toward Recycling (ATR) Scale, (b) the 12-item Pro-Environment Scale (Dunlap & Van Liere, 1978), and (c) 30 items pertaining to attitudes toward the transportation of nuclear waste (Larsen, 1994b) was administered to 50 male and 50 female undergraduates (mean age = 21.50).

Phase 3: Attitudes Toward Recycling and the Preservation of River Salmon. Two separate surveys were conducted. In the first survey a 20-item scale about attitudes toward declining salmon runs (Larsen, 1994b) was administered with the ATR Scale. The survey was administered to 39 male and 41 female undergraduates (mean age = 20.95). In a separate study the ATR Scale and the Salmon Run (SR) scale were included in a survey along with a 21-item scale that measured attitudes toward political participation (Milbrath, 1968; Johnson, 1981). The respondents were 45 male and 65 female undergraduates (mean age = 19.30).

Phase 4: Attitudes Toward Recycling and Prisoners' Rights. This survey included the ATR Scale and a 20-item scale that measured prisoners' rights (Larsen, 1994b). The respondents were 18 male and 62 female undergraduates (mean age = 20.75).

Phase 5: Attitudes Toward Recycling and Birth Control. The ATR Scale was combined with Wilke's (1967) 22-item Birth Control Scale. The respondents were 43 male and 35 female undergraduates (mean age = 23.41).

Discussion

The results indicated that the ATR Scale had satisfactory internal homogeneity and moderate construct validity coefficients, findings that support the use of this scale in environmental research aimed at understanding attitudes toward recycling. The 20 items selected from the item pool had moderate to high part-whole correlations and an impressive corrected Spearman-Brown coefficient.

The ATR Scale was significantly correlated with scales measuring other environmental issues, supporting the notion of a coherent basis for environmental attitudes. People who favored recycling were also opposed to the transportation of nuclear waste on the nation's highways. Other environmental issues correlated with positive attitudes toward recycling were general pro-environmental attitudes, a desire to protect depleted salmon runs in the Pacific Northwest, and positive attitudes toward birth control.

Almost all the items in the ATR might be useful in other Western countries, but comparative testing is needed. In addition, some of the findings, such as those regarding the salmon runs, are more salient in the Pacific Northwest. Whether the present findings and the ATR Scale might also be useful elsewhere in the world must also be determined.

Finally, the relationship between positive attitudes toward recycling, political participation, and prisoners' rights suggest that there is a connectedness between positive environmental attitudes, personal responsibility, and broader social concern.

References

Baldassare, M., & Katz, C. (1992). The personal threat of environmental problems as predictor of environmental practices. *Environment and Behavior,* 24(5), 602–616.

Dunlap, R. E., & Van Liere, K. D. (1978). The "new environmental paradigm." *Journal of Environmental Education,* 9(4), 10–19.

Edwards, A. L. (1957). *Techniques of attitude scale construction.* New York: Appleton-Century-Crofts.

Howenstein, E. (1993). Market segmentation for recycling. *Environment and Behavior,* 25, 86–102.

Johnson, E. S. (1981). *Research methods in criminology and criminal justice.* Englewood Cliffs: NJ: Prentice-Hall.

Lansana, F. M. (1992). Distinguishing potential recyclers from nonrecyclers: A basis for developing recycling strategies. *Journal of Environmental Education,* 23(2), 16–23.

Larsen, K. S. (1994a). Attitudes about the transportation of nuclear waste: The development of a Likert scale. *Journal of Social Psychology,* 134, 27–34.

Larsen, K. S. (1994b). *Unpublished environmental scales.* Corvallis: Oregon State University.

Milbrath, L. (1968). The nature of political beliefs and the relationship of the individual to government. *American Behavioral Scientist,* 12, 28–34.

Oskamp, S., Harrington, M. J., Edwards, T. C., & Sherwood, D. I. (1991). Factors influencing household recycling behavior. *Environment and Behavior,* 23(24), 494–519.

Samdahl, D. M., & Robertson, R. (1989). Social determinants of environmental concern: Specification and test of the model. *Environment and Behavior,* 21, 57–81.

Simmons, D., & Widmar, R. (1990). Motivations and barriers to recycling: Toward a strategy for public education. *Journal of Environmental Education,* 22(1), 13–18.

Van Liere, K. D., & Dunlap, R. E. (1980). Environmental concern: A review of hypotheses, explanations, and empirical evidence. *Public Opinion Quarterly,* 44, 181–197.

Vining, J., & Ebreo, A. (1992). Predicting recycling behavior from global and specific environmental attitudes and changes in recycling opportunities. *Journal of Applied Social Psychology,* 20, 1580–1607.

Vining, J., & Ebreo, A. (1994). What makes a recycler? A comparison of recyclers and nonrecyclers. *Environment and Behavior,* 22(1), 55–73.

Wilke, W. H. (1967). Birth Control Scale. In M. E. Shaw & J. M. Wright (eds.), *Scales for the measurement of attitudes* (pp. 136–137). New York: McGraw-Hill.

REVIEW QUESTIONS

1. What is a Likert scale? Why was it used in this study?

2. What is the Attitudes Toward Recycling (ATR) Scale? What does it measure?

3. What was the relationship between positive attitudes toward recycling and other environmental issues?

THE REVERSE SOCIAL DISTANCE SCALE

Motoko Y. Lee, Stephen G. Sapp, and Melvin C. Ray

These researchers created a "reverse" Social Distance Scale by modifying Bogardus's Social Distance Scale to measure minority groups' perceptions of the social distance established by the majority group between itself and minority groups. As you read this article, notice the reasons that using a reverse social distance scale can affect the number of respondents who were willing to answer the survey.

Motoko Y. Lee, Stephen G. Sapp, and Melvin C. Ray, "The Reverse Social Distance Scale," *Journal of Social Psychology,* 136 (1), 1996, pp. 17–25. Reprinted with permission of the Helen Dwight Reid Educational Foundation. Published by Heldref Publications, 1319 Eighteenth St., NW, Washington, DC 20036-1802. Copyright © 1996.

The social distance between a minority group and the majority group—the most powerful group, but not necessarily the largest—has been postulated by the present authors to be based on the minority group's reaction to its perceived rejection or acceptance by the majority group, rather than on the majority group's reaction to the minority group. Thus, Bogardus's Social Distance Scale (1925), which was created from the perspective of the majority group, cannot be used to explain the nature of this type of social distance. To assess a minority group's perceptions of the distance established by the majority group between itself and the minority group (rather than the distance a minority group has established between itself and the majority group), researchers need a different type of measure.

The literature contains no mention of such a scale, and although numerous accounts of minority perceptions of prejudice appear in the writings of W. E. B. Du Bois (Weinberg, 1992) and others (e.g., Cleaver, 1967; Finkenstaedt, 1994; Grier, 1968; Silberman, 1964; West, 1993), such accounts tend to be qualitative. A review of the following studies provides additional evidence of the need for a "reverse" Social Distance Scale.

Netting (1991) reported that Chinese immigrants in Canada tended to reject Whites and other groups instead of seeking acceptance from them. "Anglos would accept Poles, the only white minority represented in the study, and Chinese. However, Chinese would not accept Anglos" (p. 101). If the goal is understanding a minority viewpoint, then it is more important to assess the distance perceived by the Chinese immigrants as having been created by the White Canadians than it is to assess the actual social distance between the two groups, because the former perspective is that of the minority group. Left unanswered by Netting's study was the question of whether the Chinese and the Polish immigrants' perceptions of acceptance by the Anglos were the same or similar.

Muir and Muir (1988) used Bogardus's Social Distance Scale in their study of White and Black middle-school children from the Deep South. These researchers found that, by their early teens, most of the White children had adopted an adult pattern of relating to Blacks, consisting of civil acceptance and social rejection, whereas a majority of Black children accepted Whites socially as well as publicly. The Black middle-school students were found to be more tolerant of the White middle-school students than the White students were of the Black students. The Black children's perception of the extent of their social acceptance by the White children—a factor that would have provided more information about the Black children's acceptance of the White children—was not examined.

McAllister and Moore (1991) used Bogardus's Social Distance Scale in Australia to measure majority and minority groups' perceptions of social distance from each other. McAllister and Moore attempted to explain the variation in the groups' perceptions without considering the conditional nature of the social distance established by the minority groups between themselves and the majority group. The factors that were considered by McAllister and Moore accounted for very little of the variation in social distance that was created by the two immigrant minority groups—far less than the amount of variation that was accounted for in relation to the Australian majority group ([R.sup.2] = .02 for the combined European immigrant group and .01 for the Southeast Asian group vs. .11 for the Australians, 1991, p. 100).

Tuch (1988, p. 184) tried to account for the variation in social distance among Blacks and Whites toward each other's groups, using several socioeconomic predictors. As in McAllister and Moore's study, the variables that were selected explained considerably less about the Blacks' social distance from the Whites (7%) than about the Whites' social distance from the Blacks (27%).

Wilson (1986) observed that studies addressing the correlates of Blacks' racial distance preferences have been few, and their results, inconsistent. In addition, Wilson observed that social variables predicted the social distance preferred by Blacks much more poorly than they predicted the social distance preferred by Whites.

The common finding in these studies—that the selected variables explained Blacks' preference for social distance toward Whites more poorly than they explained Whites' preference for social distance toward Blacks—suggests that important explanatory variables that would account for the social distance preferences of minority groups toward the majority group were lacking in this research. To explain the minority variation in social distance, researchers need a measure of the minority's perception of the social distance established by the majority group between itself and the minority group, because this perception is assumed to be the basis upon which minorities will establish their preferred social distance from the majority group. Even Bogardus (1959, p. 77), in his study of factors that would determine the distance between nations, called people of other nations' friendliness and open-heartedness the "nearness factors."

Method

Our objectives in the present study were to assess the feasibility of a "reverse" Social Distance Scale, to determine whether such a scale would differentiate among different minority groups, and to revise the scale, if necessary, based on participants' responses. We mailed a questionnaire to approximately 1,000 minority students (U.S. citizens and permanent residents) at a state university in the spring of 1993. We received 108 completed and usable questionnaires. The present results, although not generalizable, were satisfactory in light of our objectives.

The extremely low return rate for the questionnaire was probably a reflection of indifference to or avoidance of the topic of rejection/acceptance by the majority group. Responding to our Reverse Social Distance Scale may have been difficult for certain minorities. Several students, all of whom were Black, returned the questionnaire without having answered the Reverse Social Distance Scale question. These students wrote comments such as, "Do not ask these questions. I am an American" or "This type of question perpetuates the division between whites and blacks." If, as we suspect, this type of reaction was common among those who did not return their questionnaires, then the nonparticipants' perceptions about rejection/acceptance by the majority group may have differed from those of the participants. This possibility was not explored in the present study but should be investigated.

We created the Reverse Social Distance Scale by modifying the items on Bogardus's Racial Distance Scale (Miller, 1991, p. 382). The proposed scale items (distance criteria) were as similar as possible to those on Bogardus's scale, but we did make some modifications so that the items would appear realistic to college students. In contrast to Bogardus's scale, which assesses respondents' willingness to accept members of other groups in various roles (e.g., as a fellow citizen, as a neighbor), the Reverse Social Distance Scale assesses respondents' perceptions of how other groups accept them in these roles.

Items that were likely to have been experienced by college students were phrased "Do they mind . . . ?," and the other items as "Would they . . . ?" The items and the instructions for the Reverse Social Distance Scale were as follows:

Considering typical Caucasian Americans you have known, not any specific person nor the worst or the best, circle Y or N to express your opinion.

Y N 5. Do they mind your being a citizen in this country?
Y N 4. Do they mind your living in the same neighborhood?
Y N 3. Would they mind your living next to them?
Y N 2. Would they mind your becoming a close friend to them?
Y N 1. Would they mind your becoming their kin by marriage?

We did not include Bogardus's Social Distance Scale in the present study because we wanted to avoid any contamination that might result from the use of Bogardus's scale and the Reverse Social Distance Scale on the same questionnaire. We did include the Twenty Statements Test (TST; Kuhn & McPartland, 1954), however; the respondents were asked to write 20 responses (at most) to the question "Who am I?"

Results

The aggregated data for the three groups are reported in Table 1. The category entitled other minorities included diverse groups, such as Japanese Americans, Chinese Americans, Native Americans, and other Americans, whose ancestors had immigrated from countries such as India, Sri Lanka, Vietnam, and Laos. These groups were combined into one because none of them was large enough to be considered individually in the analysis.

The results indicated that there was a significant difference among the three means. The African American students' mean score was significantly higher than those of the other two groups, indicating that, on average, the African American students perceived the distance established by the Caucasian Americans to be greater than the other two groups did. The latter two groups did not differ significantly from each other. The reason we conducted these tests of significance was to determine the magnitude of the differences in the sample, not to make generalizations about the results.

Although the scale's coefficient was high enough to be acceptable, we examined a few cases in which the responses seemed contradictory and used the respondents' comments to revise the instructions for the scale and the wording of some items. The original version of the instructions contained the adjective "typical" (Bogardus used "stereotypic"), but one respondent criticized this term as stereotyping. Because the purpose of the scale is to assess perceptions of the distance associated with the collective majority group, or the generalized other of that group, not perceptions of the distance associated with specific individuals in that group, we recommend that future researchers use the word "most," instead of "typical" or "stereotypic," in the instructions to the scale.

There were also some contradictions with regard to the responses for the citizenship item. A few persons perceived that Caucasian Americans minded having them as fellow citizens even though the Caucasian Americans did not mind them living in the same neighborhood. These participants may have equated the concept of citizenship with rights and duties and, therefore, have viewed it as encompassing more than living in the same

TABLE 1. ANALYSIS OF VARIANCE RESULTS

Group	N	M	SD
African Americans	48	3.65	1.74
Hispanic Americans	25	1.60	1.12
Other minorities *	35	1.80	1.80

Between groups: F(2, 105) = 23.8, p = .001

Note: Means with different subscripts differ significantly at .05.

* This category included Japanese Americans, Chinese Americans, Native Americans, and Americans whose ancestors had come from India, Sri Lanka, Vietnam, and Laos.

community. Although the citizenship item was included in Bogardus's scale, future researchers would do better to replace this item with one that pertains to a simpler concept, such as living in the same community.

We examined TST responses for the students whose scores were at either end of our scale: strong acceptance (1) or strong rejection (6). Eleven of the 48 African American students received a score of 6; of these 11 students, 6 used "African" or "Black" as their first identifier, 1 used this type of label as his or her 19th identifier, and 4 did not use a racial identifier. Six African American students received a score of 1; of these 6 students, 3 used a racial identifier in their first response to the TST, and the other 3 did not use a racial identifier at all.

None of the 25 Hispanic students received a score of 6, but 17 received a score of 1.

Of these 17 students, 4 used an ethnic identifier in their 2nd, 5th, 6th, or 15th response, and the remaining 13 did not use an ethnic identifier.

Of the 35 (predominantly Asian) students in the Other Minorities group, only 1 received a score of 6. This participant used a racial identifier in his or her fourth response. Eighteen of the students in the Other Minorities group scored 1; of these students, 10 did not use a racial/ethnic identifier, 6 used a racial/ethnic identifier in their first response, 1 used a racial/ethnic identifier in his or her second response, and 1 used a racial/ethnic identifier in his or her ninth response.

Discussion

The Reverse Social Distance Scale assesses minority groups' perceptions of the social distance established by the majority group between itself and minority groups. The scale differentiated between the African American students and the other two minority groups, Hispanics and Other Minorities, in the present study, but not between the latter two groups.

Researchers (McAllister & Moore, 1991, pp. 96–97) have discussed several alternatives that might account for social distance, including social learning theory (Allport, 1954), theory focusing on social experience of education (Harding, Proshansky, Kutner,

& Chein, 1969), economic competition theory (Baker, 1978), contact theory (Tajfel, 1982), and the theory of authoritarian personality (Adorno, Frenkel-Brunswik, Levinson, & Sanford, 1950). However, these theories seem to be more applicable to majority group prejudice toward minority groups than to minority group prejudice toward the majority group.

Researchers have tended to ignore the influence of minority group perceptions regarding their acceptance or rejection by the majority group on the degree of social distance minority groups establish between themselves and the majority group. As Walsh (1990) indicated, researchers (e.g., Griffitt & Veitch, 1974; Van den Berghe, 1981) have recognized the role of the majority group's acceptance or rejection of minority groups on the social distance between the majority and minorities; nevertheless, Bogardus's Social Distance Scale has continued to be researchers' (e.g., Walsh's) major tool.

We assumed that minority groups in multiethnic or multiracial societies do not isolate themselves by choice, but prefer to be accepted by the majority group and to have equal access to resources and rewards. We also assumed that minority group members perceive a social distance that has been established by the majority group, between their own group and the majority group, even though minority groups' perception of this distance may differ from that of the majority group. The social distance minority groups perceive as having been established by the majority group influences the degree of social distance the minority group will establish between itself and the majority group; therefore, we expected the relationship between the Reverse Social Distance Scale and Bogardus's Social Distance Scale to be positive. We did not explore this relationship, however, because we did not include Bogardus's Social Distance Scale in the present study, to avoid any contamination of the results.

Tajfel and Turner (1986) suggested that self-identification with one's own-group is dependent upon one's evaluation of the comparisons between one's own-group and outgroups, regarding the attributes and characteristics that are valued by one's own-group. These researchers posited that members of a group whose social identity is not satisfactory will either try to improve their group's identity or leave their present group to join a group whose identity is more positive. Thus, the member of a minority group's perceived rejection or acceptance by the majority group is likely to affect the way this individual feels about the social identity of his or her own-group.

In line with Tajfel and Turner's reasoning, we examined the responses of the highest and lowest scorers on the Reverse Social Distance Scale. Six of the 11 respondents who received a score of 6 (strongest perceived rejection) used a racial/ethnic identifier in their 1st response to the TST. These participants (the first category described by Tajfel and Turner, 1986) would be likely to distance themselves from the majority and to try to establish their own separate identities. The participants who used a racial identifier in their 19th TST response and the 4 participants who did not use a racial identifier at all would be likely to try to establish their own separate self-identity or to find another group to identify with (Tajfel and Turner's second category).

The 41 respondents who received a score of 1 (strongest perceived acceptance) would be unlikely to distance themselves from the majority. Four respondents used a racial/ethnic identifier in their 5th, 6th, 9th, or 15th response on the TST, and 26 did not use a racial/ethnic identifier at all. The 14 respondents who used a racial/ethnic identifier in their 1st or 2nd response to the TST might distance themselves from the majority group to the extent that they would prefer to limit intimate relationships (i.e., mate, kin) to members of their own-groups.

The relationship between the participants' scores on the Reverse Social Distance Scale and their choices of self-identifiers provided some insight about the possible effect of minority groups' perceptions of the social distance established by the majority group on minority group members' self-concept. More research is needed, however, to explore the consequences of minority groups' perceptions of social distance for the degree of social distance minority groups establish between themselves and the majority group, as well as the consequences of these perceptions for minority groups' self-concept.

References

Adorno, T. W., Frenkel-Brunswik, E., Levinson, D. J., & Sanford, R. N. (1950). *The authoritarian personality.* New York: Harper.

Allport, G. W. (1954). *The nature of prejudice.* Reading, MA: Addison-Wesley.

Baker, D. (1978). Race and power: Comparative approaches to the analysis of race relations. *Ethnic and Racial Studies, 1,* 316–335.

Bogardus, E. S. (1925). Measuring social distance. *Journal of Applied Sociology, 9,* 299–308.

Bogardus, E. S. (1959). *Social distance.* Yellow Spring, OH: Artichild.

Cleaver, E. (1967). *Soul on ice.* New York: McGraw-Hill.

Finkenstaedt, R. L. H. (1994). *Face-to-face: Blacks in America, White perceptions and Black realities.* New York: William Morrow.

Grier, W. H. (1968). *Black rage.* New York: Basic Books.

Griffitt, W., & Veitch, R. (1974). Preacquaintance attitude similarity and attraction revisited: Ten days in a fallout shelter. *Sociometry, 37,* 163–178.

Harding, J., Proshansky, H., Kutner, B., & Chein, I. (1969). Prejudice and ethnic relations. In G. Lindzey & E. Aronson (Eds.) *Handbook of social psychology* (2nd ed., Vol. 5, pp. 1–76). Reading, MA: Addison-Wesley.

Kuhn, M. H., & McPartland, T. S. (1954). An empirical investigation of self-attitudes. *American Sociological Review, 19,* 68–76.

McAllister, I., & Moore, R. (1991). Social distance among Australian ethnic groups. *Sociology and Social Research, 75,* 95–100.

Miller, D. C. (1991). *Handbook of research design and social measurement* (5th ed.). Newbury Park, CA: Sage.

Muir, D. E., & Muir, L. W. (1988). Social distance between Deep-South middle-school Whites and Blacks. *Sociology and Social Research, 72,* 177–180.

Netting, N. S. (1991). Chinese aloofness from other groups: Social distance data from a city in British Columbia. *Sociology and Social Research, 75,* 101–103.

Silberman, C. E. (1964). *Crisis in Black and White.* New York: Random House.

Tajfel, H. (1982). *Social identity and intergroup relations.* Cambridge: Cambridge University Press.

Tajfel, H., & Turner, J. C. (1986). The social identify theory of intergroup behavior. In S. Worchel & W. G. Austin (Eds.), *Psychology of intergroup relations* (pp. 7–24). Chicago: Nelson-Hall.

Tuch, S. A. (1988). Race differences in the antecedents of social distance attitudes. *Sociology and Social Research, 72,* 181–184.

Van den Berghe, P. (1981). *The ethnic phenomenon.* New York: Elsevier.

Walsh, A. (1990). Becoming an American and liking it as functions of social distance and severity of initiation. *Sociological Inquiry, 60,* 177–189.

Weinberg, M., (Ed.). (1992). *The words of W. E. B. Du Bois: A quotation sourcebook.* Westport, CT: Greenwood.

West, C. (1993). *Race matters.* Boston: Beacon.

Wilson, T. C. (1986). The asymmetry of racial distance between Blacks and Whites. *Sociology and Social Research, 70,* 161–163.

REVIEW QUESTIONS

1. Explain why the "reverse" Social Distance Scale was created?

2. What were the findings from this project?

3. What is the difference between the social distance of minorities and that of majorities? Explain them.

BIAS TOWARDS GAY PATIENTS BY PSYCHOANALYTIC CLINICIANS: AN EMPIRICAL INVESTIGATION

Arthur H. Lilling and Richard C. Friedman

In this study, matched vignettes were used to investigate the attitudes and the clinical assessment of psychoanalysts toward gay patients. The analysts rated their reactions on the Semantic Differential to homosexual and heterosexual patients with identical histories. They also rated what they perceived as the degree of impairment in psychological functioning on the Global Assessment of Functioning and made a DSM-III-R diagnosis based on the vignettes. The results in this study indicated that psychoanalysts maintained a subtle, yet significant negative bias toward homosexual patients, particularly those that have serious psychopathology and a negative bias toward the mentally ill in general. Watch for the way the scale was used in this survey and how the researchers used the vignettes.

Lilling, H., & Friedman, R. C. 1995. Bias towards gay patients by psychoanalytic clinicians: An empirical investigation. *Archives of Sexual Behavior,* 24 (5): 563–571. Reprinted with permission from Kluwer Academic/Plenum Publishers.

Introduction

Much ambiguity and conflict about human sexual orientation exists among contemporary mental health professionals. One reason for this is that models of psychological development and functioning have probably altered more radically in recent years with regard to homosexuality, heterosexuality, and bisexuality (however these are defined) than any other form of human behavior.

During the period between World War II and the publication of DSM-III (American Psychiatric Association [APA], 1980), homosexuality was equated with psychopathology in keeping with what was then a generally accepted psychoanalytic perspective (Lewes, 1988; Bayer, 1981). According to this paradigm, successful resolution of oedipal and pre-oedipal conflicts during development results in heterosexuality and also in integration of the personality. Psychoanalysts of that time viewed homosexuality as a motivated response to unconscious irrational fears of heterosexuality (Bieber et al., 1962; Socarides, 1978). The first two editions of the *Diagnostic and Statistical Manual* published by the American Psychiatric Association and used to definitively characterize mental disorders were based on psychodynamic principles derived from psychoanalysis. These manuals had great influence on many cultural institutions. Although homosexuality is no longer considered a mental disorder, ideas equating homosexuality with pathology still influence policies in many areas of society. Similarly, some clinicians appear to continue to endorse the older models of DSM-I and II (Socarides and Volkan, 1991).

Recently, the American Psychological Association carried out a questionnaire study of members with regard to bias towards gay and lesbian patients. Twenty-five commonly occurring clinical situations were identified in which bias appeared to be manifested by mental health clinicians (Garnets et al., 1991). Similar observations have been made of psychiatrists (Panel, 1993).

In this report we discuss an investigation of bias towards gay patients by psychoanalysts. We felt that such an investigation would be timely for a number of reasons. Psychoanalytic psychology had heavily stressed pathological aspects of homosexuality. Until quite recently (Lewes, 1988; Isay, 1989; Friedman, 1988) psychoanalysts were among those most strongly opposed to deletion of homosexuality as a category of mental disorder from the *Diagnostic and Statistical Manual of The American Psychiatric Association* (Bayer, 1981); psychodynamic concepts continue to be highly influential in clinical work; and there is an urgent need for clinical guidelines for treatment of the psychiatrically disturbed segments of the gay population. Although bias against gay and for lesbian patients by mental health professionals has been investigated (Rudolph, 1989), bias specifically manifested by psychoanalysts has not.

Method

Subjects. Subjects for this study were 82 psychoanalysts who were either graduates from the Adelphi Post-doctoral Program in Psychoanalysis and Psychotherapy, or the New York University Postdoctoral Program in Psychotherapy and Psychoanalysis, or members of the American Academy of Psychoanalysis, or American branch of the International

Psychoanalytical Association, or the Institute for Psychoanalytic Training and Research (IPTAR). Subjects were selected randomly from the mailing lists of the above associations. Of approximately 900 individuals contacted by mail, 82 usable packets were returned, a return rate of 9.11%. Of those, 53 (64.6%) were male and 29 (35.4%) were female; their age range was 37–85 with a median of 57 years; 25 subjects had M.D.s and 51 had Ph.D.s; the remaining subjects had degrees in either nursing or social work. The average number of years since the degree was awarded was 27.0 (SD = 13.6), and the average number of years practicing since analytic training was completed was 17.0 (SD = 11.8). For current theoretical orientation, 35.4% designated Freudian as their first choice, 29.1% designated Interpersonal as their first choice, and 16.5% selected Object Relations. The subjects were also asked to rate themselves on the Kinsey Scale (Kinsey et al., 1948). Of the subjects, 89.5% described their fantasy level at 0 (exclusively heterosexual) or 1 (only incidental homosexual) fantasy. Of the 3 subjects who rated themselves 4 (predominantly homosexual) or higher, all were women. Thus, the subject pool was basically heterosexual.

Instruments. The basic research strategy was to assess differences in ratings made by psychoanalysts of clinical vignettes that were identical except for the patient's sexual orientation.

There were two sets of two vignettes. Each vignette within a set matched perfectly in all descriptors except for sexual orientation which was indicated by a passing reference to the name of the patient's lover. The first set was intended to describe individuals with less severe psychopathology than those in the second set. The vignettes were labeled as follows: 1 (low pathology, homosexual: Keith/Jim), 2 (low pathology, heterosexual: Keith/Anna), 3 (high pathology, homosexual, Roger/Kenny), and 4 (high pathology, heterosexual, Roger/Nancy). Each subject received either Vignettes 1 and 3 or Vignettes 2 and 4; that is, each subject had either two vignettes in which the lover's name was male (Keith/Jim and Roger/Kenny) or two vignettes in which the lover's name was female (Keith/Anna and Roger/Nancy). Thus, the pairs of vignettes were intended to display either two homosexual patients who differed in level of psychopathology or two heterosexual patients who differed in level of psychopathology. The purpose of pairing the vignettes in this manner was to avoid giving any subject both a homosexual and a heterosexual vignette. It was thought that such a pairing might create a response set in which subjects would seek to avoid displaying a more negative attitude towards the homosexual vignette thereby confounding the subject's true attitude towards the patient.

The subjects were asked to rate the vignettes on semantic differential scales consisting of 11 adjective pairs in total adjective pairs loaded on the general evaluative dimension, adjective pairs loaded on the activity dimension, and 3 adjective pairs loaded on the potency dimension. The reason for using all three dimensions was to tap as much subtlety as possible in the evaluations of the patients by the respondents. Each adjective pair was rated on a 7-point Likert-type scale. In addition to the semantic differential rating scales, the subjects were asked to make a DSM-III-R (APA, 1980) Axis I and/or Axis 11 diagnosis as well as to indicate their assessment of the patients on the Global Assessment of Functioning (GAF) Scale (Axis V of the DSM-III-R).

Results and Discussion

The analysis was conducted by means of the SPSSX package using two-way between-subjects factorial analysis of variance (2 x 2 ANOVA), paired t-test analyses, and one-way repeated measures analysis of variance, as appropriate.

Given a return rate of 9.11%, no generalization about the attitudes and clinical practice of psychoanalytic practitioners in the general population could be made. This is a preliminary study, however. These individuals were of diverse theoretical orientation, had substantial clinical experience, and were of different disciplines. The responses they displayed to homosexual and heterosexual patients are of clinical interest.

The most striking finding is that the identical clinical description of a moderately disturbed male patient was reacted to differently by psychoanalysts if the lover was male rather than female. On the GAF the high-pathology homosexual patient was given an average rating of approximately 55, whereas the high-pathology heterosexual patient was given a healthier average rating of approximately 60. These differences are clinically meaningful in addition to being statistically significant. The description in DSM-III-R of the functioning level between 61 and 70 is as follows.

> Some mild symptoms (e.g., depressed mood or mild insomnia) OR some difficulty in social, occupational, school functioning (e.g., occasional truancy, or theft within the household), but generally functioning pretty well, has some meaningful interpersonal relationships.

The description of the functioning level between 51 and 60 is:

> Moderate symptoms (e.g., flat affect and circumstantial speech, occasional panic attacks) OR moderate difficulty in social, occupational, or school functioning (e.g., few friends, conflicts with co-workers).

The fact that M.D.s gave significantly higher GAF scores than Ph.D.s may reflect specific differences in training and clinical experience. It is possible that M.D.s diagnose and treat more disturbed patients compared to Ph.D.s so that they are inclined to have a different baseline for conceptualizing level of pathology. This finding, although not directly relevant to the purpose of this study, is interesting and worthy of further investigation. M.D.s may have different working concepts of severity of psychopathology which may extend to the areas of diagnosis and treatment.

The high-pathology homosexual vignette (Vignette 3: Roger/Kenny) was rated significantly more negatively on the SD than the high-pathology heterosexual vignette (Vignette 4: Roger/Nancy) on the General Evaluative Dimension (adjective pairs: bad/good, sick/healthy, immoral/moral, undesirable/desirable, and negative/positive) and the Activity Dimension. Negative bias toward homosexual patients was not observed in the low-pathology patients.

Thus, there were two kinds of bias that emerged among the respondents. First, a bias towards high pathology vs. low pathology patients, and second, a bias towards homosexual vs. heterosexual patients. It was the interaction between homosexuality and high pathology that yielded the most powerful statistical result. The homosexual "Roger" character (Vignette 3) also was most frequently diagnosed with a Borderline Personality, whereas the heterosexual "Roger" character was most frequently diagnosed with an Obsessive-Compulsive Disorder (this difference was not statistically significant). Some psychoanalytic authors have emphasized the association between homosexuality and borderline psychopathology (Socarides, 1978). We cannot help but wonder whether this clinical, theoretical perspective might not have led to a widespread tendency to judge a patient to be borderline because he was homosexual rather than because symptoms characteristic of borderline psychopathology were elicited in the history and mental status examination. The existence of a negative response towards more pathological but not higher functioning patients raises serious questions of bias specifically towards the mentally ill. These findings are robust regardless of which subject subgroup is analyzed—that is, M.D.s, Ph.D.s, Freudians, and Interpersonalists responded similarly.

Although psychoanalysts are among the most highly trained mental health professionals, psychoanalytic education is quite selective. Most educational programs focus on higher functioning patients who can tolerate the demanding requirements of the psychoanalytic situation. It is possible that prolonged emphasis on the clinical needs of higher functioning patients foster subtly negative attitudes towards lower functioning ones.

We were not able to ascertain the degree to which psychoanalysts had insight into their biases. We suspect that more frequently than not in day-to-day clinical work such insight may be lacking and that hidden bias may adversely influence patient treatment. Further study into the unconscious evaluative attitudes of analysts is warranted particularly in conjunction with a measure that could evaluate the efficacy of treatment.

Also indicated is educational emphasis on attitudinal awareness particularly with respect to the seriously disturbed patient population. In this study the respondents were predominantly heterosexual. This raises the question of whether gay patients and the concerns that gay therapists are better able to provide appropriate treatment may not sometimes have merit. Bias among gay psychotherapists has not been studied, however, and probably should be in the future.

The numerous ways in which bias may influence the treatment of gay and lesbian psychotherapy patients have been a topic of recent scrutiny (Garnets et al., 1991). Among gay and lesbian groups, a partial list of those with serious psychiatric disturbances include patients who are suicidally depressed, HIV+, engage in high risk sexual activity, and/or are substance abusers. The psychotic, the severely character disordered, and the bipolar gay populations also require particularly diligent therapeutic interventions. It is hoped that ongoing research into the attitudes and beliefs of health care providers will lead to improvement in patient care.

References

American Psychiatric Association. (1980). *Diagnostic and Statistical Manual of Mental Disorders,* 3rd ed., APA, Washington, DC.

Bayer, R. (1981). *Homosexuality and American Psychiatry: The Politics of Diagnosis,* Basic Books, New York.

Bieber, I., Dain, H., Dince, P., Drellich, M., Grand, H., Gundlach, R., Kramer, M., Rifkin, A., Wilbur, C., and Bieber, T. (1962). *Homosexuality: A Psychoanalytic Study,* Basic Books, New York.

Friedman, R. C. (1988). *Male Homosexuality: A Contemporary Psychoanalytic Perspective,* Yale University Press, New Haven, CT.

Garnets, L., Hancock, X. A., Cochran, S. D., Goodchilds, J., and Peplau, L. A. (1991). Issues in psychotherapy with lesbians and gay men: A survey of psychologists. *American Psychologist* 46: 964–972.

Isay, R. A. (1989). *Being Homosexual,* Farrar, Straus & Giroux, New York.

Kinsey, A. C., Pomeroy, W. B., & Martin, C. E. (1948). *Sexual Behavior in the Human Male,* Saunders, Philadelphia.

Lewes, K. (1988). *The Psychoanalytic Theory of Male Homosexuality,* Simon & Schuster, New York.

Panel. (1993). *Anti-homosexual Bias in Psychiatry.* Presented at the annual meeting of the American Academy of Psychoanalysis.

Rudolph, J. (1989). Effects of a workshop on mental health practitioners, attitudes towards homosexuality and counseling effectiveness. *Counseling and Human Development* 68: 81–85.

Socarides, C. W. (1978). *Homosexuality,* Free Press, New York.

Socarides, C. W., and Volkan, V. (1991). *The Homosexualities and the Therapeutic Process,* International University Press, Madison, CT.

REVIEW QUESTIONS

1. What kind of instrument was used in this study? How was it used?

2. Who were the respondents in the study? How do you think the results might have been different if the respondents had been college students? High school teachers?

3. How were the results analyzed?

Chapter 7: Sampling

As you have previously learned, one of the goals of research is to describe or identify specific characteristics about a specific group or population. This isn't too difficult if the group you are studying is small, such as a group of 10 or 12 children in a daycare setting. In this case, all you would need to do is observe or interview all of the children. However, this process of figuring out who to study becomes more difficult if the group is larger. Let's say you want to find out about the quality of life of all the female students in the United States and compare their answers to those of the male students. This could involve lots of students, and it would be nearly impossible for you to interview or observe all of them.

You probably would not be able to include all of the student **population** in colleges and universities in the United States because contacting all of them would be time consuming and cost too much money. Therefore, the next step is to decide how to select a **sample** that is **representative** of the population you have in mind. This is not as simple as you might think because one of the goals is that your sample must *accurately* reflect the larger population so you can **generalize** about the population you are studying. For example, let's say you want to conduct a study of college students. You have found that the college students at your particular school have an average age of 21. Fifty-one percent of them are female, and they have an average income of $8,000 a year. So, you want to collect data on the students and you visit a computer programming class in the evening to hand out your survey. You find that of the 40 students you surveyed, 80 percent were male, the average age was 35, and the average income was $40,000 a year. Does this sample represent your college population? No. You must decide what sampling method is appropriate for the research you are conducting. In this chapter, you will learn about two types of sampling methods, probability sampling and nonprobability sampling.

PROBABILITY SAMPLING

Probability sampling is designed to allow a determination of how likely the members of the sample are to be representative of the population from where they are drawn. In other words, the researcher decides which segment of the population will be used for the project to accurately portray the parameters of the larger population. Most commonly, the elements of the population are people, but could be animals or events, thus enabling the researcher to make an estimate of the extent to which the results of the sample are going to differ from the entire population. The most common way of accomplishing this is by random selection. **Randomization, or random selection** means that every subject in the population has the same chance of being selected for the sample, and therefore, the sample group should possess the same characteristics as the larger population. You can randomly select your sample in a number of ways. **Simple random sampling** is a procedure that generates numbers or cases strictly based on chance. Selection could be as simple as rolling the dice and getting heads or tails. You can also use phone numbers as a way of randomly selecting numbers with the help of a computer and **random-digit dialing.** Random-digit dialing is most useful because if a phone number is no longer in service or no one is home, then the program automatically replaces that number with the next random number.

Systematic random sampling is just a little different from the simple random sample method. In this type of sampling, every nth element is selected from a list after the first element is randomly selected within the first n cases. This type of sampling is convenient when the population elements are arranged consecutively. To use this type of method, you must first randomly select the first number to be sampled. Then you must decide on your **sampling interval,** which is the total number of cases in the population divided by the number of cases required in the sample. So, if you have 500 students in your population and you want 50 students to be in your sample, your sampling interval would be 10. Next, you would count using your sampling interval from the first randomly selected case and include every nth case in your sample.

Stratified random sampling uses information that is already known about the total population before sampling. This makes the sampling process more efficient. To begin, all elements of the population are distinguished based on their characteristics. This forms the **sampling strata.** Next, the elements are sampled randomly within the strata. For example, if your school is 3/4 women and 1/4 men, then your sample should look the same way. Your sample is a **proportionate stratified sample** if each stratum is represented exactly in proportion to the population. A **disproportionate stratified sample** varies from the population.

Cluster sampling is used when a sampling frame is not available; however, cluster sampling requires more information before the sampling than the previous methods do. Clusters are naturally occurring elements of the population. Thus, city blocks would be clusters for sampling people who live in cities and businesses would be clusters for sampling employees. To begin, you must draw a random sample of clusters, which requires a list of businesses or city blocks. You then draw a random sample of elements within each cluster. If you are interested in a cluster sample of employees, you would first record the addresses of all businesses and then you could separate them into categories such as the following:

Category	Number	Percentage
North	469	20.8
South	738	32.8
East	653	29.0
West	392	17.4
Total	2252	100.0

Next, you must decide how large a sample you want. If you decide to use 100 businesses in each category, you would use a simple random selection within each category to come up with your sample.

As you already know, your project is well designed if the sample represents the population from which it has been selected. But **sampling errors** can occur. A sampling error is the difference between the characteristics of a sample and that of the population. The less representative of a population a sample is, the larger the room for error is. For example, let's say you have a probability sample from a population of 3,880 television viewers and you want to see how close the mean age of the sample is to the population. When you figured out the average age of the first sample of 50 television viewers, it was 39.96. If the average age of the population was 42.06, then the sample was 2.1 years younger than the population. This difference of 2.1 years is the sampling error, which represents the variability of a mean in a probability sample from the mean of the population. All samples will have some sort of sampling error.

NONPROBABILITY SAMPLING

Nonprobability sampling is used when probability sampling would either be too expensive or obtaining a precise representation is not important to the study. Nonprobability sampling is also used when it is not possible to obtain or define a full population. Although nonprobability sampling is used frequently, you cannot expect the sample you obtain to be representative of the population. Most often, a nonprobability sample is used because the respondents are easy to find or they contact the researcher after finding out about a study and ask to participate. For instance, Schroer (2001) has been studying white supremacist groups on the Internet. Because it would be impossible to send out a survey using random sampling to all people, Schroer uses the Internet to find his subjects. Therefore, he doesn't interview all the people in these types of groups, but rather he interviews those he found and who are willing to talk with him.

You can use four different types of nonprobability sampling methods. **Convenience sampling** means using subjects who are available to you. This type of sampling can happen as a result of "hanging out" with the people you are interested in studying. You can hang out on a street corner, at your library, or in a music store to find your subjects. For instance, Williams (1989) was interested in learning about the teenage cocaine scene. To interview the teenagers, Williams spent years getting to know the kids and asked questions of those who would talk to him. It would be impossible to survey all teens that use cocaine, so a convenience sample is much more realistic in these types of studies.

A **quota sample** is somewhat similar to a stratified random sample. Convenience samples consist of whatever subjects are available and there is no concern with representativeness, whereas quota sampling sets quotas to ensure that the sample population somewhat resembles the larger population from which it draws. Maybe you are interested in studying the students on your campus to learn about their smoking behaviors. The first thing you might want to do is find out the demographic information of students in your school. Let's say the student population of your school is 51 percent male, 49 percent female, 87 percent white, 8 percent African American, 2 percent Native American, and 3 percent Asian. With all this information, you might collect your data by going to classes, hanging out in the library, or attending college events. Your objective is to end up with a sample that has the same percentages as your population. The problem is that you won't really know for sure if the sample is representative relative to other characteristics of the student body.

A **purposive sample** is one in which each sample element is selected for a specific purpose. If you were interested in studying women who are HIV infected to find out about their quality of life, it would be difficult to have a random sample. Therefore, you would need to find a group of women who have HIV, then those women become your sample. Let me give you another example. I study the quality of life of women who have some type of bleeding disorder where they have an inability to clot (Wysocki, 1999). Once I began this project, I realized that some of the women who had a bleeding disorder had become HIV infected because of the blood products they had received. I wanted to interview these women for a number of reasons. I felt obligated to allow their "voices" to be heard, but I knew that they only had a short time to live, and I wanted to find out about their lives. In other words, I had a purpose for selecting the sample of women for my study.

Snowball sampling is when one member of a population is identified and that person identifies another person who could take part in the study. This type of sampling is common when the researcher is interested in studying difficult to reach populations such as criminals, gang members, prostitutes, or people with specific diseases. In my bleeding disorder study, I had no idea which individuals in my sample were the ones living with HIV or AIDS. So, I had to ask a respondent, who gave me a name of one individual, and that individual gave me the name of another. Unfortunately in this case, the list of women who were living with HIV/AIDS was much smaller than the list of those women who had already died from the disease. In the following articles, you will the see various ways researchers use sampling to study the populations they are interested in.

REFERENCES

Schroer, T. (2001). Social control and White racialists: The freedoms of the Internet. In *Readings in Deviant Behavior,* 2nd ed., edited by Alex Thio & Thomas Calhoun. New York: Allyn & Bacon.

Williams, T. 1989. *The cocaine kids: The inside story of a teenage drug ring.* Reading, MA: Addison-Wesley.

Wysocki, D. K. 1999. The psychosocial and gynecological issues of women with bleeding disorders. *Female Patient* (both the OB/GYN and Primary Care Editions), 24:13–20.

INFOTRAC COLLEGE EDITION SUGGESTED READINGS AND DISCUSSION QUESTIONS

1. Look up the article "Collective memories, political violence and mental health in Northern Ireland." What type of sampling was used? Would another type of sampling have worked? Why or why not?

2. In the article "Family Communication Patterns and Personality Characteristics," a convenience sample was used. Why? Could the researchers have used a probability sampling? Why or why not?

3. Type the words "sampling" and "Internet" into InfoTrac College Edition. Find three articles. What do they say about samples found online? Is it a good idea to gain respondents online?

SEX IN AMERICA

Robert T. Michael, John H. Gagnon, Edward O. Laumann, and Gina Kolata

This example of a probability sample has been called one of the most comprehensive, representative surveys of sexual behavior in the general adult population of the United States. After explaining the huge flaws in previous studies on sexuality, the authors explain how they used a stratified, multistage area probability sample of clusters of households. Within each selected household, one English-speaking adult between 18 and 59 years of age was randomly selected as the respondent. Interviews were completed with 3342 persons, 78.6 percent of those who were eligible to participate. As you are reading this chapter, watch for information about how the authors made sure they had a representative sample.

Of all the studies that purport to tell about sex in America, the vast majority are unreliable; many are worse than useless. As social scientists, we found that the well-established survey methods that can so accurately describe the nation's voting patterns or the vicissitudes of the labor force rarely were used to study sexuality. And the methods that were used in many of the popular studies had flaws so deep and so profound that they render the data and their interpretations meaningless. In fact, the field is so impoverished that experts still find themselves citing data gathered by Alfred Kinsey during the late 1930s and into the early 1950s, a time when America was very different than it is today.[1] Many of the popularized studies that came after Kinsey, like *The Hite Report* or the *Redbook* survey, are even worse, because they ignored what social scientists had learned and used methods guaranteed to yield worthless results.

Most Americans believe that the factors that determine their sex lives lie mostly or solely within themselves. Their sexual drives, their hormones, their individual desires, are all that matter. This is in large part a legacy of the long history of attempts to study and control sexuality, dating back to studies in the past century that focused on "deviants" and sex criminals.

The era of large sex surveys began with Alfred Kinsey who felt that standard sample survey methods were a practical impossibility when it came to the subject of sex, so he compromised. And when he published his results, Kinsey shocked the nation with his findings and evoked a public response so strong that most social scientists decided to steer clear of sex research.

An evolutionary biologist from Indiana University, Kinsey was a professor of zoology, an expert on gall wasps. Using the methods he was most comfortable with, Kinsey began his study on human sexuality by first giving a questionnaire about sexual practices to the students in his classes. Finding this method unsatisfactory, he turned to face-to-face interviews and then began reaching out to different social groups. Eventually, he and his three associates interviewed nearly eighteen thousand people. It was a long and arduous task. It took him six months to persuade the first sixty-two people to be interviewed, but as he got better at interviewing it became easier to recruit respondents. The problem was not who he interviewed but how he found them.

Kinsey knew that the ideal situation would be to select people at random. That way it would be guaranteed that those he interviewed represented the general population. But Kinsey just did not think it was possible to coax a randomly selected group of Americans to answer truthfully when he asked them deeply personal questions about their sex lives.

Kinsey's compromise was to take his subjects where he could find them. He and his associates went to college sororities and fraternities, college classes and student groups, rooming houses, prisons, mental hospitals, social organizations of many kinds, and friendship groups in which one interview might lead to others. For a fourteen-year period, he even collared hitchhikers in town.

To make his data more credible, Kinsey often attempted to interview 100 percent of the members of his groups. He'd try to get every single student in a classroom or every single boarder in a rooming house to answer his questions.

It sounds impressive. After all, if he interviewed eighteen thousand people and if he got anywhere near 100 percent of the groups he approached, why would his data be unreliable?

One problem was that the people Kinsey interviewed could not stand in for all Americans. A fraternity here, a college class there, a PTA from a third place, and a group of homosexual men from somewhere else do not, taken together, reflect the population of the United States.

Instead of studying randomly selected members of the population, Kinsey interviewed what is called a sample of convenience, a sample that consisted of volunteers that he recruited or who came to him. This introduced two problems. First, the people he interviewed could not be thought of as representative of anyone in the population other than themselves. They got into the sample because they were relatively convenient for Kinsey to find and persuade to participate, or because they offered to participate on their own. Consequently, while they may have told the truth about their own sex lives, neither Kinsey nor anyone else can know how to generalize from these people to say anything useful or accurate about the whole population or about any particular subset of the population.

The second problem was that many of Kinsey's respondents volunteered to be in the study. For a sex survey, it seems likely that those who do volunteer and those who do not have different behavior, different experiences, and different attitudes about sex. If so, the data that are collected from volunteers will give an inaccurate picture of the whole population. By including the sexual histories of those who especially want to be counted in the survey, that survey gives a biased picture. This is true for any survey, not just one on sexual behavior. Many studies have suggested that people who volunteer for surveys are not like people who do not volunteer,[2] and there is some evidence that people who volunteer for sex surveys have wider sexual experience than those who do not. In addition, there is evidence that people who engage in highly stigmatized behaviors, such as incest, may refuse to be interviewed or would not volunteer to do so.

So, since Kinsey did not select his respondents in a way that permitted generalization, the data he obtained are at best interesting facts about the people he interviewed but are not useful for making statements about the population at large such as that half the husbands in America had had extramarital sex and had been improved by extramarital sex. Kinsey's data on homosexuality were most troubling for a society who thought sex between men was rare. He reported that one man in three had a sexual experience with another man at some time in his life. Ten percent of the men that Kinsey interviewed had had sex exclusively with other men for at least three years. It is this figure that may be the basis for the widely quoted "one person in ten in the United States is gay."

Even as Kinsey's studies shocked and fascinated the nation, they also elicited strong criticism from people who thought that sexuality should not be studied by scientists with questionnaires. The blistering attacks on Kinsey were so effective that surveys of sexuality were not only born with Kinsey—they almost died with him too.

Kinsey's study was followed, a decade later, by a new type of sex study, initiated by William Masters, who was a gynecologist, and Virginia Johnson, who was his research associate at Washington University in St. Louis. Masters and Johnson watched and described the sex act, performed in the laboratory by subjects that they paid. Their book, *Human Sexual Response,* was an instant bestseller, even as it disturbed many Americans. The very idea that people would agree to be volunteers in their studies (and be paid for it!) was shocking to many, who viewed the transactions as a form of prostitution.

Still, demands for facts about sexual life in America continued unabated. In the absence of systematic, scientific studies of the American population, a series of popular "reports" on sexual practices proliferated to fill the void. There was the *Playboy* report, the *Redbook report, The Hite Report,* and, most recently, *The Janus Report,* whose flaws were even more profound than those that plagued the studies by Kinsey.

In all these studies, only people who volunteered to complete the survey were included. But the people who were asked to volunteer were by no means representative of all Americans. The five million readers of *Playboy* are already a heavily selected population—they tend to be young, white men, richer than the average American, and men who are interested in sex. The nearly five million readers of *Rebook are* mostly white women in their late twenties to late thirties, married, and more affluent than the average American woman. If you asked readers of a different sort of magazine, like *Christian Century* or *Reader's Digest,* to fill out a questionnaire, you'd expect to get very different answers.

Shere Hite sent out surveys to women whose names she got from chapters of the National Organization for Women, abortion rights groups, university women's centers, and university newsletters. She also put notices in the *Village Voice,* in three magazines *(Mademoiselle, Brides,* and *Ms.),* and in church newsletters, asking readers to send to her for questionnaires. She, too, was concentrating on highly selected members of the population.

But suppose you don't care about the behavior of people not included in these surveys. Wouldn't a survey of *Playboy* readers at least tell you about sex among young, affluent white men? The problem is that very few of even those invited to answer the surveys chose to do so, which raises the question of just who these respondents are. Only 1.3 percent of the five million *Playboy* readers returned the questionnaire. In the *Redbook*[3] survey, the issue of *Redbook* magazine containing the questionnaires sold 4,700,000 copies. Barely 2 percent of the *Redbook* readers filled out and returned the survey. And of those 100,000 replies, the magazine analyzed only 2,278. Shere Hite, in her book *The Hite Report: A Nationwide Study of Female Sexuality,* said she distributed 100,000 questionnaires and got 3,000 back, a 3 percent response rate.[4]

Even though both magazines and Shere Hite trumpeted the sheer numbers of responses, large numbers in themselves do not mean anything. If too many people decline to answer your questions, you start to worry about the ones who opted out. Were they significantly different from those who participated? If, as in the *Playboy* survey, 1.3 percent of the target population answers your questions, you should be very suspicious that the people who answered are atypical for some reason and that their replies do not represent the sexual practices even of the population that received the survey.

It may sound paradoxical, but the percentage of replies is far more meaningful than the absolute number of them. If you ask 1,200 people to answer your questions, and 1,000 agree to do so, you can generalize to the target group with more accuracy than you can in 50,000 replies from a group of 1,000,000 who were asked. In the first case, 83 percent of those you asked answered your questions. In the second case, only 5 percent of those you asked replied to you, which leaves you wondering how they differed from those who did not reply.

The most recent of these "reports," *The Janus Report*,[5] by Samuel S. Janus and Cynthia L. Janus, was slightly different. The Januses said they distributed 4,550 surveys and got back 2,795 that were "satisfactorily completed." They argued that their data were credible because their respondents reflected the U.S. population. The way they got this so-called match, however, was by looking at census data on key variables, such as age, marital status, and religion, and then seeking respondents who would match the proportions found in the general population.

For example, the census said that 19 percent of the population was between eighteen and twenty-six, so the Januses sought out enough volunteers in that age group to fill in 19 percent of the slots for respondents in their survey. But it's not how many respondents are of a particular age that's so important—it's how you find them.

The Januses wanted to get enough older Americans to make their survey sample resemble the census data. So they went to sex therapy clinics and looked for older people. Does it matter where they found the old people? We have no way of knowing who these older people were, but the fact that they were at a sex therapy clinic makes it probable that they have sex partners, unlike many older Americans, and that they want to have sex. In fact, the Januses report that over 70 percent of Americans age sixty-five and older have sex once a week. A reputable national survey (the General Social Survey), which did not preselect people, found that just 7 percent of older Americans have sex that often.

Many of these sex reports also had an additional problem—that of knowing who *had* responded. Fraudulent responses—from people who filled out the questionnaires as a lark, making up sexual adventures or pretending not to have had them—would be counted just like anyone else's. A man might have pretended to be a woman and filled in a *Redbook* questionnaire, or a woman might have said she was a man and answered the *Playboy* questions. One busy man could have filled out many questionnaires for *Playboy*.

Yet these pseudo-studies provided a picture of a very sexually active nation. And because these studies have been so widely publicized and are cited so often, many Americans walk around thinking they are among the few who do not have a lot of sex partners, thinking that even if they are satisfied, they must be missing something.

Our team, working through the National Opinion Research Center, a survey research firm associated with the University of Chicago, was awarded the contract to design this study called the National Health and Social Life Survey (NHSLS). In our original study design we wanted a sample size of 20,000, which would enable us to analyze separately data from people who are members of small subpopulations. For example, if 4 percent of the population were gay, a sample size of 20,000 men and women would yield about 400 homosexual men and 400 homosexual women, enough for us to analyze their responses separately.

In the process of designing our survey, it was clear that we would not be able to achieve this sample size with the limited resources. We received only enough money to study 3,500 adults, enough to be confident about the accuracy of the data as a whole, but the sample would not be large enough for detailed analyses of small minority groups. We knew, because we used established statistical sampling techniques, that our respondents represented the general population. In addition, we purposely included slightly more blacks and Hispanics so that we would have enough members of these minority groups to enable us to analyze their responses separately, with confidence that they made statistical sense.

We would have liked to have done the same for homosexuals, including more gay men and lesbians so that we could analyze their replies separately. However, homosexuals are not so easily identified, and for good reason, because their preferences for a partner of the same gender should be private if they want them to be. But that means we could not so easily find an expanded representative sample of homosexuals as we could find blacks or Hispanics. And that means that we could not analyze homosexual behavior separately, asking, for example, how many partners gay men and lesbians have in their lifetimes or where they met their partners. But we included homosexual sex as part of sex in general, so when we ask a question such as, "How often do you have sex?" we do not distinguish between homosexuals and heterosexuals.

The most important part of our study was the way we selected the people to be interviewed. It can be tricky, and subtle, to pick out a group that represents all Americans. For example, you might say you will go to every neighborhood and knock on the door of the corner house on each block. But that would not give you a representative sample because people who live in corner houses are different from other people—as a rule, they are richer than their neighbors on the block because corner houses tend to cost more. Or you might say you'll find married couples by taking every couple that got married in June. But then you would end up with too few Jews because there is a proscription in Judaism against marrying in certain weeks that often fall in June.

Of course, the most obvious way might be to randomly select individuals from households across the country. But finding and interviewing people scattered across the United States can be very expensive, so social scientists have found a cheaper, but equally valid, way of identifying a representative sample. Essentially, we choose at random geographic areas of the country, using the statistical equivalent of a coin toss to select them. Within these geographic regions, we randomly select cities, towns, and rural areas. Within those cities and towns we randomly select neighborhoods. Within those neighborhoods, we randomly select households.

This method gave us 9,004 addresses. Naturally, since the addresses were generated by a computer, many of the addresses either did not have a residence on them or had a residence on them that was empty. Others had a household but no one who lived there was eligible for our survey—they were not between the ages of eighteen and fifty-nine or did not speak English. We determined that 4,635 of the original 9,004 household addresses were ineligible for one of those reasons, so that left us with 4,369 households that did have someone living in them who was eligible to participate in the study. Although it may seem that our sample shrank quite a bit from the original 9,004 addresses, that is normal and to be expected. We did not say we wanted a random sample of addresses for our survey. We wanted a representative sample of Americans who were aged eighteen to fifty-nine and who spoke English.

We selected the individual in a household to interview by a random process. In effect, if there were two people living in a household who were in our age range, we flipped a coin to select which one to interview. If there were three people in the household, we did the equivalent of flipping a three-sided coin to select one of them to interview.

The difference between this method and the method used by, say, *Playboy* magazine, is profound. In the *Playboy* survey, anyone who wanted to be interviewed could be. In our survey, we did not let anyone be interviewed unless we selected them. If we selected a man who offered his wife in his stead, saying he was too busy to be interviewed, we declined to interview her. And if he adamantly refused to be interviewed, his refusal counted against us. He is a nonrespondent, even though his wife might have been eager to fill in for him.

Our method is neither unusual nor remarkable. But our method is right. There is universal agreement among all social scientists: this is the way you do it.

Of all the eligible households, our interviewers completed 3,432 interviews, so we have the remarkable outcome that nearly four out of every five persons we wanted to interview, across the nation, were willing to sit down and answer a ninety-minute questionnaire about their sexual behavior and other aspects of their sex lives. This response rate is even more remarkable because it includes as nonresponders people who simply could not be found to be interviewed.

No other fact in this study is as important as the fact that four out of five randomly selected adults were willing to give an interview and to give us honest responses, judged by all the ways we can think of to check their veracity. We had a variety of checks and cross-checks to test the honesty of the responses and the respondents passed with flying colors.

Once we had the data, we asked whether the 3,432 respondents, as a group, were representative of the population of those aged eighteen to fifty-nine in the United States. We could not do this in advance because, unlike the Januses, we were not looking for people to fit into the census niches. Instead, we were selecting people at random, with no way of knowing ahead of time what their age, sex, race, religion, or education was.

In fact, our sample turned out to be exactly like other highly reputable and scientifically valid national samples. We compared our group to those of the Current Population Survey, the General Social Survey, and the National Survey of Families and Households, looking at such characteristics as marital status, ages, educational levels, race, and ethnicity. We found no evidence suggesting that our sample was not fully representative of the population aged eighteen to fifty-nine.

Table 1 shows a few of the comparisons we made, using our unweighted sample that excludes the extra blacks and Hispanics that we added on purpose. We compared our group to the Census Bureau's Current Population Survey of over 140,000 people for 1991 as the benchmark. It is the best information that demographers can get about the characteristics of the population.

The similarities between our sample and the Current Population Survey of the Census Bureau extend to age, education level, and marital status, as the table illustrates. This

TABLE 1. COMPARISON OF SOCIAL CHARACTERISTICS IN NHSLS AND U.S. POPULATION

	U.S. Population	NHSLS
Gender		
Men	49.7%	44.6%
Women	50.3	55.4
	100%	100%
Age		
18–24	18.2%	15.9%
25–29	14.3	14.5
30–39	29.5	31.3
40–49	22.7	22.9
50–59	15.3	15.3
	100%	100%
Education		
Less than high school	15.8%	13.9%
High school or equivalent	64.0	62.2
Any college	13.9	16.6
Advanced	6.3	7.3
	100%	100%
Marital Status		
Never married	27.7%	28.2%
Currently married	58.3	53.3
Divorced, separated	12.4	16.2
Widowed	1.6	2.3
	100%	100%
Race/Ethnicity		
White	75.9%	76.5%
Black	11.7	12.7
Hispanic	9.0	7.5
Other	3.3	3.3
	100%	100%

Notes: NHSLS unweighted cross-section sample of 3,159.

Gender: Bureau of the Census, Current Population Survey, 1991. *Age, Race/Ethnicity:* Bureau of the Census, Current Population Survey, 1991. *Education:* Bureau of the Census, Current Population Survey, 1990. *Marital Status:* Bureau of the Census, Current Population Survey, 1992.

extraordinary similarity of our sample to the U.S. population, from which we randomly selected our respondents, provides assurance that the respondents who were interviewed were representative of the population of all Americans aged eighteen to fifty-nine.

We also looked at the proportions of men and women who answered our questions. We knew from the census data that 49.7 percent of Americans aged eighteen to fifty-nine are men. Among our respondents, 44.6 percent are men. Other surveys that are of high quality, like the General Social Survey and the National Survey of Family and Households, had virtually the same percentages of men and women as we have. The General Social Survey has 43.8 percent men and the National Survey of Families and Households had 43.0 percent men. So we can say with confidence that the people who agreed to participate in our survey of sexual behavior were just like the population at large in their gender. We were not disproportionately interviewing—or failing to interview—either men or women.

Now there are many people in the nation who are not represented in our survey. We can speak with confidence about the behavior of the noninstitutionalized, currently housed population aged eighteen to fifty-nine. We can say nothing about those who currently live in institutions like hospitals or jails or about the homeless or about those who are under age eighteen or older than fifty-nine. Our sample did not include those groups. But 97.1 percent of American adults aged eighteen to fifty-nine in the nation are represented, and this is the first large-scale study of the broad and inclusive dimensions of the sexual patterns and experiences of this large majority of Americans. All this checking of our data has convinced us that this sample is an excellent one from which we can make generalizations about sex in America and we do so with confidence.

Notes

1. Alfred C. Kinsey, Wardell B. Pomeroy, and Clyde E. Martin, *Sexual Behavior in the Human Male* (Philadelphia: W. B. Saunders Co., 1948); Alfred C. Kinsey, Wardell B. Pomeroy, Clyde E. Martin, and Paul H. Gebhard, *Sexual Behavior in the Human Female* (Philadelphia: W. B. Saunders Co., 1953).

2. Norman M. Bradburn and Seymour Sudman, *Pulls and Surveys: Understanding What They Tell Us* (San Francisco: Jossey-Bass Publishers, 1988).

3. Carol Tavris and Susan Sadd, *The Redbook Report on Female Sexuality* (New York: Delacorte, 1975).

4. Shere Hite, *The Hite Report* (New York: Dell, 1976).

5. Samuel S. Janus and Cynthia L. Janus, *The Janus Report on Sexual Behavior* (New York: John Wiley and Sons, 1993).

REVIEW QUESTIONS

1. Describe why previous studies on human sexuality such as *Playboy, Redbook,* and *Hite* were not representative of people in America.

2. Was this a random survey and why? What steps did the researchers go through to make sure it was random?

3. How did the final sample compare with people in America from other studies?

ALCOHOLICS ANONYMOUS AND THE USE OF MEDICATIONS TO PREVENT RELAPSE: AN ANONYMOUS SURVEY OF MEMBER ATTITUDES

Robert G. Rychtarik, Gerard J. Connors, Kurt H. Dermen, and Paul R. Stasiewicz

Using nonprobability sampling, the purpose of this study was to systematically assess the attitudes of Alcoholics Anonymous (AA) members toward the newer medications used to prevent relapse and to assess their experiences with medication use, of any type, in AA. The researchers used media solicitations and snowball sampling techniques to gather 277 AA members who were surveyed anonymously about their attitudes toward the use of medication for preventing relapse and their experiences with medication use of any type in AA. Do they address ethical issues that came up in their research?

Members of Alcoholics Anonymous (AA) are often assumed to have strong negative attitudes toward the use of medication for alcohol problems. A common view is that AA members believe the alcoholic, to recover fully, must achieve sobriety solely on his or her own without reliance on another drug. Anecdotes about alcoholic clients stopping antipsychotic, antimanic, or other medications at the urging of AA members, often with adverse consequences, are legend in the alcoholism treatment field. Unfortunately, we were unable to find any systematic data on AA members' attitudes toward medication use. Data on the extent to which AA members discourage medication use also are lacking. In the only report we could find, Mason et al. (1996) note that a "small number" of depressed alcoholics stopped desipramine early because of "conflicts" with the AA philosophy.

Official AA literature (Alcoholics Anonymous, 1984) advocates that "no AA member play doctor" and advises members against telling others to throw away pills. Concern remains, however, that participation in AA or other self-help groups could result in conflict over the use of medications and interfere with substance abuse treatment (Freed and York, 1997; Rao et al., 1995). This concern has become more salient with the introduction of new medications for the prevention of relapse (e.g., naltrexone). Research to date suggests that these medications may significantly decrease relapse rates among alcoholics (O'Malley et al., 1992; Volpicelli et al., 1992), but compliance is essential (Volpicelli et al., 1997). If AA members are encouraged to stop taking the medication, their risk of relapse could increase, undermining any medication benefit. The potential impact of negative AA medication attitudes is large. The dominant treatment philosophy in the United States is based on the 12 Steps of AA and encourages AA affiliation as an essential part of recovery.

The purpose of the present study was to assess systematically (1) AA members' attitudes toward the use of medication for preventing relapse, (2) members' inclination to

Rychtarik, R. G., Connors, G. J., Dermen, K. H., & Stasiewicz, P. R. Alcoholics Anonymous and the Use of Medications to Prevent Relapse: An Anonymous Survey of Member Attitudes. Reprinted with permission of *Journal of Studies on Alcohol,* 61, pp 134–138, 2000. Copyright by Alcohol Research Documentation, Inc., Rutgers Center of Alcohol Studies, Piscataway, NJ 08854.

advise a fellow member to stop the medication and (3) members' exposure to AA pressure, either personally or on others, to stop taking a medication, no matter what type.

Method

Participants were among 304 individuals in the Buffalo, New York, area responding to newspaper advertisements seeking AA members for an anonymous phone survey of members' attitudes and opinions. Three callers declined participation; one caller terminated the interview prior to providing opinion data. An additional 23 callers were eliminated from the sample because they had not attended an AA meeting in the last 3 months. The final sample of 277 was a mean age of 50.64 and averaged 13.88 years of education; 62% were men and 94% were white (4% black). On average, participants had attended AA for 12.87 years and had attended an average of 36.30 AA meetings over the past 3 months. A majority (66%) had been AA sponsors. Geographically, participants were drawn from AA meetings throughout the Buffalo metropolitan area.

A daily, except Saturday, newspaper advertisement was placed in the major city newspaper over a 2-week period. The advertisement solicited the help of AA members for a brief anonymous phone survey of members' attitudes and opinions. No further mention of the purpose of the survey was noted. Callers responding to the advertised phone number were told that the survey would take about 5 minutes. They were then advised that the survey would ask about their AA attendance and their opinions about a newly approved medication which reduced urges to drink among alcoholics in the early stages of recovery.

Callers were told that the survey was neither promoting nor discouraging use of the medication; instead, the survey was requesting the caller's open, honest opinion. Callers were also informed that no identifying information would be obtained. Those callers agreeing to participate were then administered a brief structured interview by one of 10 trained research staff asking demographic, AA attendance, opinion and experience questions. Interviewers had received instruction in interview administration procedures and were provided standard responses to potential respondent queries. Upon completion of the survey, the caller was asked to tell other AA members about the survey and to encourage them to call.

Measures

Demographic. The participant's age, race (coded 0 = nonwhite, 1 = white), gender (0 = female, 1 = male) and years of education were obtained.

AA Attendance. The reported number of years since the caller's first AA meeting and the number of meetings attended in the past 3 months were recorded. The participant was also asked whether he or she had ever been an AA sponsor (0 = no, 1 = yes). Finally, the participant was asked for the general geographic area (e.g., town, section of the city) where he or she usually attended meetings. Common divisions within the Buffalo metropolitan area were used to divide the area into seven regions.

The proportion of the total sample within each geographical area ranged from 12% to 16%. The geographic measure was used to assess whether AA members' opinions about medication varied by area. In particular, this measure provided for an indirect assessment of possible differences in member attitudes across different AA meetings. We chose not to ask callers for specific information on the name or location of their most frequently attended meeting(s) to avoid the potential for identifying callers at specific meetings with the demographic data collected.

Medication Opinion Measures. Participants were instructed to listen while the following short story was read to them:

> Joe is an alcoholic. He has begun treatment for his problem at a local outpatient program, and has a counselor who sees him regularly, and he also has started attending AA. The treatment program's doctor has prescribed a medication for him that will help to reduce his urges to drink during the first six months of his recovery. The medication is not addicting, it is not habit-forming and it will not alter his mood.

Upon completion of the story, the caller was asked a series of questions. First, the caller was asked to choose, on the following 5-point Likert scale, the response that best described his or her thoughts about Joe's use of the medication: (1) it's a good idea, (2) it might be helpful, (3) not sure or don't have an opinion, (4) don't like the idea but it's ok for him to try it, or (5) don't like the idea and think he should not take it. The caller was then asked whether he or she would recommend that Joe stop taking the medication (0 = no, 1 = yes) if he or she were Joe's sponsor or learned of the medication use during the meeting.

AA and Medication Experience. The caller was then asked whether he or she, or someone known to them, had ever been discouraged by AA members from taking a medication that a doctor had prescribed (no matter what type; 0 = no, 1 = yes). Those participants responding affirmatively were asked to describe the medication used. In addition, the participant was asked whether he or she, or the other person, had continued taking the medication (0 = no, 1 = yes). Finally the time in years since the last such incident was recorded. Medication type was subsequently coded into the following categories: antidepressants, pain medication, anxiolytics, disulfiram, lithium, antipsychotics, naltrexone, other unspecified mood altering medications and medications of other types.

Results and Discussion

Opinion About Medication for Preventing Relapse. Of the sample, 53% reported use of the medication was either a good idea (20%) or might be a good idea (33%), while 13% reported not knowing or not having an opinion; 17% reported not liking the idea but said it was all right for the individual to use it; an additional 17% reported not liking the use of the medication and believing the individual should not take it. However, only 12% said that as a sponsor or AA member they would recommend a member stop taking the medication.

General Medication Experiences and AA. Almost a third (29%) of the sample said they had personally been encouraged by other AA members to stop taking a medication. An additional 20% said that they knew only of others encouraged to stop a medication, while 1.8% were missing data on this variable. The mean for the last occurrence of such pressure was 5.89 years ago (median = 2.5 years). The medication categories and the percentage of these participants and others discouraged from using them were as follows: antidepressants (36%), pain medications (20%), anxiolytics (14%), lithium (6%), antipsychotics (2%), naltrexone (2%), disulfiram (7%), other unspecified mood altering medications (3%) and other medications (11%). Among participants who said they knew of someone else who had been discouraged from using a medication there was a high degree of uncertainty over whether the individual had continued to use it. Outcome results are therefore limited to the 77 participants who said that they themselves had been encouraged by an AA member to stop using a medication and for whom data on subsequent medication compliance was not missing. Of these participants, 69% said that they had continued taking the medication despite being encouraged to stop; 31% said they had stopped using the medication at the encouragement of AA members.

A higher number of AA meetings attended in the last 3 months was associated significantly, but to a small degree, with a more negative opinion toward use of relapse-preventing medication ($r = .16$, $n = 277$, $p = .007$). Among callers personally experiencing some pressure to stop a medication, those who actually stopped also tended to have less favorable attitudes toward the medication ($r = -.28$, $n = 77$, $p = .013$) and were somewhat more likely to recommend that it be stopped ($r = -.23$, $n = 77$, $p = .044$).

Predictors of Opinion About Relapse-preventing Medication. The set of demographic variables did not contribute significantly to the prediction of opinion toward the medication. AA attendance variables did contribute significantly. In the full model only number of meetings attended significantly contributed to the prediction of participants' opinions. Those attending more AA meetings in the past 3 months were more likely, to a small but significant degree, to have less favorable attitudes toward the use of the medication.

Neither demographic nor AA variable sets contributed significantly to the prediction of whether one would recommend that another member stop taking the medicine.

Predictors of General Medication Experiences. As a set, demographic variables contributed significantly to the prediction of having personally been discouraged from using a medication, of any type, by AA members or knowing of others who had been discouraged. Only age, however, contributed significantly in this step of the model. AA attendance variables also contributed significantly beyond that of demographic variables. Older individuals were less likely, while members who had been sponsors were more likely to report having experienced pressure to stop a medication. No variable was significantly associated with personally having stopped using a medication in response to AA encouragement. Data on the years since the last occurrence of pressure to stop a medication were available from 130 (92%) of those exposed to pressure on either themselves or others.

Both demographic and AA attendance variables contributed significantly as they were entered into the prediction of years since the last episode. Only age contributed significantly among the demographic variables as they were entered. In the final full model ($R = .55$, $F = 10.49$, 5/124 df, $p = .000$), age, sponsorship history and meetings attended in the past 3 months contributed significantly to the prediction of the number of years since the last incident occurred Younger participants reported more recent experiences whereas those individuals who had served as a sponsor reported the last incident to have occurred more years ago. Individuals who attended more meetings over the past 3 months said that the last incident had occurred more recently.

A distinctive feature of the present study was the use of the media to recruit AA members. Ogborne (1993) noted the potential of media advertisements for this purpose but few studies have used it. Media recruitment offers several advantages over other methods for soliciting AA members. First, as Ogborne suggested, the method maintains respect for the traditions of AA. Members' anonymity is maintained and the research does not require involvement or permission of one or more AA groups. Second, the method allows for sampling from a wider range of AA groups and members than is possible when in-person recruitment methods are used. Studies that rely on clients in or discharged from treatment appear to sample only from a select group and do not sample those members with long periods of sobriety and involvement in AA who are not in treatment. In the present study, it was particularly important to sample from this latter group since these individuals would likely have a significant influence on newcomers to the fellowship.

Media recruitment of AA members, however, has limitations. Specifically, the sample in the current study consisted only of those self-selecting to call in response to the advertisement or calling after having been told of the study by a previous caller. The extent to which the sample population typifies all individuals attending AA is a concern. The pattern of demographic and AA attendance characteristics of the current sample, however, was comparable to that found in the random sample survey of 7,200 AA members conducted by AA World Services (Alcoholics Anonymous, 1997). That sample was somewhat younger (44 years of age) than the current sample, but the racial (86% white) and gender (33%) compositions were comparable. In addition, the higher educational status of the current sample appears consistent with the large proportion of members in the national survey reporting relatively high occupational levels. Meeting attendance in the national survey was also nearly identical to that of the current study (i.e., averaging more than two meetings per week). Overall, the comparability between the present sample and the larger random sample of AA members adds credence to the generalizability of the current results.

Nevertheless, other participant selection factors may have been operating to influence the nature of the population sampled. Further research in this area is needed, including longitudinal research on the experiences of individuals attending AA while taking relapse preventing and other medications. Over-sampling of racial minority groups also appears needed in this line of research to examine potential racial differences in opinion and experiences. Finally, evaluating the medical appropriateness of either continuing or stopping the medication use reported in the sample was not feasible. Though many medications listed by participants have no addictive properties, other medications could be problematic.

In the latter case, some judicious advice from fellow AA members to discuss the medication with a physician would be appropriate.

Other limitations of the current study should be noted. First, the sample recruited was predominantly one of relatively long-term AA members. Still, we felt this sample was most appropriate for the goals of the study since these individuals were likely to have the most conservative view of medication use and also the most influence. Second, a nonalcoholic comparison group was not surveyed. The results provide no data on the attitudes of AA members relative to those of the general population or of treatment-seeking samples with no AA experience. Third, we did not assess the proportion of the total sample using a medication while attending AA. So, we do not know the percentage of respondents on a medication who experienced pressure to stop. Fourth, we did not attempt to distinguish callers according to whether they were advertising responders or snowball responders.

Differences in the characteristics and opinions of these two samples may exist. Fifth, the complete anonymity procedures used, though a strength, also precluded us from implementing safeguards to prevent multiple interviews of the same person. Sixth, we did not assess inter-interviewer reliability. The interview, however, was very brief, standardized and administered by trained research staff. Under these circumstances, error from interviewer variability would appear to be low.

References

Alcoholics Anonymous. 1984. *The AA member: Medications and other drugs* (brochure), New York: Alcoholics Anonymous World Services.

Alcoholics Anonymous. 1997. *1996 membership survey,* New York: Alcoholics Anonymous World Services.

Freed, P. E., & York, L. N. 1997. Naltrexone: A controversial therapy for alcohol dependence. *Journal of Psychosocial Nursing and Mental Health Services,* 35: 24–28.

Mason, B. J., Kocsis, J. H., Ritvo, E. C., & Cutler, R. B. 1996. A double-blind, placebo-controlled trial of desipramine for primary alcohol dependence stratified on the presence or absence of major depression. *Journal of the American Medical Association,* 275: 761–767.

Ogborne, A.C. 1993. Assessing the effectiveness of Alcoholics Anonymous in the community: Meeting the challenges. In McCrady, B. S., & Miller, W. R. (Eds.) *Research on Alcoholics Anonymous: Opportunities and alternatives,* New Brunswick, NJ: Rutgers Center of Alcohol Studies, pp. 339–355.

O'Malley, S. S., Jaffe, A. J., Chang, G., Schottenfeld, R. S., Meyer, R. E., & Rounsaville, B. 1992. Naltrexone and coping skills therapy for alcohol dependence. *Archives of General Psychiatry,* 49: 881–887.

Rao, S., Ziedonis, D., and Kosten, T. 1995. The pharmacotherapy of cocaine dependence. *Psychiatiatric Annals,* 25: 363–368.

Volpicelli, J. R., Alterman, A. I., Hayashida, M., & O'Brien, C. P. 1992. Naltrexone in the treatment of alcohol dependence. *Archives of General Psychiatry,* 49: 876–880.

Volpicelli, J. R., Rhines, K. C., Rhiner, J. S., Volpicelli, L. A., Alterman, A. I., & O'Brien, C. P. 1997. Naltrexone and alcohol dependence: Role of subject compliance. *Archives of General Psychiatry,* 54: 737–742.

REVIEW QUESTIONS

1. What type of sampling method was used for this study? Why was it used rather than random sampling?

2. How did they find their respondents? Who were their respondents?

3. Do you think the sample was representative of all AA members? Did it need to be?

PART III ■ MODES OF OBSERVATIONS

■

Chapter 8: Experimental and Survey Research

What you have learned to this point are the foundations of social science research. In the next few chapters you will learn about various modes of gathering data. Research can be separated into basically two types: **quantitative** and **qualitative.** Quantitative analysis, which you will be learning more about in this chapter, is where the observations are given some sort of numerical representation. Qualitative analysis, which you will learn more about in the following chapters, is where observations are not quantified and where words, pictures, descriptions, or narratives are used as data.

To begin, you will learn about **experiments,** which are best used for topics where the researcher needs to control and explain the phenomenon being studied. Experimental design can be classified into three main types: true experimental design, quasi-experimental design, and double blind experiments. The **true experimental design** is where the researcher controls some variables while manipulating the effects of other variables. As you have learned in previous chapters, the variables used in an experiment are the independent variable and dependent variable. Therefore, the independent variable is the variable to be manipulated, while the dependent variable tells you if the independent variable had any effect on the dependent variable.

Let's say you want to conduct an experiment to determine what the affect of exercise on heart rate will be. You could hypothesize that the more a person exercises, the higher his or her heart rate. It sounds reasonable, but now you need to test this to see if your hypothesis is true. You will use only female students who are between the ages of 18–21 and will randomly assign half the females to receive the stimulus (the exercise) in the **experimental group.** The other half of the sample will not receive the stimulus and is the **control group.** You will randomly assign the women by having them number off 1 and 2. Those who are designated number 1 will go into one group, and the women designated number 2 will go into the other group. This is a true experiment because you randomly assign the subjects to one group or the other to reduce the variation between the experimental and control group and to make sure each and every subject has an equal chance of getting into each group. All true experiments have a **pretest,** which measures the outcome variable before the treatment has been given and a **posttest** to measure the outcome of both groups after the treatment has been given, as shown in Figure 8.1.

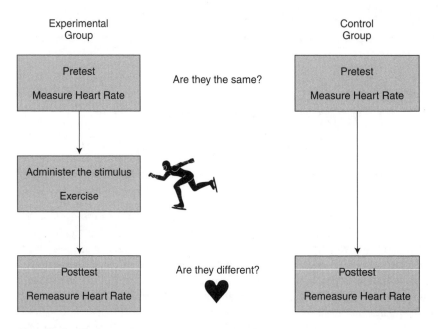

Figure 8.1. Diagram of a Basic Experimental Design

This experiment can also be illustrated by using a series of symbols commonly used to describe experimental designs:

R = random assignment to either the experimental or control group

O = represents an observation or a measurement of the dependent variable

X = those who are exposed to the experimental stimulus or the independent variable

Therefore, this experiment would look like this:

R 01   X   02   Experimental Group

R 01   02   Control Group

In this particular experiment, the dependent variable (O) is the heart rate, which is measured at point one (pretest). The subjects in the experimental group then begin to exercise (X) while the control group doesn't. Then the heart rate of each subject is measured again at point two (posttest) to see if there is a difference between groups.

A **quasi-experimental design** uses some of the same elements that the true experiment uses and even resembles a true experiment in some ways. However, in a quasi-experimental design, the researcher has little control over the exposure or non-exposure of the subjects to the independent variable. There is no random assignment; however, there is a comparison group. For example, let's say you wanted to investigate the effects of sex on anti-social behavior. The groups, boys and girls, would already be preset. You cannot change their sexes. You have two groups and pretest them all to document any anti-social behaviors. Then you would put half the boys and half the girls into two different treatment groups. Suppose members of one group receive money every time they go one hour without hitting someone and members of the other group receive reprimands every time they hit someone. At the end you would conduct a posttest to see which treatment had an effect on the boys and which treatment had an effect on the girls.

So, this quasi-experiment would look like this:

Boys 01	X1	O2 Treatment A: Money
Boys 01	X2	O2 Treatment B: Reprimand
Girls 01	X1	O2 Treatment A: Money
Girls 01	X2	O2 Treatment B: Reprimand

One of the most common types of quasi-experimental design is the **time series design,** which involves a series of repeated measures that are followed by the introduction of the experimental condition and then another series of measures.

In this type of design, the experimental group might look like this:

01   02   03   04   X   05   06   07   08

In this type of design, it could be concluded that the independent variable produced some type of effect if the changes in the dependent variable remain after repeated observations.

A **double-blind experiment** is most often used in medical experimentation. The point of a double blind experiment is to make the subjects believe they are receiving a drug, and often a **placebo,** or fake drug, is given to the control group. The idea is to observe the improvements or behaviors of the subjects after they have received either the placebo or the treatment. I will give you an example. My son needed his wisdom teeth pulled—if you have had it done, you know it can be painful. His dentist conducted experiments for a drug study and asked my son if he wanted to participate in a study on painkillers. He agreed and after his teeth were pulled, when he began to feel pain, he was given a drug. Neither the dentist nor my son knew whether he was given the real drug or the placebo. But then my son was asked to rate his pain for a specific amount of time. If the pill didn't relieve his pain, then he told the nurses and the dentist, rated it on the survey, and he was given drugs that they knew would work. So, not only did he get to participate in a study on drugs, he made money for having his teeth pulled. Not a bad deal, huh? If you live in a major city, you can often find ads in your local paper looking for people to participate in studies.

Survey research is best used for topics where the researcher asks questions and learns about the attitudes or behaviors reported by the respondent. Surveys are probably the "most frequently used mode of observation in the social sciences and the most common method reported in the *American Sociological Review*" (Babbie, 2001: 256). Surveys have become a popular way of conducting research because they are versatile, efficient, and generalizable. Although a survey is not good for testing your entire hypothesis, it certainly can enhance your understanding of a particular social issue such as the *Sex in America* survey you read about in Chapter 7. Surveys are efficient because the data can be collected from a large number of people. Surveys can be sent out in the mail, over the

Internet, given out at a mall, or conducted on the telephone. One of the largest surveys is the U.S. Census, where the government tries to obtain information about every person in the United States. Surveys are often the only way to obtain information about groups of people and therefore are a good way to generalize about the entire population.

Basically, two types of questions are used in surveys: A **close-ended question** provides the respondents a fixed set of answers to choose from. For an **open-ended question,** the respondents formulate their own responses. So, if the question asked is "What is your marital status?" a close-ended question could give four possible answers for the respondents such as married, widowed, single, or divorced. If the question were "What is your race?," there are so many possibilities to choose from, it is often easier to leave a blank and allow the respondents to fill in their responses.

Designing a **questionnaire** is not always as easy as you might think. To begin, you must go back to your hypothesis, and let your independent and dependent variables guide the questions you ask of your respondents. Remember that you are trying to figure out if the independent variable has some effect on the dependent variable. So, let's say you believe that the more education a person has, the higher his or her salary will be. The independent variable is education and the dependent variable is salary. You could just ask two questions: How many years have you been in school? And how much money do you make? However, would that be enough information and could you be sure that education is really what had an effect on the salary? Other variables might actually have an effect on your dependent variable, so you really need to make sure you are capturing the **extraneous variables,** which are those variables that are not objects of the research. So, what other things can affect how much money people make in their jobs? Age, marital status, sex, and experience could all have an effect on the dependent variable, just to name a few. Therefore, you must come up with questions that address those variables.

What kind of question could you ask that would capture your dependent variable? The question "How much money do you receive annually from your job(s)?" would capture it. You can leave a blank for an open-ended question where respondents can write in their responses, or you can give them some choices such as <$10,000, $10,000–$20,000, $20,000–$30,000, and so on. Would any other questions capture the dependent variable? If not, then you must go onto the independent variable. A question that would capture the independent variable would be "What is the highest grade you have completed in school?" Some examples of questions that would capture the extraneous variables include these:

1. What is your sex?

   Male _____

   Female _____

2. What is your age? _____

3. What is your marital status?

   Married _____

   Divorced _____

   Separated _____

   Widowed _____

   Single _____

I am sure you can come up with some other variables as well that could effect your dependent variable. The point is that you need to have questions that can capture all the variables you can think of that could affect the dependent variable in any way. If your questions have nothing to do with the variables, take them out.

Questionnaires should also be neat and well constructed. Make sure you check for grammar and spelling. If you received a questionnaire that looked terrible, you might not have any desire to take time to fill it out. There are also a few ways to distribute questionnaires. A **self-administered questionnaire** is where the respondent receives the questionnaire, fills it out on his or her own, and returns it to the researcher. Mail distribution and return is probably the most common type of distribution and one of the least expensive methods. This is where you send the questionnaire through the mail, with a self-addressed stamped envelope so your respondents can return their completed questionnaire without any expense. If the cost for the respondents' participation is low, the response rates will be higher. According to Babbie (2001), a response rate of 50 percent is adequate, 60 percent is good, and 70 percent is considered very good. The response rate can increase with follow-up mailings sent out a few weeks after the original questionnaire. One follow-up mailing can increase the response rate by an additional 20 percent, and a third follow-up mailing can add an additional 10 percent to the response rate.

Because the Internet and the World Wide Web have exploded in the last few years, more and more surveys are being conducted online. The number of individuals who have access to the Internet has grown to 81 million Americans in early 1999. Only about 90,000 Americans had Internet access in 1993. This is an increase of about 900 percent in 6 years. It is projected that by the year 2000, there will be 230 million Internet users worldwide (United States Internet Council, 1999). More and more individuals will therefore have access to online surveys.

Online surveys can be set up on a Web site with a lot of fanfare to make them appealing to the potential respondents. It seems like every time I log onto a Web site there is some sort of survey. Surveys can also be distributed and retrieved via e-mail. This tends to save time and money for all involved. In the following readings, you will see examples of how researchers use the experimental design.

REFERENCES

Babbie, E. 2001. *The practice of social research* (9th ed). Belmont, CA: Wadsworth.

United States Internet Council, 1999. State of the Internet: USIC's report on use and threats in 1999. [ONLINE] http://www.usic.org/

InfoTrac College Edition Suggested Readings and Discussion Questions

1. Using InfoTrac College Edition, enter the term "random assignment" and see what types of experiments you find. Pick five of the articles that interest you and go through them to see if you can determine what method of random assignment the researchers used to place their subjects in either the control or experimental group.

2. Type the word "experiment" and your particular discipline into InfoTrac College Edition. Thus, if you are a social work major, type "experiment and social work." What kinds of experiments are being done in your discipline? Can you figure out the independent variable, dependent variable, and the hypothesis?

3. Locate a sociological journal of your choice on InfoTrac College Edition. Look at the articles in at least two editions. What methods were used in each article? How many used experiments and how many used surveys?

INTRAOPERATIVE PROGRESS REPORTS DECREASE FAMILY MEMBERS' ANXIETY

Jane S. Leske

In this study, the authors used a four-group, quasi-experimental posttest design. They wanted to examine the effects of the current medical standards of perioperative nursing care, attention, and two types of intraoperative progress reports (that is, in person, telephone call) on family members' ratings of anxiety during their relatives' elective surgical procedures. The researchers believed, rightfully so, that surgery can be anxiety provoking to the family members of the surgical patient. Leske and her colleagues believed, and tested, whether or not the treatment and attention the family received before and during surgery would have different outcomes. As you read this study, notice how the researchers set up the experiment and the different groups that they used.

The waiting period during surgery is the most anxiety-producing time of the entire perioperative experience for patients' family mernbers.[1] Previous researchers have documented that some psychoeducational interventions (e.g., education, orientation of family members to intensive care units) reduce family members' anxiety.[2] Family members who received such interventions reported fewer fears and coped better with stress.[3] Published anecdotes suggest that after receiving intraoperative progress reports, family members described feeling more assured, having more appreciation for staff members' caring behaviors, and experiencing an increased sense of control and a reduction in stress and anxiety.[4]

Previous studies[5] have demonstrated that providing information as an independent perioperative nursing intervention reduces family members' anxiety. Questions about the types and modes of information-giving interventions remained unanswered and prompted the current study.

The purpose of this study was to examine the effects of current standards of perioperative nursing care, attention, and two types of intraoperative progress reports (i.e., in person, telephone call) on family members' ratings of anxiety during their relatives' elective surgical procedures.

Leske, J. S. 1996. Intraoperative Progress Reports Decrease Family Members' Anxiety. *AORN Journal,* 64 (3): 424–435. Used with permission.

Significance of the Study

Perioperative nurses must continue to incorporate humanistic approaches into their care of surgical patients and family members while dealing with tremendous technologic advances in surgical procedures and equipment. Previous nursing research has documented that family members may be more anxious than patients during the perioperative period. Anxiety-reducing nursing interventions may decrease family members' anxiety and improve the help they can provide to their ill relatives. These interventions, however, require further development and testing.

The following assumptions were fundamental to the purpose and design of this study.

1. Surgery is a source of anxiety for patients' family members.

2. Family members have important needs for anxiety relief during the intraoperative period.

3. Family members are able to describe their anxiety through self-report mechanisms.

The research question that guided the study was: "Is there a significant difference in reported anxiety among family members who receive either standard care, in-person intraoperative progress reports, an attention protocol, or telephoned intraoperative progress reports from perioperative nurses?" My hypothesis was that surgical patients' family members who received the in-person or telephone-call intraoperative progress reports would describe less anxiety than family members who did not receive these interventions (i.e., received the standard care or the attention protocol).

I developed the following operational definitions for this study.

- *Anxiety.* The emotional reaction evoked by a stressful situation, which produces physiologic changes secondary to sympathetic arousal (e.g., increased blood pressure and heart rate, anxiety-indicating responses to the S-Anxiety portion of the State-Trait Anxiety Inventory [STAI] Form y).

- *Attention.* A protocol checklist delivered approximately halfway through the patient's surgical procedure. This checklist, which required approximately 5 to 10 minutes to read, provided an overview of hospital routines and waiting room procedures.

- *Elective surgery.* All planned surgical procedures of a nonemergent basis.

- *Family member.* The surgical patient's adult blood relative, spouse, or significant other who waits in the hospital during the patient's surgical procedure.

- *Intraoperative progress report.* A protocol-driven progress report that was designed to relay information in person or by telephone call to family members approximately halfway through a patient's surgical procedure. The progress report lasted 5 to 10 minutes and followed a specific outline.

- *Standard care.* No intraoperative progress reports or attention protocol provided.

Anxiety is characterized by subjective, consciously perceived feelings of apprehension and tension that are associated with autonomic nervous system arousal. A three-stage cognitive appraisal of the anxiety-producing situation is essential to this psychological theory of stress. During the primary appraisal, an individual makes a distinction about the significance of the situation. The situation may evoke a variety of emotions depending on the presence and degree of the identified threat. The extent of an individual's sympathetic nervous system activation also depends on his or her interpretation of anxiety. The secondary appraisal is the process by which the individual evaluates his or her coping responses and options. Reappraisal is a change in the individual's original appraisal that results from new information or feedback from the environment. Within the context of most stressful encounters, information and emotions are combined for large portions of the cognitive appraisal process. Anxiety, however, threatens the integrity of an individual's cognitive system during the reappraisal process.

Study Design

I used a four-group, quasi-experimental posttest design to compare the effectiveness of intraoperative progress reports in decreasing family members' anxiety. I compared family members' state anxiety scores, mean arterial pressures (MAPs), and heart rates that were measured approximately halfway during their relatives' surgical procedures after providing the intervention (i.e., progress reports, attention protocol). I conducted the study during a six-month period at one community hospital located near a major metropolitan area in the Midwest.

Sample. I used power, effect size, and significance level to compute the sample size required to demonstrate significant results. Power is the probability of rejecting the null hypothesis (i.e., that intraoperative progress reports would not affect family members' anxiety). Effect size is a measure of how incorrect the null hypothesis is (i.e., how strong the effect of the independent variable [intervention] is on the dependent variables [anxiety measures]). I established the level of significance based on a formulation of the desired statistical power (i.e., .80), medium effect size (i.e., $f = .25$), and a significance level of .05. I determined that a sample size of 45 family members in each group would be sufficient to test the study hypothesis.

All adult family members of patients having elective surgical procedures at this hospital during the six-month study period were eligible to participate. Their relatives' surgical procedures needed to last at least 30 minutes (i.e., from the time of incision) for progress reports to be clinically feasible. Family members had to be available in the waiting room during surgery; identify themselves as family members of these patients; be able to speak, read, and understand English; and be at least 18 years of age.

Measures. I measured family members' state anxiety scores using the S-Anxiety portion of the STAI Form Y. This self-report scale evaluates qualities such as current feelings of apprehension, tension, nervousness, and worry. The reliability and validity of this inventory are well documented. The S-Anxiety portion of the STAI Form Y consists of 20 statements to which I asked family members to respond. In their responses, they rated their feelings of anxiety while waiting for their relatives' surgical procedures to be completed. The responses to each statement are scored on a Likert-type scale, ranging from "not at all" anxious (i.e., one) to "very much so" (i.e., four). Examples of statements on this scale include "I feel calm" and "I am worried." I summed the response numbers for each statement and obtained scores that were in the formed range for this scale (i.e., 20 =

low anxiety to 80 = high anxiety). The Cronbach's alpha coefficient for this study was .94, indicating a high degree of reliability.

I measured family members' brachial blood pressures using a noninvasive portable monitor with automatic oscillometry. I calculated each family member's MAP manually using this formula: ⅓ (systolic blood pressure–diastolic blood pressure) + diastolic blood pressure. I chose MAPs as the dependent variable because diastolic blood pressure is more constant than systolic blood pressure during most of the cardiac cycle and is a good estimate of arterial blood pressure. I used the pulse oximeter mode of the same monitor to determine family members' heart rates.

Each day during the study period, I numbered the scheduled surgical patients, drew numbers randomly from a hat, and selected two or three patients. I then asked the family members of these selected patients to participate in the study and did not limit the number of family members per patient who could participate. I ensured that the waiting periods of participating family members did not overlap so that potential interaction between patients' family members would not be an intervening variable (i.e., an alternative factor that affects the independent or dependent variable and over which the researcher has no control). I obtained written consent from all family members who participated.

I used a four-stage sampling procedure, assigning the first 50 family members to the control group (i.e., group one), the next 50 family members to the in-person progress report group (i.e., group two), the next 50 family members to the attention group (i.e., group three), and the final 50 family members to the telephone-call progress report group (i.e., group four). I chose this sampling method to maximize the probability of having equivalent groups and to prevent the interaction of family members in different groups.

Group One. Family members assigned to the control group received no nursing intervention because the standard of perioperative nursing care for patients' family members did not include intraoperative progress reports, When a patient's surgical procedure was approximately 50% completed, I asked his or her family members to fill out the S-Anxiety portion of the STAI Form Y and a demographic information form. After the family members completed these forms, the research assistants or I measured family members' MAPs and heart rates while they were seated.

Group Two. After I completed data collection from all 50 family members in group one, I randomly selected 50 additional family members to be in the in-person progress report group. When a patient's surgical procedure was approximately 50% completed, a perioperative nurse came to the waiting room and provided the patient's family members a 5- to 10–minute progress report that followed a previously published protocol. The nurse informed the family members of the patient's physiologic status, that the surgical procedure was approximately 50% completed, that the patient would be transferred to the postanesthesia care unit (PACU) after surgery, that the family members would be notified when the patient was being transferred from the PACU to the postsurgical unit, and that they could visit the patient after he or she was in the postsurgical unit.

The nurse who gave the report avoided mentioning specific time frames. After family members received the in-person intraoperative progress report, they completed the S-Anxiety portion of the STAI Form Y and a demographic information form, and research assistants or I measured the MAPs and heart rates in the manner described previously.

Group Three. After I completed data collection from all 50 family members in group two, I randomly selected an additional 50 family members to be in the attention group. When a patient's surgical procedure was approximately 50% completed, a research assistant verbally gave family members a protocol checklist. This checklist, which required 5 to 10 minutes for the research assistant to read, provided an overview of hospital routines and waiting room procedures. This "attention" session provided family members with the same amount of contact time as family members in the intraoperative progress report groups received. After receiving the attention protocol checklist, family members completed the S-Anxiety portion of the STAI Form Y and a demographic information form, and research assistants or I measured their vital signs in the manner described previously.

Group Four. After I completed data collection from all 50 family members in group three, I randomly selected an additional 50 family members to be in the telephone-call progress report group. When a patient's surgical procedure was approximately 50% completed, a perioperative nurse called the patient's family members from the OR and provided a 5- to 10-minute progress report. The format and basic content of this report were identical to the in-person progress report provided to family members in group two. After family members received the telephone-call intraoperative progress report, they completed the S-Anxiety portion of the STAI Form Y and a demographic information form, and research assistants or I measured the MAPs and heart rates in the manner described previously.

Family members in all groups completed the S-Anxiety portion of the STAI Form Y and a demographic information form, received the interventions, and had their vital signs measured in the privacy of a conference room near the general waiting room area. When the patients were in the PACU, I obtained information about the patients' surgical procedures from their intraoperative records.

Sample Demographics

Two hundred family members of 150 surgical patients participated in this study. Three additional family members (i.e., one selected for the control group, one for the in-person intraoperative progress report group, one of the telephone-call intraoperative progress report group) declined to participate.

Family Member Profile. The 200 family members ranged in age from 18 to 80 years (mean [M] = 47.5 years, standard deviation [SD] = 14.75 years). Sixty-four percent of the family members were female. Family members described their relationships to the patients as spouse (45%), parent (28%), child (15%), significant other (9%), and sibling (3%). Family members' educational preparation ranged from 8 to 24 years (M = 12.7 years, SD = 2 years). Eighty-nine percent of the family members had previous experience waiting for family members during surgery.

Patient Profile. The patients ranged in age from 1 to 90 years (M = 46.3 years, SD = 24.15 years). Fifty-six percent of the patients were females. The patients were scheduled for a variety of surgical procedures: general (28%), orthopedic (27%), otorhinolaryngologic (13%), ophthalmologic (13%), gynecologic (12%), urologic (4%), neurosurgical (2%), and thoracic (1%). Seventy-seven percent of the patients received general anesthesia, but some had local anesthesia (11%), regional blocks (4%), IV conscious sedation with local anesthesia (4%), epidural anesthesia (3%), or spinal anesthesia (1%). Sixty-one percent of the patients were scheduled as outpatients, but some were morning admissions (33%) or inpatients (6%). The actual surgical procedures lasted from 30 to 620 minutes (M = 103.27 min, SD = 71.95 min).

Results and Discussion

Before comparing data from the four groups, I examined all demographic variables to ensure the equivalence of the groups. There were no significant differences among the groups for any of the demographic variables except duration of surgical procedure. The mean surgical procedure durations were 78.38 minutes (SD = 36.71 min) for the control group, 99.46 minutes (SD = 48.79 min) for the in-person intraoperative progress report group, 129.29 minutes (SD = 117.81 rain) for the attention group, and 109.06 minutes (SD = 55.48 min) for the telephone-call intraoperative progress report group. Duration of surgical procedures was not related to the dependent variables (i.e., STAI-S scores, MAPs, heart rates), so I did not use it as a covariate in the analysis.

Family members in the in-person progress report group reported lower anxiety scores and had significantly lower MAPs and heart rates than family members in the control, attention, and telephone-call report groups. In addition, family members in the in-person and telephone-call progress report groups had anxiety scores, MAPs, and heart rates that were significantly different from each other. Tables 1 through 4 summarize these results.

Family members who received the in-person intraoperative progress reports recorded significantly less anxiety than family members in the control, attention, or telephone-call report groups. The control group's mean anxiety score of 43.42 was much higher than the normal sample mean of 35 that the authors of the tool reported, and the in-person report group's mean anxiety score of 28.59 was much lower than the normal sample mean reported by the authors of the tool. The mean anxiety scores of the attention and telephone-call progress report groups approximated the normal sample mean.

Family members in the in-person progress report group reported lower anxiety scores than family members in the telephone-call progress report group. It was apparent that telephone-call reports or attention reduced family members' anxiety more than no intervention, but providing in-person intraoperative progress reports was the most beneficial intervention.

Normal MAP is approximately 93 mm Hg. The MAP ranges in all four family-member groups contained the normal value. The MAPs in the control, attention, and telephone-call progress report groups were above the normal value, whereas the MAPs in the in-person progress report group were below the normal value. Adult heart rates normally range from 60 to 80 beats per minute. In this study, family members in all four groups had heart rates in the normal range, but the mean rate was lowest in the in-person progress report group.

The results of this study also confirm previous findings that family members of acutely ill patients are highly anxious. Family members in the control group reported higher anxiety levels than those reported by patients undergoing coronary artery bypass

TABLE 1. CONTROL GROUP (GROUP ONE) ANXIETY MEASURES

Measures	Range	Mean	Standard Deviation
State-Trait Anxiety Inventory Form Y S-Anxiety scores	20 to 60	43.42	12.58
Mean arterial pressures (mm Hg)	74.90 to 118.41	101.63	11.04
Heart rates (beats/min)	52 to 99	74.78	10.88

TABLE 2. IN-PERSON INTRAOPERATIVE PROGRESS REPORT GROUP (GROUP TWO) ANXIETY MEASURES

Measures	Range	Mean	Standard Deviation
State-Trait Anxiety Inventory Form Y S-Anxiety scores	21 to 51	28.56	7.10
Mean arterial pressures (mm Hg)	77.16 to 104.40	90.89	6.60
Heart rates (beats/min)	60 to 88	71.44	5.99

TABLE 3. ATTENTION GROUP (GROUP THREE) ANXIETY MEASURES

Measures	Range	Mean	Standard Deviation
State-Trait Anxiety Inventory Form Y S-Anxiety scores	20 to 60	37.30	12.32
Mean arterial pressures (mm Hg)	78.80 to 126.36	97.36	11.03
Heart rates (beats/min)	57 to 99	75.84	10.36

TABLE 4. TELEPHONE-CALL INTRAOPERATIVE PROGRESS REPORT GROUP (GROUP FOUR) ANXIETY MEASURES

Measures	Range	Mean	Standard Deviation
State-Trait Anxiety Inventory Form Y S-Anxiety scores	20 to 59	35.70	9.65
Mean arterial pressures (mm Hg)	73.76 to 128.37	97.08	12.95
Heart rates (beats/min)	62 to 98	77.00	9.20

graft (CABG) procedure, patients undergoing cardiac catheterization procedures, mothers of hospitalized children, significant others of patients undergoing CABG procedures, and family members who were learning cardiopulmonary resuscitation techniques because they had relatives with cardiac disease. The high degree of anxiety in the control group is alarming considering the lack of intraoperative nursing interventions directed toward family members of surgical patients.

The majority of patients in this study underwent ambulatory surgery procedures, which is not an unusual finding. Previous research has suggested that the presence of a caring person during surgery waiting periods is as effective as providing information in reducing family members' anxiety. Other researchers have reported that emotional support is more effective than providing detailed information in reducing patients' preoperative anxiety. The results of this study suggest that in-person provision of information reduces family members' anxiety more than emotional support, presence of a supportive person, or telephone-call progress reports.

The control group's anxiety scores, MAPs, and heart rates support individuals' primary appraisals of the waiting period during surgery as being anxiety producing. The reductions observed in these anxiety measures in the in-person intraoperative progress report group suggest that interventions may provide the coping option that family members need during the secondary appraisal process. Information provided by in-person intraoperative progress reports appears to decrease family members' anxiety, supporting the study hypothesis.

The sample size for this study was adequate, and the sample was selected randomly. The lack of a pretest measure, however, may require further research to examine causality in the effects of intraoperative progress reports on family members' anxiety. The results of this study can be generalized only to family members of patients undergoing elective surgical procedures. More research needs to be conducted to determine if similar results are obtained from perioperative nursing interventions directed to family members of patients undergoing emergency, major, or diagnostic surgical procedures.

Using research findings as a foundation for perioperative nursing practice may change nurses' attitudes about surgical patients' family members. In the current consumer-oriented health care climate, implementing new interventions (e.g., in-person intraoperative progress reports, family-focused perioperative nursing care) may make a difference in a facility's surgical market share. The benefits of nurse-family member interactions during the intraoperative period should not be underestimated. Adequately assessing family members' anxiety and appropriately intervening to decrease the stress associated with surgical experiences have important implications for perioperative nursing practice.

References

1. Silva, M. C. Caring for those who wait, *Today's OR Nurse,* 6 (June 1984) 26–30; E. H. Raleigh, M. Lepezyk, & C. Rowley. Significant others benefit from preoperative information, *Journal of Advanced Nursing,* 15 (August 1990) 941–945.

2. Kathol, D. K. Anxiety in surgical patients' families, *AORN Journal,* 40 (July 1984), 131–137; Silva et al., Caring for those who wait, 26–30; Raleigh, Lepezyk, & Rowley, Significant others benefit from preoperative information, 941–945;

C. W. Chavez & L. Faber, Effect of an education orientation program on family members who visit their significant other in the intensive care unit, *Heart & Lung,* 16 (January 1987) 92–99.

3. J. A. Reider, Anxiety during critical illness of a family member, *Dimensions of Critical Care Nursing,* 13 (September/October 1994) 272–279; T. M. Davis et al., Preparing adult patients for cardiac catheterization: Informational treatment and coping style interactions, *Heart & Lung,* 23 (March/April: 1994) 130–139.

4. R. Eldridge, Surgery progress reports: Support for cardiac surgery patients' families, *AORN Journal,* 40 (August 1984) 241–246; R. Craig, D. Cioni, & C. Morrison, The forgotten: Families of your surgical patients, *Journal of Post Anesthesia Nursing,* 1 (August 1986) 170–174; S. G. Donnell, Coping during the wait: Surgical nurse liaison program aids families, *AORN Journal,* 50 (November 1989) 1088–1092; J. S. Mitiguy, A surgical liaison program: Making the wait more bearable, *MCN: American Journal of Maternal Child Nursing,* 11 (November/December 1986) 388–392.

5. Leske, J. S., Effects of intraoperative progress reports on anxiety of elective surgical patients' family members, *Clinical Nursing Research,* 1 (August 1992), 169–173, 266–267; M. J. Johnson & D. I. Frank, Effectiveness of a telephone intervention in reducing anxiety of families of patients in an intensive care unit, *Applied Nursing Research,* 8 (February 1995) 42–43; A. W. Keeling & P. D. Dennison, Nurse-initiated telephone follow-up after acute myocardial infarction: A pilot study, *Heart & Lung,* 24 (January 1995) 45–49.

REVIEW QUESTIONS

1. What were the independent and dependent variables in the experiment? What was the hypothesis?

2. Explain the four-group, quasi-experimental posttest design used in this study.

3. What were some of the limitations of this study?

Sex in America—The Sex Survey

Robert T. Michael, John H. Gagnon, Edward O. Laumann, and Gina Kolata

In Chapter 7, you read a portion of this study devoted to the issue of sampling in sexuality research. This portion of the study describes how the researchers became interested in the study of sex, how they designed and administered the survey, and how the survey questions compared with the questions given in other big national surveys. Notice how much thought and planning must go into a survey to make sure it provides valid and reliable information.

The long history of attempts to study sexuality had as a dominant theme this idea that sexuality comes from within, that it is a feature of the individual, and that to understand sexual behavior we have to understand the individual's sex drives and hormonal surges and even genetic predispositions. As a consequence, the popular explanations of sexual behavior, the belief that the individual is the sole actor on the sexual stage, are an echo and a legacy of previous sex studies.

Our viewpoint is very different. We are convinced that sexual behavior is shaped by our social surroundings. We behave the way we do, we even desire what we do, under the strong influence of the particular social groups we belong to. We do not have all the latitude we may imagine when we look for a partner, nor do we have all the choices in the world when we decide what to do in bed. The choices we make about our sex lives are dramatically affected by our social circumstances.

Previous surveys, however, fed Americans' thirst for information on sexual practices and their results were often cited uncritically and the pseudo-studies of Kinsey (1948), Masters and Johnson (1966), Hite (1976), and Janus (1993) provided a picture of a very sexually active nation. Because these studies have been so widely publicized and are cited so often, many Americans walk around thinking they are among the few who do not have a lot of sex partners, thinking that even if they are satisfied, they must be missing something. Our study, called the National Health and Social Life Survey, or NHSLS, has findings that often directly contradict what has become the conventional wisdom about sex. They are counterrevolutionary findings, showing a country with very diverse sexual practices but one that, on the whole, is much less sexually active than we have come to believe.

Our survey, in contrast to the "reports" that preceded it, was a truly scientific endeavor, using advanced and sophisticated methods of social science research. Although these methods had been developed and used in the past for investigations of such things as political opinions, labor force participation and hours of work, expenditure patterns, or migration behavior, they work equally well in studying sexual behavior. Like studies of less emotionally charged subjects, studies of sex can succeed if respondents are convinced that there is a legitimate reason for doing the research, that their answers will be treated nonjudgmentally, and that their confidentiality will be protected.

Our study was completed only after a long and difficult struggle that shows, if nothing else, why it has been so enormously difficult for any social scientists to get any reliable data on sexual practices. The fact that it succeeded in the end was more a matter of our research team's stubbornness and determination than it was a mandate for this information to emerge.

The survey was conceived in 1987, as a response to the AIDS crisis. The human immunodeficiency virus, which causes AIDS, had been identified in 1984. By 1987, it was abundantly clear that it was not going to be easy or quick to find a vaccine or a cure for the disease. As the AIDS epidemic spread across the land, medical scientists began to focus on how to prevent the disease, and which groups of people were most at risk. The disease was infectious, scientists realized, and one of the ways it was spread was through sex. This understanding immediately gave rise to three questions: How quickly was the disease going to spread? Who was most at risk for getting AIDS through sexual contact? How can people be persuaded to change risky behaviors?

But to answer those questions and to contain the epidemic, scientists needed to know about sexual practices in America and they needed to know about people's attitudes toward sex. Yet after years during which sexual research was treated as somehow beyond the pale, public health officials and some policy workers realized that they had almost no data that would enable them to answer these pressing questions. They were left with the forty-year-old Kinsey data, which everyone recognized to be highly problematical. Those findings were out of date and, moreover, were not even an accurate reflection of the population of Kinsey's era. Although it seemed useless to rely on Kinsey to try to analyze the spread of HIV and staunch the epidemic, in the absence of other data, scientists had to turn to his data to estimate, for example, the numbers of men who had sex with men.

Faced with the national emergency of the AIDS epidemic and the dearth of needed data, scientists and administrators at several agencies of the federal government, including the National Institute of Child Health and Human Development, the Centers for Disease Control and Prevention, the National Institute on Aging, and the National Institute of Mental Health, supported the idea of doing a national survey of sexual practices. Leading scientists in these agencies had wanted more general studies of sexuality to examine such issues as teen pregnancy, sexual dysfunction, and child abuse, and they realized that the AIDS crisis finally made such a study politically feasible as well as crucially important.

After scientific blue-ribbon panels, such as one established by the Institute of Medicine, spoke out strongly in favor of a national sex study, the government took the first step toward conducting one. In July of 1987, the National Institute of Child Health and Human Development invited researchers to apply for a grant to design such a study, with the understanding that the best design would be used to conduct the survey. The institute also asked for proposals for designs of a parallel study on adolescent sexual practices.

But our national squeamishness about asking questions about sex and our collective ambivalence about knowing the answers surfaced right away. Even the name of the request for proposals—"Social and Behavioral Aspects of Fertility Related Behavior"—illustrated this simultaneous inching forward and pulling back. Nowhere in that title was there any hint that this was supposed to be a sex survey. And even though such a survey was intended, the original funding was to be only for a year, to determine whether the survey was feasible. Then, after a design was established, the government would issue another request for proposals on actually carrying out the study.

Our team, working through the National Opinion Research Center, a survey research firm associated with the University of Chicago, was awarded the contract to design the study. But even with this support from the federal health establishment, there was still much resistance to such a study elsewhere in the government. In the months that followed, there was a constant pressure to compromise, to pare down a sex survey into an AIDS study.

Many government officials wanted to steer clear of topics that might be important to an understanding of sex but that were not obviously related to the spread of AIDS. For example, they did not want the survey to ask about masturbation, reasoning that masturbation was a private matter and unlikely to have anything to do with the transmission of the AIDS virus. As researchers, facing the problem of limited knowledge, we wished to cast our net widely. Nothing was known about masturbation in relation to sexual practices. Do people masturbate as a substitute for sexual intercourse? Is it used to enhance sexual arousal? Do men use it to prevent premature ejaculation?

Another consequence of the focus on disease and health problems was an argument that if a couple was monogamous, the questioning should cease then and there. The attitude was that we should not be asking these sex questions of "respectable" Americans. In short, some officials assumed they already knew what the answers would be and they knew what behaviors were acceptable and innocuous and which people to leave alone.

Eventually, even this narrow inventory of AIDS-related questions turned out to be too controversial for the government. In September 1991, Senator Jesse Helms introduced an amendment to a bill on funding for the National Institutes of Health that specifically prohibited the government from paying for such a study. The amendment passed, by a vote of 66 to 34, dooming the effort.

Nonetheless, we had been able to work on interview questions and methodology during the period when it looked as if the government might go ahead with the project. Part of the feasibility study that we conducted allowed us to test questions, conduct focus groups, do pilot interviews, and to design the sample. This work laid the groundwork for a full-scale study of sexuality.

When the Senate refused funding to continue the study, we turned to private philanthropic organizations for support. Freed of political constraints, we decided to make this a sex survey that would go far beyond the original purpose of helping to fight AIDS. We would treat sexual behavior like any other social behavior, using established methods to study it. Our hope was to glean data that would help not only with the fight against AIDS, sexually transmitted diseases, and unwanted pregnancies, but that also would help us understand what enabled some sexual partners to stay together for years while others break apart after only one or a few encounters. We also hoped to learn what were the key features of sexual relationships that were both emotionally and physically satisfying.

A much trickier problem arose when we wrote our questionnaire. We had to decide how, and with what language, to ask people about their sex lives. We did not want to confuse people by using technical language. Even words like *vaginal* and *heterosexual* were not well understood by many people, we found. Yet we did not want subtly to make the interview itself sexy or provocative or offensive by using slang terms. We wanted to create a neutral, nonjudgmental atmosphere in which people would feel comfortable telling us about one of the most private aspects of their lives.

We also needed to make the questions flow naturally from one topic to another and without prejudicing people's replies because of the order of the questions. We began by asking people about their backgrounds, their race, education, and religion, for example, and moved on to marriages and fertility. Then we gradually moved on to ask about sex. We asked for many details about recent sexual events and we asked for fewer specifics about events further in the past, reasoning that inability to recall details from long ago could result in erroneous, if well-intentioned, answers.

We decided to administer the questions during face-to-face interviews, which lasted an average of an hour and a half. By asking people directly, we could be sure that the respondents understood the questions and that the person who was supposed to be answering really did answer. These were to be questions that would gently lead people through their entire sexual history without making them anxious or bored, and without antagonizing them. At the same time, we wanted the questions to be neutral, so that there was no "right" answer. And we wanted a certain covert redundancy that would allow us to check answers for consistency.

Once we had the questions, we needed trained and experienced interviewers who could put people at their ease and gain their trust. To help us select interviewers whom people would talk to, we used focus groups, asking people of different races and backgrounds whom they would feel most comfortable with. To our surprise, almost everyone, including blacks, Hispanics, and men, preferred middle-aged white women. In the end, we selected 220 interviewers, mainly women in their thirties and forties. These interviewers were for the most part veterans of several other survey projects and all had a professional attitude and commitment to working on this particular survey under the careful management of the National Opinion Research Center.

After selecting the interviewers, we flew them to Chicago for further training, instructing them about how to conduct our survey and suggesting the kinds of difficulties they might encounter. For example, they might hear vernacular terms that might, in ordinary circumstances, embarrass them. As professionals, they could not let their own reactions become apparent to the respondents. We also encouraged the interviewers to tell us their own ideas about how to interview people about sexuality. The interviewers had a very high morale because they saw this study as stretching the limits of what is possible in a scientific survey. It was a professional challenge for them to make this study a success, and they had a shared sense of collective purpose.

In order to be sure that people who were identified as part of the study would agree to participate, the interviewers used all their powers of persuasion, returning again and again to the homes of people who declined, in some cases even paying the most recalcitrant to encourage them to agree to be interviewed. The participants were guaranteed anonymity. We have destroyed all identifiers from our completed interviews; thus, we could not name or find these people again if we wanted to. We also checked our data and found those reluctant respondents answered no differently than the others.

The interviewers began work on Valentine's Day, February 14, 1992, and continued until September of that year, which enabled them to spend as long as seven months in their attempts to find people and persuade them to participate in the study. In most surveys, interviewers spend two to three months tracking down and questioning respondents.

The survey was an expensive proposition, far different from mailing out questionnaires and tallying those that came back, as others have done. But we could be assured that the designated person answered our questions and not someone else. Each interview cost, in the end, an average of about $450, including the interviewer training, the several trips to the residence when necessary to do the interview, and entering the data into a computer for analysis.

Our interviewers clearly persuaded the prospective respondents of two key things. First, that the information they gave would be of value in understanding sexual behavior in America and in informing public health officials, counselors, and policymakers about the sexual matters we were addressing. And second, that the information they provided would be obtained in privacy, held in confidence, and not be associated with them personally. The success of this survey is a testament to the skill of the professional interviewers and the goodwill of the public.

The first question, of course, is: Were the respondents telling us the truth about their sex lives? Why should we believe that anyone, sitting in a face-to-face interview with a stranger, would answer honestly when questioned about his or her most intimate, personal behavior, including behavior that might be embarrassing to admit?

Survey researchers have several ways to check on the veracity of their data, and we used many of them. First, we had several questions that were redundant, but because they were asked in different ways at different times in the long interview, it would be difficult for a subject to dissemble convincingly. For example, we asked people twice how many sex partners they had had. The first time was as a simple question early in the interview, and the respondent was asked to write down the answer privately and place it into an envelope that was then sealed; the interviewer sent this envelope into the office without opening it. The second time was about an hour later, when the respondent was reviewing a lifetime sexual history. In this case, the number of partners was summed over various periods in the respondent's life. We found that the numbers came out essentially the same both ways, increasing our confidence that people were telling the truth.

We also inserted eleven sex questions from another survey into our survey to see if our respondents gave replies that corresponded to the results of that survey. That other survey, the General Social Survey (also conducted by NORC), did not mention to the respondents when the interview began that there were any sex questions and the sex questions only constituted about two minutes of a ninety-minute interview. Our survey, in contrast, stressed that sexual behavior was the primary focus of the whole study. So this comparison lets us see if the emphasis on sex had any influence on the type of people who answered our questions or on the type of answers they gave. This is one of the only ways we know of to see if there is any indication that our respondents did not tell us the truth about their sex lives or did not have sexual histories that were similar to those of the population at large. The comparison of our results to those of the 1991 General Social Survey is displayed in Table 1.

The table shows our respondents' replies to two of the eleven questions as compared to the replies of respondents in the General Social Survey. The answers were remarkably similar. For example, about 11 percent of the men in both surveys said they had no sex partner within the past twelve months, while 68 percent or 69 percent said they had one sex partner in the past twelve months. The women's replies were just as similar in the two studies. The match between the responses in both surveys was extraordinary. We could not expect to get more corroboration or similarity if we asked about any other behavior.

The top panel of the table assures us of an important fact; that our respondents appear to have taken the interview seriously and responded honestly. Or, at least, they responded

TABLE 1. COMPARISON OF SEX PARTNER DATA IN NHSLS AND GSS

Q: "How many sex partners have you had in the past twelve months?"

| | Men | | Women | |
Response	GSS	NHSLS	GSS	NHSLS
0	11.6%	11.1%	13.4%	13.7%
1	69.4	67.6	76.4	75.5
2	9.2	9.6	6.7	6.3
3	2.4	4.8	3.6*	4.5*
4	2.4	2.8	—	—
5–10	3.9	3.1	—	—
11+	1.2	1.0	—	—
	100%	100%	100%	100%

*Three or more partners

Q: "Have your sex partners in the past twelve months been exclusively male, both male and female, or exclusively female?"

| | Men | | Women | |
Response	GSS	NHSLS	GSS	NHSLS
Exclusively male	2.8%	2.6%	99.4%	98.3%
Both male and female	0.6	1.0	0.2	0.5
Exclusively female	96.6	96.3	0.4	1.2
	100%	100%	100%	100%

with remarkable consistency with those in that other survey conducted in quite a different context. There is no indication in the distribution of the number of sex partners in the past twelve months that people thought the question was a joke and wrote down some funny numbers. There may well be some error in our data, as in all measurements, but the respondents here seem to be trying to answer the questions we asked.

The lower panel of the table is one of several pieces of information we have about homosexuality in the population, a topic we discuss at length [later]. Looking at the information here, it is striking how similar the answers are in the two surveys: a little more than 2.5 percent of the men in both samples who had sex partners in the previous twelve months said their partners were exclusively men during that period and another 0.5 percent to 1 percent said they had sex with both men and women. This leaves 96 percent of men who had sexual intercourse in the past year reporting that they had sex only with women during that time. For women, around 1 percent said they had sex exclusively with other women, another half of 1 percent or less said they had sex with both men and women. This leaves nearly 99 percent of women reporting that they had sex exclusively with men in the past twelve months.

Finally, we checked our data on sexual behavior against several other very recent and well-conducted studies that each looked at a part of the general picture we were assembling. Our study, and all of these others, came to the same basic conclusions, greatly strengthening the argument that our data can be trusted.

A final reason we trusted our data was the reports of our seasoned interviewers. They reported back to us that the participants enjoyed the interview, that they found it a rewarding and often illuminating experience to be gently led through their sex lives and attitudes about sex. In fact, they said it was an affirming event to talk about their sexuality and their sexual history in a nonjudgmental way. The interviewers reported that they had the sense that the respondents were telling the truth.

References

Shere Hite, *The Hite Report* (New York: Dell, 1976).

Samuel S. Janus and Cynthia L. Janus, *The Janus Report on Sexual Behavior* (New York: John Wiley and Sons, 1993).

Alfred C. Kinsey, Wardell B. Pomeroy, and Clyde E. Martin, *Sexual Behavior in the Human Male* (Philadelphia: W. B. Saunders Co., 1948).

William H. Masters and Virginia E. Johnson, *Human Sexual Response* (Boston: Little Brown, 1966).

REVIEW QUESTIONS

1. How was the questionnaire administered in this study? Would there have been a better way?

2. How did the researchers make sure that the respondents were telling the truth? What did they find?

3. Do you think that the answers would be more or less accurate if this type of survey was done over the Internet rather than face-to-face? Why or why not?

THE INTERNET AND OPINION MEASUREMENT: SURVEYING MARGINALIZED POPULATIONS

Nadine S. Koch and Jolly A. Emrey

Using the Internet as a means to obtain survey data has increased in the last few years. However, the validity of online surveys is often questioned. This study addresses the issues of self-selection, selection bias, and response rates by examining population data for a group of Internet users who responded to a series of online surveys posted on a gay and lesbian Web site. The demographic data collected from the online study sample was compared with national data on gays and lesbians to determine if differences existed between participants and nonparticipants. Watch for the different ways the researchers went about making sure that their sample was reflective of other samples.

Social scientists are increasingly interested in studying the attitudes of subgroups whose members are not easily identified. The use of standard survey research methods is not always feasible, especially when reliable sampling frames of certain subgroups are difficult or impossible to acquire. In such situations, purposive samples have been relied upon. It is clear that self-selected samples pose problems of statistical inference and generalizability. However, such samples allow research on rare and marginalized populations that would otherwise not be conducted. Nonprobability sampling techniques have been used to study such subgroups as Vietnam veterans (Rothbart, Fine, and Sudman, 1982), members of Alcoholics Anonymous (Fortney et al., 1998), Mexican American gang members (Valdez and Kaplan, 1999), and fundamentalist and rural Christian congregations (Jelen, 1992, 1993; Wald, Owen, and Hill, 1988). Presumably, most social scientists would agree that it is preferable to conduct research with admitted limitations rather than to ignore certain topics altogether because of methodological difficulties.

The Internet has not been considered a good source of survey respondents because of selection effects. However, Internet surveys are an extension of survey research techniques (i.e., purposive samples) that, although not optimal in the classic textbook sense, are used quite frequently in sampling populations where adequate sampling frames are not available. Although online surveys have been in use for a number of years, problems of self-selection have precluded the calculation of response rates and degree of selection bias. To date, no self-selected, easily accessible online survey has reported response rates and degree of selection bias. This study addresses those problems by examining population data for a group of Internet users who responded to online surveys, enabling us to provide a calculation of both response rate and selection bias. We find that participants in the online survey are nearly indistinguishable from nonparticipants and are demographically comparable to their nationwide cohort. The overall response was slightly more than 16 percent, similar to response rates for nontargeted, mass mail surveys. In short, we

Koch, N. S., and Emrey, J. A. 2001. The Internet and opinion measurement: Surveying marginalized populations. *Social Science Quarterly,* 82 (1): 131–138. Reprinted with permission from Blackwell Publishing, Ltd.

argue that online surveys should not be dismissed outright as a research tool for difficult-to-reach populations.

Sample Selection Bias

Sample selection bias is a serious concern for researchers, and attention has focused on the causes of, diagnosis of, and corrections for sample selection bias (Berk, 1983; Groves, 1987; and Winship and Mare, 1992). Researchers are often confronted with a dilemma when researching populations that are difficult to find. How does one study a particular subgroup without compromising the validity of the data, especially when employing non-traditional sampling methods? As Rothbart, Fine, and Sudman (1982: 408) argue, "The problems involved in sampling rare populations, and therefore the methods for their solutions, are becoming increasingly important in survey research . . . social researchers are increasingly being asked to conduct studies of persons with special characteristics—such as laid-off workers or people with certain categories of illness—so as to provide policy-relevant data." Winship and Mare (1992: 327) in their research on sample selection bias also acknowledge this research dilemma by pointing out that "nonrandom selection is both a source of bias in empirical research and a fundamental aspect of many social processes."

The three general questions of concern for this paper are: (1) How do those accessing the Internet Web site where the survey(s) are posted differ demographically from their cohorts in the general population? (2) How do those who participated in the online survey differ demographically from those who visited the site but elected not to participate? and (3) What is the overall response rate to online surveys?

Methodology

A series of three surveys were posted on a gay/lesbian Web site (http://www.qcc.org). In addition, a Computer Center was established at a community gay/lesbian center to provide computer access to those without home computers. As of June 1997, there had been over 10,000 visits to this Web site. In order to use the Web site, users were required to complete an online demographic profile. The demographic data collected on the over 10,000 gay/lesbian users of this Web site will be compared to demographic information on gays/lesbians in the general population.

To evaluate survey response rates, we compare the response rates to the general demographic questionnaire of all users with the response rates to the three online attitudinal surveys posted on the Web site beginning in May 1996 and ending in June 1997. The first survey posted on the site was voluntary. The second online survey was "semimandatory." The importance of participating in this second survey was stressed, yet an option was given where the user could continue to access the site if (s)he "promised" (s)he would complete the survey at a later time. Since no oversight mechanism was installed to make certain a user kept his/her promise, participating "at a later time" was more or less optional. The third survey was mandatory. The Web site could be accessed only upon the users completion of the survey.

In addition to calculating an overall response rate to the online surveys for those accessing the Web site, we categorized users as participants or non-participants. Analysis was performed to discern any differences between those who elected to respond to online surveys and those who chose not to participate.

Results

Internet Sample versus National Cohort. Because online surveys are subject to selection bias, there is an increased likelihood of obtaining a skewed sample. Therefore, it is necessary to investigate the characteristics of those initially self-selecting. Gays/lesbians accessing the gay/lesbian Web site at www.qcc.org were compared with gays/lesbians in the general population. The 1992 Voter Research and Surveys (VRS) exit poll (Edelman, 1993) sample of national voters included a sexual orientation variable, providing a useful comparison.

This study's sample and VRSs gay/lesbian sample were compared across six demographic variables: education, income, age, race, party identification, and ideology. The two samples are similar with regard to education. The difference in education categories between the two samples makes sense when we incorporate the results of the income variable in the analysis. Differences between the groups can be found on the basis of age, with the Internet sample being younger. From these data, it appears that the Internet sample is somewhat more racially diverse, with more Hispanics, Asians, and members of other racial/ethnic backgrounds represented.

The Internet sample is distinct in terms of political party identification. Over 25 percent of the Internet sample indicated "no party affiliation." Those indicating some party identification did so at a lower rate in each category than those participating in the national sample. With regard to political ideology, the two samples are similar. Although Table 1 illustrates some differences, overall the distribution of responses on the six demographic variables across the two samples tends to be similar, with only slight under- and overrepresentation in some categories.

Statistical Analysis of the QCC Data: A Logistic Regression Model. The literature and our initial analyses suggested that important explanatory variables in differentiating gay/lesbian participation in online surveys were income, age, education, gender, and access to the Internet. A logistic regression model was constructed to further assess what differences existed between those participating in the attitudinal surveys and those answering only the required demographic questions.

Our initial analysis also led us to conclude that any differences among those who participated in the attitudinal surveys were most likely due to greater familiarity with the Internet and greater ease of access to the technology (Walsh et al., 1992). Therefore, our hypothesis for the logistic regression model is that users who participated in the attitudinal surveys are more familiar with the Internet and have greater ease of access to this technology than users who chose not to participate.

To measure familiarity with the Internet, all Web site registrants were asked if this was their first use of the Internet and how many hours per week each spent on the Internet. Registrants were also asked how they accessed the QCC Web site. For purposes of model specification we collapsed all responses into two categories: home and other (included accessing the site from the Gay and Lesbian Community Center (QCCSITE). The

TABLE 1. INTERNET AND NATIONAL (VRS) SAMPLES OF GAYS AND LESBIANS

	Internet Sample	National (VRS) Sample
	N = 10,633	N = 466
Education		
<H.S.	4%	4%
H.S.	11%	21%
Some coll.	34%	31%
College	28%	21%
Postgrad.	23%	23%
Income		
<$30,000	39%	48%
$30–50,000	27%	29%
>$50,000	34%	23%
Age		
<45 years	88%	70%
45 years +	12%	30%
Race		
White	72%	84%
Black	4%	10%
Hispanic	8%	4%
Asian	6%	*
Other	10%	2%
Party Identification		
Dem.	43%	50%
Repub.	12%	18%
Indep.	14%	23%
Other	4%	10%
No Affil.	28%	*
Ideology		
Lib.	48%	51%
Mod.	36%	42%
Conserv.	9%	8%
Rad.	7%	*

*Indicates data unavailable. "Asian" and "radical" were not included as response categories in the VRS survey.

dependent variable in this model is participation, a dichotomous dummy variable with 1 = participating in an online survey and 0 = not participating in an online survey.

The ten independent variables included in this model are first time use of the Internet (NETUSE); hours spent per week on the Internet (HOURS); access to the Internet (ACCESS); (QCCS1TE); (OWN); (PREVIOUS); and income, education, gender, and age. NETUSE and HOURS are included in the model to attempt to ascertain users' expertise and level of comfort with the Internet. PREVIOUS indicates whether or not a user had visited the Web site before. As with familiarity of the technology, familiarity with the Web site may affect future participation in an attitudinal survey. ACCESS, QCCSITE, and OWN tap into the availability and accessibility of the Internet.

Our analysis of this model indicates that those persons participating in the surveys differ somewhat from the nonparticipating population, but not in any substantive manner. Although six of our ten independent variables did perform at statistically significant levels, each reported only slight (less than 3.5 percent) changes in the predicted probabilities. The variables ACCESS and GENDER appear to have the greatest effects at 3.49 percent and –3.54 percent respectively. Income appears to have a negative effect on this model. Those making the most money were 2 percent less likely to have participated in a survey.

Participants in Voluntary, Semivoluntary, and Mandatory Online Surveys versus Nonparticipants. Three additional logistic regression models were run to assess differences between those respondents who participated in each of the three (voluntary, semivoluntary, mandatory) online surveys and those who did not participate. The differences between those participating in the voluntary survey and those who did not participate in any of the surveys are not particularly substantive. The most meaningful differences appear to be with regard to age. Older persons were more likely to voluntarily participate in the survey. The QCC site variable was statistically significant in this model, indicating that participants in the voluntary survey were 2 percent less likely to have participated in the survey if they were accessing the Web site from the computer facilities at the Gay and Lesbian Community Center. This may be due to limited access to equipment and time limitations imposed. Although the effect was statistically significant at the .05 level for this variable (QCCSITE), its substantive impact is very small.

Those who participated in Survey 2 or the "semimandatory" survey also differed little from those who participated in the voluntary survey and those who did not participate in any of the three surveys. Two variables were shown to be statistically significant in the Survey 2 model. The QCCSITE variable indicated that those registering from the computer facilities at the Gay and Lesbian Community Center were almost 9 percent less likely to participate in the semimandatory survey than those who registered from other sites. INCOME was also shown to be significant in this model, with those of higher income less likely to participate.

Our third survey was mandatory. When we compare the two groups in this model (those who participated in the mandatory survey versus nonparticipants) we find that fewer variables produced statistically significant results in our model. These findings are expected, since one would anticipate that the participants in a mandatory survey (which had the greatest number of survey participants overall) should most closely resemble our population. The two variables, which performed at a statistically significant level in this model, were ACCESS and QCCSITE. Although each was statistically significant, they did not predict at levels that would indicate to us that our participants in the mandatory surveys differed much from the nonparticipants.

Conclusion

The independent variables yielded little explanatory power as to differences between participants and nonparticipants in our study. We believe that we can walk away from this exercise with cautious optimism and some interesting conclusions regarding the use of online surveys. First, selection bias appears to have occurred prior to respondents' participating in the surveys. Although this is somewhat reassuring, selection bias remains a problem with this new methodology. Second, the demographic characteristics of the participants and nonparticipants are practically indistinguishable. In fact, the demographic characteristics of our study of gays/lesbians comported well with the VRS national sample of gays/lesbians. Hence, we can generalize from our nonrandom sample to our population with a modicum of confidence. Finally, we can compare the response rate for our online surveys with those of more traditional mail-in surveys. Our overall response rate was approximately 16.4 percent. Although this is not an exceptionally high response rate, it is well within the range of reported response rates for more well established mail survey techniques.

References

Berk, R. 1983. "An Introduction to Sample Selection Bias in Sociological Data." *American Sociological Review* 48: 386–397.

Edelman, M. 1993. "Understanding the Gay and Lesbian Vote in 1992." *Public Perspective* 4: 32–33.

Fortney, J. B. Booth, M. Zhang, J. Humphrey, and E. Wiseman. 1998. "Controlling for Selection Bias in the Evaluation of Alcoholics Anonymous as Aftercare Treatment," *Journal of Studies on Alcohol* 59: 690–697.

Groves, R. 1987. "Research on Survey Data Quality." *Public Opinion Quarterly* 51 (Suppl.): S156-72.

Jelen, T. 1992. "Political Christianity; A Contextual Analysis." *American Journal of Political Science* 36: 692–714.

———. 1993. "The Political Consequences of Religious Group Attitudes." *Journal of Politics* 55: 178–190.

Rothbart, G., M. Fine, and S. Sudman. 1982. "On Finding and Interviewing the Needles in the Haystack: The Use of Multiplicity Sampling." *Public Opinion Quarterly* 46: 408–421.

Valdez, A., and C. Kaplan. 1999. "Reducing Selection Bias in the Use of Focus Groups to Investigate Hidden Populations: The Case of Mexican-American Gang Members from South Texas." *Drugs and Society* 14: 209–224.

Wald, K., D. Owen, and S. Hill. 1988. "Churches as Political Communities." *American Political Science Review* 82: 531-548.

Walsh, J., S. Kielser, L. Sproull, and B. Hesse. 1992. "Self-Selected and Randomly Selected Respondents in a Computer Network Survey." *Public Opinion Quarterly* 56: 241–244.

Winship, C., and R. Mare. 1992. "Models for Sample Selection Bias." *Annual Review of Sociology* 18: 327–350.

REVIEW QUESTIONS

1. What were the independent variables used in this study?

2. How did the researchers compare their survey data? What did they use? What were the results?

3. Do you believe that using the Internet is a good way to gather data? Why or why not? What type of study would you like to do on line?

Chapter 9: Field Research and Unobtrusive Measures

ANALYSIS, AND INTERVIEWING

The first thing you need to do before conducting most research is to look at the world around you. What do you see? I bet if you think about it, you have been a researcher for a long time without even realizing it. You might have even made some observations and come to some conclusions about the various things you see around you. Well, we all do.

Let me give you an example. I like to go to auctions. I originally didn't know that I liked auctions. When I first moved to Nebraska, I needed furniture. Friends told me about an auction where I would find really great deals. So, every Wednesday night I would go to the auction wearing my backpack, and I watched what was going on around me as I graded my students' papers. I had never been to an auction before and found that many things were happening. Auctions aren't just about buying furniture and other items. People in the audience socialized and appeared to know each other. The men working the front tables, who showed the merchandise, had different methods of holding items and talking about the items depending on what the item was and how much money they wanted to receive as a bid. They were putting on a show for the audience. Everyone seemed to have a different way of bidding on items. Some would scratch their noses, others would lift their hats, some would pull on their ears, and for some, the bid was so subtle it was impossible, at least for me, to even see. I soon realized by watching and paying attention that there were many other things happening at the auction that I never would have known about without observing the behaviors for months.

Fieldwork can also be called **ethnography** or **participant observation.** This type of observation is just "let's hang out" and watch what happens around us, which can be fun. But watching and participating in the auction also helped me develop questions about auctions, such as the rituals, socialization, and economic systems that take place within an auction. Field researchers can explore all kinds of situations. Let me give you some examples. Tamotsu Shibutani (1978) was a research assistant for the University of California's Evacuation and Resettlement Study who had observed the evacuation of the Japanese into resettlement communities. Shibutani became part of Company K, a unit in the U.S. military during World War II. Company K had some problems such as rampant absenteeism, insubordination, violence, and protests, along with very bizarre behavior portrayed to the people outside of the unit. However, because Shibutani (1978: vii) was on the inside, he could view the behaviors through the "eyes of the participant," so he was able to chronicle "one of the more disorderly units in United States military history and form a sociological generalization concerning the process of demoralization" among the members of Company

K. Collecting data in this type of environment isn't always as easy as you might imagine. Shibutani wrote his notes and sent them through the mail almost daily to his friends and relatives who kept them for him until after his term in Company K ended.

In another study, Mitch Duneier (1992), a young white man, spent time in the Valois "See Your Food" Cafeteria on Chicago's South Side for four years while he was a graduate student at the University of Chicago. He began to notice a group of poor, working-class Black men who congregated at a table that became known as "Slim's Table." Over the years, he got to know the men, observed their behaviors, found out about their lives and listened to their troubles. He was able to refute stereotypes by spending time with Slim, a car mechanic who was more or less the respected master of the table where the diners met once or twice a day for their 45 to 90 minutes each meal. Duneier also observed Slim, an elderly white diner, who substituted Bart as his father figure and cared for him. The diners formed a moral community that transcended the roles and images commonly shown about Black men and as a result, Duneier was able to discredit many of the previous studies on Black men that often generalized about working-class Blacks, but from essentially middle-class researchers' points of view. This study helps to confirm the inaccuracies about Black stereotypes that are shown in the popular media, and Duneier was only able to accomplish this by spending time in the field with these men.

Being a participant observer has some drawbacks, however. How much of your participation can influence the activities and behaviors of the people you are studying? While observing is an important aspect of field research, you must also take notes. How do you do it? The field notes must provide extensive descriptive detail about the situation you are observing. **Jotted notes,** which are written in the field, are short and meant to trigger your memory for a later time. **Direct observation** notes involve the researcher writing the notes soon after leaving the field. These notes should be detailed, with concrete information and sayings from the respondents. Maps and diagrams should also be included in the notes. For instance, William Whyte (1965: 13), in his book *Street Corner Society: The Social Structure of an Italian Slum,* watched what took place on a street corner in a slum district known as "Cornerville." This city was inhabited almost exclusively by Italian immigrants and their children. The area was known as a problem part of the city, but many in the city feared Cornerville was home to corrupt politicians, poverty, and crime. Because the only way to gain knowledge about Cornerville was to live there and participate in the activities, Whyte did exactly that. One of the first things Whyte does is describe in detail the history of Doc's gang called the Nortons. To show the status of the individuals involved, Whyte diagramed the Nortons during the spring and summer of 1937 (see Figure 9.1)

We can't be on that street corner, so the information shown to the reader by the researcher is terribly important. The information needs to be very specific, contain as much detail as you can, and be as accurate as possible.

INTERVIEWING

Observing will help you determine what types of questions to ask your respondents when you **interview** them. If a specific place or situation is new to you, as the auction was for me, then observing for a few months allows you the ability to understand the situation in a very different way than if you had just decided to start asking questions of people. A **questionnaire** involves written questions that are given to the respondents through the mail,

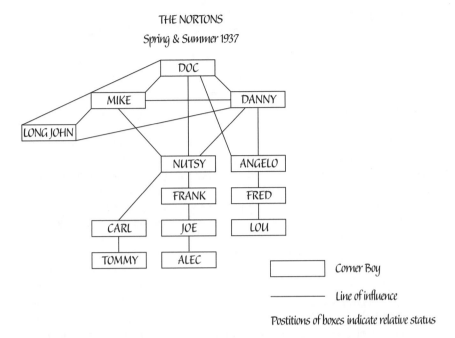

Figure 9.1. Whyte's Diagram of the Status of the Individuals Studied

From *Street Corner Society: The Social Structure of an Italian Slum,* by W. F. Whyte, 1965. Reprinted by permission of the University of Chicago Press.

email, Internet, or in person, whereas an interview involves the interviewer asking the questions and recording the answers given.

When you go into the field to collect data and observe what is going on, you have the opportunity to gather a rich set of data and ask questions of the people you are studying. Interviews in the field are usually unstructured, as in-depth as possible, and informal. Interviewing is also interactive and is different than the survey research we have previously discussed—it is more intensive because of the thoroughness of the questioning. Intensive interviewing relies heavily on open-ended questions to develop a comprehensive view of the respondents' behaviors, attitudes, or actions.

Follow-up questions or probes allow the researcher to consider the subjects' answers and ask for clarification. What happens if you question a subject regarding his or her feelings about a new homeless shelter and the subject responds, "I don't like the new homeless shelter"? A follow-up question might be "Why don't you like it?"

CONTENT ANALYSIS

Another type of research is **content analysis.** This involves quantitative measurement of the content of messages and communications being studied. In other words, content analysis is a technique for gathering and analyzing the content of where the researcher can study cultural artifacts to look for trends, patterns, and themes. You can use many cultural artifacts—such as books, films, fashion, textbooks, and billboards—in this type of analysis. The key to content analysis is that the data is not created for the purpose of the study, but rather the data are found the way they are and then studied systematically (Reinharz, 1992).

For instance, Brabant and Mooney (1997) were interested in sex-role stereotyping in the Sunday comics. The researchers believed that even though women's social positions had changed during the last 20 years, the media had not portrayed that change at all. Using studies conducted in 1974 and 1984 as guides, Brabant and Mooney collected cartoons in 1994 and analyzed each strip for the frequency or appearance of husbands and wives, where they were located (inside or outside the home), tasks they were doing, frequency of reading appearances, and whether or not the wives wore an apron. The researchers wanted to see if there was a difference in the way gender roles were portrayed between years. The authors found that even though male appearances inside the home increased, female appearances were higher than males over the three-time period. Furthermore, although the number of women who wore aprons decreased over time, men were never pictured wearing aprons.

In another example, Kinnick (1998) compared the newspaper coverage of male and female athletes during the 1996 Summer Olympic Games. The profiles of athletes in five leading U.S. newspapers were examined for incidence of gender bias in reporting and photography. Although the study found evidence of gender bias for a number of criteria, female athletes were found to have received similar or more favorable treatment than male athletes, and no evidence of gender bias was found in terms of quantitative representation of female athletes or in the placement and prominence of stories. This study suggests that the coverage of female athletes has been improving.

Although items such as the Sunday comics or a photograph of a female athlete standing alone do not really mean much to us, a content analysis has implications for the way people, items, or behaviors are portrayed to the rest of us.

HISTORICAL RESEARCH

The next type of research that you will learn about in this chapter is called **historical research.** History looks at past and present events, which can include diaries, graduation records, maps, religious artifacts, books, court transcripts, clothing, or photographs. Though you might think that historical research is really only about gathering the facts about a significant event, such as a war to document it, historical method is not just gathering those facts but, rather, interpreting them. Without the interpretation, there is no research.

The historical researcher makes an effort to go back as far as possible to the primary source. A **primary source** gives the direct outcome of specific events or experiences in someone's life. If you want to research the life of women in the 1920s in a specific area, you would use primary sources such as newspaper clippings, diaries, and eyewitness accounts of the women's lives. You would want to give meaning to the lives of the women you are researching. Using the primary sources ensures the integrity of the study you are conducting.

Secondary sources are just as valuable as the firsthand accounts of the events. Although the secondary sources are at least once removed from the primary sources, they can give you important information about the primary sources. Secondary sources can include bystanders who were not involved in an incident, but were given accounts by someone who was there. One problem with secondary sources to consider is how much trust you can put into the secondary sources understanding of the primary sources. Furthermore, a researcher who conducts historical research must make sure that the data is reliable and valid. This is accomplished through authenticity and accuracy. **Authenticity** is also known as external criticism because it asks if the data are genuine or fake. It isn't always easy to tell if the document is truly a primary source. However, authenticity is established based on indicators such as the printing techniques used, the language, the writing styles, and when the document was established. **Accuracy,** also known as internal criticism, is concerned with the trustworthiness of the source. For instance, if you are investigating teen behavior in the 1940s and your source suggests that teens were promiscuous, would you find that trustworthy considering what you know about events during that period?

Narrative

Very few mainstream research methods books mention **narrative** or **oral history** as a way of collecting data. According to Reinharz (1992), this oversight appears to be because mainstream social scientists tend to find little value in studies that are subjective. Furthermore, there is little training and discussion about this method in most research methods classes.

Sometimes called oral history or biographical work, narrative is a way of listening to the voices of those who are being studied and is a way of uncovering "hidden histories, contesting academic androcentrism, and reinstating the marginalized and dispossessed as makers of their own past" (Miles & Crush, 1993: 84). Narrative research is also used to analyze documents, to reanalyze previously published oral histories from a different perspective, to identify empirical patterns, and to examine groups quantitatively (Reinharz, 1992).

According to Reinharz (1992: 133), "The researcher's purpose is to create a written record of the interviewee's life from his/her perspective in his/her own words." Boetcher Joeres and Laslett (1993) state that personal narratives are a way of studying the problems of women [and men] from all cultures and walks of life. Telling their histories is a way to pay tribute to the people being studied, which you will see in the readings that follow.

References

Boetcher Joeres, R. E., & Laslett, B. 1993. Personal narratives: A selection of recent works. *Signs,* 18(2): 389–392.

Brabant, S., & Mooney, L. A. 1997. Sex role stereotyping in the Sunday comics: A twenty year update. *Sex Roles,* 37(3/4): 269–281.

Duneier, M. 1992. *Slim's table: Race, respectability, and masculinity.* Chicago: University of Chicago Press.

Kinnick, K. N. 1998. Gender bias in newspaper profiles of 1996 Olympic athletes: A content analysis of five major dailies. *Women's Studies in Communication,* 21(2): 212–228.

Miles, M., & Crush, J. 1993. Personal narratives as interactive texts: Collecting and interpreting migrant life-histories. *Professional Geographer,* 45(1): 84–95.

Reinharz, S. 1992. *Feminist methods in social research.* New York: Oxford University Press.

Shibutani, T. 1978. *The derelicts of company K.* Berkeley: University of California Press.

Whyte, W. F. 1965. *Street corner society: The social structure of an Italian slum.* Chicago: University of Chicago Press

INFOTRAC COLLEGE EDITION SUGGESTED READINGS AND DISCUSSION QUESTIONS

1. Look up the article "Phenomenological and participatory research on schizophrenia: Recovering the person in theory and practice" in InfoTrac College Edition. What problems did the researcher have while doing the participatory research?

2. Locate the article "The margins of underdog sociology: Implications for the West Coast AIDS Project." In this article, the researchers discuss the problems associated with going out into the field to collect data. Could they have used another method to gather data from the same population? Why or why not?

AMATEUR STRIPPING AND GAMING ENCOUNTERS: FUN IN GAMES OR GAMING AS FUN?

Julie Ann Harms Cannon, Thomas C. Calhoun, and Rhonda Fisher

This observational study used Goffman's (1961) theories on games and gaming encounters to investigate both the audience and the staff as they are involved in an amateur stripping competition. The study's authors also use Goffman's discussion of "front stage" and "back stage" interactions in the competition. Unlike professional stripping literature, this study highlights the importance of incorporating the meanings that both the audience and the staff members contribute to this encounter that come from using both field work and interviewing as the methodology. As you read this article, think about the ways in which the researchers managed to participate in the setting, while at the same time obtaining the information that they wanted.

The research on professional stripping has been extensive. Research on amateur stripping, however, is a relatively recent development. Currently, studies of amateur stripping have focused on observational analyses (Calhoun, Cannon, and Fisher 1996), gender differences in male and female amateur stripping competitions occurring within a heterosocial setting (Fisher, Cannon, and Calhoun, forthcoming), and the motivational accounts of amateur strippers (Calhoun, Cannon, and Fisher 1998).

Unlike professional stripping, which can be considered an occupation, amateur strippers voluntarily remove their clothing in public, in hopes of securing limited prize monies and/or other gifts (e.g., compact disks, swimwear, clothing). However, and most important for our research, amateur strippers perform without guarantee of any financial compensation. As it turns out, money is not the primary motivating factor for amateur performers (Calhoun et al. 1998). Amateurs engage in the competition because they find it fun.

Interestingly, most research on professional and amateur stripping has focused on the strippers themselves, yet no studies, to our knowledge, have adequately addressed the interactions between the staff and the audience members. This is understandable given that professional stripping differs dramatically from the amateur stripping competition.

The purpose of the present study is to discuss the ways in which the staff and audience of an amateur stripping club, Kato's, manipulate the dancers to keep the competition fun and profitable. Using the work of Erving Goffman (1961), we discuss the "gaming encounter" of the amateur stripping competition, which necessarily includes the audience and staff. Given that these groups ultimately work together and most determine the "winners" of the amateur stripping competition, it is crucial to understand the implicit rules of the amateur stripping competition. Although the explicit rules are fairly simple in that the participants (a) must not expose buttocks or genitalia (i.e., strippers cannot be nude or wear underwear that is too revealing, such as G-strings), (b) cannot touch audience members, and (c) have three minutes to perform their routine, the implicit rules (discussed in greater detail later) of the amateur stripping competition are much more revealing. Viewing the competition from this perspective de-centers the dancers, allowing us to view them as mere pawns in a more complex competition occurring between the audience and staff. In this study we use Goffman's (1961) work on games and gaming encounters to investigate the sociological imperative of untangling the "front stage" and "back stage" interactions of the amateur stripping competition (Goffman 1959).

The amateur stripping contest offers us the opportunity to assess the applicability of Goffman's (1961) game theoretical perspective to the study of a relatively new social behavior, amateur stripping in a heterosocial setting. We examine how the manipulations of the dancers by the audience and staff constitute a gaming encounter quite different from the interactions described in the literature on professional stripping behavior. As noted previously, amateur stripping involves much more than the game rules of the competition. More specifically, a dancer cannot win the competition without assistance—this is true whether or not she or he follows the explicit or implicit contest rules. To understand the outcome and goal of the competition, it is essential to talk with two key players in this gaming encounter—the staff and audience members.

Method

Subjects and Setting. Amateur strip night occurs each Thursday at a bar known as Kato's.[1] Thursday is the main night out for college students in this large midwestern city with a population of just over 200,000. At Kato's, there are two contests taking place. The men's competition begins at approximately 10:30 P.M., and the women's competition begins shortly thereafter.

During our eight-month investigation we were able to observe, on an average evening, 5 male and 5 female participants in the weekly dance contest. Some nights the number of participants in each contest was as high as 11. Only on one occasion did the number of participants fall below 3 per contest.

We interviewed 6 staff members (5 men, 1 woman), 9 audience members (4 men, 5 women), and 19 dance contestants (10 men, 9 women). The racial-ethnic composition of each of the categories was representative of Kato's (primarily White, with some African American, Asian, and Hispanic participants). For the purposes of this research, our findings are based solely on the responses of the audience members and staff.

Anyone who pays the $2 cover charge on entry can participate in the competition. Each contest carries a cash prize—$100 for first, $50 for second, and $25 for third place. The atmosphere at Kato's is quite similar to that of a typical nightclub or disco. The lighting is dim, the music is loud, and the dance floor is the main attraction. Alcohol is available from the beer stand at the main entrance and from bars on the first and second levels. Customers may be seated at tables or booths located on both levels. The dance floor, however, is on the first level, and this is where most customers seek seating. The second floor has a balcony overlooking the dance floor, and those who prefer it, or who cannot find seating on the first floor, sit or stand and look on from above. The activity on the second level is less specifically focused on the contest. It is often difficult to obtain a good view of the competition from this location. Dancing occurs before and immediately following the stripping contests. Finally, customers may play pool at any time during the evening on either floor even while the dance contest is in progress.

The heterosocial setting provides patrons with the sense that they are at a "typical" dance club. Thus, Kato's is not seen as a seedy men's stripper bar or an all-women's night club where stripping is the only focus. The environment is supportive and friendly in that there is a core of patrons who regularly socialize. Most of these patrons arrive at Kato's at least one hour before the contest as seating is limited. During the wait, individuals may dance alone or in groups of two or three; they may even participate in a very large group dance called the Electric Slide. The atmosphere is one that creates the sense that men and women are on an equal playing field (Calhoun et al. 1996).[2]

However, there are actually two separate contests occurring at Kato's on amateur night, with men always performing first and women second. During each contest, the participants dance by themselves or with a partner to the music of their choice. After each contestant has had the opportunity to dance for at least three minutes, the dancers are brought back out on the floor as a group for the final "cheer-off." The announcer for the competition encourages the audience to cheer for their favorite dancers, and those receiving the loudest applause win. The announcer and staff subjectively determine which dancer received the best response.

The atmosphere during the contests is generally speaking quite rowdy or chaotic. As previously noted, the men's competition is always the first of the evening. At this time, women circle the dance floor, often jockeying for the best location. There is some pushing and shoving between the women, but seldom does it result in physical confrontation. As soon as the men's competition is over, there is a very aggressive readjustment of floor space and atmosphere as men advance to the inside perimeter of the dance floor to view the women who will participate in the main event. Because many women do not retreat, the dance floor becomes extremely congested. The security staff repeatedly ask the men to move back. Consequently, the women are pushed farther away from the dance floor. During the observation period, it was not unusual for men to literally crawl over the top of female researchers to gain a strategic spot on the inside of the perimeter. Not surprisingly, fights were common occurrences on amateur night at Kato's (Calhoun et al. 1996).[3]

Data Collection and Techniques. As noted earlier, the data for this study were collected over an eight-month time period from the population of male and female dancers, staff, and audience members observed at Kato's. During the beginning stages of the project, we engaged solely in observational research. It was essential for us to become regulars at Kato's. Although note-taking during the competition was somewhat difficult and often focused a great deal of attention on our work, we took this as an opportunity to let customers and staff know about the project. Additionally, once audience members, staff, and participants realized what we were doing at Kato's they were eager to offer suggestions and observational responses that would prove quite helpful later in our research efforts.

Each of the participants agreed to participate by written consent.[4] The participants were given information regarding the nature of the project during the initial contact and at the time of the interview. Participants were also informed that a copy of the research findings would be available at Kato's on completion of the project.

Because this study was of a potentially sensitive nature, steps were taken to protect the identities of the participants. Participants were notified that real names would not be used in the final report of the research findings, that they could refuse to answer any question, and that the interview could be terminated at any time during the conversation.

Typically, participants were contacted at Kato's after the amateur stripping competition; however, some contacts were made by means of snowball sampling techniques. Interviews were conducted at a variety of locations, including our offices, participants' and investigators' residences, restaurants, and professional and amateur stripping establishments. Additionally, a few interviews were conducted over the telephone. Data were collected by using a semistructured interview format. Although all interviews were directed by the interview schedule, conversations were not limited only to the scheduled questions. Participants were encouraged to discuss all aspects of amateur stripping that had the potential for the development of future research. All interviews were audiotaped and completely transcribed for future analyses.

Findings

Games and Gaming. Again, Goffman (1961) argued that games and gaming encounters involve very different types of interaction strategies. Whereas games involve very formal and explicit rules, gaming encounters are generally more spontaneous and depend on implicit rules or expectations. Amateur stripping, we argue, can be viewed as a game in that it has formally and explicitly stated rules. However, and more important in terms of stripping behavior in general, amateur stripping can also be viewed as a gaming encounter between the audience and staff. It is this dynamic that is the most compelling component of the amateur dance contest.

More specifically, the strippers themselves, although central to the fun, do not control the gaming encounter. Jay, the disc jockey, in discussing this aspect of the competition, stated,

> In everyday life they [the dancers] can be very good-looking people, very tight if you will, be very strong, and have one percent body fat, and nobody will talk to them because they're just that way. But once they get on stage and people look at them and see how tight they are, then it's a different story because now they're just an object, whereas before they were a person.

Thus, the dancers themselves may only manipulate the audience through the presentation of self (i.e., having a good body or dressing in sexy or provocative clothing). However, a positive outcome cannot be ensured by an attractive physique or costume. Ultimately, the audience determines the outcome of the competition, and this decision may not be based on appearance or any other component of self-presentation the dancer may use.

In addition to addressing the nature of the stripper's role in the competition, Jay also discussed the importance of creating an alternative reality—a reality in which the body takes precedence over internal attributes or personality. As Goffman (1961) noted, this alternative reality is critical to the maintenance and creation of fun in any gaming encounter. In the world of amateur stripping, individuals become merely objects of desire subject to the evaluation of audience members and staff—evaluations based solely on physical attributes or entertainment value.

Socially Creating and Manipulating Fun. First, it is important to reiterate the primary goals of the amateur stripping competition—fun and profit. Although these goals are unique, ultimately the two are intrinsically linked. Fun for the audience typically equals profit for Kato's. The staff at Kato's work hard to make sure that the audience members are having fun, as this is ultimately more profitable for Kato's. Paul, the manager of Kato's and announcer for the competition, spoke to this directly:

> Lately, I've been having to cut it [the amateur contest] off at a certain amount of people [performers] because a lot of people, they like to come down for strip night, but they also want to dance too. And so I try to get it over as close or before midnight as possible . . . a lot of people brought it to my attention that they are bothered by the fact that they don't get a chance to dance.

This balance between the contest and the socializing is very important at Kato's. Although the competition itself is generally considered to be central to the creation of a fun experience, people also come to Kato's to dance and socialize.

Ultimately, the entire staff works to get the customers excited about the competition. However, the bulk of this responsibility falls on the manager's shoulders as he is ultimately accountable for success of Kato's. Paul had this to say in reference to the competition and the creation of fun and profit at Kato's:

> I would say that it's more important to get a lot of good-looking guys out there dancing and get the girls all fired up because hopefully it will carry over to Friday and Saturday night. They'll say, boy, I was down there Thursday night and I had a really good time . . . Let's go check it out Friday and Saturday night and see what's going on.

It is essential that the fun of amateur night be extended to the weekend at Kato's. The amateur contest is a way to bring patrons to the establishment on weekends and thus to ensure the club's profitability.

Interestingly, as the previous quotation suggests, men and women do not necessarily have the same definition of fun. Ron, an audience member, stated,

> I think women tend to see it [the men's competition] more as a fun thing. This is the stereotype of even watching it [male stripping] on TV and stuff where

women will be like, "This is fun." And, it's more of a social fun event. But the men will go there themselves to get a jolly, just to play out the fantasies in their heads. But I think women do it in a big group of friends.

More specifically, women attend the amateur contest as form of entertainment and social solidarity with other women, whereas men attend to achieve a type of sexual stimulation or gratification.

However, the disc jockey also takes responsibility for pumping up the crowd. Jay described his work:

Well, basically you welcome people down. You don't usually do a lot of speaking over the mike, but when we do it's usually for a drink special. While you're doing a drink special, you're saying "Hey, you know [Kato's] Thursday night, it's amateur strip night. You know why you're here." . . . I think in the future, as I'm there a little longer, I'm sure it's gonna turn into me pumping the crowd up a little more. I think we're [the staff] going to be having more talks about that because I think it's a good thing.

Again, fun equals profit. While the customers wait for the contest to begin, Jay keeps them entertained and works to build enthusiasm about the competition. Simultaneously, he encourages the audience members to buy drinks. Alcohol is used for profit in two ways. First, the more drinks the customers buy, the more money the bar makes. Second, the more people drink, the more likely they are to lose their inhibitions and strip—this is critical in terms of the spontaneity of the competition and the creation of fun.

Implicit Rules of the Amateur Contest. As noted above, anyone who pays the $2 cover charge to attend the amateur contest is eligible to participate as a performer. Yet, there are also implicit rules about men's and women's performances and about who is actually supposed to perform at Kato's.

Audience members have very different views about what makes a winning male-female performance. Ron, in speaking about the performances, stated,

I think you have to be self-confident but not arrogant. Like, I think it's always good to have some kind of gimmick . . . don't be like a plain Jane dude. [You should] always [be] working on a little dance. Have a routine to catch people's attention.

However, the requirements are very different for women, according to Ron: "I think it is important to look timid, [yet] look confident. [You should] look like you don't do this all the time." Jay (the disc jockey) offered a similar opinion:

I found that women that almost have a playful, midwestern kind of look to them have done well. You know whether they're professional or not, but they kind of come out there and they just kind of tease the audience. And they're good at it.

However, the bottom line seems to be the same for both men and women. He continued by saying, "I guess . . . the main thing is that whether you've stripped [or] danced before, if you can get out in front of people, and you're comfortable with your body, you [are] probably going to do pretty well."

There are definite beauty standards at Kato's. However, Paul, the manager of Kato's, described the variety of women who perform during the dance competition:

> I like the fact that we have a lot of different types of girls. Sure, in a perfect world they'd all look like supermodels. But we get a lot of different types of people. I'm sure a lot of guys like heavier girls. A lot of guys like perfect girls. A lot of guys like flat-chested girls . . . I have no problem with anybody dancing.

Although Paul extolled the virtues of diversity in the female form, he acknowledged the ideal type of female performer.

Interestingly, those who participate in the competition should be "natural" beauties. Kim, a regular audience member, addressed the issue of dancers with breast implants: "I don't think it's fair to the other girls. Because some of the girls, they're good and they [the audience] usually are not used to the ones that aren't professionals." These sentiments call into question the nature of the implicit rules at Kato's. Although technically anyone who follows the explicit rules regarding time limits, degree of nudity, and physical contact can participate in the competition, compliance with these rules is not enough to ensure success. The participants must be aware of the implicit rules, or "beauty codes" (Calhoun et al. 1996), if they are to win the competition. However, as noted previously, these rules are gender based.

The Rules Change for Fun's Sake. Although there are explicit rules as well as implicit rules operating during the amateur contest, the rules are almost always subject to change (except for those that are legally sanctioned, such as the degree of nudity and the prohibition against dancers and audience members touching one another). Jay (the disc jockey) spoke of the time limit per performance: "Well, that three-minute rule is basically just a minimum. We say 'We're going to let you out there for at least three minutes.' Most people are out there for about three and one-half." During our observations of the amateur stripping contest, we repeatedly viewed extended performances. When the audience is having fun, it is profitable for Kato's to allow the dancers to continue past the three-minute time limit.

Additionally, the staff at Kato's is known to be inflexible regarding the nudity and contact restrictions. However, although there appears to be a show of enforcement by the security staff, many violations of these explicit rules occur while the staff is preoccupied with another facet of the contest. Specifically, dancers have been known to reveal more clothing than explicitly allowed (i.e., to have removed underwear or worn G-strings) and also to touch audience members. In fact, breaking the explicit nudity and contact rules is often an implicit rule of the competition. Audience members encourage this type of activity and are quite enthusiastic when it occurs. Again, controlled spontaneity or fun takes precedence over the explicit rules. The audience has more fun if some rules are violated, thus potentially creating a more profitable evening for Kato's.

Spontaneous Involvement. As noted previously, spontaneity is essential to fulfilling the goals of amateur strip night (i.e., fun for the audience and profit for the staff). The audience and staff must work together to facilitate the desired effects or outcomes—the transformation of the mundane or everyday into a fun and profitable evening. This involves the complete involvement of these two groups. However, in amateur stripping, spontaneity is actually socially created and subject to manipulation.

Again, it is important to note that the game of amateur stripping is very different than stripping as a gaming encounter. People have definite expectations about Thursday night at Kato's that do not actually correspond to the rules of the competition. Paul (the manager) discusses the atmosphere on amateur strip night versus an off-night at Kato's:

> Thursday nights about 10:15 or so, people start gathering around the dance floor. Thursday nights they're geared for kind of one thing, the strip contest . . . You can feel it in the air. You feel the difference in the air down here. It's a lot more tense down here on Thursday nights. I don't mean tense in a physical way, like there's going to be a fight breaking out or anything, but people are expecting something on Thursday nights. They are expecting to see the girl of their dreams out there dancing. Girls are expecting to see the hunk from the Playgirl calendar out there dancing. There's a lot of expectations, I guess, on Thursday nights. Fridays and Saturdays there are no expectations. They want to come down, have drinks, have some fun, and dance.

Part of the fun of the amateur night is the chaos, as Paul describes it. The audience seems to enjoy that element of uncertainty and spontaneity.

Tension, like spontaneity, is also an essential dynamic of the amateur stripping competition. The tension is used to manipulate the dancers and to stimulate the audience. As Goffman (1961) noted, tension in gaming encounters results from the interaction of the formal and implicit rules or the mixing of the real world with the socially created fantasy of the gaming encounter. It is precisely the stress of these interactions that sets the tone for the amateur stripping contest and contributes to the fun and profit.

In her discussion of the order of the competition, Sonya speaks directly to the tension component of the amateur gaming encounter: "They're building excitement, like a warm-up band before a concert."

Incidents, Integrations, and Flooding Out. It is a constant effort and necessity to maintain the socially constructed world of the gaming encounter. "The dynamics of an encounter [are] tied to the functioning of the boundary-maintaining mechanisms that cut the encounter off selectively from wider worlds" (Goffman 1961: 66). This is particularly true of the amateur stripping competition. The audience members and staff must constantly work together to keep incidents from interrupting the flow of events. However, this is not always possible or desired, as discussed below.

Amy, a waitress at Kato's, described the following incident in which a dancer violated one of the implicit appearance rules of the competition:

> A month or two ago a real old lady stripped. I think she was about 50 or so, and the whole crowd just . . . I never sell beer usually too much during the strippers because everyone just doesn't want to lose their place. And I've had tons of people come up to me and they're like, "This is disgusting."

This incident was disturbing to the patrons of Kato's, but the disruption was useful in terms of profit—Amy was able to sell more beer. Also, the woman provided the audience with an opportunity to articulate the implicit rules—knowing who is not supposed to strip also provides individuals with information about who should participate in the competition.

Another incident occurred when a seemingly intoxicated woman proceeded to take her turn in the competition. She was clearly in a world of her own, which violated the expectations of a shared experience between audience members and dancers. Further, she attempted to remove more clothing than was legal. Normally, this behavior would not disturb the audience members, but the woman did not meet the beauty norms at Kato's. In this way she broke the interaction frame, and the bouncers were forced to remove her from the floor.

Again, as Goffman (1961) noted, it is critical to integrate these incidents into the proper frame of the encounter in some way. The most obvious way is to remove the participant and explain the regulations of the competition. However, it is also possible for the announcer to make a joke about the performance and allude to the "proper participant."

Discussion and Conclusions

This study sought to assess the importance of Goffman's (1961) concepts of the game and gaming encounters in an investigation of amateur stripping competitions. We found that although technically amateur stripping can be viewed as a game with explicit rules, it is better viewed as a gaming encounter whereby both explicit and implicit rules operate simultaneously. Additionally, we discovered that the staff and audience members are influential in determining the outcome of the competition. Although explicit sanctions can be applied to norm violators, the actual application of sanctions depends on the mood of the audience and the needs of the staff (i.e., fun and profit).

The implicit rules are determined primarily by the audience and staff, with the dancers being manipulated for fun and profit. We do not argue that the dancers cannot manipulate both the audience and staff, for this is indeed the case. However, we argue that this is not the primary reason for the event. Specifically, the event exists to meet the needs of the management. This translates into profit for the management, fun for the audience, and potential monetary gain for the participants.

It is up to the audience and staff to keep the environment spontaneous and fun. This is accomplished through the implementation of beauty codes, allowing specific rules to be violated by some participants in varying degrees, and ensuring that the fantasy of amateur strip night is maintained. We also found that some violations by the dancers could not be integrated into the interaction frame, thus creating a break in the fantasy-constructed reality—which is critical to attracting a large crowd weekly.

The significance of this study is that amateur stripping, we argue, is a demonstration of the larger social norms governing interactions. As with most encounters, there are norms, implicit and explicit, that dictate the interactional patterns between the participants. Amateur stripping also illustrates the impact that rules have on framing situations and, more important, on dictating the nature of the interaction. Fun is not an inherent component of stripping behavior. Rather, in the case of amateur stripping, fun is socially constructed from week to week and from participant to participant on the basis of the needs of the management and the mood of the audience.

Although this study highlights the complex interactions of audience and staff at an amateur stripping competition, additional research is needed. In the future, research should consider the racial and ethnic composition of those who participate in this behavior. Given the diversity of audience members and participants at Kato's and other urban establishments, it is likely that key differences may be identified in terms of identity formation, beauty standards, motivations, and so on. In addition, class may be a significant factor and should be investigated. Although Kato's is situated in a college town, the patrons and participants may be quite different from the college population in terms of socioeconomic status. For this reason, attention must be given to the regional characteristics of the community and patrons. Finally, given the nature of this behavior and the methods currently used to study it, it would be beneficial to assess the impact of researcher as insider versus researcher as outsider. For example, the researcher as insider might become privy to additional knowledge about the participants and their involvement in other types of behavior, including those that are clearly deviant.

Notes

1.   All names referred to in this work are pseudonyms.

2.   This information is abstracted from the article cited.

3.   See previous footnote.

4.   One of the male participants agreed to participate over the phone. His verbal consent was audiotaped at this time. Although we sent him a consent form, it was never returned.

References

Calhoun, Thomas C., Julie Ann Harms Cannon, and Rhonda Fisher. 1996. "Amateur Stripping: Sexualized Entertainment and Gendered Fun." *Sociological Focus* 29(2): 155–166.

Calhoun, Thomas C., Julie Ann Harms Cannon, and Rhonda Fisher. 1998. "Explorations in Youth Culture & Amateur Stripping: What We Know and What We Don't." Pp. 302–326 in *Youth, Youth Culture and Identity,* edited by Jon Epstein. Maiden, MA: Blackwell Publishers.

Calhoun, Thomas C., Rhonda Fisher, and Julie Harms Cannon. 1998. "The Case of Amateur Stripping: Sex Codes and Egalitarianism in a Heterosocial Setting." Pp. 47–61 in *The Ritual Tapestry: Social Rules and Cultural Meanings in America,* edited by Mary Jo Deegan. Westport, CT: Greenwood Press.

Goffman, Erving. 1959. *The Presentation of the Self in Everyday Life.* New York: Anchor Books.

———. 1961. *Encounters: Two Studies in the Sociology of Interaction.* Indianapolis: Bobbs-Merrill.

REVIEW QUESTIONS

1.   Earlier in the book we found that data without theory and theory without data is often empty and without purpose. What theory was used in this project? How did this particular theory drive the research question?

2.   What did the researchers need to do so they could conduct fieldwork in a strip club? How did they manage to blend in?

3.   If this study was conducted using the conflict theory, what types of research questions could have been asked?

The Evolution of Al-Anon: A Content Analysis of Stories in Two Editions of Its "Big Book." (Mutual Help for Alcohol-Related Problems: Studies of Al-Anon and of Alternatives to Alcoholics Anonymous)

Jane E. Martin

This study compares the 1985 with the 1965 edition of Al-Anon Faces Alcoholism *in which the range of relationships to the alcoholic is examined in the stories. Using a content analysis as the methodology, the authors investigate the addition of the stories of the Adult Children to show that there is less emphasis on acceptance, more expressions of anger, and that fewer alcoholics in the stories find sobriety in AA. As you read this study, notice how the researchers do the analysis and how they document change over time.*

This article an historical look at Al-Anon that uses primary sources to conduct a content analysis that compares the 1985 with the 1965 edition of *Al-Anon Faces Alcoholism.* This book is the counterpart to the "Big Book" of Alcoholics Anonymous and the content analysis based on a comparison of two editions of Al-Anon's "Big Book," *Al-Anon Faces Alcoholism* (1965; 1985). These are the Al-Anon counterparts to the original "Big Book" of Alcoholics Anonymous, first published by Alcoholics Anonymous in 1939. AA's "Big Book" contains the personal stories of alcoholics. It was originally published to help AA members work their program and to illustrate for them what can happen when they do. They are generally success stories and are selected for their exemplary quality. As such, they may not represent the average alcoholic but, rather, ideal images of recovering alcoholics.

The same is true of the Al-Anon stories. This analysis of the Al-Anon books was undertaken in order to examine how images of the ideal Al-Anon member are portrayed by the organization and what, if any, changes in those images have occurred over time and thus are reflected in the second edition. It should be kept in mind that these texts are not chosen for their literary merit but for what their content represents, for the messages they convey. They are a tool of the Al-Anon movement, part of a kit, a formula for survival—and serenity.

Martin, J. E. 1992. The evolution of Al-Anon: A content analysis of stories in two editions of its "Big Book." (Mutual Help for Alcohol-Related Problems: Studies of Al-Anon and of Alternatives to Alcoholics Anonymous). *Contemporary Drug Problems,* 19 (4): 563–585.

Purpose of the Fellowship

The Al-Anon Family Groups fellowship grew out of Alcoholics Anonymous and so has the same roots. Philosophically, the Al-Anon/AA roots lie in the principles of the Oxford Group movement, a religious revivalist organization founded by a Lutheran minister, Dr. Frank Buchman. The founders of AA, Bill Wilson and Bob Smith (Dr. Bob), together with others of their early core groups, based the Twelve Steps for recovery on these principles. Essentially, they were: surrendering one's life to God in recognition that one cannot manage it alone; being honest with oneself and others about past wrongs; making amends for past wrongs; doing good deeds without the knowledge of anyone else; and praying for help to live these principles (*Lois Remembers,* 1979, p. 92).

The early "AA" meetings, from approximately 1935 to 1937, were actually Oxford Group meetings. During this period Bill Wilson and Dr. Bob began to realize that their work would be best accomplished by meeting exclusively with alcoholics, so they started meeting outside of the Oxford Group within their own homes. It was at these meetings that the wives of the alcoholics began to talk and draw on one another for support. They met in the kitchens of these homes and chatted while preparing coffee and refreshments for the men. Prior to more formal organization of the family groups, the wives' groups tended more toward gossip and complaint meetings than actual twelve-step meetings. Often, however, wives and other family members would sit in on the AA meetings rather than wait in the kitchen.

Dr. Bob's wife, Annie, and Bill Wilson's wife, Lois, together with the third AA's wife, Anne B., are considered the co-founders of Al-Anon. It wasn't until 1940, however, that constructive gatherings for the families of AAs began to evolve. . . . while they [the AAs] met in the assembly room below, a handful of us wives got to know each other in the sky-lighted studio above. By 1948, 87 groups had applied for a listing in the AA directory, but since this directory was only for AA, Lois and Anne B. formed a Clearing House Committee in New York City. By this time Al-Anon was producing publications such as leaflets and newsletters and was getting media attention as well. In 1954 the number of groups was growing at a rate of about one every three days. At this point the Clearing House Committee incorporated and became a nonprofit organization known as the Al-Anon Family Group Headquarters, which was overseen by a board of trustees and an executive committee. In 1957, Alateen was established under the umbrella of Al-Anon for the teenage children of alcoholics. At present, the Family Group Headquarters has registered approximately 33,000 Al-Anon and Alateen groups, of which about 20,000 are in the U.S. and Canada. World membership is estimated to be somewhere around 600,000 (personal communication, Archivist, Al-Anon Family Group Headquarters, December 1992).

Methods

An informal content analysis of the personal stories contained within the two editions of *Al-Anon Faces Alcoholism* was conducted. The first edition was published in 1965 and the second in 1985. About half of the stories from the first edition were reprinted verbatim in the second edition; the other half were deleted and 23 new stories were added to the second edition. The most useful and revealing approach to the analysis appeared to be not in terms of the two editions, but rather in terms of three distinct types of stories:

those deleted from the first edition, those retained from the first to the second, and those new to the second.

As each story was read, it was coded for concrete items of interest as well as for qualitatively meaningful comments, concepts, or ideologies. The concrete items of interest were: (1) the respective roles of the Al-Anon/alcoholic dyad (e.g., wife/husband, mother/daughter, etc.); (2) the gender of each person in these roles; (3) the outcome of the story—i.e., whether or not the alcoholic found sobriety in AA; (4) whether the Al-Anon member had more than one alcoholic in his or her life; and (5) whether there is mention of other alcoholism in the alcoholic's family.

Not every story could be coded along each parameter, but those that could be coded on any parameter were tallied and proportions calculated. This tabulation procedure was done in order to get a sense of the more pervasive images that Al-Anon may have been displaying at the time each edition was released. Al-Anons who tell of more than one alcoholic in their life—often called "dual" Al-Anons—were coded where possible on their primary alcoholic relationship (e.g., spouse, father). In those few cases where the primary alcoholic relationship is not directly apparent, it is considered to be the alcoholic with whom the Al-Anon was most recently involved upon entering the Al-Anon program.

The qualitative coding took three forms: (1) indicators of ideal image or behavior; (2) group philosophy; and (3) mention of dates, places, or historical events (of which there were few) that helped to place the story in some context. The third turned out to be insubstantial and was not pursued in the present study. This broad approach to the analysis of the stories generated a large amount of data. The present description of findings will be limited to only the most important themes. Following a descriptive summary of the coded items, the themes from the deleted- and retained-story sections will be summarized. Those from the new-story section will be covered in more detail, and finally a few of the unifying theoretical concepts will be discussed.

Descriptive Summary of Coded Stories

There was a total of 55 stories in both editions of *Al-Anon Faces Alcoholism:* 15 deleted in the second edition, 17 retained from the first to the second, and 23 new to the second edition. Two stories, one deleted and one retained, were not classified, since they were composed of small excerpts and did not constitute stories per se. A second retained story was not classified because it was a slightly abstract story in which the writer had no clear social role or alcoholic counterpart. Altogether, 52 stories were analyzed. Table 1 presents the story types by gender in the Al-Anon/alcoholic dyad. The gender distribution of male and female Al-Anons and alcoholics is similar in both types of first-edition stories: most of the Al-Anons are female and most of the alcoholics are male. In contrast, more male Al-Anons are represented in the new stories than in the old ones, while the gender of the alcoholics does not appear to change.

The social roles of the Al-Anons are shown in Table 2 by type of story, and Table 3 shows the social roles of the alcoholics by type of story. Again, the social roles of the Al-Anons and alcoholics in the first-edition stories (both deleted and retained) are basically similar in nature and appear in the same proportions. Though the wife/husband and husband/wife dyads dominate all three story types, the new stories reflect an expansion of

TABLE 1. GENDER DISTRIBUTION OF AL-ANONS AND ALCOHOLICS, BY TYPE OF STORY

Gender	Deleted	Retained	New
Al-Anons			
Female	86% (12/14)	87% (13/15)	59% (13/22)
Male	14% (2/14)	13% (2/15)	41% (9/22)
Alcoholics			
Female	29% (4/14)	31% (5/16)*	32% (8/25)*
Male	71% (10/14)	69% (11/16)*	68% (17/25)*

* These groups contain more alcoholics than Al-Anons due to sets of parents counted as individuals.

TABLE 2. SOCIAL ROLES OF AL-ANONS (FREQUENCY), BY TYPE OF STORY

Role	Deleted	Retained	New
Wife	8	8	6
Mother	2	2	1
Husband	2	2	3
Sister	1	2	—
Daughter	—	—	4
Father	—	—	3
Lover (*)	1	—	2
Son	—	—	2
Alateen	—	1	2
Total	14	15	23

* The writer in the first-edition story was engaged to the alcoholic.

Al-Anon's helping sphere to other groups, primarily children of alcoholics and those in nonmarital love relationships.

Story outcomes—whether or not the alcoholic found sobriety in AA—are presented by gender and type of story in Table 4. In the first-edition stories, close to the same overall proportions of alcoholics in each category of story found sobriety in AA. There are some gender differences, but they are not substantial in light of the small numbers. The new stories, on the other hand, show a definite pattern: the proportion of women alcoholics who find sobriety in AA dropped to 50% and the proportion of male alcoholics dropped to 24%, bringing the overall proportion down to half of what it was in the first-edition stories. This could have reflected a move on the part of Al-Anon to make the stories more true to life, but more likely it simply reflects the increased diversity of Al-Anons in the second edition and the inclusion of many adult children of alcoholics whose parents never found sobriety.

TABLE 3. SOCIAL ROLES OF ALCOHOLICS (FREQUENCY), BY TYPE OF STORY

Role	Deleted	Retained	New
Husband	8	8	6
Wife	2	2	3
Daughter	1	2	2
Son	1	—	2
Sister	1	—	—
Brother	—	2	—
Lover (*)	1	—	2
Parents (sets)	—	1	2
Father	—	—	5
Mother	—	—	1
Total	14	15	23

* The alcoholic in the first-edition story was engaged to the Al-Anon.

TABLE 4. ALCOHOLICS (%) WHO FOUND SOBRIETY IN AA, BY TYPE OF STORY AND GENDER

Gender	Deleted	Retained	New
Female	75% (3/4)	60% (3/5)	50% (4/8)
Male	56% (5/9)	73% (8/11)	24% (4/17)
Overall	62% (8/13)	68% (11/16) (*)	32% (8/25)

* The number of alcoholics is greater than the number of stories due to sets of alcoholic parents counted as individuals.

This "found sobriety in AA" outcome measure was initially intended to make note of happy and sad or positive and negative endings. However, it soon became apparent that for the Al-Anons whose stories were selected for publication, there was no such thing as a sad, negative story; they were all success stories. Though there are five cases where the alcoholic died as a result of drinking, and these are indeed sad, the Al-Anons in each case found serenity through the Al-Anon program and expressed gratitude to the program for offering them a new way of life that they would then share with others. This way of thinking about things is completely in line with the Al-Anon philosophy that it is possible to achieve serenity and even happiness while continuing to live with an active alcoholic (or, presumably, without one).

Finally, the proportion of Al-Anons who described more than one alcoholic in their lives was examined; these were referred to as "dual" Al-Anons. The proportions were 14% (2/14) in the deleted stories, 20% (3/15) in the retained stories, and 39% (9/23) in the new stories. Four of the five dual Al-Anons in the first-edition stories were mothers of alcoholics in their primary alcoholic relationship and wives of alcoholics in their secondary alcoholic relationship ("secondary" here is used to label the relationship that is not the main focus of the story). In the new stories, the Al-Anons in their primary relationships were wives, lovers, children, and a father. Their secondary relationships were even more diverse: children, wives, a father-in-law, a doctor, and a nurse. Across both editions, the majority of dual relationships were found to involve a parent in either the primary or the secondary role. In fact, a dominant theme throughout the new stories is acknowledgement of the lasting effects of living with alcoholic parents.

This portrayal of Al-Anons in touch with multiple alcoholics in their lives may indicate that Al-Anon has aimed to attract a wider variety of people. It also reflects the growing recognition of the effects of alcoholism outside of the marital relationship.

Qualitative Assessment

If one compares *Al-Anon Faces Alcoholism* (1965; 1985) with AA's "Big Book" (*Alcoholics Anonymous,* 1976), one finds that the Al-Anons' stories are quite different from the alcoholics' stories. First, they are relatively brief. While many of the "Big Book" stories are eight to ten pages long, the Al-Anon stories are only two to four pages. Second, they contain very little detail. Many "Big Book" stories describe early childhood and family experiences, first alcohol use, first alcohol problems, jobs, marriage, relevant dates and historical events. Al-Anon stories, on the other hand, tend to begin with life with the alcoholic, describe the development of the problem, describe the crises that brought the writer into Al-Anon, and then describe the program philosophy used and how it helped with their problems. There is very little given in the way of dates, historical events, real people or real places. There is also little about the life of the Al-Anon as an individual prior to life with the alcoholic.

Al-Anon stories in both editions lack precisely the sort of detail that brings the AA "Big Book" stories to life. The Al-Anon stories are mini-dramas that begin with the down side and end with the up side but seem to reflect very little of the personal character of the writer. The stories have a slightly unsettling glibness about them that the AA stories, at any rate the old-timer stories, do not. This is undoubtedly a function, at least in part, of how abbreviated the stories are. For instance, one wife writes about how her husband used to become violent with her when he was drunk but would not remember anything that had happened once he was sober. One night when drunk he broke through their bedroom door and tried to strangle her. She screamed and was rescued by a neighbor. The next day, upon seeing evidence of what he had done and hearing the neighbor verify what he had tried to do, the husband finally called AA. Next she writes: "That was many years ago. We are happier than we've ever been. I know how much I owe to Al-Anon. If it hadn't been for the wonderful people in my group, I'd have left Jim and he might be dead today" (1st ed., p. 177). This story strangely minimizes the author's own brush with death and focuses more on how she may have saved the alcoholic who tried to kill her.

Deleted Stories. In general, each story category has a unique pattern. The deleted stories are primarily about the problem, the crisis, and the resolution but are almost completely devoid of direct references to program philosophy (e.g., the 12 steps and slogans such as "Let go and let God"). Presumably this is why they were left out of the second edition. The way of referring to problems in the deleted stories is less refined, and incorporates less program philosophy and less jargon, compared with the retained stories.

Also among the deleted stories is one by an Al-Anon husband writing in his capacity as a medical doctor. In a clear tone of professional arrogance and sexism, he warns Al-Anons not to advise others to leave their spouses since they may not understand the whole story. He then goes on to explain why there may be problems with the resumption of sex once the (implicitly male) alcoholic is sober:

> She may not even realize that she unconsciously resists her husband's advances, and that the resulting dissatisfaction may be increasing his dependence on alcohol. She doesn't blame herself because she may not realize that she has never really met his need. . . . Where there has been a happy and normal sex relationship before alcoholism became a serious problem, there is always hope, after sobriety, that patience and tolerance will once more restore it. . . . A nagging, suspicious woman is not likely to produce desire in a husband. (1st ed., pp. 86–87)

In early Al-Anon, this sort of advice from a professional was apparently acceptable. According to more refined Al-Anon thinking, no one is to blame for the alcoholic's illness, not even the alcoholic, though a more kind, loving approach with the alcoholic is believed to improve situations dramatically and perhaps diminish the desire for alcohol.

Retained Stories. In contrast to the deleted stories, the retained stories can be characterized by how relatively packed they are with traditional program philosophy. Placed within the second edition, they might be thought of as ensuring that a solid Al-Anon foundation is maintained as the cultural diversity of its members expands.

The first story within each edition was retained and is called "Serenity Does Not Depend on Sobriety." It is exceedingly traditional in terms of both Al-Anon philosophy and the author's social role as wife and mother. This story is exemplary in that the woman rose from the depths of despair, and an attempted suicide, to serenity and happiness in spite of her husband's continued drinking. A few excerpts will illustrate her message:

> I owe my life to the help of Al-Anon and AA friends, to our priest. . . . Now I accept the fact that I am powerless. I now take care of myself and try to improve myself. . . . Al-Anon is as necessary to me as the food I eat and the air I breathe. It is a wonderful help in facing all problems. . . . Perhaps God's wish for me is to help other wives and families. Thoughts of this kind are a great comfort to me. I no longer feel I'm deprived when I miss this party or that outing, when I can't go here or there. I consider what I have. . . . I must fulfill the role I was intended for: a wife, a mother, a member of society. I cannot do it as a self-pitying neurotic. . . . Al-Anon's purpose is to show us how to help ourselves. . . . There are blue days, of course. When they come, I say to myself, "You have no time for self-pity. . . ." The best therapy I have found is to keep busy. I take my house apart and clean and clean. I lose myself in a good novel. I have my hair done. . . . I do not look at our problem as a cross to bear but as something that has been sent to show me a beautiful new way of life I would not have known otherwise. (2nd ed., pp. 92–93)

This woman's story might be very inspiring to some who find themselves in the same situation. The emphasis is on accepting her situation as God's will, recognizing her powerlessness (note that it is a generalized powerlessness), and keeping the focus on herself. Her tone is still that of a martyr who has surrendered.

The tone of another retained story (second story in the second edition) is also very traditional, but much more positive.

> The first thing I really learned was that I must bring myself to release my husband and my children from my direction and domination. . . . The Fourth (step) suggests an inventory of ourselves, and this is certainly of vital importance. . . . Such faults as a tendency to self-pity, possessiveness, resentment and fear, for example, can be rechanneled into attitudes motivated by love. Pride can be transformed into human dignity, which is pride plus humility, instead of selfishness. . . . I know the value of becoming more flexible. . . . I'm also trying to get rid of habitual "expectancy." . . . When an alcoholic finds this way of life, he often grows so fast that we must learn to grow with him or the relationship may be in danger. (2nd ed., pp. 96–98)

This wife sounds very encouraging, as though she made some constructive changes in her life through working the program. No doubt, releasing others to live their own lives and examining one's own faults can help improve life. Yet here, as in other stories throughout the two editions, important feelings like fear and resentment are defined as the Al-Anon's faults. The basic message is that the Al-Anon should not have these feelings; if she does, there is something wrong with her and she needs to work her program better in order not to have them. The alcoholic cannot be expected to share the responsibility for these feelings, since he is not responsible for his illness. An additional message is that if the alcoholic begins to recover and grow, the Al-Anon may endanger the relationship if she does not grow with him. There is something akin to a "blaming the victim" twist within this Al-Anon philosophy.

These two exemplary Al-Anon stories, as well as many others, portray an ideal image of the Al-Anon as calm and selfless in all situations, almost saintly. In this image there is no room for anger or self-pity. Perhaps the extremely high value Al-Anon places on the ideal image of the serene Al-Anon wife represents the implicit social sanction against women expressing their anger or making demands on others.

New Stories. The variety of Al-Anons, the increasing complexity of the alcoholic relationships, and the broader scope of issues discussed in the new stories represent the growth in cultural diversity and the corresponding expansion of Al-Anon's helping sphere. In the new stories we see new people (adult children of alcoholics, non-marital partners, including a gay man) and new issues (incest, communication, sexual relationships, sexual identity). Several of the new issues are addressed in a way that suggests a broadening of the therapeutic purposes of Al-Anon. One husband, writing about how he protected his alcoholic wife from the consequences of her drinking, explains that he allowed the pattern to repeat itself in his professional life. Application of the Al-Anon principles helped him to resolve problems in both relationships:

> As a direct result of my denial of my problems at home, I duplicated them in my professional life. I chose a business partner who had many of the characteristics of my wife, though he himself did not have a drinking problem. . . . With this (Higher) Power I could take the necessary steps to let go of the alcoholic and her behavior and to extricate myself from a damaging business relationship. (2nd ed., p. 189)

In another instance, a woman who came to Al-Anon looking to resolve her pain over her alcoholic father suddenly became aware that her early experiences with him involved sexual abuse. Though she did seek outside help, she credits Al-Anon for helping her to overcome her emotional scars:

> My sharing with other members of Al-Anon has shown me that I am not alone in my experiences and, indeed, that incest is more often involved in the family disease of alcoholism than has previously been realized. But mine is a message of hope. Others like me can recover. . . . To achieve this goal, the love and acceptance found in Al-Anon are invaluable. (2nd ed., p. 211)

The last four stories in the second edition (all new) center on sexual relationships. Though the subject is not a new one, the direct way in which it is addressed is new. Discussion of the sexual relationship in the first edition was limited to the MD's "professional" comment cited earlier. One man, discussing the sexual conflicts that eventually led to his divorce, concludes:

> For me, the key to a secure sexual identity is a strengthening of my self-worth through diligent practice of the Al-Anon program. (2nd ed., p. 213)

Another man, who blames some of his marital problems on his lack of a healthy sexual identity, found help in Al-Anon as well, and says:

> I can only urge others to recognize that, in the course of our illnesses, our relationships degenerate in many ways. But with the help of AA and Al-Anon they can blossom once more in an even more beautiful manner and take on deeper meaning for both husband and wife. (2nd ed., p. 216)

These statements about what the program can do for the marital relationship reach well beyond the simple traditional Al-Anon goal of serenity independent of whether the alcoholic is still drinking or not.

Adult Children of Alcoholics. A theme pervasive among the new stories is that conveyed by the adult children of alcoholics (ACA's): being raised by one or more alcoholic parents creates long-lasting emotional deficits such as heavy sadness, low self-worth, and an inability to develop healthy, trusting, intimate relationships:

> I am the adult child of two alcoholic parents, and my life is dominated by that fact. (2nd ed., p. 158)

> I believe that my self-destructive behavior before I found Al-Anon stemmed from my great lack of self-worth. . . . Thus, without parental love, I grew up far from well-adjusted. I was always searching for someone to love and for someone to love me, and without exception I sought out those people most like my parents. I was, in fact, perpetuating the pain of rejection by seeking love and acceptance from those least able to give it. (2nd ed., p. 206)

> Now, with the help of the Al-Anon program, I feel that if I don't take care of myself, I will continue to suffer. There is a growing desire in me not to do that any longer. (2nd ed., p. 112)

Although the principles of the program remain the same, the recovery process of the ACA's in Al-Anon seems to be of a nature different from that traditionally described by wives. Different recovery "tools" are emphasized. Most no longer live with their alcoholic parent(s) (though many end up with an alcoholic partner), so there appears to be less emphasis on detachment or on examining one's own faults. Rather, the emphasis is on an acknowledgment of the illness they grew up with, the emotional needs that were never met, and the behavior patterns they developed to cope with it all.

The goals of serenity and happiness remain the same, but they are achieved differently. There appears to be less emphasis on accepting the will of God (though God is mentioned in each story) and more on getting the needed nurturing, love, and acceptance from the Al-Anon group. For some, the relevant Higher Power may be the group. The process of working the Al-Anon program and participating in groups is referred to as a healing process; it begins to fill with self-worth the void that has always been there.

Some children of alcoholics describe in these stories a particular youthful coping strategy. They describe stuffing their feelings below the surface, numbing out, or tuning out (though only one ACA reports the use of substances).

Unlike stories by the more traditional wives, it appears in stories by children of alcoholics that the process of recovery necessitates the acknowledgment and expression of latent pain and repressed anger. The adult son quoted above explains:

> My depression turned out to be grief. I had cried over losing what I had never had: my father's love. . . . Slowly, my numb feelings came back to life. Thirty-two years of anger, pain, anxiety and fear poured out, and finally from the depths of me came the desire for a relationship with my father. (2nd ed., p. 202)

Some ACA's, however, do not describe such a catharsis. Rather, they describe a more passive process of "coming to terms" with their anger through knowledge and acceptance of the "disease of alcoholism." One ACA nurse describes her conflict prior to acceptance:

> My group suggested, in a caring way, that I had not yet accepted alcoholism as a disease and that when I did, I would feel differently. . . . I thought that over for a while. If I embraced the disease concept of alcoholism, I'd have to stop hating my dad. (2nd ed., p. 101)

Importance of the Disease Concept. The disease concept of alcoholism is the cornerstone on which Alcoholics Anonymous, and consequently Al-Anon, is built. As the dominant ideology of Al-Anon, it may have served an important function in the early years for both the alcoholic husband and the Al-Anon wife. It may have kept wives from rebelling against their self-centered husbands, husbands who even after sobriety could not be held responsible because they were still sick. Any wife who did not support her husband in his program one hundred percent could be seen as responsible for his relapse.

The co-founders of Al-Anon, Lois Wilson and Annie Smith, were extremely devoted wives, and the historical references (*Lois Remembers,* 1979, and *First Steps,* 1986) suggest that they had unusually harmonious relationships with their husbands even during the drinking years. In her memoirs Lois describes how it was with Bill:

> Once he started, he seldom stopped until he became so drunk he fell inert. He was not violent when in his cups and was deeply remorseful afterward. When he

finally realized he couldn't stop, he begged me to help him, and we fought the alcohol battle together. (*Lois Remembers,* 1979, p. 73)

I love my husband more than words can tell, and I know he loves me. He's a
splendid, fine man—in fact, an unusual man with qualities that could make him
reach the top. His personality is endearing; everybody loves him; and he is a born
leader. Most kindly and big-hearted, he would give away his last penny. He is
honest almost to a fault. (*Lois Remembers,* 1979, p. 77; an entry from her diary
in Bill's drinking days)

Dr. Bob described Annie as having "a cheerfulness, sweetness, and calm that were to
remain with her throughout the years" (*First Steps,* 1986, p. 8). Annie's son, Bob Jr., described her as timid, shy, and selfless, yet able to rise out of her timidity as the situation
demanded (*First Steps,* 1986, p. 9).

These were the women who first decided to apply the AA program to themselves.
They were kind, patient, and selfless, almost saintly. Lois's one outburst of anger toward
Bill, when she threw her shoe at him, so shocked her that she realized then she needed the
program to ensure that she would not behave that way again. It seems that these two
women were almost perfect wives. Their "almost perfect" image appears to have been in-
stitutionalized as the ideal Al-Anon image, since it is dominant in many of the wives' published stories. But the image may be difficult to live up to, if not self-defeating. It is
unlikely that many wives have such "good" alcoholic husbands, and it is equally unlikely
that many alcoholic husbands have such loving, patient wives. The co-founders of AA and
Al-Anon were unique people.

To the extent that the recurrent story themes selectively represent the most important
values and ideals of the Al-Anon organization, it appears to be very important that the Al-
Anon accept the disease concept, and thus accept the alcoholic, without asking any critical questions with respect to why the alcoholic is afflicted:

One of my most persistent errors was that I still felt I had to know why. . . . I
don't want to know why he drinks, I decided. It is enough for me to accept the
fact that he is sick, that he drinks because he cannot help himself and that nothing I know or say or do is going to change that. Surely understanding what
caused the disease is no part of knowing that he is an alcoholic. (1st ed., p. 147)

Again, this message that one should not question the disease concept, or whether the alcoholic fits into that concept, may serve the alcoholic well. It is said to give the alcoholic the
freedom to recover. In reality, it may help to create an atmosphere of passivity and acceptance around the alcoholic that allows him or her to take advantage of his or her disease status. On some level it also serves the Al-Anon well because it allows her (or him) to live with
the problem without constantly feeling that she (or he) must do something about it. For most
people, major changes come hard, and the inertia of the status quo can be powerful. For
some people, particularly women who are dependent on their alcoholic spouse for economic
or other reasons, the philosophy not only allows them a valid reason to go on living with
their partner, but it empowers them to change the one thing that they can themselves.

Is Al-Anon Changing? Theoretically, in terms of the Twelve Steps, the program remains
unchanged. But in other fundamental ways Al-Anon has changed. It has diversified. The

ideal Al-Anon image of the selfless, detached, but serene wife (or other family member) continues to run through many of the second-edition stories, but not all. In the second edition we see new faces. Second-edition stories were written by other types of partners, by relatives, by friends, and particularly by adult children of alcoholics. The new faces are not all serene; many are angry. There is an emphasis on recognition of the damage done and a resolve to heal, an emphasis that is more emotionally and psychologically oriented than the original. There is less emphasis on serenity and surrender to a higher power. If the new stories are any indication, the program appears to be more adaptable to the individual.

References

Al-Anon Faces Alcoholism (1965). First edition. New York: Al-Anon Family Group Headquarters, Inc.

Al-Anon Faces Alcoholism (1985). Second edition. New York: Al-Anon Family Group Headquarters, Inc.

Al-Anon Family Groups (1987). New York: Al-Anon Family Group Headquarters, Inc.

Alcoholics Anonymous (1976). Third edition. New York: Alcoholics Anonymous World Services, Inc.

First Steps: Al-Anon: 35 years of beginnings (1986). New York: Al-Anon Family Group Headquarters, Inc.

Lois Remembers (1979). New York: Al-Anon Family Group Headquarters, Inc.

REVIEW QUESTIONS

1. What types of information was the author trying to obtain in this study?

2. What variables were coded and how were they coded?

3. What were the conclusions?

Thinking Through the Heart

Ann Goetting

As you read this article by Ann Goetting, think about how she uses narrative to find out about women who have successfully left abusive relationships. By listening to the stories of the women, Goetting was able to describe some very clear symptoms and patterns that take place in abusive relationships. It isn't enough to just listen to the voices of our respondents—it is important to learn from their experiences.

The Project in Development

This book is the product of an idea long in incubation, with antecedents reaching back into my youth. My father's unpredictable episodes of rage followed by fits of hollow kindness, in the daily context of condescension, trepidation, and humiliation, introduced me to battering before it had a name. No one in the household was spared my father's wrath, which continues to affect every member of my family today. The hardest part, as I see it now, was my inability to understand what it was all about. It was that ignorance that victimized me and rendered me powerless all those years. Later, as a family studies scholar and criminologist, I was drawn to the notion of studying and teaching about family violence. The knowledge and insights gained by that work provided the framework necessary to free me, to a great extent at least, from that childhood legacy of battering. It is that sense of liberation that inspired this book. Battering thrives on ignorance and is snuffed out by understanding. I want everyone to understand battering because I want it to stop.

The project called for biographical accounts of American women that described the battering process from inception through exit. Diversity in terms of ethnicity, age, social class, religion, geographical region, sexual orientation, and general experience was a critical consideration. There was no intention to create a representative sample, because the goal was to demonstrate patterns and provide instructive cases rather than to generalize. Armed with this vision, I set out to find the women.

A nationwide call for participants to abuse shelters and other organizations and agencies sympathetic to battered women elicited a substantial response. Additionally, a personal search concentrating on my university and community yielded several participants. I first gathered basic background information from each woman and then shifted my attention to her battering and exit processes. My work was theory driven, always focused on the patriarchy and established patterns of battering and getting out. The texts I have created to tell women's stories combine information supplied by them—from autobiographical essays, diaries, newspaper and magazine articles, letters, and interviews—with my own interpretations. Their stories are filtered through me. I met with all except two of the participants, Lucretia and Raquelle, and in all cases I was invited into their homes. I wrote a story only when I was certain that I "knew" the woman well enough.

Early on, as I approached the third or fourth essay, the original concept of the project underwent dramatic revision. It was when I was preparing Colette's story that I knew for certain that I could not sterilize women's biographies by excluding critical dimensions that may at first blush seem unrelated to the subject at hand—battering.

I had read and heard Colette's heart-rending account of her treacherous childhood that culminated in the blood-drenched suicide of her clinically depressed mother. My image of Colette in the telling is frozen in time: visiting her on a cool summer afternoon in shaded, open sunroom, her clear-eyed candor and her serene style. A small framed black-and-white photo of her fashionably suited mother as a young Frenchwoman rested on a shelf nearby. Then, as Colette concluded the story of her own battering, I heard the tale of the death by car accident of Colette's only child at age six—with whom Colette had endured and escaped years of abuse. There were more framed photos on display to relay the significance of Michelle's life and death. Here was a woman's life story whose integrity should not be violated in the name of research on battering (Riessman, 1993: 4). It is only in the context of Colette's story of her youth that her account of her battering rings true.

At that point the book in progress became a collection of life stories of women who had endured and safely left abusive men—not just stories of abuse and escape. The stories are more honest this way. They are stories packed full of women's issues and human issues: contextual knowledge at its best. The thematic link is the abuse and the getting out. I revised the biographies completed before Colette's, then went on to construct the rest contextually. So now the book teaches about childhood, good and bad alike; eating disorders; homelessness; clinical depression culminating in suicide; alcoholism; sibling relationships; baby smuggling; drug trafficking; homosexuality; motherhood; and adult child-parent issues. And it provides glimpses into Puerto Rico; Israel; Star Lake, New York; Wind River Indian Reservation; professional baseball; a Michigan outlaw militia; and the dreadful personal toll exacted by the United States involvement in the Vietnam War. When placed in context, issues surrounding battering seem neutralized and perhaps even dwarfed by the other life processes and events experienced by some of these women.

The construction of the biographies progressed at a brisk and even pace and without a hitch for one year beginning in February 1995. Each essay was a joint endeavor for me and the storyteller. I sent her my first draft, and from there we revised and refined together until we were both satisfied with the product. The women were allowed choice in revealing or suppressing first names and other identifying features. Some participated in the project as a gesture of liberation—a "coming out" of sorts. Their disclosure of their identity symbolizes their pride in having escaped a life of fear and oppression. Other women chose pseudonyms and withheld other specifics in order to protect family members. Using first names only, and leaving the real undifferentiated from the contrived, was my decision.

The stories are uneven. Some are eloquently expressed and nuanced exposes, while others are stilted by comparison. The variation in tone and texture reflects the uniqueness of the teller. Some women found comfort and even elation in the reflection process from their now safe spot, while others could barely tolerate remembering. Additionally, some women were basically more verbally expressive, articulate, and uninhibited than others. These variations produced detectable differences in the biographies, making an important contribution to understanding women's diversity. That women's lives cannot be packaged in some standard way is clearly evidenced by this collection. Nevertheless, every story is worth the telling, and each makes a unique contribution to the product of our combined efforts: a better understanding of battering and getting out and their consequences.

Ethnic diversity is an important part of this collection of life stories of battered women. A small but telling research literature apprises us of the enhanced problems that battered women of color face because of their minority status (Hendrickson, 1996; Mousseau & Artichoker, 1993; Bachman, 1992; White, 1995; Zambrano, 1985, 1994; Moss et al., 1997). Six women in this book—Sharon, Lucretia, Freda, Rebecca, Annette, and Blanca—are women of color, and their life experiences, when compared with those of White women, reflect reported differences between minority and White battered women. Themes of racism as well as sexism permeate the stories of these six women in predictable ways.

> I have no war stories related to the production of this book; without exception, the women were generous, gracious, and patient teachers. This feminist project has made my journey to feminism well worth the trouble (see my autobiographical essay: Goetting, 1996).

The Truth About Biography

Concerns with accuracy have surrounded the literary form of narrative or lifetelling, including biography, for a couple of decades (Goetting, 1995). Do people tell the truth about their lives? The answer to that question is succinctly articulated by the legendary Cree hunter who traveled to Montreal to offer court testimony regarding the effect of the new James Bay hydroelectric scheme on his hunting lands. He would describe the way of life of his people. But when administered the oath he hesitated: "I'm not sure I can tell the truth . . . I can tell only what I know" (Clifford, 1986: 8). We tell the truth pretty much as we know it, but that may not be someone else's "truth."

Some scholars of narrative speak of lifetelling as fiction. They claim that memory is faulty and leaves but a quiver of recognition of times past, which we then adjust into story. In that sense biography is "something made," "something fashioned"—the original meaning of fiction. The claim is not that life stories are false but rather that they are interpretations constructed around a string of imperfect recollections. These scholars point out additionally that lived experience is mediated by language, which is also imperfect. Often there are not words to accurately describe what has happened to us. Lived experience is further mediated by the context in which it is told. The version offered by Colette that day in her sunroom may be different in tone and texture from the version she told her current husband during their courtship years earlier. Biography, as a special form of narrative, further "distorts" the lived experience by adding the biographer's layer of interpretation to those of the storyteller. The perspective of the biographer can add a critical dimension to a story. My biography of Colette is surely different than would be, for example, O. J. Simpson's version of that same life. In sum, biography is not simply a "true" representation of an objective "reality"; instead, memory, language, the context of the telling, and the interpretations of both storyteller and biographer combine to create a particular view of reality. The counterpoint to lifetelling as fiction rather than truth is that it is truth if truth is properly defined. It is argued that in spite of inherent distortions, lifetelling does reveal truths. These truths do not disclose the past "as it actually was" by some arbitrary standard of objectivity; instead, they are reconstructed and, therefore, superior truths. We continue through our lifetime to interpret old events from new positions. Each time, we tell the story differently, and with each telling the story matures and gains depth. My story as a ten-year-old of my father's rages was different than the story I tell today of the same times and incidents. From this perspective on truth, biography is better than having been there because it adds the element of seasoned consciousness to the original experience. In the words of Georges Gusdorf (1980):

> In the immediate moment, the agitation of things ordinarily surrounds me too much for me to be able to see it in its entirety. Memory gives me a certain remove and allows me to take into consideration all the ins and outs of the matter, its context in time and space. As an aerial view sometimes reveals to an archaeologist the direction of a road or a fortification or a map of a city invisible to someone on the ground, so the reconstruction in spirit of my destiny bares the major lines that I have failed to notice, the demands of the deepest values I hold that, without my being clearly aware of it, have determined my most decisive choices. (38)

Our real concern with biography is not whether it is "truth" or "fiction" but what it can teach us about human feelings, motives, and thought processes. For example, in this book we are far less interested in knowing who hit or slapped whom how often than we are with knowing how a woman feels about being hurt by her partner, how she reacts and why. Biography does not supply us with verifiable truths; rather, it offers a special kind of impassioned knowing. A final note on truth as it applies specifically to these biographies: certainly a curiosity about "his side of the story" is reasonable. Would these women's abusers tell the same stories about the relationship? Would they minimize or deny what they are accused of in these pages? First, it must be emphasized that we live in a gendered universe, where men and women are considered to be two distinct types of people and are treated accordingly. In that sense men and women occupy two different worlds and, in so doing, define and understand little, if anything, similarly (Tannen, 1990; Szinovacz, 1983). It is no surprise, therefore, that when researchers separate couples and inquire about shared activities and the dynamics of their relationship, those couples seem to describe two different relationships altogether (Szinovacz, 1983). It is that phenomenon that inspired sociologist Jessie Bernard (1972) to title her now classic essay of American marriage "Marriage: Hers and His." Battering is no exception to the rule. Two sound studies of couples in relationships where the woman is physically abused (one, from the United States [Szinovacz, 1983]; the other, Scottish [Dobash et al., 1998]) inform us that women report more types of violent victimization and in greater frequency than their male partners admit to. Furthermore, more women than men report injuries from the abuse and, again, women report higher frequencies. All in all, women perceive more violence in these relationships and tend to judge it as more serious. I suspect that the abusers of the women in this collection would tell very different stories and that they would minimize and deny the abuse of which they are accused.

Winning with Biography

Biography enjoys popularity among readers of every stripe. It offers privileged access to understandings of the human condition in all of its complexity. The life of the emotions, the life of the mind, the physical life, and the social life are told in context to produce a comprehensive whole. It is all there within easy grasp: the obscurities, the reasonings, the motivations, the passions. German sociologist Wilhelm Dilthey touts biography as the highest and most instructive form of knowledge about humanity (translated by Kohli, 1981). From that perspective the best way to truly understand a category of human experience, such as escape from battering, would be through examination of a diverse assemblage of biographies focusing on that experience—in this case life stories of battered women who got out.

In addition to providing a superior method of understanding the human experience, reading biography helps us make sense of our own lives by connecting us with others. It activates us to construct a benchmark against which to compare our own existence, thereby prompting us to rethink that existence. We continually test our own realities against such stories and modify our perceptions accordingly. In that way biography transforms us. In the process of this personal transformation, this reconceptualization of our life, we typically are comforted and sometimes elated by the newfound connections that inspired the journey. Finding people in situations comparable to ours who have discovered similar truths fortifies us with consensus and affirmation. We are no longer alone and vulnerable. Jane Tompkins (1989) tells it best:

> I love writers who write about their own experience. I feel I'm being nourished by them, and that I'm being allowed to enter into a personal relationship with them, that I can match my own experiences with theirs, feel cousin to them, and say, yes, that's how it is. (170)

By delivering sensitive insight and inspiring a reinterpretation of life through human connectedness, reading biography can forge informed life change. The sociologist C. Wright Mills's promise of "the sociological imagination" (1959) instructs us that insights into social context can supply the resources necessary not only to understand one's own life but to at least partially control its outcomes. Similarly, social theorist Max Weber insists that humans can succeed only if "each finds . . . the demon who holds the fibers of his very life" (Gerth & Mills, 1946: 156).

It becomes apparent that reading biography can be personally rewarding and a joy to experience. It has the potential to nourish and fortify us and to propel us into a constructive path of personal renewal. Biography represents reason informed by passion, arguably the most powerful form of knowledge production. Robbie Pfeufer Kahn (1995) refers to that process as "thinking through the heart." The women whose stories grace these pages have generously and bravely embraced this process to one point of completion, many specifically in hopes that their stories would find, inform, soothe, and intelligently activate battered women. This book personifies "thinking through the heart."

References

Bachman, R. 1992. *Death and violence on the reservation: Homicide, family violence, and suicide in American Indian populations.* New York: Auburn House.

Bernard, Jessie. 1972. Marriage: Hers and his. *Ms.* December: 46–49, 110–111.

Clifford, James. 1986. Introduction: Partial truths. Pp. 1–26 in *Writing culture: The poetics and politics of ethnography,* James Clifford & George E. Marcus (eds.). Berkeley: University of California Press.

Dobash, Russell, Rebecca Dobash, Kate Cavanagh, & Ruth Lewis. 1998. Separate and intersecting realities: A comparison of men's and women's accounts of violence against women. *Violence Against Women* 4(4): 382–414.

Gerth, H. H., & C. Wright Mills (eds. & trans.). 1946. *From Max Weber: Essays in sociology.* New York: Oxford University Press.

Goetting, Ann. 1995. Fictions of the self. Pp. 3–19 in *Individual voices, collective visions: Fifty years of women in sociology,* Ann Goetting & Sarah Fenstermaker (eds.). Philadelphia: Temple University.

Goetting, Ann. 1996. Ecofeminism found: One woman's journal to liberation. Pp. 174–179 in *Private sociology: Unsparing reflections, uncommon gains,* Arthur B. Shostak (ed.). Dix Hills, NY: General Hall.

Gusdorf, Georges. 1980. Conditions and limits of autobiography. Pp. 28–48 in *Autobiography: Essays theoretical and critical,* James Olney (ed. & trans.). Princeton, NJ: Princeton University Press.

Hendrickson, Roberta M. 1996. Victims and survivors: Native American Womenwriters, violence against women, and child abuse. *Studies in American Indian Literatures* 8(1): 13–24.

Kohli, Martin. 1981. Biography: Account, text, method. Pp. 61–75 in *Biography and society: The life history approach in the social sciences,* Daniel Bertaux (ed.). Thousand Oaks, CA: Sage.

Mills, C. Wright. 1959. *The sociological imagination.* New York: Oxford University Press.

Moss, Vicki A., Carol Rogers Pitua, Jacquelyn C. Campbell, & Lois Halstead. 1997. The experience of terminating an abusive relationship from an Anglo and African American perspective: A qualitative descriptive study. *Issues in Mental Health Nursing* 18: 433–454.

Mousseau, Marlin, & Karen Artichoker. 1993. *Domestic violence is not Lakota/Dakota tradition.* Sisseton, SD: South Dakota Coalition Against Domestic Violence and Sexual Assault. To obtain free copy, call 1-800-572-9196, or write P.O. Box 141, Pierre, SD 57501.

Pfeufer Kahn, Robbie. 1995. *Interviewing the midwife's apprentice: The question of voice in writing a cultural ethnography of patriarchy.* Paper presented at annual meetings of the American Sociological Association, Washington, DC.

Riessman, Catherine Kohler. 1993. *Narrative analysis.* Thousand Oaks, CA: Sage.

Szinovacz, Maximiliane E. 1983. Using couple data as a methodological tool: The case of marital violence. *Journal of Marriage and the Family* 45: 633–644.

Tannen, Deborah. 1990. *You just don't understand.* New York: William Morrow.

Tompkins, Jane. 1989. Me and my shadow. Pp. 169–178 in *Gender and theory: Dialogues on feminist criticism,* Linda Kauffman (ed.). Oxford: Basil Blackwell.

White, Evelyn C. 1995. *Chain chain change: For Black women in abusive relationships.* Seattle: Seal.

Zambrano, Myra M. 1985. *Mejor sola que mal acompanada: Para Ia Mujer Golpeada/For the Latina in an abusive relationship.* Seattle: Seal.

———. 1994. *No Mas! Guia Para la Mujer Colpeada.* Seattle: Seal.

REVIEW QUESTIONS

1. How did the researcher gather her respondents?

2. Why does Goetting believe that narratives are "more honest?"

3. What is the "truth about biography?"

Chapter 10: Existing Data and Evaluation Research

You have learned in the previous chapters the various ways of collecting data and conducting research that are most common to social science researchers. In this chapter, you will learn about different types of research that do not involve your own data collection. Rather, in this chapter you will learn first about using data that has been collected by someone else and about evaluation research where the researcher evaluates a program or a study.

The first type of research involves using **existing statistics** that can come in the form of numerical information, reports, or other official documents. Using existing statistics would be ideal for a project where the goal is to find out about information that has been collected by large bureaucratic organizations. Often this data is gathered for policy decisions or as a public service. Existing statistics can be used as supplemental data for any topic you are interested in. For instance, suppose you are writing a report about the positive aspects of private education. You may look for statistics that have been gathered by the Department of Education and find the differences in SAT and ACT scores between private and public high school students. In other types of research, it might not make sense for you to collect all your own data from scratch. Using existing data can save you time, money, and energy. And, at the same time, existing statistics give you a place to begin figuring out what you will be studying.

Using existing statistics is most appropriate when the researcher is interested in testing a hypothesis that involves variables that can also be found in reports by official agencies such as those that address economical, political, and social conditions. There is so much existing data available for you to look at that it can be mind-boggling. Much of existing data is free and can be found either on the Internet or in your library. Some examples of **primary existing data** are the following:

- *Statistical Abstract of the United States,* which was published the first time in 1878 and has been published annually since then. The *Statistical Abstract* is a compilation of official reports produced by more than 200 U.S. government and private agencies. Many other governments publish similar reports. For instance, Canada produces the *Canada Yearbook* and New Zealand publishes *New Zealand Official Yearbook.*

- *Standard and Poor's Register of Corporations, Directors and Executives* lists more than 37,000 U.S. and Canadian companies and provides information on the corporations, their products, officers, and sales figures.

- *Dictionary of American Biography* was first published in 1928 and updates information regularly. The *Dictionary* lists the careers, travels, and titles of publications of famous people.

- *Vital Statistics on American Politics* provides information on the campaign spending practices of every candidate for Congress. It details their primary and final votes, ratings by various political organizations, and a summary of the voter registration regulations by state.

- *The General Social Survey* (GSS) is a regular, ongoing study that has been conducted using personal interviews of U.S. households conducted by the National Opinion Research Center (NORC). The sample sizes for this project have been around 1500 for each of the 19 years the survey has been conducted. Each interview lasts about 90 minutes, and the data from this study would be beneficial if your project is in any of the following areas: Economic Studies, Education Studies, Epidemiology and Public Health Studies, Health Services Studies, Statistics and Methodology Studies, and Substance Abuse, Mental Health, and Disability Studies.

Here is another example. Let's say you were interested in conducting a project to investigate if the rates of AIDS are higher in some countries than others. To begin, you could go to the U.S. Census Web site at http://www.census.gov. Using their subject A–Z listing, you would look under A and find a section called AIDS then AIDS Surveillance, where you can find the AIDS Surveillance Data Base. From here, you could find the AIDS prevalence rate of various countries and them compare (U.S. Census Bureau, 1999). You could then incorporate the U.S. Census data into own your research project and draw some of your own conclusions about some of the differences you find.

Existing statistics can also come from **secondary data,** which allows you to reanalyze the data from a previously collected survey. The primary focus when using secondary data is on the analysis rather than on the data collection. This type of data is used more frequently because it is inexpensive, it permits comparisons between individuals, groups, and nations, and it allows for replication. It also permits new research questions to be asked that were not asked in the previous study.

Evaluation research is widely used to measure the effectiveness of a program, policy, or a specific way of doing something. Evaluating is common and we all do it. Think back to the last test you took. After the test was completed, what did you think? Did you think, "I should have studied more," or "I really get nervous with multiple choice tests," or "I think I passed the test, but just barely"? You were evaluating yourself. Evaluation research is very similar to experimental research. Although the goal of basic research is to understand the social world, evaluation research is designed to evaluate the effectiveness of various types of programs to measure whether or not the program is working.

Social programs tend to address social problems such as homelessness, drinking and driving, and HIV/AIDS prevention. Because public policy and funding for social programs tend to depend on the need for the program and its success in helping those who use the program, it is important to be able to evaluate it. Many federal granting agencies are even starting to require that social agencies have an evaluative researcher involved in the project from the beginning to make sure that the effectiveness of the program can be well documented. Suppose you are interested in reducing the rate of teen automobile fatalities, and you believe that developing a program to encourage teens not to drink and drive would be effective. You can obtain information about fatalities in your area, then after many months of putting the program together and presenting it to high school students in the area, you want to see if it reduces the number of fatalities. You can also develop a survey asking students about their drinking and driving patterns before the program and retest them after the program to see if their behaviors changed. In the following articles, you will see how researchers use the data from large studies to investigate the phenomenon they are studying.

REFERENCES

General Social Survey Data [ONLINE]
    http://www.norc.uchicago.edu/projects/gensoc.asp

U.S. Census Bureau. 1999. Estimates of HIV-1 Seroprevalence [ONLINE]
    www.census.gov/ipc/www/hiv1.html

INFOTRAC COLLEGE EDITION SUGGESTED READINGS AND DISCUSSION QUESTIONS

Using InfoTrac College Edition, type in the words "Census data" to locate articles such as "Trends in Asian American racial/ethnic intermarriage: A comparison of 1980 and 1990 census data." Many other articles use sex, race, or religion as variables. Find five articles that use the Census data and address those variables. Explain how the researchers used the data. Was the data used for the entire study or was it just used to find out preliminary information?

WHAT SOCIOLOGISTS DO AND WHERE THEY DO IT —THE NSF SURVEY ON SOCIOLOGISTS' WORK ACTIVITIES AND WORKPLACES

Robert J. Dotzler and Ross Koppel

In this article, data from the National Science Foundation Survey of Doctoral Recipients was used to investigate what sociologists do besides working in an academic setting. The researchers found that only 45.8 percent of Ph.D. sociologists actually teach sociology and that other jobs that a sociologist could have, besides teaching, are either ignored or dismissed. Rather than sending out a survey and asking sociologists what they do as a job, the researchers were able to use existing data that had been collected by the National Science Foundation, which saved not only time but money. As you read this article, watch for the questions that the researchers "asked" the data and how they went about finding their answers.

Dotzler, Robert, J., and Ross Koppel. 1999. What sociologists do and where they do it—The NSF survey on sociologists' work activities and workplaces. *Sociological Practice: A Journal of Clinical and Applied Sociology,* 1(1): 71–83. Reprinted with permission from Kluwer Academic/Plenum Publishers.

Introduction

Sociologists' self-perceptions are inconsistent with the reality of their professional activities. The discipline *as taken for granted* sees itself primarily as professors teaching sociology. Recent data from the NSF survey of Ph.D. sociologists, however, reveal that this view is anachronistic and more wrong than right. Less than one-half of all sociologists—45.8%—teach sociology. The majority of our colleagues spend their days managing and administrating, conducting applied or basic research, teaching in areas other than sociology, and engaging in a wide range of tasks that are divergent from the traditional image.

We do not know why sociologists persist with a traditional, classroom-based image, but we do know that this image is profoundly consequential to the way sociologists interact with each other and with the larger society. As a discipline, we tend to ignore or dismiss the *doing* of sociology in favor of the *teaching* of sociology or of theoretically focused research. As a discipline, we usually view sociology's use in society as something teachers do on the side—a perception that these data show to be false. Moreover, we argue that the perception is detrimental to the influence and role of sociology. Consider the role of the other sciences, both the social and the physical. Are their statuses and strengths *eroded or enhanced* by their practitioners? Are economists, biologists, psychologists, physicists, or anthropologists perceived as working primarily within the classroom? Sociology appears to be special in its adherence to a traditional image, despite its distorting and ultimately disempowering effects.

This report on sociologist's activities and types of employment is based on the 1995 Survey of Doctorate Recipients, which is produced every two years by the National Research Council under contract with the National Science Foundation. The survey was conducted the week of April 15, 1995, of all individuals with an earned doctorate. We were fortunate to obtain support and encouragement from NSF staff and contractors who devised many tables for this research.

We envision this article as the first of several that provide insight into our profession, our work lives, and our labor supply and demand. In future publications, we expand our analysis to include information on cohort effects (e.g., the great job dearth of the 1970s; see Koppel, 1993), quality and the status of the Ph.D. granting institutions, pay differences by employer type, gender, and region.

In this first analysis of the data we ask:

- What do sociologists do? What are the principal tasks and job descriptions?

- Where do sociologists work? What proportion are in academic institutions, in practice settings, in private industry, in not-for-profits?

- How do academic and practicing (applied) sociologists differ in their principal tasks?

A general caveat: It is probable that those in applied fields and in non-education institutions were more difficult to find and less likely to respond than sociologists in academe. Thus, we suspect, but cannot document, systematic underrepresentation of applied/nonacademic sociologists in all of the data presented here.

Most sociologists work in educational employment settings. However, as we shall see, many of those in educational institutions do not teach and, even of those who teach, sociology is not always the subject.

TABLE 1. TYPE OF EMPLOYER*

	Number	Percent
Educational institution	8,901	72.9
Noneducational institution	3,310	27.1
Total	12211	100.0

*All data for Ph.D. sociologists employed during week of April 15, 1995; weighted 1995 SDR data. Actual sample size, 1300.

TABLE 2. TYPE OF EDUCATIONAL EMPLOYER

	Number	Percent
Precollege education	63.1	.08
College		
2-year	406.2	4.6
4-year	7451.3	83.7
Medical School	313.9	3.5
University research	579.9	6.5
Other	87.1	0.9
Total	8901.6	100.0

Table 1 gives us a sense of the size of the profession as well as the distribution between educational and noneducational employers for those with earned Ph.D.s up to age 76—a figure of 12,221. Of these, approximately five-sevenths (72.9%) work in educational institutions; about two-sevenths (27.1%) do not. The latter figure of 27.1% represents some 3300 Ph.D. sociologists working outside of educational institutions. Note that the data are weighted to reflect the actual number of sociologists in the profession. The actual sample size is 1300.

Table 2 reflects the distribution for those employed by educational institutions. We can see that fully 83.7% of the almost 9000 Ph.D. sociologists working in educational institutions work in the traditional four-year college setting. Note that 6.5% of those in educational institutions work at "university research" jobs; medical schools represent another 3.5%. Precollege education occupies less than 1% of sociology's teachers.

Of the 3300 or so working in noneducational institutions (see Table 3), we see that about one-quarter (24.9%) are in private for-profit institutions; another one-quarter (25.3%) are in private not-for-profit institutions. Almost one-fifth (19.5%) are self-employed, and almost 30% work in government: state, local, military, and federal.

By combining Tables 2 and 3 (see Table 4), we get a sense of the great diversity of employment settings. Although educational institutions still predominate, a notable percentage

TABLE 3. TYPE OF NONEDUCATIONAL EMPLOYER

	Number	Percent
Private for profit	823.8	24.9
Private not for profit	835.8	25.3
Self-employed	614.2	18.6
Government		
State and local	459.8	13.9
Federal and military	512.7	15.5
Other	63.6	1.9
Total	3,309.9	100.0

TABLE 4. TYPE OF EMPLOYER FOR THOSE IN EDUCATIONAL AND NONEDUCATIONAL SETTINGS

	Number	Percent
Private for profit	823.8	6.7
Private not for profit	835.8	7.0
Self-employed	614.2	5.0
Government		
State and local	459.8	3.8
Federal and military	512.7	4.2
Other noneducation	63.6	.5
Precollege education	63.1	.5
College		
2–year	406.2	3.3
4-year	7451.3	61.0
Medical School	313.9	2.6
University research	579.9	4.7
Other	87.1	.7
Total	12,211.4	100.0

of sociologists work in private, private not-for-profit, government, and self-employment settings.

We now shift focus from employer category to the more central question of principal job codes. Moreover, we examine these data for all sociologists (Table 5). We present the information for sociologists in education (left-hand column); sociologists in noneducational settings (middle column), and all sociologists combined (last column). These data are among the most powerful to emerge from this recent NSF survey of sociologists. They are based on the respondent's own classification of "best principal job code."

TABLE 5. BEST PRINCIPAL JOB CODE FOR SOCIOLOGY PH.D.S WITH EDUCATION EMPLOYERS, NONEDUCATION EMPLOYERS, AND BOTH TYPES OF EMPLOYERS*

	Education Employer (%)	Noneducation Employer (%)	Both
Clergy and other religious		4.5	1.2
Computer science programmers, analysts	0.2	5.2	1.8
Health workers	0.2	5.2	1.9
Artists, TV, public relations		3.9	1.0
Lawyers, judges	0.2	3.4	1.1
Management and administration	15.0	38.0	20.3
Statisticians	0.2	3.3	1.0
Sales and service		4.2	1.5
Economists	.02	1.0	0.4
Psychologist and clinical		2.4	0.7
Sociologists	4.6	17.1	8.0
Other social scientist	1.0	8.6	3.1
Elementary education	0.2		0.1
Secondary-social sciences	0.2		0.1
Postsecondary teaching			
Sociology	62.7		45.8
Assorted, not sociology	16.3		11.7
Social workers		1.8	0.5
Other occupations	0.2	1.5	0.4
Totals	100.0	100.0	100.0
(wt. N)	8,901.6	3,309.7	12,211.0

*Numbers do not equal 100% because of rounding, which is exacerbated by collapsing of cells.

Look first at the left column, which comprises principal tasks for those employed by educational institutions: The leading category, not surprisingly, is teaching sociology (62.7%). This is followed by management (15%) and by sociologists teaching subjects other than sociology (16.3%). Sociologists as sociologists—presumably research and practice—is next at 4.6%. (We are obliged to use categories employed by the National Science Foundation's questionnaire and data reduction structure (cf. National Science Foundation 1995a, 1995b, 1996a, 1996b).

Look next at the middle column, which comprises principal tasks for those employed by noneducational institutions. We see that management and administration is the modal category, at 38%—almost two-fifths of the group. Sociologists (as researchers, policy experts, etc.) are another 17.1%. These are followed by "other social sciences," 8.6%; computer systems experts, programmers, and analysts, total 5.2%; clergy, 4.5%; entertainment, TV, and the arts, 3.9%; and judges/lawyers, 3.4%.

Now, we move to the data and column that we find most revealing—the combined or "both" column, on the right. The most significant finding is the fact that, when examined as a discipline, less than one-half—45.8%—of sociologists teach sociology. This is, we argue, a noteworthy and oft-ignored reality of our profession. Other notable findings in this right-hand column include:

- It is striking that 20.3% of all sociologists work in management and administration. That is, slightly over one-fifth of all Ph.D. sociologists concern themselves primarily with coordination, administration, or management of organizations, government agencies, educational institutions, policy, etc.

- As we saw in the other columns, sociologists as "sociologists" comprise another 8% of the profession.

- Teaching other social sciences in postsecondary educational settings totals 11.7% of all sociologists. This includes teaching of psychology, social work, health specialties, law, computer science, marketing and business, math, and education.

- Work in computer systems and programming occupies less than 2% of the profession.

- Note that very few are working as statisticians (1%), social workers (0.5%), and psychologists (0.7%).

These new NSF data allow us to extend the analysis of what sociologists do (Table 6). Specifically, the survey asked respondents about their primary work activity—a question that allows more nuanced responses than the previous question on "best principal job code." We present these findings for sociologists in noneducational institutions. These data manifest the work of practicing sociologists, who apparently are occupied with conducting applied research, running institutions or agencies, advising clients or colleagues, building computer systems, and making money (for the institutions, if not themselves).

- Fully one-third, 33.7%, are engaged in applied research as their *primary* activity.

- Managing, leading, planning, coordinating, developing, designing, and supervising occupies almost one-half of the work of nonacademic sociologists (48.1%), if we add: managing and supervising (17.4%); employee relations (1.2%); sales, purchasing, marketing, customer service, and public relations (6.6%); quality or productivity management (0.8%); professional service (10.7%); production, operations, and maintenance (0.1%); design (2.6%); development (3.6%); and accounting, finance, and contracts (5.1%).

We emphasize that the exact meaning of some of these categories has not been defined entirely to our satisfaction. As noted previously, we are dependent on the classifications established by the NSF survey. We understand, for example, that "professional service" refers to dealing with clients or performing professional sociological work. Thus, this category could easily be considered "applied research."

The questions reflected in the previous two tables required sociologists to select one major category to define their "primary work" or "best job code." Of course, our work lives often defy a single definition or single category. Often our work days or work weeks are too diverse to be reflected in one designation. The next table and set of comparisons

TABLE 6. PRIMARY WORK ACTIVITY OF SOCIOLOGY PH.D.S EMPLOYED IN
NONEDUCATIONAL INSTITUTIONS

	Number	Percent
Accounting, finance, contracts	170	5.1
Applied research	1,116	33.7
Basic research	74	2.2
Computer applications, programming, systems development	253	7.6
Development	120	3.6
Design	88	2.7
Employee relations	41	1.2
Managing and supervising	575	17.4
Production, operations, maintenance	3	0.1
Professional Services	354	10.7
Sales, purchasing, marketing, customer service, public relations	217	6.6
Quality or productivity management	27	0.8
Teaching	94	2.8
Other	177	5.3
Total	3,309	100.0

address that reality. Table 7 reflects the work at which the respondents spend 10 hours or more per week. As might be expected, the question, from which it is derived, allows multiple responses—reflecting the fact that there is more than one 10-hour period in a week.

Moreover, just as in the format for Table 5, we provide these data for sociologists: (1) employed in educational institutions, (2) employed in noneducational institutions, and (3) all sociologists (both groups combined). Thus, the left column shows the breakdown of major work activities for sociologists in education; the middle column shows the breakdown for sociologists employed by noneducational institutions; and the last column is for the combined population.

This table contains several powerful discoveries:

- The first row reveals that over 50% of those employed by both educational and noneducational institutions spend at least 10 hours or more per week of their time on applied research. Almost 53% of those employed by educational institutions spend at least 10 hours per week on applied research; the comparable figure for those with noneducational employers is 59.1%. This is a finding of signal importance. It reflects a central reality (versus the current image) of sociology as something other than pedagogy and supports the need for greater attention to sociological practice and the use of sociology in society.

- The second row illustrates the large role that management and administration occupies for *both* those employed by educational institutions and those who are not in educational institutions. "Management and administration" is a major job for almost

TABLE 7. MAJOR WORK ACTIVITIES (10 HOURS OR MORE PER WEEK) OF SOCIOLOGY PH.D.S IN EDUCATIONAL INSTITUTIONS, NONEDUCATIONAL INSTITUTIONS, AND BOTH

Work Activity	Education Employer (%)	Noneducation Employer (%)	Both (All, %)
Applied research	52.8	59.1	54.5
Management and administration	37.7	55.2	42.4
Employee relations	26.2	41.9	30.4
Computer applications	18.2	35.8	23.0
Accounting, finance, contracts	9.0	32.0	15.2
Sales, purchasing, marketing	7.1	31.3	13.7
Development	10.5	28.5	15.4
Professional services	17.3	26.8	19.9
Quality and productivity management	6.2	24.4	11.1
Design	5.9	23.5	10.6
Basic research	58.3	16.8	47.1
Teaching	90.5	15.2	70.1
Production, operations	0.6	3.5	1.3

two-fifths of academic and for four-sevenths of the nonacademic samples. Moreover, as we have seen in the previous analyses, if we add the time spent on accounting, employee relations, productivity management, development, etc., it appears that most sociologists are involved in several forms of management and supervision. This finding is consistent with the earlier tables and reflects a theme we have seen before.

• We are surprised by the differences in basic research. Almost three-fifths of those employed by educational institutions state that this is an important time allocation, whereas less than one-fifth of those who are not in educational institutions make similar claims. Frankly, we thought there would be more similarities between the two groups. Perhaps there is some normative pressure or ambiguity in definitions. Similarly, we were very surprised to see the noneducational institution employees spending almost twice as much time with computer applications as the educational employees. Perhaps academe is less digital than we thought or the nonacademic world is more high-tech than we supposed.

• Of course, teaching predominates among the educational employees, but we note that almost one in six noneducational institution employees is involved in teaching.

Implicit in several of the tables reviewed above is the question: why are some people in academe and others in practice? We do not have as complete an answer as we would wish, but we can address some elements of that question.

The NSF survey asked if one's current work is related to one's doctorate (Table 8). This is a question that must be examined in light of a heavy dose of cognitive dissonance.

TABLE 8. IS WORK RELATED TO DOCTORATE FOR THOSE EMPLOYED IN NONEDUCATIONAL INSTITUTIONS?

	Number	**Percent**
Closely related	1361.7	41.2
Somewhat related	1356.8	41.0
Not related	591.3	17.9
Total	3309.0	100.0

TABLE 9. IF WORK NOT RELATED TO DOCTORATE, WHY?

	Number	**Percent**
Pay and promotion	265	44.9
Working conditions	227	38.4
Location	264	44.7
Career change	205	34.7
Family	50	8.5
Job not available	332	56.3
Other	137	23.2

Note: More than one answer is possible.

Nevertheless, the results are of interest. Note that, at this point, we have data only for those *not* in educational institutions. (Was the assumption that all those in educational settings are working in areas related to their doctorates?)

We find that even for those employed in nonacademic institutions, slightly over two-fifths (41.1%) state their work is closely related to their doctorates, while another two-fifths (41%) report that their work is somewhat related. Thus, less than one-fifth (17.9%) state that their work is not related to their doctorates.

As we suggested above, there is much room for individual conceptual wiggling about what "related" means and the interpretations of both doctorate and current work. Nevertheless, over 82% of those not in educational settings claim their work is related to their doctorates. We await data on those in educational settings.

We are able to examine the reasons *why* work is not related to doctorate for those with noneducation employers. In the first of two tables (Table 9) more than one answer is possible: The major response is "job not available," although "pay/promotion" and "location" are also frequently noted. This is not a surprising finding.

The next table (Table 10) presents the findings where only the *most important* reason is allowed. We see the importance of nonavailability of a job in one's field. Note that "family," which was given in the earlier table, is not listed here.

TABLE 10. IF WORK NOT RELATED TO DOCTORATE, MOST IMPORTANT REASON FOR
THOSE WITH NONEDUCATIONAL EMPLOYMENT

	Number	Percent
Pay and promotion	115	19.5
Working conditions	64	10.8
Location	14	2.4
Career change	54	9.1
Job not available	280	47.4
Other	64	10.8
Total	591	100

Summary and Conclusions

Our major findings confront what we argue is a false and anachronistic image of what sociologists do. The data reported here, tabulated for this study by the National Science
Foundation, reveal that most sociologists are not primarily classroom teachers of sociology. Moreover, even if we include all classroom-based sociologists in the analysis, most
of the members of the profession spend most of their time working on applied research,
administering and managing, advising on policy or programs, and dealing with computers, contracts, or clients.

What we find is that a lot of sociologists are out in society practicing sociology. We
suggest that this is a valuable activity both for our discipline and for society. Our concern
is that our failure to reflect this reality within the discipline undermines our strength as a
profession. How we understand what we do and how we present ourselves to others is
consequential. (Need we recite W. I. Thomas's dictum?) Until very recently, however, the
American Sociological Association (ASA) devoted limited attention to the practice of sociology. We argue that the ASA and sociologists, for the long-term health and integration
of the discipline, should devote more resources to the practice sector.

Our data address the reality and the image of sociology as a strictly university-based
profession. We argue that the "use-value" of sociology is as meaningful as its "knowledge
value." Any reasonable understanding of the role of social sciences in society suggests that
neither will flourish without the flowering of both. The rise of the "market" perspective and
of the focus on a discipline's role in society, even within the walls of academe, calls for a
better balance between "use-value" and "knowledge-value" within the discipline.

Contrary to the views of many (e.g., Halliday & Janowitz, 1992), these data indicate
that a large number of Ph.D. sociologists work in roles very different from those of the
college-based teacher/scholar. Our objective, however, is not to challenge academic sociology. We want to see it grow and flourish. Our argument is that it will grow and flourish best
if the practice side of sociology is better cultivated and understood by sociologists across
the board. The creation and expansion of jobs in the sociological practice sector depend in
no small way on the university-based sociologist's understanding of and involvement with

this sector. Equally important, the perceived and actual utility of sociology as a discipline is enhanced by sociological practice. Both academe and practice will benefit if sociologists are equipped technically and intellectually for work in practice. This will require a transformation of our current graduate programs.

We envision this article as the first of several that examines the NSF sociology Ph.D. dataset. We hope to provide insight into our work lives and into our labor supply and demand, cohort effects, pay differentials, quality/status of Ph.D.-granting institutions, gender, part- and full-time status, and region. We are negotiating with the NSF to obtain the dataset so that we can run multivariate analyses and can free the NSF staffers from their roles as intermediaries—although they have been both kind and helpful. We hope that better information about what sociologists do will help all of us better understand, guide, and use our discipline in society.

References

Halliday, Terence, & Morris Janowitz (eds.). 1992. *Sociology and its publics: The forms and fates of disciplinary organization.* Chicago: University of Chicago Press.

Koppel, Ross. 1993. Looking for the "lost generation" in the wrong places. *ASA Footnotes,* May, 1993.

National Science Foundation. 1995a. Guide to NSF Science and Engineering Resources Data, NSF 95–318, Arlington, VA.

———. 1995b. NSF Survey Instruments Used in Collecting Science and Engineering Resources Data, NSF 95–317, Arlington, VA.

———. 1996a. Selected Data on Science and Engineering Doctorate Awards, 1995. NSF 96–303, Arlington, VA.

———. 1996b. Characteristics of Doctoral Scientists and Engineers in the United States, 1993. NSF 96–302, Arlington, VA.

———. 1997. Characteristics of Doctoral Scientists and Engineers in the United States, 1995. NSF 97–319, R. Keith Wilkinson. Arlington, VA.

REVIEW QUESTIONS

1. How is the data for the National Science Foundation Survey of Doctoral Recipient collected and how often?

2. What did the researchers find out from the survey they used?

3. Do you think they should have sent out their own survey, rather than having used the existing data? Why or why not?

PROFESSORS WHO MAKE THE GRADE (FACTORS THAT AFFECT STUDENTS' GRADES OF PROFESSORS)

Vicky L. Seiler and Michael J. Seiler

Evaluation research can take many forms, such as the evaluation of a program, or a drug, or a research project. In this study, the authors evaluate the factors that affect professors' scores on student teaching evaluations and shows how faculty evaluation scores are related to how much students learn and what happens when students grade their teachers. This study demonstrates that the professor and the course characteristics significantly affect professors' evaluation scores and student learning. While reading this article, watch for the way in which the researchers used evaluation and any problem that you think you see with the way this study was done. Does it tell the complete story?

Introduction

The Accounting Education Change Commission (AECC) states that the first objective of accounting educators is to teach students effectively (1). The AECC also says that the best way to ensure continuous improvement in the classroom and in all areas of teaching is to develop measurement and evaluation systems that encourage these improvements. In short, the AECC maintains that teaching should be the primary consideration for universities when promoting and granting tenure. Indeed, the importance of teaching is directly emphasized by colleges and universities (7, 13, 15, 18, 24, 26, 27, 28).

Because so much time and importance are associated with teaching, these institutions of higher learning should make sure they are able to evaluate a professor's teaching effectiveness as accurately as possible. There are several ways: self-assessment; peer review; supervisor ratings; and, alumni, outside consultant and student evaluations.

Not surprisingly, the primary method used by colleges and universities is the student evaluation. According to Hooper and Page (11), there are several reasons:

First, students are the customers of the university. Hence, their satisfaction with how they are taught is what really matters. Second, compared to other groups, students can be argued to be the best qualified to evaluate faculty members since they have the unique opportunity to continually observe their professors throughout the semester. As such, their evaluation is not biased by "a bad day" or "a good day," as can be the case with a one-time external reviewer. Third, students provide an inexpensive way to collect data. And fourth, student evaluations are anonymous. Conversely, with a peer review, professors know exactly who is evaluating them. For professional reasons—such as not wanting to make enemies, black-balling yourself in the eyes of the reviewed member, etc.—faculty members are much less likely to objectively review their peers.

Seiler, V. L and Seiler, M. J. 2002. Professors who make the grade (factors that affect students' grades of professors). *Review of Business,* 23 (2): 39–44. Used with permission.

In spite of these advantages, there are some potential problems with student evaluations, however. For example, students have enough time with their professor, but do they possess the skills to know how the professor should teach? A classic example is given by Naflulin, Ware and Donnelly (16), where an actor who knew nothing about the subject being taught posed as a professor. This "teacher" made jokes, smiled a lot and was a great communicator—receiving excellent student evaluations even though his performance had little or no educational content.

These potential drawbacks notwithstanding, student evaluations continue to be the primary and, in some cases, the only method used to evaluate teaching performance in the classroom (29). In its seven sections, this study examines which factors affect professors' scores on student teaching evaluations and how these factors influence students' learning. This article also determines whether professors' evaluation scores are related to students' learning—using "Structural Equation Modeling (SEM)," a methodology not used in previous articles examining teacher evaluations. SEM is a statistical method that combines features of multiple regression, and factor and path analyses to examine both observed and latent variables.

And finally, we will discuss the potential benefits and implications of our study, as well as why we think others should employ SEM in future research on teaching evaluations.

Data

We obtained teaching evaluations from a mid-sized American Assembly of Collegiate Schools in Business (AACSB) accredited university in the Midwest. Students from this school's accounting department completed a total of 520 evaluations.

The university's department of accounting offers 17 classes at the undergraduate and Master of Business Administration (MBA) levels. Of these 17, eight are undergraduate, nine are MBA, seven are required, 10 are elective; and, six are given during the day, 11 at night. Most importantly, we found no difference in response rates between the graduates and undergraduates.

Various combinations of tenured and part-time professors teach the accounting classes, and 10 instructors were involved in this study.

The Evaluation. Exhibit 1 provides the actual teaching evaluation survey this university uses. The surveying instrument is a standard, 34-item questionnaire, employing a seven-point semantic differential scale (1 = lowest possible score; 7 = highest). Often if a student likes a professor, he/she will circle all answers to the right, thus grading on a global basis (halo effect or yea/saying), rather than item-by-item. The converse is also true (nay/saying). Professors and administrators do not like this practice because it prevents them from determining where improvements can be made. To reduce this bias, the survey states approximately one-third of the questions in reverse order.

The first six survey questions are asked to obtain background information on the responding student. questions 1 through 3 are to be filled out by both undergraduates and MBA students, while only graduate students complete questions 4 through 6. All students answer questions 7 through 34, which are the focus of our analysis.

Items describing overall professor characteristics are listed in questions 7 through 18. questions 19 and 20 ask for professor comparison ratings. Course-specific items are asked

EXHIBIT 1. STUDENT EVALUATION SURVEY

Part I: Background Information

Q1 Year in School

Q2 Undergraduate Major

Q3 Undergraduage G.P.A. (Graduate Students ONLY)

Q4 Graduate G.P.A.

Q5 Where Is Undergraduate Degree From?

Q6 If Graduate, Number of Courses Taken

Part II: Descriptive Items on Professors

Listed below are 12 sets of tiems. Mark the box on the answer sheet that corresponds to the letter on the scale which best describes your feelings about the instructor for each of the 12 sets. Please indicate only one letter for each set.

Q7	Fair	A B C D E F G	Unfair
Q8	Muddled Thinking	A B C D E F G	Clear Thinking
Q9	Irresponsible	A B C D E F G	Responsible
Q10	Thoroughly Knowledgeable	A B C D E F G	Unknowleable About the Subject Matter
Q11	Helpful	A B C D E F G	Not Helpful
Q12	Unoriginal	A B C D E F G	Original
Q13	Enthusiastic	A B C D E F G	Unenthusiastic
Q14	Encourages Critical Thinking	A B C D E F G	Discourages Critical Thinking
Q15	Poor Listener	A B C D E F G	Good Listener
Q16	Humorless	A B C D E F G	Humorous
Q17	Likes Teaching	A B C D E F G	Doesn't Like Teaching
Q18	Lacks Confidence	A B C D E F G	Highly Confident

Q19 In comparison to faculty members *outside* the College of Business Administration, how would you rate this professor?

A	B	C	D	E	F	G
One of Worst	Very Poor	Below Average	Average	Above Average	Very Good	One of Best

Q20 In comparison to faculty members *within* the College of Business Administration, how would you rate this professor?

A	B	C	D	E	F	G
One of Worst	Very Poor	Below Average	Average	Above Average	Very Good	One of Best

Part III: Descriptive Items Concerning the Course

Listed below are 14 sets of items. Mark the box on the answer sheet that corresponds to the letter on the scale which best describes your feelings about the course for each of the 14 sets. Please indicate one letter for each set.

Q21	Standards Undemanding	A B C D E F G	Standards Extremely Demanding
Q22	Course Materials Stimulating	A B C D E F G	Course Materials Boring
Q23	Course Materials Very Relevant	A B C D E F G	Course Materials Irrelevant
Q24	Written Assignments Very Valuable	A B C D E F G	Written Assignments of No Value
Q25	Magnitude of Work Very Heavy	A B C D E F G	Magnitude of Work Extremely Light
Q26	Course Is of High Value	A B C D E F G	Course Is of Little Value
Q27	Content Too Much for One Terrm	A B C D E F G	Content Too Little for One Term
Q28	Syllabus Highly Useful	A B C D E F G	Syllabus of No Use
Q29	Course Very Challenging	A B C D E F G	Course Offered No Challenge
Q30	Teach. Methods Highly Appropriate	A B C D E F G	Teach. Methods Highly Inappropriate
Q31	Course Objectives Clear	A B C D E F G	Course Objectives Unclear
Q32	Class Well Organized	A B C D E F G	Class Poorly Organized
Q33	Content Exceeded Expectations	A B C D E F G	Content Did Not Exceed Expectations

Q34 All in all, how much do you feel you learned from this course?

A Great Deal   A B C D E F G   Nothing at All

EXHIBIT 2. HYPOTHESIZED MODEL

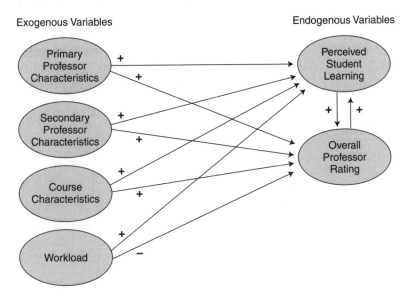

All exogenous variables are latent, while all endogenous variables are single indicator variables

in questions 21 through 33. Finally, question 34 asks the student to rate how much he/she has learned in the course.

Methodology

According to the university, there are many questions that ask almost the same thing. Twenty-five of the 34 questions, for example, are aimed at answering only two general questions: "How good is the professor?" and "How good is the course/class?"

This particular university reports each question's rating to its professors individually, but only ranks the professors based on their average score on three summary measures.

The first category measures the instructor's characteristics as a teacher and consists of questions 7 through 18. The second measures the relative rank of the instructor in the business school and the university, and consists of only questions 19 and 20. The third measure examines course content and consists of questions 21 through 34.

Our analysis focused on the first and third categories. As just mentioned, the first measure attempts to answer the question, "How good is the professor?" while the third measure attempts to answer, "How good is the course/class?"

We performed an exploratory factor analysis to determine if these categories were accurate. We used the statistical package, LISREL VII, to determine the causal relationships between the independent and dependent variables. The factors produced in the analysis became the latent exogenous variables used in SEM. Also in the model were two endogenous variables: question 20, "professor's rating," and question 34, "amount students learned." Exhibit 2 shows the hypothesized relationships among the variables.

EXHIBIT 3. FACTOR ANALYSIS FOR SURVEY QUESTIONS 7–18 AND 21–33

Pattern Matrix Coefficients Greater Than .30 Are Shown for Each Variable

		Factor				Cronbach Alphas	Percentage of Explained Variation
		1	2	3	4		
Factor 1	**Primary Professor Characteristics**					.9124	41.8%
Q7	Fairness	.7830					
Q8	Thinking	.6869					
Q9	Responsible	.7554					
Q10	Knowledgeable	.7470					
Q11	Helpful	.5117					
Q15	Listener	.5100					
Q17	Likes Teaching	.5374					
Q18	Confidence	.4372					
Q30	Teaching Methods	.5279					
Q32	Class Organization	.6597					
Factor 2	**Secondary Professor Characteristics**					.7371	5.5%
Q12	Original		.6689				
Q13	Enthusiasm		.5804				
Q14	Encouragement of Critical Thinking		.5518				
Q16	Humorous		.6938				
Factor 3	**Course Characteristics**					.8001	4.5%
Q22	Course Materials Stimulating			.7911			
Q23	Course Materials Relevant			.5832			
Q24	Value of Written Assignments			.6126			
Q26	Value of Course			.6424			
Q28	Syllabus			.4028			
Q31	Course Objectives			.3019			
Q33	Course Expectations			.3907			
Factor 4	**Work Load**					.8406	8.4%
Q21	Demanding Standards				.6472		
Q25	Magnitude of Work				.8571		
Q27	Course Content				.8378		
Q29	Challenging				.5742		

EXHIBIT 4. GOODNESS-OF-FIT MEASURES FOR THE FINAL STRUCTURAL EQUATION

Goodness-of-Fit Measures	Value
Chi-Square Value	2.87
Degress of Freedom	3
p-value	0.412
Chi-Square Value/D.F.	0.957
Goodness-of-Fit Index	0.998
Adjusted Goodness-of-Fit Index	0.985
Root Mean Square Residual	0.013

Results

To evaluate the underlying dimensions of the surveying instrument, we conducted a factor analysis on responses to items 7 through 18 and 21 through 33. We used oblique rotation due to correlations among the factors, an eigenvalue cutoff of 1.0 and factor loadings over 0.30 (9) to assess the dimensionality of the instrument. The resulting four factors explained 60.3 percent of the overall variation in the model.

Cronbach alphas were utilized to determine reliability estimates of latent constructs. Exhibit 3 shows which variables compose each latent construct, the name of each construct and the corresponding Cronbach alpha values.

Our analysis yields several interesting results. For one, the university's contention that survey questions 7 through 18 ask the same general question, "How good is the professor?" is itself questionable. While it seems these questions seek to answer the same general question, the factor analysis yielded strong results indicating the presence of two distinct factors. Along the same lines, questions 21 through 33 share two factors, not one. Specifically, we found that four questions (21, 25, 27 and 29) break out of the second category, "How good is the course/class?" These questions form their own factor, which measures the amount of work required in the class.

Exhibit 4 shows the goodness-of-fit measures for the final model. The first measure, a chi-square test, indicates the model's overall fit. The hypotheses are as follows:

[H_o]: The fitted model is the same as the perfect model.

[H_a]: The fitted model is not the same as the perfect model. (1)

Since the chi-square's corresponding p-value (0.412) is greater than the alpha value of .05, we do not reject H_0 and conclude that the model is not significantly different from the perfect model. A second indicator of the model's fit is the ratio, chi-square/degrees of freedom. If the ratio is below 5.0 (n>200), the model's fit is good [12]. At .957, the ratio for our model is exceptional.

A third and fourth measure of fit criteria are the goodness-of-fit index and the adjusted goodness-of-fit index. The perfect model has a measure of 1.0. Any value greater than .9 is considered to be a good fit [25]. Our goodness-of-fit equals 0.998 and the adjusted goodness-of-fit equals 0.985—both extremely good measures.

And a fifth measure of fit is the root mean square residual, in which a value closer to zero indicates a better fit (the closer to zero, the better the fit). Our root mean square residual equals 0.013, again indicating a good fit [21].

Exhibit 5 presents the effects of the exogenous variables on the endogenous variables (gamma paths) for the final model. Maximum likelihood estimates (unstandardized solutions), standardized solutions, standard errors and t-statistics are given for each of the effects. We found that the factor "work load" did not have a significant relationship with either of the endogenous variables and was thus eliminated from the final model. Also, secondary professor characteristics do not significantly affect overall professor rating. Hence, this path was also eliminated in the final model.

Significant Causal Relationships. There were significant positive causal relationships between professor and course characteristics, and professor summary evaluation scores and student perceptions of how much they learned overall. There was also a positive causal relationship between professor summary evaluation scores and perceived student learning. These paths were statistically significant at the 99 percent confidence level. The final model is shown in Exhibit 6.

In addition to verifying statistically significant relationships, the factor analysis of the evaluation data (Exhibit 1) revealed that four variables form an additional factor, which is inconsistent with the university's position. However, upon running SEM, the factor consisting of these variables did not prove to be statistically significant. Thus, we believe these four questions are of no use in the evaluation and should be eliminated.

Implications. The SEM analysis provides clear empirical results that can easily translate into policy implications and decisions for colleges and universities. The 14 professor and seven course characteristic variables provide a good measure of the latent constructs.

These constructs affect both the level of perceived learning and the overall professor rating. Professor rating affects perceived learning, but the converse is not true. Finally, the latent construct, "workload," does not affect either professor rating or perceived learning. Therefore, it should be removed from the evaluation survey entirely.

The bottom line is that administrators can use the evaluation instrument in Exhibit 1 —incorporating the adjustments we've just recommended—to more accurately measure professor performance in the classroom. Administrators should test their current evaluating instrument, which is most likely different from the one we've set forth. They can use our SEM methodology to determine if they are measuring what they are attempting to measure. In doing so, they will be able to make more accurate tenure/promotion decisions, and professors will be able to teach more effectively.

Conclusion

We examined 520 student evaluations from accounting students at a mid-sized AACSB-accredited university in the Midwest. We used Structural Equation Modeling to determine the significant relationships between professor and course characteristics, and professors' ratings and students' perceived learning.

A word of caution should be noted. The data in this study were gathered from just one department in one university—so we are not generalizing our results to other departments

EXHIBIT 5. MAXIMUM LIKELIHOOD ESTIMATES OF THE EFFECTS OF THE EXOGENOUS
VARIABLES ON THE ENDOGENOUS VARIABLES FOR THE FINAL LISREL MODEL

	Endogenous Variables					
	Perceived Student Learning			Overall Professor Rating		
Exogenous Variables	ML-Est.	SE	T-Test	ML-Est.	SE	T-Test
Primary Professor Characteristics	.34 (.24)	.06	5.55*	.67 (.49)	.05	13.72*
Secondary Professor Characteristics	.50 (.37)	.05	11.22*			
Course Characteristics	.68 (.40)	.05	14.03*	.17 (.13)	.05	3.79*

Note: Standardized solutions are in parentheses.

*Statistically significant at the 99% confidence level.

EXHIBIT 6. FINAL MODEL

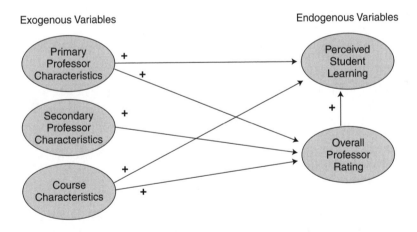

All arrows shown here represent statistically significant relationships at the 99% level of confidence.

or universities across the country, nor should you. Instead, we believe we provide a solid
foundation on which future research can, and should, be directed.

Important questions for further research might include whether it's necessary to develop department-specific and/or university-specific models describing the relationships
among professor and course characteristics and teaching evaluations, or whether general
models would be more appropriate.

In any case, we believe colleges and universities can benefit from using the results of this study and any subsequent studies using SEM. It's a sophisticated technique that can be used very effectively in the area of teacher evaluations.

References

1. Accounting Education Change Commission. "AECC Urges Priority for Teaching in Higher Education," *Issues in Accounting Education,* 5, 1993, 330–331. . . .

7. Cornwell, R. "The Evaluation of Faculty Performance," *Collegiate News and Views,* 1984, 9–13. . . .

9. Hair, J., R. Anderson, R. Tatham, and W. Black. *Multivariate Data Analysis,* Fourth Edition, Prentice Hall, 1995, 385. . . .

11. Hooper, P. and J. Page. "Measuring Teaching Effectiveness by Student Evaluation," *Issues in Accounting Education,* 1986, 56–64.

12. Kettinger, W., and C. Lee. "Perceived Service Quality and User Satisfaction with the Information Services Function," *Decision Sciences,* 25, 1995, 737–766.

13. Kreuze, J., and G. Newell. "Student Ratings of Accounting Instructors: A Search for Important Determinants," *Journal of Accounting Education,* 5, 1987, 87–98. . . .

15. McKeachie, W. "Student Ratings of Faculty: A Research Review," *Improving College and University Teaching,* 1967, 4–8.

16. Naflulin, D., J. Ware, and F. Donnelly. "The Dr. Fox Lecture: A Paradigm of Educational Seduction," *Journal of Medical Education,* 48, 1973, 630–635. . . .

18. Porcano, T. "An Empirical Analysis of Some Factors Affecting Student Performance," *Journal of Accounting Education,* 2, 1984, 111–126. . . .

21. Rupp, M., and R. Segal. "Confirmatory Factor Analysis of a Professionalism Scale in Pharmacy," *Journal of Social and Administrative Pharmacy,* 6:1, 1989, 31–38. . . .

24. Street, D., C. Baril, and R. Benke. "Research, Teaching, and Service in Promotion and Tenure Decisions of Accounting Faculty," *Journal of Accounting Education,* 12, 1993, 43–60.

25. Taylor, S., A Sharland, B. Cronin, and W. Bullard. "Recreational Service Quality in the International Setting," *International Journal of Service Industry Management,* 4:4, 1993, 68–86.

26. Tompkins, J., H. Hermanson, and D. Hermanson. "Expectations and Resources Associated with New Finance Faculty Positions," *Financial Practice and Education,* 6, Spring/Fall 1996, 54–64.

27. Tripathy, N., and G. Ganesh. "Evaluation, Promotion, and Tenure of Finance Faculty: The Evaluators' Perspective," *Financial Practice and Education,* 6, Spring/Fall 1996, 46–53.

28. Wright, P., R. Whittington, and C. Whittenburg. "Student Ratings of Teaching Effectiveness: What the Research Reveals," *Journal of Accounting Education,* 2, 1984, 5–30.

29. Yunker, P., and J. Sterner. "A Survey of Faculty Performance Evaluation in Accounting," *Accounting Educator's Journal,* 1988, 63–71.

REVIEW QUESTIONS

1. What were the hypotheses in this study?

2. What methodology did the researchers use in this study? Why?

3. List three of the findings of this project.

PART IV ■ ANALYZING DATA

■

Chapter 11: An Introduction to Statistics

Now that we have talked about the foundations of research and the various methods you can use in a research project, you must learn what to do with the information you collect. In this chapter, you will learn about **descriptive statistics,** which describe numerical data and can be categorized by the number of variables involved. For instance, univariate has one variable, bivariate has two variables, and multivariate has more than two variables.

RESULTS WITH ONLY ONE VARIABLE

Univariate statistics describe one variable. The two most common ways to describe the numerical data of one variable is with **graphs** or **frequency distributions.** Graphs have an advantage because they provide a picture that makes the results easier to comprehend. The graph in Figure 11.1 shows the religions of the individuals in the study.

At the same time, a frequency distribution shows the exact numbers of the cases and the values that have been reported. The following is a frequency distribution. There is only one variable for both the graph and the table.

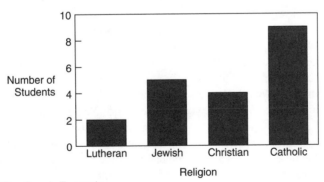

Figure 11.1. Bar Graph Example

Religion	Frequency
Lutheran	2
Jewish	5
Christian	4
Catholic	9
Total	20

The primary goal is to accurately display the distribution's shape and to show how cases are distributed across the values of the variable. You must be wary of three features: central tendency, variability, and skewness that can be represented in either graphs or frequency distribution. **Central tendency** is where your data is displayed in the form of averages. You may either use the mode, which is the most frequent attribute either grouped or ungrouped; the mean, which is the average; or the median, which is the middle attribute in the ranked distribution of observed attributes. Let's suppose you are interested in looking at a group of children who range in age from 4 to 10, as shown here:

Age	Number
4	3
5	4
6	6
7	8
8	4
9	5
10	2

The **mode,** which is also termed **probability average,** is the easiest way to measure because you look for the most frequent value. In our case of children, the mode would be 7-year-olds because there are eight of them. If there were two groups with eight children in them, the distribution would be **bimodal.**

The **median** represents the middle value, or the point that divides the distribution in 50th percentiles. To accomplish this, you must find the middle value and have an equal number of cases above or below it. If there are an equal number of cases, then the median point falls between two cases and is computed by adding the values of the two middle cases and dividing by 2. You do not know the precise ages of the children because the data is grouped, so you need to find the middle numbers and divide them by 2 as shown in Table 11.1.

Sometimes the median is better because it is the middle score and reflects the point in the distribution above which half the scores fall and below which half the scores fall. The arithmetic average or the **mean** takes into account the values of each case in a distribution. You compute the mean by adding the values of all the cases and dividing by the total

TABLE 11.1. EXAMPLE OF THREE "AVERAGES"

Age	Number		
4	3		
5	4		
6	6		
7	**8**	Most frequent	Mode=7
8	4		
9	5		
10	2		

Age	Number		
4	3	4 x 3 = 12	
5	4	5 x 4 = 20	Mean = 6.91
6	6	6 x 6 = 36	
7	8	7 x 8 = 56	
8	4	8 x 4 = 32	
9	5	9 x 5 = 45	
10	2	10 x 2 = 20	
		221 total/32 cases	

Age	Number		
4	3	1–3	
5	4	4–7	
6	6	8–13	
7	8	14 15 16 17 18 19 20 21	
		7.06 7.19 **7.31** 7.44 7.56 7.69 7.81 7.94	Median = 7.31
8	4	22–25	**Midpoint**
9	5	26–30	
10	2	31–32	

number of cases. You must be careful, though, because the mean value can be drastically affected by extreme scores and is not always the best indicator of the score distribution.

The central tendency is just one aspect of the shape of the distribution, is only one numbered summary of the distribution, and might not give you the total picture. Even though two distributions can have the same measures of central tendency, they can differ how they spread about the center. The problems can be mitigated if you report a summary of the **dispersion** of responses. One way to measure the dispersion is the **range,** which calculates the true upper limit of the distribution minus the true lower limit. In the case of the children, we know that the mean for the children is 6.91, but their ages range from 4 to 10. Another way to report dispersion would be through **interquartile range** (IQR). The IQR is the numerical measure that locates a particular value in a data set. More precisely, the pth percentile is the value that has p percent of the data below second half $(1 - p)$ percent of the data. The IQR = Q3 – Q1, and the IQR between Q1 and Q3 is 50 percent of the data. Thus IQR gives an idea how varied the data is—the bigger the IQR, the larger the variability is.

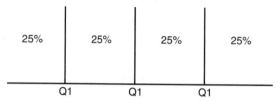

Here is an example. There are two classes of 12 students each and their scores on their exams are as follows:

Class 1   66 67 70 74 75 77 78 81 82 85 89 90

Class 2   50 58 61 66 70 77 78 82 89 93 95 96

For both classes, median is 77.5. However, by calculating the IQR for class 1 as follows,

$$Q1 = \frac{3rd\ value + 4th\ value}{2} = \frac{70 + 74}{2} = 72$$

$$Q3 = \frac{9th\ value + 10th\ value}{2} = \frac{82 + 85}{2} = 83.5$$

We find the IQR = 83.5 – 72 = 11.5. For class 2

$$Q1 = \frac{3rd\ value + 4th\ value}{2} = \frac{61 + 66}{2} = 63.5$$

$$Q3 = \frac{9th\ value + 10th\ value}{2} = \frac{89 + 93}{2} = 91$$

The IQR = 91 – 63.5 = 27.5

So, even though the medians of the two classes are the same, by computing IQR we get an idea about the dispersion in the two data sets. Because 27.5 > 11.5, there is a greater variability in the second data set than in the first.

RESULTS WITH TWO VARIABLES

Whereas a univariate statistic describes a single variable, the **bivariate** statistic tells you about the statistical relationship between variables. The purpose of bivariate statistics is to compare between groups. Let's say you want to explore the sex differences between students and whether or not they voted during the last election. Your independent variable is sex and your dependent variable is voting. To show the comparison, the table would look like Table 11.2.

TABLE 11.2. VOTING BY SEX

Voting	Men	Women
Yes	68%	56%
No	32%	44%
Total	100%	100%
	(496)	(362)

We can tell by looking at the table that more men voted than women during the last election.

When you read a table or create a table, you need to consider certain things:

- A table should have a heading or a title that succinctly describes what is contained in the table.

- The original content of the variables should be clearly presented. The information is especially critical when a variable is derived from responses to an attitudinal question because the meaning of the responses will depend largely on the wording of the question.

- The attributes of each variable should be clearly indicated. Complex categories will have to be abbreviated, but the meaning should be clear in the table and the full description should be reported in the test.

- When percentages are reported in the table, the base upon which they are computed should be indicated. It is redundant to present all the raw numbers for each category because these could be reconstructed from the percentages and the bases. The presentation of both numbers and percentages often make a table confusing and more difficult to read.

- If any cases are omitted from the table because of missing data, their numbers should be indicated in the table.

RESULTS WITH MORE THAN TWO VARIABLES

A **multivariate table** is one that has more than two variables. The same steps are used to read and create a multivariate table as in the bivariate table. The main difference is that you are looking for some type of explanation by using more than one independent variable. Let's say that you are interested in how many people voted in the last election by sex and their age. The table might look like Table 11.3.

The results indicate that more women voted in the last election than men and that more women who were over 40 voted than did those who were under 40. Although fewer men than women voted in the last election, more men who were over 40 voted than did those men who were under 40. The following readings in this chapter will give you an overview of how statistics are used in social science research. This is not meant to be a complete overview of statistical analysis, but just enough to wet your whistle until you learn more in class.

TABLE 11.3. MULTIVARIATE RELATIONSHIP: VOTED IN LAST ELECTION, BY SEX AND AGE

Voted in Last Election	Men	Women
Under 40	21%	30%
	(240)	(364)
40 and older	34%	50%
	(325)	(416)

ELEMENTARY APPLIED STATISTICS: FOR STUDENTS IN BEHAVIORAL SCIENCE

Linton C. Freeman

Although Freeman wrote the book from which this chapter is taken in 1965, this material still provides a clear and concise explanation of statistics for students. As you read, notice how he explains the scales used in research.

The field of statistics can perhaps be best understood as a special language. And like any language, it allows us to think about things and to communicate our thoughts to others. It is not special in the sense that it will allow us to think or talk of anything different from what we can in our ordinary speech. It is special, however, in that it encourages us to talk in a more precise manner than we could in another language. It is this emphasis on precision that is the strength of statistics. If rigorous thought and precise communication are our aims, statistics is the language for us.

Like other languages, the language of statistics includes words and rules of grammar; these are the tools of a language. Statistics, however, is a limited language with a limited set of tools. In statistics we can talk only about the characteristics of things we can observe. Before the techniques of statistics can answer the questions put to them, they must be provided with data—with the raw materials of observation.

Some statistics require data of one sort, some another, but all statistics need data that are based on observations. This chapter will be concerned with an examination of the observational data required by all statistics and with the various kinds of observational data which are used by the several different statistics. Three forms of data will be discussed: nominal scales, ordinal scales, and interval scales. However, before we can examine specific types of data we must consider some of the general characteristics of all data that are useful for statistical analysis.

Freeman, L. C. 1965. *Elementary applied statistics: For students in behavioral science* (pp. 3–16). New York: Wiley. Used with permission from the author.

Variables

In any scientific study it is necessary that we observe and record some characteristic or characteristics of the world of our experience. We deal with things we see or touch or smell or hear; these things are all observable. But observability alone is not enough; they must also be capable of differing. If some observable characteristic of an object changes when it is observed again and again, or if it differs between one object and another, it is said to *vary*. In the language of the statistician it is called a *variable*. A variable, then, is an observable characteristic of something which is capable of taking several values or of being expressed in several different categories. Thus weight is a variable, for all objects do not weigh the same amount and a single object may change its weight from time to time. And age is a variable, and college grades, and strength and sex and speed and size and anything you can name which is (1) characteristic of objects or persons, (2) observable, and (3) differs from observation to observation. These, then, are the raw materials of statistical analysis. They are the data that constitute the subject matter of statistics.

Scales

If the data of a variable are to be put to use in a statistical analysis, they must be recorded in some systematic fashion. Each variable must be defined operationally; that is, it must be described in terms of the steps which are required in recording its changing values. Such a definition requires both a description of the characteristics to be observed and specification of the categories among which variation will be recorded. Statisticians often call this procedure of operationally defining variables *scaling;* the resulting descriptions are called *scales*.

In many, perhaps most, cases the scale of a variable will be dictated by common usage. Thus, in our society, the variable age is usually scaled in years, counting the first anniversary of birth as 1, the second as 2, and so on. Except for very young children, such a count is made in years, rounding not to the nearest whole year, but rather to the last anniversary passed. Thus a man who tells you he is 21, may have been born 21 years and 2 days earlier or perhaps 21 years and 362 days. We are already provided, therefore, with a standardized operational definition of age and a means of scaling that variable.

It is important to remember that the scale used to record a variable is not a part of the variable itself. The values taken by a variable are a part of its operational definition. Although some variables have generally accepted sets of values or categories, others, particularly in social science, have no well-established scales of measurement. These variables require that the investigator himself determine the categories among which they may be expected to vary. In studying a variable like social class, for example, one investigator might devise a scale which would yield three classes, say, upper, middle, and lower, but another investigator might specify four classes: upper, middle, working, and lower. Then, too, some variables, like popularity, might require that we start fairly fresh, without much precedent of common usage to go by, and work out an entirely new scale. A person's popularity might be scaled according to the frequency of his contacts with others, or by asking his associates their opinions of him, or in any number of ways. The important thing is to work out a rigorous way of defining a variable operationally before trying to launch into statistical analysis.

Constructing scales, then, is the outcome of operationally defining variables. And scales are necessary to provide data in any statistical study. However, scales are not all alike. They vary from extremely simple affairs consisting only of two unordered categories to quite complex devices including a long series of equally spaced classes starting from a real zero point. We shall discuss three of the most important types of scales.

Nominal Scales. The simplest scale consists of nothing but a set of categories. The basic operation of scaling consists of classifying observations into categories. Any two observations may be equal (in terms of the variable in question) and they are therefore classified into the same category, or they may be unequal, which leads to their classification into different categories. The categories therefore must be mutually exclusive and collectively exhaustive. That is to say, each observation can be classified only into *one* category of the set and each can *always* be classified into some one of them. Sex, for example, is such a nominal scale; all people can be classified into the category male or the category female, and no one may be classified as both.

Usually the classes in a nominal scale are named as they are in the preceding example. Sometimes, however, they are assigned numbers. Assignment of numbers to players in various positions in college football is an example of this practice. Some teams, for example, assign numbers 1 through 29 to quarterbacks, 30 through 39 to fullbacks, 40 to 49 to halfbacks, and so on. These numbers do not imply order; they are simply names which designate categories. Thus an end who wears number 87 is not any "better" or "higher" than a quarterback who wears 27. Eighty-seven merely indicates that its bearer plays a different position from the man who wears 27.

This example illustrates an important characteristic of nominal scales: although numbers may be used to designate classes, these numbers have very few of the usual attributes of numbers. They may not be added; two halfbacks with numbers in the forties do not equal one end with a number in the eighties. In fact, they permit no arithmetic operations at all. These numbers are merely labels for categories. Different labels designate different categories. The original labels may be exchanged for any other set providing that each is replaced by one and only one new label. They may be names (halfback, fullback, and so on) or numbers (40s, 30s, and so on) or even letters, but in any case no order is implied. These scales do not allow us to "measure" variation in any strict sense. Instead, variation is labeled—categories are named along with criteria for classifying observed cases into one or another category.

Many of the variables studied by behavioral scientists are of this nominal or classificatory type. A human ecologist may be interested in regions—say, Northern, Southern, Eastern, Western—and an anthropologist may be concerned with types of descent systems—matrilineal, patrilineal, bilateral—or a family sociologist with marital status—single, married, widowed, divorced. Each of these variables represents scaling at its simplest form where characteristics of objects are merely categorized into various classes.

In each of these examples, and in all nominal scales, observation leads to the classification of each case into one and only one of an unordered set of classes. There may be any number of classes from two on up, but every time they must be mutually exclusive and together they must permit the classification of any observable case. Because of this emphasis on classification alone, nominal scales are often called just *classifications*.

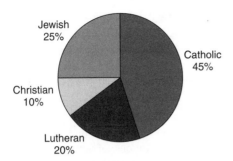

Figure 1. A Pictorial Representation of a Nominal Scale—Religion

Many statistical writers use the word qualitative to describe nominal scales. They distinguish between these unordered or qualitative scales and scales which are ordered or quantitative. Essentially, however, this is just a distinction between two levels of strength or complexity of scale types. As we shall see, quantitative scales take more into account; they are simply more complex schemes for classifying observed data.

Ordinal Scales. Like nominal scales, ordinal scales are made up of sets of mutually exclusive classes. Ordinal scales, however, possess one additional attribute: the classes form an ordered series. Whereas nominal scales only classify, ordinal scales classify *and order* the classes.

Suppose we are interested in scaling the variable "hardness" for three substances, say diamonds, glass, and wood. We may use "scratchability" as our criterion, and we should then attempt to scratch each substance with each of the others. We will probably find that the diamonds will scratch the glass and the wood and that they will be scratched by neither of these substances. And the glass will scratch the wood and the wood will scratch neither. Relative to hardness, then, we are able to establish a hierarchy—a rank ordering— in which the diamonds rank hardest, the glass less hard, and the wood least hard. In this example we should establish three ordered classes ranging from hardest to least hard.

Ordinal scales, then, establish an ordered series of classes. These classes may be named as in the preceding example (hardest, less hard, least hard), or they may be assigned numbers, which is the more common approach. Thus, diamonds rank 3 in hardness, glass 2, and wood 1. These numbers express the important attribute of order in such scales; they allow us to talk in such terms as "harder than," "higher than," or "more than." However, they do not imply how much harder, higher, or more. Diamonds are harder than glass, but on the basis of such a scale, we do not know how much harder they are. And we do not know whether diamonds are as much harder than glass as glass is harder than wood. Rank 3 is higher than either rank 2 or rank 1 in hardness, but we cannot assume that it is twice as hard as 2 or three times as hard as 1 or anything of that sort. Ordinal scales permit discussion of "moreness" or "lessness," but they make no assumptions as to how much more or less.

Since ordinal scales include a record of order, the labels assigned to their categories must preserve that order. Any labels may be used (new ones may be substituted for old) as long as the original order is preserved. This was done when we substituted the numbers 3, 2, 1 for the labels hardest, less hard, least hard, in the preceding scale. But we may, with equal legitimacy, name our categories 9, 4, and 1 or even 1285, 103, and 18. Because the magnitude of the differences among these values has no significance, any new values may be substituted as long as the order is not changed. This procedure is called an *ordinal* or *monotonic transformation.*

Pairs of observations on an ordinal scale, like those on a nominal scale, may be equal (that is, they may belong to the same class or category) or they may be unequal and therefore belong to different classes. If two observations represent different categories in an ordinal scale, either the first must be greater than the second or the second greater than the first. At no point may their order be ambiguous.

Anything which can be recorded in an ordinal scale can, of course, be simplified and treated as if it were not ordered. When we are not concerned with order, we can simply ignore it and treat ordinal data as if they were nominal. However, if we simplify our ordinal scale into a nominal form, we are often neglecting to use the information supplied by the index. So, in general, it is not wise to simplify a scale, for in doing so we are throwing information away.

Social class as measured by sociologists is an ordinal scale. It enables one to rank persons—to speak in such terms as "higher than" or "lower than," but never to answer how much higher. And attitude tests usually produce ordinal scales. We can talk of "more pro-" or "more anti-," but again the order is the end result; and we are usually unable to determine degrees of difference.

In conclusion, then, although nominal scales classify, ordinal scales classify and order. The ordinal scale provides us with a ranked series of mutually exclusive classes. These are often called simply *ranks.*

Interval Scales. Interval scales have all the qualities of ordinal scales plus one more. Not only do they provide an ordered series of classes, but the intervals between any two pairs of adjacent classes are equal. In this case the distance between 1 and 2 is the same as that between 8 and 9, 112 and 113, or between any two adjacent classes. Temperature as it is usually measured is an interval scale. The one degree between 70° and 71° is the same as the one between 89° and 90°. This enables us not only to compare individual cases, but to talk about how many units more or greater one case is than another. We are not restricted to reporting merely that today is colder than yesterday as we would be if we used an ordinal scale; we can say that it is 13° colder.

To construct an interval scale it is necessary to establish some standard unit of measurement. For any two observations that are not equal, the degree of their difference must be expressible in terms of the standard unit.

The units of measurement may, of course, be changed. A constant may be added to the number for each observation or each may be multiplied by a constant. Changes of this sort will affect neither the order nor the relative magnitude of differences in such scales; they are called *linear transformations.*

Interval scales are less common than the simpler forms in behavioral science data. However, we do deal with such variables as number of children and frequency of interaction that can be expressed as interval scales. Three children is the same increase over two as two is over one. And seven interactions is the same frequency less than eight as four is

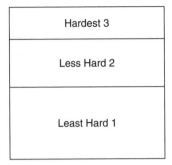

Figure 2. A Pictorial Representation of an Ordinal Scale—Hardness

less than five. Some of these are even more complex forms of scales, but here they are all grouped together under the classification of interval scale.

We can also always simplify interval scales. A variable like height, for example, need not be recorded in the interval scale of feet and inches. It may be defined in terms of a pair of ranks; say everyone over 5 ft. 5 in. would be ranked as 2 (tall) and everyone below that figure as 1 (not so tall). Or to simplify further, even the notion of order may be dropped and the two categories can be treated merely as nominal categories.

This consideration points up the essential distinction among our three types of scales. Nominal scales classify—they can be visualized as sets of categories, each with a different name, which together exhaust the possibilities (Fig. 1). In ordinal scales, however, categories within the scale are ordered (Fig. 2). And the classes within interval scales are both ordered and equal in size (Fig. 3).

These distinctions are important in choosing statistics for the analysis of data. The field of statistics has a long, but unearned, reputation for producing lies. It is altogether too easy to find a pair of items like the following:

Advertisement of the Sunny Dells Development Association, September 1, 1963: Sunny Dells is a good place to live. The average family income in our town is $11,400 a year.

Pamphlet distributed by a reform political candidate, September 5, 1963: Our taxes must go down if our town is to survive. Present rates are excessive when we stop to consider that the average family in Sunny Dells earns only $6800 per year.

Clearly, there is something wrong here. The typical family in Sunny Dells obviously cannot earn both $11,400 and $6800 a year. Can it be that one or both of these averages has lied?

The truth is not that statistics lie, but that liars use statistics. In a fact-minded culture like ours, the statistical argument has great appeal. The "average" can be determined by any of a half-dozen different procedures, and sometimes these will provide quite different results. The not too honest purveyor of statistics can take advantage of this situation and provide the consumer with an average which is not necessarily appropriate to the problem but one which is best designed to make his point. It is up to the consumer of statistics,

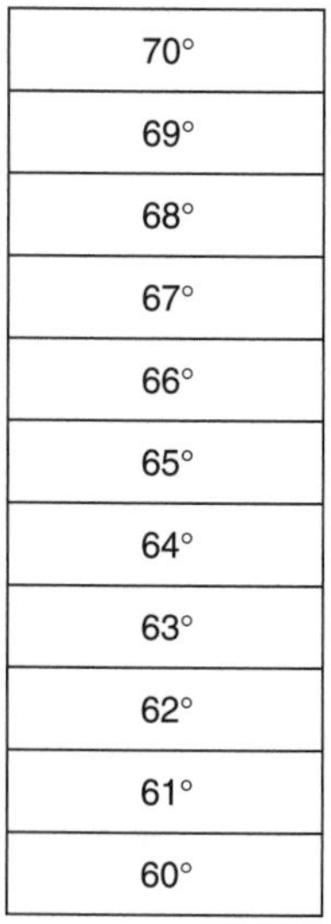

70°
69°
68°
67°
66°
65°
64°
63°
62°
61°
60°

Figure 3. A Pictorial Representation of an Interval Scale—Temperature

therefore, to learn enough about the range of techniques that are available and their proper use to protect himself from this kind of statistical hard sell. A person who has a reasonably good grasp of the field of statistics will seldom be misled by the inappropriate use of a statistical technique.

The honest user of statistics must always keep one fact in mind: in some instances the use of one statistical procedure is appropriate; in others it is not. The choice of a statistic in a particular situation must be based on two considerations: (1) the nature of the available data and (2) the type of problem at hand. . . .

Three Jobs for Statistics

Hundreds of statistical techniques are available to the contemporary scientist or statistician. Of these, probably no more than twenty or thirty are used regularly in social science, but even twenty or thirty distinct techniques can be quite a confusing array unless they can be understood in terms of their uses.

Fortunately, for the user of statistics, most of the procedures we find can be roughly classified in terms of just a few basic applications. Social scientists generally confine their applications of statistics to three: (1) summarizing observations on a single variable, (2) describing association between variables, and (3) making inferences. Other applications may occasionally be found, but these three are the only ones that occur commonly in social science. They will be discussed in this chapter.

In general, people seem to be both neat and lazy. We express our inclination toward neatness by filing away everything we observe in a more or less orderly fashion in our minds or in our books. And the laziness shows when the filing system is examined, for instead of filing complete statements of our experiences, most of us are content with brief (and often not too accurate) summaries of the things that we know.

One of the primary activities of the social scientist, or of any person for that matter, is reporting things he has observed. "This is a hot day," we say, or "My class is small this year." Here, in each instance, we are describing one characteristic of one object. In the first instance, a day is the object, and its temperature is the characteristic. In the second, a group of students is the object, and their number the characteristic.

Usually, however, we are not concerned with describing a single case. Rather, we want to describe some characteristic of several objects. We might say something like, "Saturday and Sunday were both hot," or even, "Saturday, Sunday, Monday, Tuesday, Wednesday, Thursday, and Friday were all hot." Obviously, however, as soon as we try to deal with more than a few cases such a description becomes extremely cumbersome. Thus, instead of long-winded enumerations of all the days that seemed warm, we usually report merely that, "The weekend was hot," or "The whole week was a scorcher." We use a linguistic shortcut to summarize our experience.

In each of these examples we have used ordinary English to describe or summarize something we have observed. If our powers of observation are adequate, and if we have some facility with the language, we can communicate reasonably well in this fashion. A good deal of ambiguity, however, still remains. This is where statistical procedures come in handy. If we use statistical language, our communication can be less ambiguous. We can adopt scaling procedures and instead of saying "This is a hot day," we should say, "The temperature is 107 in the shade." And instead of "My class is small this year," we may report that "My class contains three students." Here the mode of expression suggested by statistical scaling obviously yields more precise statements and leads therefore to more effective communication.

When our observations are many, statistical techniques may be used to summarize them. Ideally, such a summary should be brief, and yet it should reflect, as much as possible, the sense of the original observations. An adequate summary should enable us to record and to communicate our observations.

There are many statistics which may be used to summarize observations. Among the most useful are those that belong to a set we call *averages*. There are many kinds of averages, but they are alike in that they all attempt to determine a typical observation to represent the entire distribution. So instead of "Last week was hot," we may say, "The average temperature was 88° last week." The latter statement is much more precise than the former.

If we calculate an average to summarize a particular set of observations, we are always left with the question of how satisfactorily it accomplishes that summary. The use of an average suggests a need for further information that will reveal just how typical this typical observation is. Statistics of this latter type are called *indexes of variation;* they help us to make judgments about the adequacy of our averages. We can, for example, think about two very different temperature patterns, each with an average of 88°. One week, let us say, fluctuates between 68° and 108°. The other week remains around 88°; it varies no more than 20 degrees one way or the other. An index of variation is used to summarize this pattern of change or difference. Together, an average and an index of variation provide a summary of a set of observations.

Many more examples can be given, but these should illustrate the point. The language of statistics is more precise than other languages; it allows us to make more accurate reports and summaries of the characteristics of things we observe.

Describing the Relationship Between Two Variables

A second aspect of communication involves the description of relationships or association. One of the primary aims of the social scientist is to reduce the apparent complexity of man's social life. If we look around us, we see that men differ in their attitudes, their values, even their conceptions of what is true and what is false. Sometimes they congregate in large cities, and sometimes they go off by themselves and live as hermits. They vote differently, earn different amounts of money by different means, and spend it in different ways. They worship different gods and follow different leaders. Some men conform to all the rules of their fellow men and others seem always unwilling or unable to restrain themselves. Men are strong or weak, kind or unkind, open or withdrawn; the range of behavior men exhibit seems almost limitless.

The social scientist, however, need not be intimidated by this seemingly endless range of variation. For he has found that the behavior of his fellows—like the behavior of stars or atoms or falling bodies—is not completely random and unpredictable. It is usually possible to specify conditions under which at least part of this variation disappears. When such conditions have been specified, a relationship has been established.

Among Eskimos, for example, persons differ with respect to their occupations. However, within the various age-sex statuses, the differences disappear almost completely. Mature men hunt, mature women prepare hides, and so on. Thus the variable, occupation, does not vary when the variable, status, is taken into account. The two variables are related; they are related in such a way that knowledge of one implies knowledge of the other, and our world is—in one degree—less complex.

Any description of relatedness between observable characteristics may be viewed as a matter of guessing. When we say that in Chicago the season and temperature are related, we are asserting that if we know the value taken by one of these variables, we can guess the value of the other more accurately than we can without such knowledge. If we are told that the temperature in Chicago is 92° on a certain day, we guess that the day occurred in summer. And if we are asked to guess the temperature of a winter day, we pick a figure in the twenties or thirties. Clearly, this relationship is not perfect; occasionally in January the thermometer has reached 68° and sometimes in August it has dropped to 37°. But such occasions have been rare; in general, the relationship holds.

There may be a very large relationship or a very small one, but if we can guess one variable from another at all, we have a useful knowledge. There is a very small relationship between smoking and lung cancer. Yet this relationship, small as it is, may be helpful in finally discovering the causes and cure of cancer.

From this discussion it is clear that we can describe and discuss relationships between variables in everyday English. However, as in describing a single variable, the lack of precision in our language places unnecessary restrictions on our discourse. Whereas in English we must say that this and that are highly related (or not so highly related), in statistical language we can affix a precise number to their relationship. This number tells us the exact degree of their relatedness—precisely how much a knowledge of one variable helps us in guessing the other. Using this statistical tool, called the *coefficient of association,* we can describe relationships in a rigorous fashion. So again, precision is our reward for using statistical language.

Inference

Thus far, our discussion has been confined to the role of statistics in helping us to describe and summarize things we have experienced. However, statistics can be useful also in generalizing from past experience, in making predictions about the cases we have yet to see.

Every day each of us makes a series of decisions based on generalizations of relationships we have perceived in the past. When we leave home in the morning, we may look at the sky and decide whether to wear a raincoat. We know that one attribute of the weather (whether the sky is overcast or not) has in the past often been related to another attribute (whether it rains or not), and we assume that this relationship will continue to hold. We do not then just arbitrarily decide to take or leave our raincoats (we do not toss a coin); instead we judge in terms of a generalization of our past observations of the relationship between overcast skies and rain. Similarly, our decision to go to college may be based on our prior knowledge of the relationship between amount of education and potential earning as it has applied to others. Here we predict that the same rule will apply to us. And our desire to avoid a course in statistics may result from our earlier perception that the amount of mathematics in a course is generally related to its difficulty.

In this manner we use our knowledge of a past relationship between things as a guide for future behavior. Whenever we have been able to guess one characteristic of something on the basis of our knowledge of another, we assume that the relationship will continue to hold. In effect, we look at a few cases and generalize from these to the cases we have yet to see. This procedure seems to serve as a useful general guide for behavior.

Clearly, however, some generalizations are better than others. That is, some of our predictions stand up in light of further observations, whereas others do not. Our grandmothers, for example, thought that the emotional experiences, good and bad, of a pregnant woman would be reflected in the physical and emotional makeup of her child. Generalizations of this sort are probably built on the occurrence of a chance case or two and they persist without further follow-up. Although this generalization is patently false, our common folklore is still full of such nonsense. We try to avoid generalizing on the basis of too few cases, and we try to make sure that the cases are typical. But our ordinary linguistic tools let us down. How few cases are too few? And how can we tell if those we have observed are truly typical of the whole set?

Again, statistical procedures are helpful. The procedures of statistics include some which are called *statistics of inference;* these are designed to help us answer the questions we have raised. Common sense tells us that the more cases we observe the more probable are our generalizations. These statistics tell us how sure we should be on the basis of any given number of cases. So again precision is the reward of the user of statistics.

Statisticians distinguish two types of statistics of inference: *estimates* and *tests of significance.* Estimates refer to direct generalizations of observations. The average income of college graduates, for example, is an estimate based on studies of some, but not all, college graduates. Tests of significance, however, are concerned with comparing our observations with some hypothetical state of affairs. We may guess, for example, that there is a relationship between education and income in America. It would be prohibitively expensive to try to study the whole population of Americans, but we could take a sample of that population. Suppose that for the cases in our sample we did find some relationship between education and income. A critic may argue that the observed relationship is peculiar to our sample—that if we had studied the whole population of Americans, no such relationship would have been indicated. A test of significance would enable us to determine the precise probability that such was the case. It would allow us to determine the likelihood of getting an apparent relationship in our sample if there were none in the population.

In both cases the basic problem is one of generalizing from observed data to the larger population of cases from which the observations were drawn.

REVIEW QUESTIONS

1. Describe the four scales Freeman talked about in this chapter.

2. What scale would you use if your variable were social class? Why?

3. What scale would you use if your variable were temperature? Why?

NOTHING NEW UNDER THE SUN? A COMPARISON OF IMAGES OF WOMEN IN ISRAELI ADVERTISEMENTS IN 1979 AND 1994

Anat First

First compared two studies that were done in 1979 and 1994 to see how women and men were portrayed in printed Israeli advertisements. As you read the following introduction, watch for the variables. Would this be a univariate, bivariate, or multivariate study?

Gender Advertisements and Social Implications

Both critical theory and cultural studies emphasize the central role of advertising in the formation of our symbolic reality (Kellner, 1995; Goffman, 1979; Schudson, 1993). In Western culture, politicoeconomic reality and the symbolic reality presented by the advertising world are related. Kellner (1995) notes that "all ads are social texts that respond to key development during the period in which they appear" (p. 334). Goffman, in *Gender Advertisements* (1979), speaks of advertising as a world of "commercial realism" in which we are given "realistic" images of domestic life and male-female relationships, "in

First, A. 1998. Nothing new under the sun? A comparison of images of women in Israeli advertisements in 1979 and 1994. *Sex Roles: A Journal of Research,* 38(11–12): 1065–1078. Reprinted with permission from Kluwer Academic/Plenum Publishers.

which the scene is conceivable in all detail . . . providing us with a simulated slice of life" (p. 15). Schudson (1993) describes advertising as "'capitalist realism' . . . [which] does not claim to picture reality as it is but reality as it should be—life and lives worth emulating" (p. 215). Both Goffman and Schudson emphasize reality within a specific culture as a site of reference for advertisements.

Goffman's *Gender Advertisements* (1979), a landmark volume on the depiction of gender in advertising, provided the theoretical framework for both studies. Goffman suggested that advertising conveys cultural ideas about each sex, sometimes in a subtle form, at other times more explicitly. He categorized gender "behavior displays" and the present study uses five of them: (1) Relative Size: "One way in which social weight—power, authority, rank, office renown—is echoed expressively in social situation is through relative size, especially height" (p. 28). (2) The Feminine Touch: "Women, more than men, are pictured using their fingers and hands to trace the outline of an object or to cradle or caress its surface . . . or to effect a just barely touching" (p. 29). Winship (1981) noted that women in advertisements are frequently represented in a "fragmented" way or "cropped" and signified by their lips, legs, hair, eyes or hands, which stand for the "sexual woman." (3) Function Ranking: "In our society when a man and a woman collaborate face to face in an undertaking, the man—it would seem—is likely to perform the executive role" (Goffman, 1979, p. 32). Function ranking can also be tested in terms of activity or passivity, and also, according to Schudson (1993), in terms of product prestige. (4) The Ritualization of Subordination: "A classic stereotype of deference is that of lowering oneself physically in some form or other of prostration. Correspondingly, holding the body erect and the head high is stereotypically a mark of unashamedness, superiority and disdain" (Goffman, 1979, p. 40), and (5) Licensed Withdrawal: "Women more than men, it seems, are pictured engaged in involvement which removes them psychologically from the social situation at large" (Goffman, 1979, p. 57).

The Analysis of Gender Advertisements

Previous studies have analyzed the changing nature of women's role portrayals in magazine advertisements. Sullivan and O'Connor (1988) found that current ads in some ways more accurately reflect the diversity of women's social and occupational roles more than do those of the 1960s and 1970s. Yet, in some professional magazines like medical journals the portrayals of women continue to be stereotyped and outdated (Hawkins & Aber, 1993).

Another perspective on the study of the portrayal of women emerges from research that views communication as "symbolic action" and advertising as commercial pictures that reflect "actual or putative leadership and symbolization of some structure or hierarchy or value presentable as central to society." (Goffman, 1979). Gender representation is a dominant feature of modern advertising, and it provides an ideal place to examine the encoding of cultural norms and value in ritualized format (Jhally, 1987).

Griffin, Viswanath, and Schwartz (1994) outline a persistent problem regarding the best method for analyzing advertising images: How do we designate and evaluate meaningful coding units? This methodical question is so central to the study of women in advertising that it provides a convenient way to discuss the extant body of research.

In Western societies, women constitute a sociopolitical minority even when they are the majority numerically. As a minority, women can be—and have been—studied in ways that parallel the research on other minority groups. Greenberg and Brand (1994) report that work on minorities and the media can be grouped into three major sets. The first counts the presence or absence of minorities in media. The second set consists of studies that attempt to assess the status and role of a minority. The third examines the extent to which the minority characters interact with majority characters. Research on women and the media can be similarly characterized by the types of analyses conducted (for example, see, Lazier & Kendrick, 1993). The current paper falls within this last set.

This paper integrates visual and content analysis utilizing a quantitative method, similar to Griffin et al. (1994) or Belknap and Leonard (1991). A comparison of two studies (in 1979 and 1994), it employs Goffman's (1979) categories in both studies and tested the frequency with which particular roles and symbols appear in different newspapers and magazines across those categories.

The Israeli Scene

Israel has often been perceived as offering women greater equality than do most Western nations. For example, the mandatory participation of Israeli women in military service is a practice that has drawn world attention. The fame of Israel's first woman Prime Minister, Golda Meir, has also contributed to that image (Rapaport, 1993). Yet in Israel, as in most modern Western democratic societies, the prevailing social outlook identifies women with the private sphere where they are responsible for the family and household, while men are associated with the public sphere, and are thus eligible for status in the labor market, in the army, and in politics. Israeli women's acceptance of these traditional identities has predisposed them toward roles centering on family affairs. The role of Israeli women in the family is constructed by two processes. The first is the fact that Israel is a "garrison state" and that women do not have a major role in this apparatus (Yishai, 1996). In reality female roles in the military are mostly nonessential and noncombat. The second process is related to the nature of Israel as a Jewish state, in which Jewish religious norms and laws apply to women, for example, marriage and divorce laws, which are inherently unequal in their application, are governed by the religious courts. Recently, however, women have gained greater access to several public fields formerly monopolized by men, particularly education and management. One effect of this growth has been to weaken the perception that only men are suited for activity in the public sphere and that the private sphere is the exclusive charge of women. These developments in the traditional sociocultural order have enabled women to become more involved in political activity, which has further contributed to systematic change in the country's social framework (Benjamin-Kurtz, 1996).

In 1978 a national committee presented the results of its study of women and the mass media in Israel. Its conclusions included a critique of the portrayal of women in Israeli advertising. The committee found that advertisements in the Israeli media tended to present women in sexist, negative, and harmful images, often directly contradicting the idea of equality. The original study of gender and Israeli advertisements presented here was conducted in 1979 (see First, 1981). Fifteen years later, in 1994, another study was conducted using the same methods of investigation and categories to look for indications of change in the representation of gender in advertising. This paper presents a comparison between these two time periods.

Methodology

The Sample. The combined sample from the study (1979) and the restudy (1994) consisted of 2,497 full-page or larger advertisements that appeared in prominent daily newspapers, women's magazines, and men's magazines in Israel in the given periods. This included 1678 advertisements collected during the twelve months of 1979 and 819 advertisements collected from January 1st to July 1st, 1994.

The sample of advertisements from women's magazines came from two sources—all the issues of *Na'amat* and *At* from the relevant periods. *Na'amat,* a women's political periodical owned and published by the largest women's organization in Israel, is affiliated with the Trade Union Federation and the Labor Party. *Na'amat* provided the sample with 51 advertisements in 1979, and with 20 more in 1994. *At* was the foremost commercial women's magazine in 1979, and at that time put forward some feminist views. In 1994, it was still a leading women's magazine. In 1979, 346 advertisements from *At* were included, with 88 more being sampled in 1994.

In 1979, 338 advertisements from all the issues of *Monitin*—a men's monthly magazine—were included. The magazine closed after several years, however, and we did not select another men's magazine to replace it in our 1994 data set, because none existed.

The sample also covered all the weekend newspaper advertisements, which had three sources. The first, *Ha'aretz,* is a morning paper widely read by government officials and other elites. *Ha'aretz* provided 381 advertisements in 1979 and 328 advertisements in 1994. In 1979, we also selected 572 advertisements from *Ma'ariv,* an evening newspaper that had the second largest circulation in Israel at the time.

The 1994 advertisements were drawn from another newspaper, however: *Yediot Acharonot,* then the most popular evening newspaper in Israel. The reason for changing newspapers springs from the fact that in 1994 *At* and *Ma'ariv* were owned by the same family, and so it was decided to substitute *Yediot Achronot* for *Ma'ariv* in the 1994 study. *Yediot Acharonot* contributed 383 advertisements to the 1994 study.

These figures indicate that the studies tested the whole population of Israeli advertisements over the given periods. The analysis that follows, however, concerns only those advertisements that depicted at least one adult human being. In 1979, 746 advertisements portrayed at least one adult, whereas 628 did so in 1994. That is, at least one adult appeared in only 1374 out of 2497 advertisements.

The Coders. The content of the sampled advertisements was coded by two trained individuals who worked independently. The coders were given a codebook that defined and delineated visual and textual categories based on Goffman's work, and they were engaged in a discussion about what was and was not included in each category.

In 1979, the analysis was undertaken by two coders, a man and a woman, aged 30–40, with some academic education. In 1994, it was performed by two other judges, also a male and a female, aged 25–30, students in the Department of Mass Communication and Journalism at the Hebrew University of Jerusalem. The reliability ($p < .05$, CR > 1.96) of the coding process in 1979, as well as in 1994, was tested by means of the model presented in Singer (1964). In both studies there was a little disagreement between coders, but when a disagreement did arise, discussions were held until consensus was reached.

Coding Units. Drawing heavily on Goffman's work, both studies used five behavior groupings. It is noteworthy that in the 1979 research there was a disagreement on the category "relative size" and it was not included in that study. The categories are not necessarily mutually exclusive.

• *Relative Size.* This category was determined by comparing the height of parties pictured in the advertisements. The results of this comparison were coded using a scale from one to four: (1) the man is shown as taller than the woman in an exaggerated manner, (2) the man is reasonably taller than the woman, (3) the man and woman are of the same height, and (4) the woman is shown as taller than the man in an exaggerated manner.

• *The Feminine Touch.* The feminine touch was measured by pictures involving the use of the whole body or only one part of it (fingers, the face, legs, lips); self-touching; cradling the object; using provocative body positions; and relevance of the exposed part of the body to the product.

• *Function Ranking.* To capture this variable, the professions were coded and were rated using Hartman (1979) and Krous and Hartman's status scale (1993), which ranks employment status in Israeli society.

• *Licensed Withdrawal.* Types of facial expression were coded indicating that the individual is not completely absorbed in the immediate reality presented in the advertisement. These included the following expressions—fear, shyness, anxiety, plus turning one's gaze away from another—all of which show a loss of control.

Findings

Overall, we found that in printed advertisements in Israel, women were and still are depicted as sex objects, parts of their body are used to highlight advertisements' headlines, and they are displayed in various forms of subordination, although there was a change for the better regarding some aspects of function ranking between the two periods. There were two major differences between the studies. The first was the increased number of men in the advertisements. The second was the increased number of women performing behavior displays that turn them into sex objects. It seems that those who produce the advertisements have not altered their basic conceptions about the behavior and symbolic meaning of women. Some changes have occurred, however, mostly concerning the prominence of features of the same behavior group, and in some cases the association of a number of those features with men as well as women.

Relative Size. A difference of height among the human figures depicted was found in only 14% of the 1994 sample (this variable was not tested in the 1979 sample). However, in most of the cases (10%), the men were taller in an exaggerated manner, men and women were the same height in 3% of the cases, and women were taller than men in only 1% of the advertisements. Even though the incidence of relative size was sparse, when it did occur the stereotypical patterns emerged very clearly.

Feminine Touch. At least one feminine touch phenomenon occurred in almost all of the advertisements (90%) in both periods. As indicated in Table 1, the appearance of every

TABLE 1. PROFESSIONAL STATUS OF MEN AND WOMEN IN 1979 ADVERTISEMENTS
VS. 1994 ADVERTISEMENTS (IN PERCENTAGES)*

	1979		1994	
	Women N=83	Men N=179	Women N=77	Men N=78
Low (1–3)	14	20	5	10
Average (4–6)	63	38	50	45
High (7–9)	23	42	45	45
Total	100	100	100	100

*The percentages are rounded: 1979, chi-square 23.38, df 4, $p < 01$; 1994, chi-square 36.11, df 8, $p < 01$.

behavioral aspect increased between the periods. For example, in 1979 women were shown touching themselves in 27% of the cases (out of 746 ads), and in 1994 this kind of behavior appeared in 52% of the ads (out of 628 ads). The percentages of men touching themselves also grew between the periods (from 6% to 31%) but a significant gap (chi-square 37.885, df 2, $p < 00$) between the percentages of women and of men still remained in 1994. In 1994, we looked at the relevance to the product of the appearance of a man or a woman in the advertisement and found that in only 40% of the cases was the appearance of an adult relevant. There was a significant difference (chi-square 21.404, df 2, $p < 00$) between the relevance of male nudity (31%) and of female nudity (49%).

Function Ranking. In the 1979 study, most of the women were presented in roles that were associated with average status: on the scale of nine levels, they ranked between four to six. Occupations at these levels include secretary, nurse, and saleswoman. However, in the restudy, women were represented equally in both average status (50%) and high status levels (45%), as shown in Table 1. A number of other differences were found in the depiction of men's and women's professions. Whereas in the earlier study men were represented twice as much as women overall, in the restudy both gender groups were equally represented and achieved the same percentages in the high status levels. The trend of over-representing men in low status occupations continued, although it decreased between the two studies.

Other aspects of function ranking were also analyzed in 1994. The first additional feature was activity versus passivity. We found that 71% of the men were depicted as active as against 54% of the women (chi-square 25.366, df 1, $p < 00$). The second feature was product price. Women were more likely than men to be associated with cheap products whereas men were more likely to be associated with expensive ones (chi-square 13.886, df 3, $p < 00$).

Ritualization of Subordination. Overall, about 70% of the 1979 advertisements featured some aspect connected to the subordination of women, as opposed to 60% of the advertisements in the restudy. In both studies, there was a significant difference between women and men (1979, t = 17.67, m1 = 0.53, m2 = 0.23, p < .01; 1994, t = 3.57, m1 = 13.39, m2 = 12.25, p < 00). There is a major transformation over time regarding the kind of behavior that indicates modes of subordination. In the 1979 study, 15% of the women were depicted in an erect position, as opposed to 44% of the men. However, in the 1994 study, 73% of the women were portrayed in an erect position, compared to 68% of the men. This change recurs across several indicators of ritual subordination. For example, in the first study 38% of the women and 3% of the men were shown leaning backward, while in the restudy 16% of the women and 11% of the men were leaning backward. On the other hand, we rarely found women and men lying on the floor in the first study, yet in the restudy 15% of women and 7% of the men were shown lying on the floor. Additionally, the depiction of women in a "clownish" position doubled in 1994 (from 6% to 14%) while the percentage for men remained constant (8%).

In both studies, women were more associated than men with the kinds of smiles that testify to agreement. However, there is a difference in the depiction of men between the two studies. For example, in the first study we did not find a single man depicted with a smile that suggested embarrassment, while in the restudy, 5% of the men were smiling in an embarrassed fashion.

Licensed Withdrawal. In both studies women were more associated than men with the kinds of facial expression that testify to a situation of licensed withdrawal. The most interesting finding is the consistency of male expressions as shown in Table 2. Significant change over time in the presentation of female expressions primarily concerns expressions of control, which doubled from the first to the second study. Also, the "other" category changed its character between the studies. In the study this category refers mainly to expression of passion while in the first study it applied to neutral expressions.

Finally, in both studies, no differences were found between the newspapers and journals examined with regard to our hypotheses.

Discussion

The title of this paper might suggest that nothing has changed over the years regarding the portrayal of women in Israeli advertisements. This contention was ratified. Both studies make clear that advertisements systematically portray women rather than men in situations where parts of their body are used to frame and promote the product. These features include the use of fingers, hands, face, lips, and other exposed parts of the body. However, in the restudy this tendency increased for both men and women, although the increase was especially marked for women. As regards occupational status, it was found in the first study that where such status was indicated, the distribution of men across occupational levels was significantly different from that of women. In general, more advertisements portrayed men as having an occupational status (or having an occupation at all) than portrayed women in that manner. There were more men than women at the upper and the lower levels of the status hierarchy, while at the middle levels the proportion of women was greater than men. This "landscape" had changed substantially by 1994. Women were depicted both as having professions and achieving the same status as men. The biggest change occurred at the highest status level. Women doubled their representation from

TABLE 2. EXPRESSIONS OF MEN AND WOMEN IN 1979 ADVERTISEMENTS VS. 1994 ADVERTISEMENTS (IN PERCENTAGES)*

	1979 (N = 764)		1994 (N = 628)	
Expressions	Women	Men	Women	Men
Regret	4	0	1	0
Fear	6	3	3	3
Shyness	20	12	22	12
Control	29	79	57	78
Other	41	6	17	7
Total	100	100	100	100

*The percentages are rounded: 1979, chi-square 16.21, df 2, $p < 01$; 1994, chi-square, 157.572, df 44, $p < 00$.

1979 to 1994, equaling men in the latter year. At first glance this seems like a major shift, but a deeper analysis shows that the changes were somewhat superficial. The advertisers altered part of the narrative of the relations of men and women, according to changes in the makeup of the labor force in Israeli society, changes that had occurred in most Western democracies (for example, see Ferrante, Haynes, & Kingsely, 1988; Furnham & Bitar, 1993). Effectively, the numerical representation of women had increased (to women's benefit), but the symbolic representation of women still demonstrated their inferiority.

This alteration can be read in relation to capitalist ideology overall. Testing other features of the social order, I found that men were depicted as active and women as passive. Moreover, the advertisers refer to women and men differently according to their ability to buy the product. While it seems that the occupations of the gender groups have been altered, women are still regarded as lacking money (they cannot allow themselves expensive products). Schudson (1993) claims that "there were various ways to find identity and placement in the larger world. Income was especially convenient because it provided a 'ranked identification' and consumer goods begin to be an index and a language that place a person in society and relate the person in symbolically significant ways to the national culture" (p. 158). Thus women were ranked in an inferior position to men.

The subordination of women remained steady over time. While gestures of subordination were more "graceful" in the first study, subordination became more obvious in the 1990s; women were found more often on the bed or on the floor. "Beds and floors provide places in social situations where incumbent persons will be lower than anyone sitting on a chair or standing. Floors also are associated with less clean, less pure, less exalted parts of the room" (Goffman, 1979, p. 41), and naturally lying on the floor or on a bed are expressions of sexual availability. These findings corroborate those of the "feminine touch" behavior group: that women were more represented as sexual objects in the 1990s than in the late 1970s. Moreover, a greater number of advertisements depicted men rather than women in positions of control. The most important finding was that licensed withdrawal remained the same over the years.

There is more than one way to read these findings. One approach, which has been discussed above, already provides an overall perspective on the relations between men and women. It seems that women are still portrayed as sex objects and their depiction reflects subordination and a lack of ability to control most of the situations in which they are involved.

Another approach is to interpret this portrayal of gender with reference to advertisements as part of "capitalist realism" (Schudson, 1993). In capitalist society, citizens are turned into consumers. As Kellner (1995) suggests, "mass-produced goods and fashion are used to produce a fake individuality, a 'commodity self,' an image" (p. 336), and the depiction of gender in advertising serves to convert the individual into this product-image. Thus, when confronted with the problem of gender stereotypes, instead of transforming women from products into human beings, advertisers prefer to convert men themselves from human beings into products. This process can help us explain the increasing "use" of men as sex objects in advertisements. Additionally, that there were no differences among the magazines and the newspapers examined suggests, among other things (for example, the small size of Israel's population), that the name of the game is "capitalist realism," which is dominant in all print media.

In addition, we have to read our findings in an Israeli context. First we have to note that even though much public attention has centered on the issue of the portrayal of women in advertisements, not a lot has changed over the years. On the one hand, women are better portrayed according to their professions even in a situation of "hyperritualization" (Goffman, 1979), since they have achieved increased representation in different status levels of the labor market. On the other hand, women in 1994 were in worse shape according to the other behavioral aspects as demonstrated above.

Last, whereas researchers have found that some basic values have indeed changed in Israeli society between the 1970s and the 1990s (Adoni, 1995), the basic values and attitudes toward women are much the same, as manifested by the content of Israel's advertisements. I would stress that while some chauvinistic characteristics were reduced, the various subordination behaviors of women are still common; women are still seen as sex objects, and even in more provocative forms than in the past.

References

Adoni, A. (1995). Literacy and reading in a multimedia environment. *Journal of Communications, 45,* 152–172.

Belknap, P., & Leonard, W. M. (1991). A conceptual replication and extension of Erving Goffman's study of gender advertisements. *Sex Roles, 25,* 103–118.

Benjamin-Kurtz, G. (1996). Attitudes, perceptions and behavior patterns of men and women in the central committees of Israeli political parties. Thesis accepted for the degree of Doctor of Philosophy, Bar Ilan University, Ramat-Gan (in Hebrew).

Ferrante, C. L., Haynes, A. M., & Kingsley, S. M. (1988). Images of women in television advertising. *Journal of Broadcasting and Electronic Media, 32,* 231–237.

First, A. (1981). Presentation of men and women and sex stereotypes as they are reflected in printed advertisements. Thesis accepted for M.A. degree, Tel Aviv University, Tel Aviv (in Hebrew).

Furnham, A., & Bitar, N. (1993). The stereotyped portrayal of men and women in British television advertisements. *Sex Roles,* 29, 297–310.

Goffman, E. (1979). *Gender advertisements.* New York: Harper & Row.

Greenberg, B. S., & Brand, J. E. (1994). Minorities and the mass media. In J. Bryant & D. Zillmann (Eds.), *Media effects.* Hillsdale, NJ: Lawrence Erlbaum.

Griffin, M., Viswanath, K., & Schwartz, D. (1994). Gender advertising in the U.S. and India: Exporting cultural stereotypes. *Media, Culture and Society,* 16, 487–507.

Hartman, M. (1979). Prestige grading of occupations with sociologists as judges. *Quality and Quantity,* 13, 1–19.

Hawkins, J. W., & Aber, C. S. (1993). Women in advertisements in medical journals. *Sex Roles,* 28, 233–242.

Jhally, S. (1987). *The codes of advertising: Fetishism and the political economy of meaning in the consumer society.* New York: St. Martin's.

Kellner, D. (1995). Advertising and consumer culture. In J. Downing, A. Mohammadi, & A. Sreberny-Mohammadi (Eds.), *Questioning the media.* London: Sage.

Krous, V., & Hartman, M. (1993). Changes in prestige grading of occupations in Israel 1974–1989. *Megamot,* 40, 78–87 (in Hebrew).

Lazier, L., & Kendrick, A. L. (1993). Women in advertisements: Sizing up the images, roles and functions. In P. J. Creedon (Ed.), *Women in mass communication.* London: Sage.

Rapaport, G. (1993). *On feminism and its opponents.* Tel-Aviv: Dvir Publishing House (in Hebrew).

Schudson, M. (1993). *Advertising. The uneasy persuasion.* London: Routledge.

Singer, J. D. (1964). Content analysis of elite articulations. *Conflict Resolution,* 8, 425–485.

Sullivan, G. L., & O'Connor, P. J. (1988). Women's role portrayals in magazine advertising: 1958–1983. *Sex Roles,* 18, 181–188.

Winship, J. (1981). Handling sex. *Media, Culture and Society,* 3, 25–41.

Yishai, Y. (1996). Myth and reality in gender equality: The status of women in Israel. In M. Lissak & B. Kny Paz (Eds.), *Israel towards the Year 2000: Society, politics and culture.* Jerusalem: Magnes (in Hebrew).

REVIEW QUESTIONS

1. Why were two different years used in this study?

2. How was the information coded?

3. How many variables were in this study? What were the variables? How were they measured?

Chapter 12: Writing and Reading a Research Paper

No one can read what has never been put on paper.

Howard Becker, 1986:5

Many students are daunted by the thought of a research assignment. This is often made more difficult than it needs to be. Students do not always either know how to read the papers they find in the library or how to use the sources they have gathered for their papers. Writing is important in the social sciences and reluctance to start the process is common. According to Howard Becker (1986), who has been teaching graduate students to write for years, everyone has their own writing habits that they usually don't want to share with others because they seem so silly. Becker says the time-wasting writing habits his students describe are something we all have to deal with and that it is "a common disease. Just as people feel relieved to discover that some frightening physical symptoms they've been hiding are just something that is 'going around,' knowing that others had crazy writing habits should have been, and clearly was, a good thing" (Becker, 1986: 3).

AN ACADEMIC RESEARCH PAPER

The very first thing you need to know is some basic terminology. I find that it is best that students in research methods classes use mainly **primary sources.** A primary source is the original article that describes and reports **empirical research** and **theoretical articles** that have been published in a **peer-reviewed** academic journal. An empirical research paper is a description of a systematic observation or study, whereas a theoretical article explains a theory and how it relates to the variables being investigated. Peer-reviewed means that the research paper has been blindly reviewed, usually by three other scholars in the same field, who decide if the research meets the standards of the journal. We will discuss primary sources in this chapter, but you should know that **secondary sources** are summaries of original research that you find in newspapers, magazines, and hear about on the news. Secondary sources are good because they give us ideas for studies and also give us clues about where to look for the original study. However, it is difficult to know for sure that the reporter interpreted and then reported the original research correctly. Therefore, your professor might not want you to use secondary sources.

Let me give you an example of why using secondary sources might not be a good idea, but it is something we often do in our day-to-day lives. Recently, there has been a lot of media coverage on the dangers of hormone replacement therapy (HRT) for women, even though since the 1960s both doctors and women believed that HRT was a wonder drug that kept women young, eased the symptoms of menopause, and decreased hip fractures. Since then, between 6 and 13 million American women have been placed on HRT. However, now it seems that many women have stopped taking HRT because of the media (secondary sources) reports of a study that appeared in *JAMA: Journal of the American Medical Association* (primary source). The actual study, supported by the National Institutes of Health, was to continue for 8.5 years, but ended after only 5.2 years because the preliminary data suggested that the drugs used in the study had negative effects on the respondents. However, as a budding researcher you would know not to make any decisions, especially about your health, based on secondary sources. Instead, you would know you should locate the original source before making a decision (Women's Health Initiative, 2002).

The primary source reported that in this study 16,608 postmenopausal women aged 50–79, each of whom still had her uterus, received either the HRT (n=8506) or a placebo (n=8102). The study ended early, because the preliminary reports found that increased coronary heart disease (n=286) and invasive breast cancer (n=290), along with stroke (n=212), pulmonary embolism (n=101), endometrial and colorectal cancer (n=159) were found to be higher in those women who received the drugs. We know from Chapter 3 on Ethics that the researchers are obligated to tell the women in the study their findings and not have them continue if the study could be dangerous in any way. However, it is the secondary sources that seem to be scaring women and doctors into discontinuing the drug. Should women stop taking HRT? That's an individual decision. However, now that you know how to think about this sociologically, you can read the primary sources and look for additional information on female mortality. For instance, the *Statistical Abstracts of the United States* tells us that 1,940,000 women between the ages of 45–74 were killed by firearms in 1997 (U.S. Census Bureau, 2000a), 67,520,000 died of various types of cancer (U.S. Census Bureau 2000b), and 74,900,000 died from heart disease in 1998 alone (U.S. Census Bureau 2000c). So, in comparison with other heath issues, how serious is the HRT issue?

READING A JOURNAL ARTICLE

Now let's get back to learning how to read a journal article. If you go back to a few of the articles you have been asked to read in your course, you will notice that they all follow the same basic format. There are usually six parts to an empirical research article: (1) abstract, (2) literature review or introduction, (3) methods, (4) results, (5) discussion or conclusion, and (6) references. If you are a visual person, you might look at the various parts of a paper as an hour-glass where you begin broadly with the abstract, then go to the introduction or literature review, which gets more and more narrow as you focus in on your hypothesis. Then you begin once again to broaden out as you talk about the specifics in your methods section, explaining the results and getting broader still with your conclusion. You end with the references.

Now let's take each section in detail using an article on AIDS and adolescents that I wrote with another student when we were undergraduates (Wysocki and Harrison, 1991).

Abstracts. Although abstracts are usually the first thing you will see when you read an academic research article, they are written after the rest of the paper has been completed. An

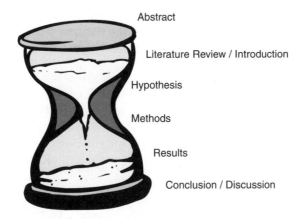

Figure 12.1. Parts of an Empirical Research Article

abstract is a very brief statement about the research hypothesis, purposes, or questions about the project. After that, a brief sentence or two describes the methodology used in the project, such as whether a survey or face-to-face interviews were conducted, or all the data was collected over the Internet. This section also should include information about the participants or the sample. Next, the results should be mentioned in almost the next to the last sentence that provides a very brief description of the findings. Finally, the last sentence often draws a conclusion for the reader.

As you can tell, abstracts are very short. The goal of an abstract is to provide readers with just enough information to help them decide whether the article is something they are interested in and something that will help with their projects. Here is example of an abstract:

> The media have had a powerful impact in shaping the public's view of AIDS. While research on the media has focused mainly on what has been directed toward adults, children and adolescents also are at risk for AIDS. The purpose of this study is to determine how magazines geared toward children and adolescents report information about AIDS. Seventy-nine periodicals geared toward children and adolescents were identified, of which 13 had articles pertaining to AIDS. Forty-six articles from eight periodicals were used for the final analysis. Most articles provided only minimal information about AIDS and very little information was given about prevention, transmission, and testing procedures. The articles did not provide a sufficient quantity and quality of information to help prevent the spread of HIV in adolescents and children. (Wysocki and Harrison, 1991)

Can you pick out which parts of the abstract each sentence fulfills?

Literature Review/Introduction. This is an important, but often confusing, part of the article. A literature review introduces the problem, develops the background by providing a history of the scholarly work on the subject, and ends with the purpose and the rationale of the study. My students sometimes think this is the only part of a research paper they find in the library that they need to read. (They then use the literature review of other authors in their papers inappropriately.) However, this isn't true and can be a problem because it's difficult to cite and often gets cited incorrectly, if at all.

Remember our hourglass? We went from broad to narrow or general to specific. That is how the literature review goes. Using the same article on AIDS and adolescents, you can see that we start broadly by introducing the issue of AIDS, how it has increased over the years, and that people who become infected with the virus are getting younger and younger.

> As of March 31, 1989, there had been 89,501 cases of AIDS reported in the United States (Centers for Disease Control [CDC], 1989). The CDC did not separate adult and adolescent cases of AIDS prior to 1986. Between 1986 and 1988, however, 335 adolescent cases of AIDS ranging in age from 13 to 19 years had been reported (Centers for Disease Control, 1989). These figures may be conservative due to reluctance of high-risk adolescents who are also drug abusers to seek medical attention. In addition, it is estimated that 21 percent of people currently diagnosed with AIDS are young adults between ages 20 to 29 (Tolsma, 1988). Because the virus frequently lies undetected for 8 to 12 years prior to diagnosis (Flora & Thoresen, 1988), these adults probably became infected during their teenage years. It seems, therefore, that a substantial number of adolescents are at risk for AIDS.

Then we began to get more specific and mentioned the reasons that adolescents were at risk, using empirical research to support the ideas along the way.

> The reasons for risk vary. Most commonly, sexual activity is the primary mode of HIV transmission among adolescents. In a 1986 Lou Harris poll conducted for Planned Parenthood, 57 percent of teenagers sampled reported having sexual intercourse by age 17 (Skeen & Hodson, 1987). In some communities the age of first intercourse was found to be as low as 12 years. An informal survey conducted by Renshaw (1989) in her Maywood, Illinois, clinic, found that of the 100 males and females sampled, the average age of first intercourse was 12.5 years and 14.5 years, respectively. In contrast, Zelnik and Shah's (1983) study found that the average age of first coitus experience was about 16 years old. Although studies vary as to the exact age of first intercourse experience, it is evident that this experience does frequently take place within the teenage years. In addition, although most of this early sexual behavior is between males and females, the Kinsey Institute has estimated that four in 10 adolescent males participate in some form of homosexual behavior (Haffner, 1988) and Brooks-Gunn, Boyer, and Hem (1988) believe that over 10 percent of adolescent males had at least one homosexual experience.

We continued to talk about more types of risks that put adolescents in danger of becoming infected by talking about the lack of condom use, sexually transmitted diseases, sexual abuse and incest, IV drug use, steroid use, tattooing, and body piercing. Then we narrowed it farther by talking about adolescents' knowledge of AIDS, and how much the media affects what adolescents know about the subject. Once again, we supported our ideas with empirical research. In this way we developed the background of the significant scholarly work done on these topics and paved the way to the rationale for the study, which was stated at the beginning of the article:

> Because researchers generally agree that media is an important source of public information (Goodwin et al., 1988), it becomes important to study how American media portrays AIDS. Of primary concern is how media influences our nation's children, whom without correct information could become a high-risk group for contracting Human Immunodeficiency Virus (HIV). The purpose of this study is to determine how popular magazines geared toward children and adolescents are reporting on AIDS, and what effect they might have in influencing a young person's current belief, knowledge, and attitudes.

So, why did I say at the beginning of this section that someone else's literature review should not be used directly in your paper? Correct! You have been paying attention. Because it is someone else's understanding of previous empirical studies that they used for their literature review—the authors' "story" leading up to the rationale or hypothesis of the project you are currently reading about. Let's say you liked what Wysocki and Harrison said in the previous chapter and in your paper you wrote the "media is an important source of public information (Wysocki and Harrison, 1991)." Would this be correct? No, actually Goodwin et al., 1988, said it. So, you would have cited it incorrectly. Why do we use literature reviews in articles? It's a great way to find out where the primary sources can be located by matching the citation in the literature review to the full reference in the bibliography section.

Methods. This section is important, as you know, because it describes in detail how the study was conducted. The methods section not only allows the reader to evaluate the research, but it should also be so detailed that another researcher can replicate it exactly. There are often subsections of the *Methods* section that are labeled and sometimes are *Participants, Materials,* and *Procedure,* depending on the organization and detail of the study. Using the same study, the methods section is as follows:

> For this study, we reviewed all periodicals (n = 79) geared toward children and adolescents, as identified in *Magazines for Libraries* and the *Children's Magazine Guide* under the sub-headings "teenagers" and "children." Of these 79 periodicals, a total of 13 had published articles pertaining to the subject of AIDS dating from January 1983 to April 1989, as shown in Table 1. All articles were obtained except those contained in *Choices, Contact, Current Events* and *Current Science.* These publications are not available in any libraries in the Phoenix Metro area, suggesting that they are minor publications with limited circulation. After reviewing the general content of each article, it was decided that even though *Rolling Stone* was listed under the subheading "teenagers," this magazine was not geared toward children and adolescents. For this reason, *Rolling Stone* was excluded from the analysis. This final sample consisted of 46 articles from 8 periodicals.

One of my students wanted to replicate this study to investigate whether or not the information in the media about HIV/AIDS now available to adolescents in the media had changed and improved over time. She took this methods section, followed it exactly, and located data from May 1989, when we stopped collecting data, to the present. Unfortunately, she found that things had not changed much.

Results. The results section summarizes the data that has been collected and explains the findings in enough detail to justify the conclusions. This section often includes tables, figures, and statistics. Sometimes this is a difficult section to read, especially if you haven't had a few statistics courses—or don't remember them. Summarizing the data in tables and figures is always helpful and very easy to do in either your word-processing program or Excel. If you want to be creative, you can also use SPSS and PowerPoint—they are both pretty user friendly. Remember to refer to the tables and figures in the text such as "The data, as shown in Table 1, suggests that there has not been an increase in the information given to adolescents about HIV/AIDS since 1982."

Discussion or Conclusion. Here, the information in the results section is evaluated and interpreted. Usually the section begins with a clear statement about whether or not the hypothesis was supported. Also using the literature review (remember, it gave information on other scholarly work to set up the current project), the author can compare and contrast the findings in this study with the studies presented in the literature review. This section also discusses what this project contributes to the current base of knowledge on the topic, what conclusions can be drawn from the study, and suggestions of future research possibilities.

So, now you might be thinking . . . "Oh, that's easy for Dr. Wysocki to say, but how am I supposed to do this for the paper that is due in the morning." Well, the answer to that is . . . you can't. You must start writing a research paper very early. It can't be done in one night. And now, you know you have to read the entire article to see how it fits with your topic.

WRITING FOR THE SOCIAL SCIENCES

Now that you know the parts of an academic paper, let's use an example to see how it is done if you have been assigned to write an academic paper. I always suggest that students find a topic that interests them. Let's say you are interested in some aspect of domestic violence. There are all kinds of interesting topics under domestic violence such as family issues, economic aspects, drug and alcohol use, or the criminal justice system. But let's say you are interested in the media and you believe that the media plays some part in domestic violence because you know that everyone is socialized by the media somehow. You also know due to court TV and the news that although domestic violence was once a private trouble, it has now become a public issue. So, let's say you believe that as media coverage increases so do acts of domestic violence—this is your hypothesis. Then what would your independent variable and dependent variables be? Correct!!!

Media Coverage  Increase in Domestic Violence
IV   DV

You have an idea for your topic, so now would be a great time to sit down, freely write out an outline for a literature review to locate scholarly work in the subject. But should you just go to the library? You could, but you might end up with lots of stuff you don't need. You don't go to the grocery store without a shopping list (because if you do you return home with lots of things you don't need), so you shouldn't go to the library without your outline.

Let's start with Domestic Violence (DV). Remember to start broadly.

1. Definition of DV
   a. National Statistics
   b. Incidents of DV to police departments
   c. Problems with reporting
   d. Comparison of DV to other crimes
      i. Murder
      ii. Theft
2. Reasons for DV
   a. Control
   b. Power
   c. Gender Differences
3. Reasons women stay in DV relationships
   a. Financial
   b. Fear
   c. Children
4. Misconceptions about DV
   a. Women could leave if they wanted
   b. They need the violence
   c. They deserve the violence

Now for Media, the Independent Variable.

1. Kinds of media
   a. Music
   b. Television
   c. Movies
   d. Newspapers
2. Socialization
   a. Socialization Theory
   b. How the media socializes us (Don't forget you need a theory because research without theory is pretty empty. So, if you believe that the news is socially constructed, you might want to use this theory.)
   c. How the media constructs our reality
3. The media's portrayal of DV

This is a very rough outline (shopping list), but enough to take to the library as a guide. Now you look up scholarly work to plug into the various parts of your outline to support what you think you want to write about.

So, is this the final outline? No, it's just a beginning. You might get into the literature and find out that someone else talks about something that you hadn't thought of. So, you can put it in your outline. Similarly, you might find out that something in your outline just doesn't fit and you don't need it . . . so out it goes. Also, after getting into the literature, you might find out that you can organize your outline differently.

PLAGIARISM

Citing properly seems to be one of the most difficult tasks in writing a research paper. However, it is also one of the most important things to learn, because failure to cite properly could put you in danger of being charged with **plagiarism.** Each discipline has its own "Ethical Standards for the Reporting and Publishing of Scientific Information," but plagiarism is using someone else's writing without crediting the author and is often grounds for failing your class or expulsion from school and wrecks havoc with your reputation.

I believe that sometimes students don't even realize they are plagiarizing. A few years ago, I gave an assignment in one of my classes and as I was grading the papers, I found I was very impressed by one student's paper. This student had been pretty quiet in class, so I was pleasantly surprised to see her do such good work on a subject I was really interested in. As I kept reading, I realized that the information sounded really familiar to me and a few pages later I realized that the student had used a chapter out of my dissertation which was available on the Internet. When I asked her why she had copied my work, she said she thought what I wrote was good, believed I would like it if she used my work, and that she didn't know it was cheating. It appears this one young student is not an isolated case and that students don't intentionally plagiarize but, rather, don't know how to cite their sources properly.

According to Donald McCabe (2001), of the 4500 high school students who answered a written survey, 74 percent reported at least one or more instances of serious cheating on tests, 72 percent on written work, and 30 percent reported more serious, repetitive cheating. Similarly, in an earlier study of 2,100 students on 21 different college campuses, ⅓ admitted to serious test cheating and ½ admitted to one or more instances of serious cheating on written assignments (McCabe and Trevino, 1996), and it is just part of student life (McCabe, 1999). Furthermore, more males cheat than females do, fraternity and sorority members are more likely to cheat than are those who are nonmembers, and those who believe their peers strongly disapprove of cheating are less likely to cheat (McCabe, and Bowers, 1996).

Although the Internet is a wonderful tool to use in research, the Internet has also provided new opportunities for students to plagiarize. As you probably know, there are plenty of places on the Internet to buy your paper if you care to pay $10 per page. Many students seem to do this, and some professors feel that Internet plagiarism is becoming more dangerous and more common than we might realize (Laird, 2001; McCabe, 1999). In fact, teachers and librarians now publish articles, Web sites, and other information to help professors catch those who plagiarize from the Internet (Lincoln, 2002). Although only 15 percent of high school students have purchased a paper from an Internet paper mill, 52 percent have reported using a few sentences directly from the Internet without citing the source (McCabe, 2001). School policies vary on this subject, but it's best to learn how to keep yourself out of trouble.

There are different types of plagiarism, and the most serious is **intentional plagiarism,** which includes cheating of any kind. This can be anything from copying directly from an article or a book you found to buying an article off the Internet. Intentional plagiarism seems to be increasingly common. **Unintentional plagiarism,** however, is even more common and occurs when you paraphrase or summarize another author's ideas, but do not give credit to the author. One of the problems I encounter most often in an undergraduate research methods class is when a student uses an academic article, reads only the literature review, and then uses information out of the literature review of an author as the student's own literature review. So for instance, Smith wrote an article on child abuse in 1990. The student goes to Smith's article and finds out that in Smith's literature review, Smith uses articles from Jones (1984), another one from Kelley (1999), and yet another one from Rodney and Roe (1997) to describe the various reasons for child abuse in our country. So, the student decides to also talk about the reasons for child abuse and uses what Smith's literature review tells us the other researchers have found. Then the student cites Smith (1990). What's wrong with this? That's right!!! The student would have had to go back to the original articles that Smith cited to make sure Smith cited them accurately and also because the student cited the studies of other researchers rather than Smith's study.

The best way to make sure you do not plagiarize unintentionally is to use a book on how to write and use citations both in your paper and in your bibliography. There are too many of these books to discuss here, and each has its own style, but having one from the *American Psychological Association, American Sociological Association,* or the *Chicago Manual of Style* would help with any papers you write. Furthermore, one more way that students get caught on plagiarizing unintentionally is to use a paper for one class that has been used and graded in another class. Would you want your children to double dip like that? Probably not . . . so you shouldn't either.

REFERENCES

Becker, Howard. 1986. *Writing for social scientists: How to start and finish your thesis, book or article.* University of Chicago Press: Chicago.

Laird, E. 2001. Internet Plagiarism: We All Pay the Price. *Chronicle Review,* July 13, pg. 5.

Lincoln, M. 2002. Internet Plagiarism. *Multimedia Schools,* 9 (1): 46–49.

McCabe, D. L. 1999. Academic Dishonesty Among High School Students. *Adolescence,* 34 (136): 681–687.

McCabe, D. L. 2001. Student Cheating in American High Schools. [ONLINE] http://www.academicintegrity.org/

McCabe, D. L., & Bowers, W. J. 1996. The Relationship Between Student Cheating and College Fraternity or Sorority Membership. *NASPA Journal,* 33, 280–291.

McCabe, D. L., & Trevino, L. K. 1996. What We Know about Cheating in College. *Change,* 28: 28–33.

U. S. Census Bureau. 2000a. No. 132. Death Rates from Heart Disease by Sex and Age: 1980 to 1998. *Statistical Abstract of the United States: 2000 (120th edition).* Washington, DC.

U. S. Census Bureau. 2000b. No. 133. Death Rates from Cancer by Sex and Age: 1990 to 1998. *Statistical Abstract of the United States: 2000 (120th edition).* Washington, DC.

U. S. Census Bureau. 2000c. No. 136. Death Rates for Injury by Firearms by Sex, Race, and Age: 1997. *Statistical Abstract of the United States: 2000 (120th edition).* Washington, DC.

Women's Health Initiative. 2002. Risks and Benefits of Estrogen Plus Progestin in Healthy Postmenopausal Women: Principal Results from the Women's Health Initiative Randomized Control Trial. *JAMA: The Journal of the American Medical Association,* 288 (3): 321–333.

AIDS AND THE MEDIA: A LOOK AT HOW PERIODICALS INFLUENCE CHILDREN AND TEENAGERS IN THEIR KNOWLEDGE OF AIDS

Diane Kholos Wysocki and Rebecca Harrison

This article was used to explain the different parts of a paper in the introduction to this chapter. The whole article has been included here, so you can see how it is done. Read the literature review and see if you can come up with the outline we might have used writing this paper. Remember to start broadly and become narrower and more focused as you go along.

Acquired Immune Deficiency Syndrome (AIDS) was unknown before 1981. By the fall of 1987, however, the majority of America's public had at least heard about AIDS through some form of media (Goodwin & Roscoe, 1988). In a poll conducted by *Newsweek,* 91 percent of those people who responded indicated that their awareness of AIDS was due to exposure given by the mass media. It is likely, then, that popular media such as magazines and television are shaping both the adult and adolescent view of AIDS.

Because researchers generally agree that media is an important source of public information (Goodwin & Roscoe, 1988), it becomes important to study how American media portrays AIDS. Of primary concern is how media influences our nation's children, whom without correct information could become a high-risk group for contracting Human Immunodeficiency Virus (HIV). The purpose of this study is to determine how popular magazines geared toward children and adolescents are reporting on AIDS, and what effect they might have in influencing a young person's current beliefs, knowledge, and attitudes.

The Risk of AIDS Among Adolescents

As of March 31, 1989, there had been 89,501 cases of AIDS reported in the United States (Centers for Disease Control [CDC], 1989). The CDC did not separate adult and adolescent cases of AIDS prior to 1986. Between 1986 and 1988, however, 335 adolescent cases of AIDS ranging in age from 13 to 19 years had been reported (Centers for Disease Control, 1989). These figures may be conservative due to reluctance of high risk adolescents who are also drug abusers to seek medical attention. In addition, it is estimated that 21 percent of people currently diagnosed with AIDS are young adults between ages 20 to 29 (Tolsman, 1988). Because the virus frequently lies undetected for 8 to 12 years prior to diagnosis (Flora & Thoresen, 1988), these adults probably became infected during their teenage years. It seems, therefore, that a substantial number of adolescents are at risk for AIDS.

Reasons for this risk vary. Most commonly, sexual activity is the primary mode of HIV transmission among adolescents. In a 1986 Lou Harris poll conducted for Planned Parenthood, 57 percent of teenagers sampled reported having sexual intercourse by age

Wysocki, D. K., and Harrison, R. 1991. AIDS and the media: A look at how periodicals influence children and teenagers in their knowledge of AIDS, *Journal of Health Education,* 22 (1), pp. 20–23. Used with permission.

17 (Skeen & Hodson, 1987). In some communities the age of first intercourse was found to be as low as 12 years. An informal survey conducted by Renshaw (1989) in her Maywood, Illinois, clinic, found that of the 100 males and females sampled, the average age of first intercourse was 12.5 years and 14.5 years, respectively. In contrast, Zelnik and Shah's (1983) study found that the average age of first coitus experience was about 16 years old. Although studies vary as to the exact age of first intercourse experience, it is evident that this experience does frequently take place within the teenage years. In addition, although most of this early sexual behavior is between males and females, the Kinsey Institute has estimated that 4 in 10 adolescent males participate in some form of homosexual behavior (Haffner, 1988) and Brooks-Gunn, Boyer, and Hem (1988) believe that over 10 percent of adolescent males have had at least one homosexual experience. Thus, many adolescents may be at risk for AIDS through both heterosexual and homosexual activity.

This risk is increased by the fact that few teenagers use protective measures such as condoms. A study done by Jaffe, Seehaus, Wagner, and Leadbeater (1988) found 46.2 percent of minority females between the ages of 13 and 21 never used condoms during vaginal intercourse and 74 percent never used condoms during anal intercourse. Sexually transmitted diseases such as chlamydia, syphilis, gonorrhea, and pelvic inflammatory diseases are found in highest numbers among teenagers 15 to 19 years of age, suggesting a high rate of unprotected activity (Brooks-Gunn et al., 1988). Sexual abuse and incest provide other avenues for HIV transmission to both young children and adolescents. Reports of abuse are steadily increasing and the rate of incestuous abuse among young females has quadrupled since the early 1900s (Russell, 1986). One study by Russell showed that of 930 subjects, 16 percent reported at least one incestuous experience before age 18 and another 12 percent before age 14.

Another mode of HIV transmission within the adolescent population is sharing needles for intravenous drug use. Unfortunately, accurate statistics reporting the prevalence of teenage drug use are lacking. Miller and Downer (1988) estimated that 61 percent of seniors in high school have experimented with some kind of drugs for recreational purposes, and 1 percent of high school seniors have used heroin, with a much higher rate existing in inner-city areas. Other studies estimate that over 200,000 teens have tried injecting drugs (Brooks-Gunn et al., 1988). It is likely that due to reluctance of adolescents to report accurately about such things as sexual activity and drug use, these estimates are low. Another concern is that some unknowingly will come into sexual contact with those that do inject drugs.

Additional possible sources of HIV transmission among adolescents are injecting steroids, sharing needles for piercing ears, tattooing, and becoming "blood brothers." Thus many behaviors place teenagers at risk for contracting AIDS.

Adolescents' Knowledge of AIDS

With so many adolescents currently at risk, AIDS education and awareness can be an important instrument to help prevent infection. Yet a 1986 survey that examined the existing AIDS education programs for the U.S. Conference of Mayors, found that only one-third provided any type of AIDS information. As a result, few adolescents have adequate knowledge about AIDS. Goodwin and Roscoe (1988) found that in their sample of 495 university undergraduates, 2 percent (nine students) were very knowledgeable about AIDS, but two-thirds of the respondents possessed only moderate knowledge. Di-Clemente, Zorn, and Tenoshok (1986) looked at the level of AIDS knowledge, beliefs, and attitudes among 1,326 San Francisco adolescents, aged 14–18. Their findings showed that some knowledge of AIDS was present: 92 percent knew that one way of contracting AIDS was through intercourse but 60 percent did not know that using condoms during intercourse can lower the risk of contracting AIDS. A Massachusetts study found even more discouraging results: 96 percent had heard about AIDS, yet only 15 percent of those who were sexually active were taking any precautions such as using condoms. In addition, the Massachusetts study found that many adolescents believed AIDS could be transmitted by kissing, sharing eating utensils, toilet seats, and donating blood. Studies such as these indicate that the AIDS information that adolescents receive is inadequate.

Adolescents, AIDS, and the Media

Current research suggests that AIDS is portrayed selectively by the media. The media, specifically popular magazines, have played a significant role in constructing and maintaining the view that AIDS is a "gay disease." Moreover, the mass media are judgmental in the way they portray the person with AIDS, showing primarily homosexuals, drug users, and prostitutes as the subjects of those media articles reporting on AIDS victims. By portraying people with AIDS as inherently different from adolescents, adolescents are given a false sense of security. As a result, they are at a greater risk for infection.

Method

For this study, we reviewed all periodicals (n = 79) geared toward children and adolescents, as identified in *Magazines for Libraries* and the *Children's Magazine Guide* under the sub-headings "teenagers" and "children." Of these 79 periodicals, a total of 13 had published articles pertaining to the subject of AIDS dating from January 1983 to April 1989, as shown in Table 1.

All articles were obtained except those contained in *Choices, Contact, Current Events* and *Current Science.* These publications are not available in any libraries in the Phoenix Metro area, suggesting that they are minor publications with limited circulation. After reviewing the general content of each article, it was decided that even though *Rolling Stone* was listed under the subheading "teenagers," this magazine was not geared toward children and adolescents. For this reason, *Rolling Stone* was excluded from the analysis. This final sample consisted of 46 articles from eight periodicals.

Results

Extent of Coverage

Of the 46 articles used for this sample, no magazine published any articles on AIDS during 1983 and 1984. In 1985, one article was published. One article was published in 1986 and 27 in 1987. A decline was evident in 1988 with sixteen articles published, and only one article on AIDS was published in 1989.

TABLE 1. PERIODICALS THAT CONTAINED AIDS ARTICLES

Periodical	Number of Articles in Year							Total Articles
	1983	1984	1985	1986	1987	1988	1989	
Choices					2	3		5
Contact						1		1
Current Events			1	3	2	1		7
Current Health						1		1
Current Science			1	4	3	2	3	13
Jack and Jill						1		1
Junior Scholastic					1	6		7
National Geographic						1		1
Scholastic Update					17			17
Science World					8	5	1	14
Seventeen			1	1		2		4
Teen					1			1

Note: Rolling Stone was listed as a teenage magazine, but we did not include it in this sample. Articles are through April 1989.

For analysis, each year was divided into four quarters. Articles within each quarter were then coded according to where they were placed in the magazine. Placement of articles was almost evenly distributed throughout all four quarters: 29 percent occurred within the first quarter, 29 percent in the second quarter, 16 percent in the third quarter, and 26 percent in the fourth quarter. Articles ranged in length from one-third of a page to four pages, with the exception of a 23-page pictorial essay in National Geographic. In addition, Scholastic Update had one issue devoted entirely to AIDS. It was concluded that positioning and brevity of the articles suggest that magazines did not consider AIDS an important topic.

Basic Knowledge

Most of the articles covered basic information about AIDS. Fifty percent of the articles noted that AIDS is caused by a virus. Forty-four percent referred to AIDS as a virus that attacks the immune system, and 35 percent stated that AIDS is life-threatening or fatal. Two articles discussed the complexities of mutant RNA and its relationship to HIV, and four felt that AZT would eliminate some of the symptoms of AIDS. *Teen Magazine* was the only one to mention the symptoms of AIDS, such as severe weight loss, high fevers, and fatigue. The article, however, did not explain how to differentiate between the symptoms of AIDS and other illnesses. Thirty-three percent of the articles stated that AIDS could not be transmitted through casual contact. One-third explained that AIDS can be transmitted sexually, 40 percent wrote about intravenous drug use as a mode of transmission, and 30 percent simply stated that AIDS was transmitted through cuts or by blood. *Current Health* magazine suggested that "children are the least likely to get AIDS" and the few who did become infected received it from their mothers.

Prevention

Most of the articles gave no information about how to protect one's self or others from contracting or transmitting AIDS, and the balance provided only minimal information. Only three articles said anything about safe sex. *Teen* discusses the importance of using condoms, but fails to explain how to put them on properly or where and what kind to purchase.

This article also suggested that readers avoid French-kissing. The November, 1985 issue of *Seventeen* instructs readers to use a condom during vaginal or anal sex, avoid contact with semen during oral sex, and avoid French-kissing anyone in a high risk group. Three years later in March 1988, *Seventeen* suggested to readers that HIV does not live in saliva and that condoms are not 100 percent effective, reflecting scientists' growing knowledge of AIDS. Hotline numbers and information were given in only 16 percent of the articles. None of the articles mentioned that people are generally infected and capable of infecting others for 8 to 12 years before diagnosis. Only one article mentioned that it takes six months for the virus to appear in the blood stream after initial infection. This article did not, however, explain how someone might mistakenly think themselves not infected and therefore unable to transmit the disease during this time. Eight percent mentioned using condoms as a way of not transmitting the virus, while the benefit of using a spermicidal such as Nonoxynol 9 was mentioned by only six percent. Eight percent of the articles stated that people are not at risk if they practice abstinence, oral sex, or have only one partner, but none of the articles defined the term "abstinence," which would likely be unknown to most teens. Similarly, it was not made clear that serial monogamy could be a risk factor for AIDS, in that each time a person develops a new sexual relationship, that person is again potentially exposed to HIV infection even if the relationship remains monogamous for its duration.

Conclusion

It is indisputable that children and adolescents are at risk for AIDS. Behavioral changes in sexual activity promoted by accurate AIDS education is of paramount importance to reduce the risk of AIDS infection. Without accurate education from many sources, the necessary behavioral changes most likely will not occur. Appropriate education about AIDS should come from all possible sources, but especially from schools, parents, television, and magazines. As shown in this study, magazines geared toward children and teenagers are failing to provide a sufficient quantity and quality of information about AIDS. Children and adolescents who fail to get correct information will be unable to make sound choices about their lifestyles, and therefore will be unprotected against AIDS. Because media is the way in which children and adolescents get most of their AIDS information, media such as magazines and television must become more responsible in the information they provide to their young readers.

References

Brooks-Gunn, J., Boyer, C. B. & Hem, K. (1988). Preventing HIV infection and AIDS in children and adolescents. *American Psychologist, 43,* 958–964.

Carroll, L. (1968). Concern with AIDS and the sexual behavior of college students. *Journal of Marriage and the Family, 50,* 405–411.

Centers for Disease Control. (1989). Update: Heterosexual transmission of Acquired Immunodeficiency Syndrome and Human Immunodeficiency Virus infection—United States. *Morbidity and Mortality Weekly Report, 38,* 423–433.

DiClemente, R. J., Zorn, J., & Tenoshok, L. (1986). Adolescents and AIDS: A survey of knowledge, attitudes, and beliefs about AIDS in San Francisco. *American Journal of Public Health, 76,* 1443–1445.

Flora, I. A., & Thoresen, C. E. (1988). Reducing the risk of AIDS in adolescents. *American Psychologist, 43,* 965–970.

Goodwin, M. P., & Roscoe, B. (1988). AIDS: Students' knowledge and attitudes at a midwestern university. *Journal of College Health, 36,* 214–222.

Herber, M. (1987). *Living with teenagers.* New York: Basil Blackwell.

Jaffe, L. R., Seehaus, M., Wagner, C., & Leadbeater, B. J. (1988). Anal intercourse and knowledge of Acquired Immunodeficiency Syndrome among minority-group female adolescents. *Journal of Pediatrics,* 1005–1007.

Miller, L., & Downer, A. (1988). AIDS: What you and your friends need to know—A lesson plan for adolescents. *Journal of School Health, 58,* 137–140.

Renshaw, O. (1989). Sex and the college student. *Journal of College Health, 37,* 154–157.

Russell, O. (1986). *The secret trauma.* New York: Basic Books. Inc.

Skeen, P., & Hodson, O. (1987). AIDS: What adults should know about AIDS (and shouldn't discuss with very young children). *Young Children,* 65–70.

Tolsman, D. (1988). Activities of the Centers for Disease Control in AIDS education. *Journal of School Health, 58,* 133–136.

Zelnick, N. I., & Shah, F. K. (1983). First intercourse among young Americans. *Family Planning Perspectives, 5,* 64–70.

REVIEW QUESTIONS

1. If you were going to do a study on AIDS and adolescents, what type of methodology would you use? How would you set it up?

2. What variables were used in this study? Can you think of any that were left out?

3. Can you make your own outline of this literature review? After you have done that, find more current literature to support your outline.

Glossary

A

abstract   a very brief statement about the research hypothesis, purposes, or questions about the project that also includes a statement about the methods, results, and conclusions

accuracy   a measure of how trustworthy and accurate a historical data source is

agreement reality   things you consider real because you have been told they are real by other people and those other people seem to believe they are real

anonymity   provided by research in which no identifying information is recorded that could be used to link respondents to their responses

authenticity   the genuineness of historical data sources

authority   those who we believe just because we think they truly know about the subject because they are in a position of authority

average   a measure of central tendency represented as the mean, median, or mode

B

bimodal   a variable that has only two attributes

bivariate   where two variables are used and analyzed for the purpose of determining the empirical relationship between the two variables

Bogardus Social Distance Scale   a measurement technique that determines the willingness of the respondents to participate in social relations with other kinds of people in varying degrees of closeness

C

census data   data collected by the government that gives the characteristics of the population

central tendency   summary of averages that includes the mode, the arithmetic mean, or the median

close-ended question   interview questions that have a clear and apparent focus and a clearly defined answer

cluster sampling   used when it is either impossible or impractical to compile an exhaustive list of elements that compose the target population

code of ethics   guidelines set up by national organizations that guide our research endeavors and protect respondents from harm

concept   a mental image that summarizes a set of similar observations, feelings, or ideas explaining exactly what is meant by the term used

conceptualization   the process of specifying what is meant by a term

confidentiality   provided by the researcher where identifying information that could be used to link the respondents to their responses is only available to designated personnel

conflict theory   according to Marx, people are always in conflict for power

content analysis   a method used to study communications processes in magazines, television, or any other type of media

control group   a statistical or experimental means of holding some variables constant in order to examine the causal influences of others

convenience sampling   an available group of subjects

cross-sectional method   a method of developmental research that is used to examine age differences rather than age changes in subjects

D

dependent variable   a variable, or factor, causally influenced by another (the independent variable)

descriptive research   research that describes a phenomenon without any attempt to determine what causes the phenomenon

descriptive statistics   simple measures of a distributions central tendency and variability

dimensions   a specific aspect of a concept

direct observation   watching the activity being studied and taking notes while watching the activities

dispersion   the distribution of values around some central value, such as the average

disproportionate stratified sample   when a sample subpopulation is disproportionate to ensure there are sufficient numbers of cases from each for analysis

double-barreled question   a single survey question that actually asks two questions but allows only one answer

double-blind experiment   an experiment where neither subjects nor staff who are delivering the experimental treatments know which subjects are getting the treatment and which subjects are getting the placebo

double-negative questions   when the appearance of a negation of a questionnaire item paves the way for easy misinterpretation

E

ecological fallacy   when a conclusion is drawn erroneously about individuals when actually the data is drawn from the observations of groups

empirical research   a statement or theory which can be tested by some kind of evidence drawn from experience

ethics   guidelines for research where the researcher makes sure that all respondents have voluntary participation and they are not harmed

ethnocentrism   the tendency to look at other cultures through the eyes of one's own culture, and thereby misrepresent the other cultures

ethnography   the study of people at firsthand using participant observation or interviewing

evaluation research   research that evaluates social programs or interventions

exhaustive   a variable's attributes or values in which every case can be classified as having one attribute

existing statistics   someone else's data that researcher's use to undertake their own statistical analyses

experiment   a research method in which variables can be analyzed in a controlled and systematic way, either in an artificial situation constructed by the researcher or in naturally occurring settings

experimental group   the group that receives the treatment in an experiment

experimental reality   things you know as real because you have had your own direct experience with experiment research that examines the cause and effect relationships through the use of control and treatment groups

explanatory research   research that seeks to identify causes or effects of the phenomenon being studied

exploratory research   research in which social phenomena are investigated without prior expectations so researchers can develop the explanations

extraneous variables   variables that represent an alternative explanation for the relationship observed between the independent and dependent variable

F

feminist theory   a theory that looks at inequality in race, gender, sex, and sexuality

fieldwork   sometimes used as a synonym for ethnography, it describes the activity of collecting data in empirical research

follow-up questions   after having a question answered by a respondent, the interviewer asks another question to follow up with the first one

frequency distribution   numerical display showing the number of cases and usually percentage of cases that corresponds to each value or groups of values of a variable

functionalist theory   a theoretical perspective based on the notion that social events can best be explained by the functions they perform and the contributions they make to the equilibrium of society

G

generalizability   the ability to draw inferences and conclusion from the data collected

graphs   a way of showing or displaying statistical answers

H

historical research   a methodology for examining how events that have occurred in the past affect events that happen in the present and in the future

hypothesis   an idea or a guess about a given state of affairs, put forward as a basis for empirical testing

I

independent variable   a variable, or factor, that causally affects another (the dependent variable)

index   a type of composite measure that summarizes several specific observations and represents some more general dimension

indicator   the end product of the conceptualization process where a specific set of indicators indicate the presence or absence of the concept we are studying

informed consent   the respondents must be informed about the purpose of the study, who the researchers are, who they work for, and exactly what the study is about before they can give informed consent to participate in the study

institutional review board (IRB)   a group of representatives who are required by federal law to review the ethical issues in all proposed research that is federally funded and that involves human subjects or can potentially harm subjects

intentional plagiarism   includes cheating of any kind, which can include copying directly from an article or a book or buying an article off the Internet

interobserver reliability   the reliability of a measurement is compared with the results obtained by at least two different observers

interquartile range (IQR)   the simplest measure of the dispersion is the range, which determines the range of scores for the middle 50 percent of the subjects

interrater reliability   the extent of consistency among different observers in their judgements, that are reflected in the percentage of agreement or degree of correlation in their independent ratings

interview   a method of collecting data, similar to an oral questionnaire, that can be either structured and focused or informal and flexible

J

jotted notes   notes taken by the researcher during the research project

L

Likert scale a method used in attitude scales that requires the individual to either agree or disagree to a set of statements using a scale

literature review introduces the problem, develops the background by providing a history of the scholarly work on the subject, and ends with the purpose and the rationale of the study

longitudinal method a method of developmental research that assesses changes in behavior in one group of subjects at more than one point in time

M

macrolevel analysis analysis and theories that deal with broad areas of society such as the political or the economic system

mean a statistical measure of central tendency, or average, based on dividing a total by the number of individual cases.

measurement techniques the method of collecting data, which can be a survey, interviews, or focus groups

median the number that falls halfway in a range of numbers; a way of calculating central tendency that is sometimes more useful than calculating a mean

mesolevel analysis analyses and theories that deal with social groups or organizations, such as classrooms and offices

microlevel analysis analysis and theories that deal with narrow or small aspects of social life, such as the differences in play between boys and girls

mode the number that appears most often in a given set of data; can sometimes be a helpful way of portraying central tendency

multivariate where several variables are used and analyzed

multivariate table a way of displaying the findings for more than two variables

mutually exclusive a variable's attributes or values are mutually exclusive if every case can have only one attribute

N

narrative sometimes called biographical work or oral history; a way of listening to the voices of those being studied to uncover hidden histories

nonprobability sampling when the likelihood of selecting any one member of the population is unknown

O

open-ended questions interview questions that provide an opportunity for respondents to respond in any way they want

operationalization   specifying the operations that will indicate the value of cases on a variable

oral history   interviews with people about events they witnessed or experienced at some point earlier in their lives

ordinal scales   measurement that assigns only rank order to outcomes

P

paradigms   a fundamental model that organizes our view of something and tells us where to look for answers. Sometimes is used interchangeably with the term *perspective*

participant observation   (fieldwork) a method of research widely used in the social sciences, in which the researcher takes part in the activities of the group or community being studied

peer reviewed   a research paper that has been blindly reviewed, by usually three other scholars in the same field, who decide if the research meets the standards of the journal

personal troubles   where the individual thinks the problems they are having are a reflection of only themselves

placebo   something that is used in place of the experimental stimulus to make the respondent think they have received the stimulus

plagiarism   using someone else's writing without crediting the author

population   the people who are the focus of social research

posttest   the test given to subjects in a randomly assigned group after the end of the experiment

pretest   the test given to subjects in a randomly assigned group before the beginning of the experiment

primary existing data   original sources of information that is used in a research study

primary sources   documentation that is firsthand information

probability average   also called the mode, the easiest way to measure because it represents the most frequent value

probability sampling   the type of sampling that is used when the likelihood of selecting any one member of the population is known

proportionate stratified sample   where a uniform proportion of cases are drawn from each homogeneous group

public issues   issues that the individual has no control over; they are because of society and more macro

purposive sample   when a sample is selected on the basis of your own knowledge of the population based on the researcher's own judgment and the purpose of the study

Q

qualitative research   research methods that emphasize depth of understanding and the deeper meanings of the human experience and that are aimed at generating theoretically richer observations

quantitative research   research that emphasizes precise, objective, and generalizable findings

quasi-experimental design   done when groups are preassigned to treatments

questionnaire   a set of structured, focused questions that employ a self-reporting, paper and pencil format

quota sampling   a nonprobability sampling procedure that is similar to stratified random sampling in that a particular stratum is the focus that ends when a specified number is selected

R

random-digit dialing   where the computer automatically makes random telephone calls

randomization   also called random selection, where every subject in the population has the same chance of being selected for the sample and therefore the sample is a reflection of the population

random sampling   a sampling method in which a sample is chosen so that every member of the population has the same probability of being included

range   a measure of dispersion composed of the highest and lowest values of a variable in some set of observations

reductionism   a fault of some researchers where a strict limitation (reduction) of the kinds of concepts are considered relevant to the phenomenon under study

reliability   the quality of measurement method that suggests that the same data would have been collected each time in repeated observations of the same phenomenon

representative sample   a sample that "appears like" the population from which it was selected in all respects that are potentially relevant to the study

research   a way of answering a hypothetical question

research methods   the diverse methods of investigation used to gather empirical or factual material. Different research methods exist. Sometimes it is useful to combine two or more methods within a single research project.

S

sampling   studying a proportion of individuals or cases from a larger population as representative of the entire population

sampling errors   the difference between the characteristics of a sample and that of the population

sampling interval   the standard distance between elements selected in the sample

sampling strata   where all elements of the population are distinguished based on their characteristics

scale   a type of composite measure composed of several items that have a logical or empirical structure among them, such as the Likert or Bogardus social distance scales

secondary data (sources)   data that has been collected by someone other than the researcher doing the analysis

self-administered questionnaire   a collection of questions that the respondents are able to answer on their own

semantic differential   where the respondents are asked to choose between two opposites on a questionnaire

simple random sampling   a method of sampling in which every sample element is selected only on the basis of chance through a random process

snowball sampling   a method of sampling in which the sample elements are selected as they are identified by successive informants or interviewees

social desirability   the appeal of the question being asked of the respondent

stratified random sampling   a method of sampling in which the sample elements are selected separately from the population strata that are identified in advance by the researcher

survey research   a method of research in which questionnaires are administered to the population being studied

symbolic interactionism   a theoretical approach that emphasizes the role of symbols and language as the core elements of all human interaction

systematic random sampling   every kth element in the total list is systematically chosen for inclusion in the sample

T

theoretical articles   explain a theory and how it relates to the variables being investigated

theory   An attempt to identify general properties that may explain observed events. Theories form an essential element of all scientific works. While the theories tend to be linked to broader theoretical approaches, they are strongly influenced by the research results they help to generate

time series design   a quasi-experimental design that consists of many pretest and posttest observations of the same group

tradition   the way things have always been and always been done in the past

true experiment design   an experiment in which the subjects are randomly assigned to an experimental group that receives a treatment or other manipulation of the independent variable and a comparison group that does not receive the treatment and whose outcomes are measured in a posttest

U

unintentional plagiarism   plagiarism that is done without intentionally stealing

units of analysis   the level of social life on which a research question is focused

univariate   where a single variable is used and analyzed

V

validity   the truthfulness or accuracy within the score of a test or interpretation of an experiment

variable   a dimension along which an object, individual, or group may be categorized, such as weight or sex

voluntary participation   when the subjects know about the study they are participating in and have made a voluntary decision to take part

Index